PENGUIN  CLASSICS

THE CONQUEST OF NEW SPAIN

ADVISORY EDITOR: BETTY RADICE

BERNAL DÍAZ DEL CASTILLO was born in Medina del Campo, Spain, in 1492. After participating in two explorations of the Mexican coast, he joined Cortes in the march on Mexico and the battles for the city. He began his *History of the Conquest of New Spain* when he was over seventy, and the last survivor of the Conquerors of Mexico. Fearing his literary abilities were not up to the task, he nearly abandoned the work, but resumed it because he felt that the other chroniclers of the period had not represented it accurately. He had received a municipal office in Guatemala and a grant of Indians, but his great estates did not yield him much wealth. He died in about 1580.

J. M. COHEN, born in London in 1903 and a Cambridge graduate, was the author of many Penguin translations, including versions of Cervantes, Rabelais and Montaigne. For some years he assisted E. V. Rieu in editing the Penguin Classics. He collected the three books of *Comic and Curious Verse* and anthologies of Latin American and Cuban writing, and frequently visited Spain and made several visits to Mexico, Cuba and other Spanish American countries. With his son Mark he edited the *Penguin Dictionary of Quotations* and its companion *Dictionary of Modern Quotations*. J. M. Cohen died in 1989. *The Times*' obituary described him as 'the translator of the foreign prose classics for our times' and 'one of the last great English men of letters', while the *Independent* wrote that 'his influence will be felt for generations to come'.

BERNAL DÍAZ

THE CONQUEST OF NEW SPAIN

TRANSLATED WITH AN INTRODUCTION BY

J. M. COHEN

PENGUIN BOOKS

PENGUIN BOOKS

Published by the Penguin Group
Penguin Books Ltd, 27 Wrights Lane, London W8 5TZ, England
Penguin Books USA Inc., 375 Hudson Street, New York, New York 10014, USA
Penguin Books Australia Ltd, Ringwood, Victoria, Australia
Penguin Books Canada Ltd, 10 Alcorn Avenue, Toronto, Ontario, Canada M4V 3B2
Penguin Books (NZ) Ltd, 182–190 Wairau Road, Auckland 10, New Zealand

Penguin Books Ltd, Registered Offices: Harmondsworth, Middlesex, England

This translation first published 1963
23 25 27 29 30 28 26 24

Printed in England by Clays Ltd, St Ives plc
Set in Linotype Pilgrim

Contents

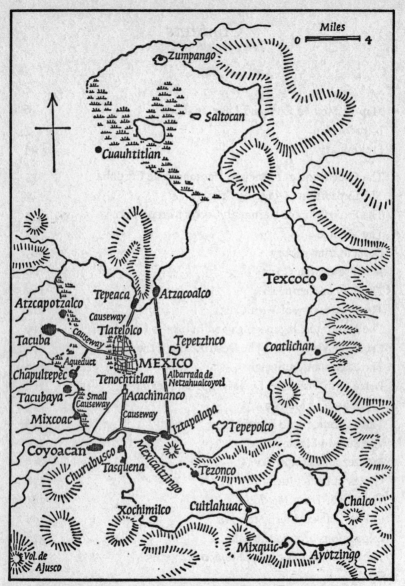

Map of Mexico City and Lake Texcoco at the time of the Spanish Conquest.

Introduction

BERNAL DÍAZ DEL CASTILLO, the last survivor of the Conquerors of Mexico, died on his estates in Guatemala at the age of eighty-nine, as poor as he had lived. Born in 1492, the year in which Columbus discovered the New World, he survived to see a great part of America subjugated by Spain. But despite the leading role he had played in the heroic overthrow of the Aztec Empire, he left his family no other riches than his 'true and wonderful' *History of the Conquest of New Spain*, of which he made his fair copy at the age of seventy-six, when he was, according to his own certainly exaggerated description, both deaf and blind, and to which he added his preliminary note at the age of eighty-four. He had been over seventy when he began it, and had at one point given it up. For on comparing the fine style of certain other chroniclers (who had told the story of Cortes' achievement with less first-hand knowledge than he had) with the roughness and lack of polish of his own language, he had been discouraged.

Certainly Bernal Díaz was not an accomplished stylist. He had, however, a graphic memory and a great sense of the dramatic. Moreover he was conscious of having taken part in a great achievement, unparalleled in modern history: the overthrow of a great Empire by a company of adventurers, inspired partly by a sense of mission and partly by a crude greed for gold. Their success, even their survival, could in his belief be accounted for only by the miraculous intervention of God and the Saints, who wished New Spain to be added to the realm of Christ and the Emperor Charles V.

So, when Bernal Díaz found the story misrepresented by Cortes' chaplain and official panegyrist, Francisco Lopez de Gomara, and also by Gonzalo de Illescas (who spoke the truth 'neither in the beginning, nor the middle, nor the end'), he decided to resume his work and carry it to completion. Many times in the course of his *History*, he refers to these chroniclers, setting right their errors and often angrily accusing them of ignorance and malice. His purpose was by no means simply to vindicate his own part in the march on Mexico. True, he frequently informs the reader that Cortes consulted his captains and soldiers – including himself – at important junctures in the campaign, and did not, as Gomara asserted, make all his decisions alone. Bernal Díaz, however, never attempts to claim a bigger role for himself than for his fellows and for long passages of his narrative he describes events at which he was not present, sometimes because of wounds, or in which his part is indicated only by the use of *we* or of *us soldiers*, where the stay-at-home historian would have had to write a plain *the*.

The narrative here translated covers the two preliminary explorations of the Mexican coast under Cordoba and Grijalva, with both of whom Bernal Díaz served, the first march on Montezuma's city, the Spaniards' expulsion and flight, and their subsequent build-up of a new army, with which they captured the island-capital of the Empire which Guatemoc had now inherited from Montezuma. Bernal Díaz' *History*, however, is a much longer book than this. It covers the long tales of intrigue in Spain, Cuba, and Hispaniola, which almost succeeded in replacing Cortes by weaker leaders who would have been content to make a few modest settlements on the coast; and it continues after the final reduction of the Mexican capital to tell of further campaigns in search of the gold which had so far evaded the Conquerors. Bernal Díaz describes also the terrible march through the forest of Honduras, Cortes' final prosperity, and his own efforts on a visit to Spain to secure some better fortune for himself, 'the oldest Conquistador of New Spain', than what came to him from his estates and his magistracy in Guatemala.

By his own confession, as we saw, Bernal Díaz was a poor stylist, and a retranslation of his whole narrative would have filled almost two volumes of this size. I have therefore pruned his story of repetitions and digressions, among other things cutting away his scoldings of Gomara and the other chroniclers and his frequent lists of men, horses, weapons, and provisions, which hold up the story. Where the omitted chapters contain facts essential to the understanding of events, I have given a brief account of them, in brackets, and I have ended my translation with Bernal Díaz' reflections on the capture of the Aztec capital. The rest can be read, by those who wish to know the tale of Cortes' later campaigns and final triumph, in W. H. Prescott's classic, *The Conquest of Mexico*.

In writing his immortal history a hundred and twenty years ago, Prescott borrowed freely from Bernal Díaz, whom he praised in terms on which I could not hope to improve:

Bernal Díaz, the untutored child of nature, is a most true and literal copyist of nature. He transfers the scenes of real life by a sort of *daguerreotype* process, if I may so say, to his pages. He is among chroniclers what Defoe is among novelists. He introduces us into the heart of the camp, we huddle round the bivouac with the soldiers, loiter with them on their wearisome marches, listen to their stories, their murmurs of discontent, their plans of conquest, their hopes, their triumphs, their disappointments. All the picturesque scenes and romantic incidents of the campaign are reflected in his page as in a mirror. The lapse of fifty years has no power over the spirit of the veteran. The fire of youth glows in every line of his rude history; and, as he calls up the scenes of the past, the remembrance of the brave companions who are gone gives, it may be, a warmer colouring to the picture than if it had been made at an earlier period. Time, and reflection, and the apprehensions for the future which might steal over the evening of life, have no power over the settled opinions of his earlier days. He has no misgivings as to the right of conquest, or as to the justice of the severities inflicted on the natives. He is still the soldier of the Cross; and those who fell by his side in the fight were martyrs for the faith. 'Where are now my companions?' he asks; 'they have fallen in battle or been devoured by the cannibal, or been thrown to fatten the wild beasts in their cages! they whose remains should rather have been gathered under monuments emblazoned with their achievements, which deserve to be commemorated in letters of gold; for they died in the service of God and of His Majesty, and to give light to those who sat in darkness – *and also to acquire that wealth which most men covet.*' The last motive – thus tardily and incidentally expressed – may be thought by some to furnish a better key than either of the preceding to the conduct of the Conquerors. It is, at all events, a specimen of that naïveté which gives an irresistible charm to the old chronicler, and which, in spite of himself, unlocks his bosom, as it were, and lays it open to the eye of the reader.

It is not surprising that an American Protestant should suspect the honesty of the Spaniards' crusading spirit. Notwithstanding the horrible decadence of the Aztec religion, the deeds of the conquerors (which included massacre, torture, and forcible conversion) were not by nineteenth-century standards very much better. Yet as one reads Bernal Díaz, one credits him and his comrades with a true sense of mission. One sees that by their own standards they were often behaving with moderation. On several occasions the Mercedarian friar (Bernal Díaz seems to have forgotten his name) urged Cortes to restrain his proselytizing zeal; and it must not be forgotten, as Prescott points out, that disbelief in Christianity, whether by conviction or from ignorance, was in that age punishable by burning.

About the heroism of the Spaniards there can be no two opinions. The risks they took were enormous, since their superiority in weapons was often cancelled by lack of powder and by the inability of their cavalry to manoeuvre. As for Bernal Díaz' attitude to Cortes, I can only endorse Prescott's opinion that 'he endeavours to adjust the true balance between his pretensions and those of his followers; and while he freely exposes his cunning or cupidity, and sometimes his cruelty, he does ample justice to his great and heroic qualities'. The same may be said of Bernal Díaz' characterization of the other Spanish captains, of the chiefs of the various Indian nations, and of many less important members of the Spanish expedition. His portrait of Montezuma ably reveals the Aztec ruler's divided mind, and the very real qualities of nobility and generosity for which the Spaniards came to respect and even to love him. His successor Guatemoc, too, is shown as a brave man and a dignified leader, whose last defence of his capital earned his enemies' admiration, which however did not prevent them from torturing him, and finally executing him for allegedly encouraging a revolt among the conquered Aztecs. The *Caciques*, the Spaniards' early enemies, who afterwards became their allies, stand out as individuals as do also the Spanish captains, Pedro de Alvarado,

Introduction

Cristobal de Olid – whose final rebellion and cruel execution by Cortes falls outside the scope of this narrative – Andres de Tapia, and Alonso de Avila. The fate of the last-named captain provides a note of heavy irony at the expense of the whole story of the Spaniards' search for gold. He was captured by a French privateer on his way back to Spain with the royal fifth – which was in fact the major part of the booty. So the much disputed spoils of Montezuma's empire finally arrived in the treasury of his most Christian Majesty of France. The only satisfaction which the Spaniards obtained was that they finally captured and executed the French pirate.

For all the roughness of his style, Bernal Díaz could sometimes be picturesque. How graphically he calls up the moment in which the Spaniards first saw from the summit of the sierra de Ahualco the valley of Mexico with its lakes and lakeside towns, its maize-fields and stone causeways, and the distant towers of the capital itself riding like a second Venice on the waters. But his writing is generally on a more pedestrian level. His narrative is not skilful, and his choice of words is restricted. Often he gossips, and often he resorts to clumsy tricks of style. But however much we may criticize his *History*, it will, in Prescott's words, 'be read and re-read by the scholar and the schoolboy, while the compositions of more classic chroniclers' – of Gomara, for instance, who wrote briefly in a polished style – 'sleep undisturbed on their shelves'. For Bernal Díaz was singularly free from the temptation to pervert his story in the interests of affections or feuds or personal vanity. To have marched with Cortes was for him sufficient glory. He did not need to increase his reputation or self-esteem by tricks of the pen.

*

Taking as my authoritative text the edition of the *Historia verdadera de la conquista de la nueva España* of Joaquín Ramirez Cabañas (fifth edition, Editorial Porrua, 1960), I have translated the greater part of Bernal Díaz' first 157 chapters, omitting only certain extraneous incidents (which I have in some cases briefly summarized) and the very frequent repetitions which mar his narrative. Ignoring his chapter-divisions, which are uneven and arbitrary, I have given each campaign or principal incident a separate section. As for the names of persons and places, I have departed from Bernal Díaz' often haphazard transliterations in favour of those most familiar either from Prescott's narrative or from present-day maps of the country. Where Bernal Díaz was in actual error as to a locality or a date, I have generally corrected him in a footnote based on the observations of Señor Ramirez Cabañas or some equally reliable scholar.

Any reader who wishes to know the subsequent story of Mexico cannot do better, as I have said, than turn to Prescott, who, for all his inevitable bias against Catholic and Aztec alike, wrote a first-rate narrative based on the best authorities he knew, and chief among them, on Bernal Díaz himself, who now for the first time is able to tell his own story to a wide English-reading public. Of previous translations, that of A. P. Maudslay is the best. Printed for the Hakluyt Society (1908–16), it is complete and fully documented. It is, however, ungainly in style and to be found only in a few libraries. The *Life of Bernal Díaz* by R. B. Cunninghame Graham (Eveleigh Nash, 1915) is in effect a résumé of the *History* made by an able writer who was an enthusiast for the deeds of the Conquistadors. It is most valuable when its author allows Bernal Díaz to speak for himself, but hardly a substitute for his *History*. Recent years have seen a great development in our knowledge of early Mexican civilization, of which the Spaniards found relics among the Toltecs of Cholula, but which was in a general state of decadence, especially among the savage Aztecs, who had only recently conquered the valley of Mexico. An able account of the thought and religion of early Mexico is given by Laurette Séjourné in *Burning Water* (Thames and Hudson, 1957), and a study of the Poetry and Symbolism of the Aztecs and their predecessors is provided by Irene Nicholson's *Firefly in the Night* (Faber and Faber, 1959).

London   J.M.C.
May 1963

THE CONQUEST OF
NEW SPAIN

Preliminary Note

I HAVE observed that before beginning to write their histories, the most famous chroniclers compose a prologue in exalted language, in order to give lustre and repute to their narrative, and to whet the curious reader's appetite. But I, being no scholar, dare not attempt any such preface. For properly to extol the adventures that befell us, and the heroic deeds we performed during the conquest of New Spain and its provinces in the company of that valiant and enterprising captain, Don Hernando Cortes – who, as a reward for his heroism, was afterwards created Marques del Valle – would require eloquence and rhetoric far greater than mine. What I myself saw, and the fighting in which I took part, with God's help I will describe quite plainly, as an honest eyewitness, without twisting the facts in any way. I am now an old man, over eighty-four years of age, and have lost both sight and hearing; and unfortunately I have gained no wealth to leave to my children and descendants, except this true story, which is a most remarkable one, as my readers will presently see.

The Expedition of
Francisco Hernandez de Cordoba

I, BERNAL DÍAZ DEL CASTILLO, citizen and governor of the most loyal city of Santiago de Guatemala, one of the first discoverers and conquerors of New Spain and its provinces, and of the Cape of Honduras and Higueras, native of the most noble and famous city of Medina del Campo, and son of its former governor Francisco Díaz del Castillo, known as the Courteous – and his legal wife Maria Diez Rejon – may their souls rest in glory! – tell you the story of myself and my comrades; all true conquerors, who served His Majesty in the discovery, conquest, pacification, and settlement of the provinces of New Spain; one of the finest regions of the New World yet discovered, this expedition being undertaken by our own efforts, and without His Majesty's knowledge.

My ancestors having always been servants of the Crown, and my father and one of my brothers being in the service of the Catholic Kings, Don Ferdinand and Doña Isabella, I wished in some sort to emulate them. When, therefore, in the year 1514 a gentleman named Pedrarias Davila went out as Governor of Tierra Firme,[1] I agreed to accompany him to the newly conquered country, and after an uneventful voyage we arrived at Nombre de Dios, as it was called. Some three or four months, however, after the settlement was made, there came an epidemic from which many soldiers died, and all the rest of us were ill with bad ulcers on the legs. In addition, there were disputes between the Governor and a rich gentleman named Vasco Nuñez de Balboa, who had conquered the province and was then commander of the army. Pedrarias Davila had given him his daughter in marriage but had afterwards been suspicious that his son-in-law might raise a rebellion and lead a body of soldiers towards the Southern Sea. He had therefore given orders that Balboa should be beheaded and certain of his soldiers disciplined.

As we were witnesses of these events, and of other revolts

1. The Spanish Main, a settlement on the coast of Panama.

among the captains, and as news had reached us that the island of Cuba had lately been conquered and settled, under the governorship of a kinsman of mine named Diego Velazquez, some of us gentlemen and persons of quality who had come out with Pedrarias Davila decided to ask his permission to go there. This he readily gave us, since he did not require all the soldiers he had brought out from Spain, the province being a small one and now entirely conquered.

Once we had received permission we boarded a good ship, and with fair weather reached the island of Cuba. On landing we paid our respects to the Governor, who was pleased to see us and promised to give us Indians as soon as there were any to spare. I was at that time twenty-four.

After spending three fruitless years in Tierra Firme and Cuba, about a hundred and ten of us, settlers from Tierra Firme or Spaniards who had come to Cuba but received no grant of Indians, decided to make an expedition to seek new lands in which to try our fortunes and find occupation. We arranged with Francisco Hernandez de Cordoba, a rich man who owned a village on the island, that he should be our leader, and he was well fitted for the post.

With this expedition in view, we purchased three ships, two of them a good capacity and the third a barque bought on credit from the Governor Diego Velazquez, who let us have it on condition that all three vessels should go to some islands, lying between Cuba and Honduras, and now called the Guanaxes Islands, and there fight the natives, whom we could then sell to him for slaves and thus pay for the barque. Realizing the wickedness of the Governor's demand, we answered that it would be against the laws of God and the king for us to turn free men into slaves; and when he learnt our plans, he decided they were better than his. So he helped us with provisions for our voyage in quest of new lands. Certain interested persons have asked me why I have recorded this proposal of Diego Velazquez, since it is discreditable to him and has nothing to do with my story. My answer is that it is in keeping with his subsequent persecution of us, in alliance with Juan Rodriguez de Fonseca, Bishop of Burgos.

We found ourselves in possession of three ships loaded with

cassava bread, which is made from a root, and we bought pigs, which cost us three pesos each. At that time there were no sheep or cattle in the island of Cuba, for it was only beginning to be settled. We added a supply of oil and some inexpensive articles for barter. We then sought out three pilots of whom the chief, who took charge of our fleet, was Anton de Alaminos, a native of Palos. We also engaged the necessary sailors, and the best supply we could get of ropes, cordage, cables, and anchors, of casks for water, and everything else we needed for our voyage, and all this at our own cost on credit.

When we had collected all our soldiers we set out for a port on the northern coast which the Indians call Axaruco, twenty-four miles away from San Cristobal, where there was then a settlement which was transferred two years later to the present town of Havana. In order that our fleet should take the right course, we asked a priest of San Cristobal called Alonso Gonzalez to come with us. We also chose for the office of Inspector a soldier named Bernaldino Iñiguez of Santo Domingo de la Calzada so that, should we by God's will come upon rich lands, or peoples possessed of gold or silver or pearls or any other kind of wealth, there should be someone to guard the royal fifth.

When all this was arranged and we had heard mass, we commended ourselves to God and His blessed Mother, and began our voyage.

On the eighth of February 1517 we sailed for Axaruco, and twelve days later doubled Cape San Antonio. Then, once in the open sea, we steered at a venture towards the west, without knowledge of the depths or currents, or of the winds that prevail in those latitudes. So we were in great hazard of our lives when a storm struck us which lasted two days and two nights and had such force that we were nearly wrecked. When the weather moderated we resumed our course, and twenty-one days after leaving port to our great joy we sighted land, for which we gave thanks to God. This land was as yet undiscovered, and we had received no report of it. From the ships we could see a large town, which appeared to lie six miles back from the coast, and as we had never seen one as large in Cuba or Hispaniola we named it the Great Cairo.

We decided that the two vessels of shallowest draught should go in as near as possible to see if there was any anchorage close to the shore; and on the morning of 4 March we saw ten large canoes called pirogues, full of the inhabitants of that town, approaching us with oars and sail. These pirogues are shaped like troughs. They are large and hollowed out of huge single logs, and many of them will hold forty Indians.

These canoes came close to our ships, and we made signs of peace, waving our hands and our cloaks as an invitation to them to come and speak to us. For at that time we had no interpreters who knew the languages of Yucatan and Mexico. They approached quite fearlessly, and more than thirty men came aboard our flagship. We gave each of them a string of green beads, and they spent some time examining the ships. Then the principal man among them, who was the *Cacique*,[1] told us by signs that they wanted to board their canoes and go back to the town. He indicated that they would return another day with more canoes, in which we could go ashore.

These Indians wore cotton shirts made in the shape of jackets, and covered their private parts with narrow cloths which they called *masteles*. We considered them a more civilized people than the Cubans. For they went about naked, except for the women, who wore cotton cloths that came down to their thighs.

Next morning the same *Cacique* came back bringing twelve large canoes with Indian oarsmen. With a smiling face and every appearance of friendliness, he made signs that we should go to his town, where they would give us food and everything else we needed, and to which they would take us in their canoes. As he invited us aboard he repeated in his language: '*Cones catoche, cones catoche,*' which means: 'Come to our houses.' For this reason we called the place Cape Catoche, and so it is still named on the charts.

When our captain and the soldiers saw these friendly demonstrations, it was agreed that we should lower our ships' boats, and all go ashore together in the smallest of them and the twelve

1. The Carib word for military chief. The *Cacique's* privileges and duties varied from nation to nation.

canoes. We saw the whole coast crowded with Indians who had come from the town, and therefore decided that we would all land at the same moment. When the *Cacique* saw us land but make no move towards the town, he again made signs to our captain that we should go with him to the houses. He gave so much evidence of peaceful intentions that after some discussion most of us soldiers agreed that we should go forward, taking all the arms that we could carry. We took fifteen crossbows and ten muskets, and started to follow the road along which the *Cacique* was going with his great company of Indians.

We advanced in this way until we came to some brush-covered hillocks. Then the *Cacique* started shouting to some bands of warriors whom he had placed in ambush to kill us. In response to the *Cacique*'s call these bands quickly fell on us with great fury, and began to shoot with such accuracy that the first flight of arrows wounded thirteen soldiers. The Indians wore armour made of cotton which reached down to their knees. They carried lances and shields, bows and arrows, slings, and many stones; and after the arrow-flights, with their feathered crests waving, they attacked us hand to hand. Wielding their lances in both hands, they did us great damage. But, thanks be to God, when they felt the sharp edge of our swords and the effect of our crossbows and muskets, they quickly took to their heels, leaving fifteen dead on the field.

A little beyond this place where they attacked us was a small square with three houses built of masonry, which served as *cues* or prayer-houses. These contained many idols of baked clay, some with demons' faces, some with women's, and others equally ugly which seemed to represent Indians committing sodomy with one another. Inside the houses were some small wooden chests containing other idols and some disks made partly of gold but mainly of copper, also some pendants, three diadems, and other small objects in the shape of fishes and of the local ducks, all made of poor-quality gold. When we saw the gold and the masonry houses we were very pleased to have found such a country. For Peru had not yet been discovered, nor was it to be discovered for another twenty years.

Whilst we were fighting the Indians, the priest Gonzalez took possession of the chests, the idols, and the gold, and carried them to the ship. In this skirmish we captured two Indians, who when they were afterwards baptized received the names of Julian and Melchior. Both were cross-eyed. Once this surprise attack was over we returned to our ships and after attending to the wounded set sail along the coast in a westerly direction.

Believing this to be an island, as our pilot assured us it was, we went forward very cautiously, sailing by day and anchoring at night. And after fifteen days we sighted what appeared to be a large town beside a great inlet or bay. Here we thought there might be a river or stream at which we could take water, of which we were very short, since the casks and other vessels we had brought were not watertight. The reason for this was that we were too poor to buy good ones. The day of our landing was St Lazarus' Sunday, and so we called the place Lazaro, by which name it is still marked on the charts. The proper Indian name for it is Campeche.

So that we could all disembark at once and not be caught as we had been at Cape Catoche, we decided to go in the smallest ship and the three boats, and to carry all our arms.

In these bays or inlets the water drops very considerably at low tide. So we had to leave our ships anchored more than three miles off shore. We disembarked near the town, where there was a pool of good water, at which the inhabitants were accustomed to drink. For as far as we could see, there were no rivers in this country. We landed the casks, intending to fill them and re-embark. But when we were ready to go a company of about fifty Indians, dressed in good cotton cloaks, who looked like *Caciques*, came peacefully out of the town, and asked us by signs what we were looking for. We gave them to understand that we had come for water, and were going straight back to our ships. They asked us by gesture whether we came from the east, and repeated the word '*Castilan, Castilan*'. But we did not understand what they meant. Then they invited us to go with them to their town, and after some discussion among ourselves we decided to go, but in good formation and very cautiously.

They led us to some very large buildings of fine masonry which were the prayer-houses of their idols, the walls of which were painted with the figures of great serpents and evil-looking gods. In the middle was something like an altar, covered with clotted blood, and on the other side of the idols were symbols like crosses, and all were coloured. We stood astonished, never having seen or heard of such things before.

It appears that they had just sacrificed some Indians to their idols, so as to ensure victory over us. However, many Indian women were strolling about most peacefully, as it seemed, laughing and amusing themselves. But as the men were gathered in such numbers, we were afraid that there might be another ambush, like that at Catoche. At this point many more Indians came up, wearing very ragged cloaks, and carrying dried reeds, which they put down on the ground. These were followed by two bands of Indian archers in cotton armour, carrying lances, shields, slings, and stones, and each of these bands was drawn up by its captain at a short distance from us. At that moment there came from another house, which was the temple of their idols, ten Indians wearing long white cotton cloaks which fell to their feet. Their hair was very long, and so clotted with blood that it would have needed cutting before it could be combed or parted. These were the priests of their gods, who in New Spain are generally called *papas*. They brought us incense of a sort of resin which they call copal, and began to burn it over us in earthenware braziers full of live coals. By means of signs they gave us to understand that we must leave their land before the firewood that they had piled there burnt out. Otherwise they would attack us and kill us. The *papas* then ordered the reeds to be set alight, and departed without more words, and the warriors who were drawn up to attack us began to whistle and sound their trumpets and drums.

When we saw these great bands of Indians threatening us so boldly we were afraid. For we had not yet recovered from the wounds received at Cape Catoche, and had just thrown overboard the bodies of two soldiers who had died. So we decided to retire to the coast in good order, and began to march along the shore towards a large rock which rose out of the sea, while the boats and the small ship laden with the water-casks coasted along close to the shore. We had not dared to embark near the town, where we had landed, since a great number of Indians were waiting for us there, and we were sure they would attack as we did so.

Once we had embarked and got the casks on board, we sailed on for six days and nights in good weather. Then we were struck by a *norther*, which is a cross-wind on that coast. It lasted four days and nights, and was so strong that it almost drove us ashore, and forced us to anchor. In doing so we broke two cables, and one ship began to drag. Our danger was very great, for if the last cable had broken we should have been driven ashore and destroyed. But, thank God, we were able to ease the strain by lashing it with ropes and hawsers.

When the weather had improved, we continued to follow the coast, going ashore as often as we could, to take fresh water. For, as I have said, our casks were not watertight. They gaped and we could not repair them. But as we were following the coast we trusted that we should find water wherever we landed, either in *jagueyes* (pools) or by digging for it.

As we sailed on our course we sighted another town about three miles back from an inlet which looked like the mouth of a river or stream. So we decided to anchor; and because the tide falls so far on this coast and ships are liable to be stranded, we stood three miles off. Then we went ashore in our boats and the smallest ship, carrying all our casks and well provided with weapons. We landed a little after midday three miles from the town, where there were some pools, some maize plantations, and a few small stone houses. As we were filling our casks, many bands of Indians came along the coast from the town of Champoton, as it is called, wearing cotton armour to the knees, and carrying bows and arrows, lances and shields, swords which appeared to be two-handed, slings and stones. They wore the habitual feathered crests, their faces were painted black and white and rust-red, and they approached us silently. They came straight towards us, as if in peace, and asked us by signs whether we came from the east. We replied also by signs that we did. We were puzzled by the words that they then called out to us, which were the same as the Indians at Lazaro had used. But we could not make out what they meant. All this happened about nightfall, and the Indians then went off to some near-by village. We posted sentinels as a precaution, for we mistrusted these great assemblies of Indians.

As we watched through the night, we heard a great band of warriors approaching from the farms and the town, and we well knew that this boded us no good. We discussed what we should do, and some were for embarking immediately. As is usual in such cases, there was no agreement. The majority thought, however, that if we attempted to do so the Indians would attack us at once, and since they were so many we should be in danger of our lives. But a few of us were for attacking them in the night, for, as the proverb goes, the first blow is half the battle.

While we were still debating, the dawn broke, and we saw that we were outnumbered by two hundred to one. So wishing one another a stout heart for the fight, we commended ourselves to God and did our best to save our lives.

Once it was daylight we could see many more warriors advancing along the coast with banners raised and plumes and drums, to join the others who had gathered during the night. After forming up in squadrons and surrounding us on all sides, they assailed us with such a shower of arrows and darts and stones from their slings that more than eighty of our soldiers were wounded. Then they attacked us hand to hand, some with lances and some shooting arrows, and others with their two-handed cutting swords. Though we fought back with swords and muskets and crossbows they brought us to a bad pass. At last, feeling the effects of our sword-play, they drew back a little, but not far, and only to shoot at us from greater safety. During the fighting, the Indians shouted to one another '*Al calachuni, calachuni*', which means in their language, 'Attack and kill the captain.' Our captain was hit by ten arrows, and I by three, one of which gave me a dangerous wound in the left side, piercing between my ribs. All the rest received severe lance wounds, and two of our men were captured alive.

Our captain saw that good fighting did not help us, since so many bands surrounded us and so many more were coming up fresh from the town, bringing food and drink with them and a large supply of arrows. All our soldiers had received two or three arrows, three of them had their throats pierced by lance-thrusts, and our captain was bleeding from many wounds. Already fifty of our men had been killed, and we knew that we had no more strength to resist. So we determined with stout hearts to break through the Indian battalions and seek shelter in our boats, which lay off shore, not far away. Thus we saved ourselves. Forming ourselves up in a close squadron, we broke through the enemy, who with fearful yells, whistles, and cries showered arrows upon us, and hurled their lances with all their might, wounding still more of us.

Then we ran into another danger. As we all jumped into the boats at the same time, and there were many of us, they began to sink. Clinging to the sides of the waterlogged craft as best we could, and half swimming, we reached the vessel of shallowest draught, which came in haste to our assistance. Many of our men were wounded again as we embarked, especially those who were clinging to the stern of the boats, for they presented a good target. The Indians even waded into the sea with their lances, and attacked us with all their might. But, thank God, by a great effort we escaped with our lives from these people's clutches.

The battle had lasted an hour, and in addition to the fifty men or more killed and the two prisoners we threw five men overboard a few days later, who had died of their wounds and of the great thirst we suffered. As I said, the town was called Champoton, and the pilots and sailors named this coast on their charts La Costa de Mala Pelea.[1]

When it was all safely over we thanked God for our escape. But as the soldiers' wounds were being dressed some of them complained of pains, for they were beginning to grow cold and the salt water caused considerable swelling. Some of them also cursed the pilot and his voyage to this island that we had discovered. For he was always insisting that it was an island, and not the mainland.

After attending to our wounds, we decided to return to Cuba. But as almost all the sailors were wounded we had not enough

1. The Coast of the Evil Battle.

men to tend the sails. So we abandoned our smallest vessel and set fire to her after removing her sails, cables, and anchors and dividing her unwounded crew among the two larger vessels. But we had even worse trouble in our lack of fresh water. Owing to the attack at Champoton and our hurried retreat to the boats, we had not been able to fetch off the casks and barrels we had filled, but had left them on shore. We had such a thirst that our mouths and tongues were cracked, and there was nothing to give us relief. Such are the hardships to be endured when discovering new lands in the manner that we set about it! No one can imagine their severity who has not himself endured them.

We kept our course very close to the land in the hope of finding some river or bay where we could get fresh water; and after three days we sighted an inlet in which we thought there might be a stream or a freshwater creek. Fifteen of the sailors who had stayed aboard and were unwounded and three soldiers whose wounds were no longer dangerous landed with pickaxes and some barrels. The creek was salty and they dug some holes on the shore. But there the water was as salty and bitter as in the creek. However, bad as the water was, they filled the casks and brought them aboard. But no one could drink it, and it pained the mouths and stomachs of the few soldiers who tried. In this creek there were so many large alligators that it has always been called El Estero de los Lagartos, by which name it is marked on the charts.

While the boats were ashore taking water, a north-east gale arose, so violent that the ships dragged their anchors and were driven towards the beach. Seeing this danger, the sailors who had gone ashore hastily brought the boats back, and had just time to throw out additional anchors and cables, so that the ships rode in safety for two days and nights. Then we raised anchor and set sail, continuing our voyage towards Cuba. The pilot Alaminos discussed our course with the two other pilots, and it was agreed that we should now make for Florida which, according to his readings of the chart, was only two hundred miles away. Once we had reached Florida, he said, the crossing would be shorter than the course by which we had come.

[The ships sailed to Florida, and there took water just in time to save the lives of the parched adventurers. There was a sharp skirmish with the Indians, after which the expedition returned to Cuba, where its leader Francisco Hernandez de Cordoba and three of the soldiers died of their wounds. A report was made to the Governor Diego Velazquez that a thickly populated country had been discovered, whose inhabitants built stone houses, wore cotton clothes, possessed gold, and cultivated maize. The objects taken from the temple at Catoche appeared much superior to anything so far found in the New World. The idols aroused particular interest, and some attributed them to the Jews who were exiled by Titus and Vespasian and sent overseas.

The Governor examined the two prisoners, Melchior and Julian, as to the existence of gold-mines in their country. They replied that there were some, but Bernal Díaz considered this to be untrue. The Spaniards understood the newly discovered country to be called 'Yucatan'. In fact the prisoners were explaining that they cultivate the Yuca or cassava, the plant of which they make their bread.

Diego Velazquez reported to the Royal Council for the Indies that he had made the discoveries himself at very great expense; and the President of the Council, Fonseca, Bishop of Burgos, advised the King – the Emperor Charles V – who was in Flanders, that this was so.

Bernal Díaz was reduced to poverty, and after a disastrous trading expedition asked for the help of the Governor, who was, as we have heard, his relative. Velazquez asked him if he would be prepared to return to Yucatan, and Bernal Díaz, after twitting him on the mistaken name and expatiating on the hardships of Hernandez' expedition, was told that such hardships are to be expected by those who set out to discover new lands and gain honour. Bernal then agreed to serve in the next expedition.]

The Expedition of Juan De Grijalva

In the year 1518 the Governor of Cuba decided to send out another fleet to the lands which we had discovered and which are called Yucatan, and he looked for four ships to compose it. Two of these had taken part in Francisco Hernandez' expedition, and the other two he bought with his own money.

At the time when he was fitting out the fleet, there were present in Santiago de Cuba, where Velazquez resided, Juan de Grijalva, Alonso de Avila, Francisco de Montejo, and Pedro de Alvarado, all of whom had come to see the Governor on business, for they held *encomiendas* [1] on the islands. All four were men of importance. Juan de Grijalva, therefore, who was a relation of the Governor, was appointed Commander-in-Chief, and the other three gentlemen each received command of a vessel. The captains contributed the provisions and stores of cassava bread and salt pork, and Diego Velazquez provided the four ships, a supply of beads and small articles of little value for barter, and some vegetables. He then ordered me to go with these captains as ensign.

As the report had spread that these lands were very rich, and the Indian Julian said there was gold, those settlers and soldiers in the island who possessed no Indians were eager and greedy to go. So we quickly collected two hundred and forty companions. Then each of us, out of his own funds, added such stores, arms, and other necessities as he could. It appears that the Governor's instructions to the expeditions were that they should obtain all the gold and silver they could by barter, and settle if they dared and if the land was suitable for settlement, but otherwise return to Cuba.

When all of us were assembled, and the pilots – three of whom had served on Hernandez' expedition – had received their

1. The right to the labour and produce of some town or village granted to a settler by the Council of the Indies.

instructions, and lantern signals had been arranged to be used at night, we set sail, after hearing mass, on 8 April 1518.

In ten days we doubled Guaniguanico or St Anton's Point, and after another ten days' sailing discovered the island of Cozumel, which we had not sighted before, for with the current that was running we were driven much farther to the leeward than when we sailed with Francisco Hernandez. We followed the southern shore of this island, and sighted a village with a few houses and a good anchorage beside it, which was free from reefs. The Captain and a number of us soldiers went ashore. But the inhabitants of the village had fled when they saw our ships under sail, for they had never seen such a thing before.

We soldiers who landed found two old men who could not run hiding in some maize-fields, and led them back to the Captain. Julian and Melchior, whom he had brought back from Francisco Hernandez' expedition, understood their language perfectly, since it was the same as their own, the islands being only some twelve miles off the coast. Through these interpreters, the Captain spoke kindly to the old men. He gave them some beads and sent them to summon the *Caciques* of the town. They went off, but never came back.

While we were waiting for them, a good-looking Indian girl appeared, and began to talk in the Jamaican language. She told us that all the men and women of the village had fled to the woods in fear. As I and many of our soldiers understood this language very well, since it is the same as is spoken in Cuba, we asked the girl in some surprise how she came to be there. She answered that two years ago she had gone out from Jamaica with ten men of the island in a large canoe, intending to fish from some near-by islets. But the current had carried them to this land, where they had been thrown ashore. The inhabitants had killed her husband and all the other men, and had sacrificed them to their idols. Thinking that this woman would make a good messenger, our Captain sent her to summon the Indians and the *Caciques* of the village, and allowed her two days to go and return. For we were afraid that if we let Melchior and Julian go off they would go back to their own country, which was not far away.

But, to return to the woman from Jamaica, the reply she brought was that none of the Indians would be persuaded to come, whatever she said. We called the village Santa Cruz in honour of the day on which we discovered it.

When Juan de Grijalva saw that it would be wasting time to stay there any longer, he gave us orders to go on board, and the Indian woman went with us. We then continued our voyage, following the route we had taken with Francisco de Hernandez, and in eight days reached the neighbourhood of Champoton, the scene of our defeat by the Indians. As the tide runs out very far in the bay, we anchored three miles from the land, and put half our soldiers ashore in the boats near the houses of the town.

The Indian inhabitants and others from the district at once assembled, as they had done before when they killed fifty-six or more of our men and wounded all the rest, as I have related. They were carrying their usual weapons: bows, arrows, lances of various sizes, some of which were as large as ours; shields, swords single and double-handed, and slings and stones. They wore cotton armour, and carried small trumpets and drums. Most of them had painted their faces black, but some had daubed themselves with red and white; and, very proud of their recent victory, they were drawn up to the shore, ready to fall on us if we landed. But we had gained some experience from our earlier expedition, and had brought with us in our boats some small cannon and a good supply of crossbows and muskets.

As we approached the shore, they began to shoot arrows, and to hurl lances at us with all their might, and although we did them great damage with our cannon, such a flight of arrows rained down on us that half our soldiers were wounded before we got ashore. But once we had landed we checked their fury with good sword-play and with our crossbows. For although they continued to shoot at us we were all wearing padded cotton armour. They continued to attack us for some time, however, before we drove them back into some swamps near the town. In this fight seven soldiers were killed, among them Juan de Quiteria, a man of importance. Our Captain Juan de

Grijalva received three arrow wounds and had two of his teeth broken; and more than sixty of us were wounded.

As soon as we saw that all the enemy had fled, we entered the town, attended to our wounded, and buried our dead. We did not find a single person in the whole place, and those who had retreated to the swamp had all disappeared. We took three prisoners in this skirmish, one of whom was a person of importance; and Grijalva sent them off to summon the *Cacique* of the town, giving them clearly to understand through the interpreters Julian and Melchior that we pardoned them for what they had done. As a sign of peace, he gave them some green beads to hand to their *Cacique*. They departed but never returned. So we concluded that our interpreters had not repeated what they were told, but the exact opposite. We stayed in the town for three days.

I remember that this skirmish took place in some fields where there were many locusts of the small variety, which jumped up and flew in our faces as we were fighting. The Indian archers were many, the arrows fell on us as thickly as hail. Sometimes we mistook them for locusts and, failing to put up our shields, were struck and wounded. But on other occasions we took the flying locusts for arrows, and were severely hampered in our fighting.

Keeping on our course, we reached what appeared to be the mouth of a very great and broad river. However it was not, as we had thought, a river, but a very good harbour. Because there was land on both sides of us, and the water was so wide that it looked like a strait, the pilot Alaminos said that here the island ended and the mainland began. Therefore we called it the Boca de Terminos,[1] and so it is named on the charts.

It was in fact a lagoon, enclosed by islands, with three entrance channels.

Our Captain Grijalva went ashore with the other captains and soldiers, and we spent three days taking soundings at the mouth of the strait. After thoroughly exploring the bay up and down to discover where it ended, we found that there was no island, but that we were lying in a very good harbour.

1. The Spanish name might be translated Boundary Bay.

On shore there were some stone buildings used as prayer-houses, which contained many idols of baked clay, wood, and stone. Some of them were female figures, others represented serpents, and there were many deers' antlers.

We thought that there must be a town near by, since a place with such a safe port would be a good site for a settlement, but we were wrong. It was quite uninhabited, and the prayer-houses merely belonged to those traders and hunters who put in there when passing in their canoes and offered a sacrifice. We found good deer and rabbit hunting, and with the help of a greyhound bitch we killed ten deer and many rabbits. When we had finished our explorations and soundings we re-embarked, but the bitch remained behind.

Making our way by day westward, close along the shore, but not daring to sail at night for fear of reefs and shallows, after three days we sighted the mouth of a very wide river, and brought our ships inshore, since it seemed a good harbour. As we came nearer in, however, we saw the water breaking over the bar at the mouth of the river. So we lowered our boats, and discovered by sounding that our two larger ships could not enter. It was agreed that they should anchor outside in the open sea, and that all our soldiers should go up the river in the two ships of smaller draught and the boats.

We took this course because we saw many Indians armed like those at Champoton with bows and arrows and other weapons, lying in canoes alongside the river banks, and therefore realized that there was a larger town close by. Moreover, as we came along the coast we had seen nets set in the sea for catching fish, and had gone by the boat which was towed behind the flagship to take the fish from two of them.

The river was called the Tabasco river after the *Cacique* of the town who was so named. But since we discovered it on this voyage, and Juan de Grijalva was the discoverer, we called it the Rio de Grijalva, and so it is marked in the charts.

When we arrived within a mile and a half of the town, we heard a great noise of wood being cut, for the Indians were setting up obstacles, strong-points, and stockades, and undoubtedly preparing to fight us. Realizing this, we landed a mile or more from the town on a headland where there were some palms. When the Indians saw us go ashore, a fleet of some fifty canoes approached, full of warriors clad in cotton armour and carrying bows and arrows, lances and shields, drums, and feather plumes. Many other canoes full of warriors were lying in the creeks, and they kept at some distance from us, as if, unlike the others, they had not the courage to approach. On seeing these preparations, we were on the point of firing on them with guns, muskets, and crossbows when, thanks be to God, we decided to call out to them. Through Julian and Melchior, who spoke their language very well, we told them that they had nothing to fear, that we wished to talk to them, and that when they heard what we had to say they would be glad we had come to their country. Moreover, we intended to give them some of the things we had brought with us. When they understood our speech, four canoes carrying about thirty Indians approached us, and we showed them some strings of green beads, some little mirrors and 'blue diamonds',[1] at the sight of which they assumed a more friendly attitude, for they thought they were *chalchihuites*,[2] which they value very highly.

Then our Captain informed them through our interpreters that we came from a distant country, and were vassals of a great emperor called Charles who ruled over many great lords and chieftains, and that they must accept him as their lord, which would be greatly to their advantage, and that in exchange for these beads they must give us poultry and provisions.

Two of the Indians replied, one of them a chief and the other a *papa* – who, as I have said, in New Spain is a sort of priest who serves their idols – saying that they would give us the provisions we asked for, and would barter their things for ours, but that, as for the rest, they already had a lord, and yet we who had just arrived and knew nothing about them wished to offer them another. They warned us not to attack them as we had done at Champoton, for they had more than three *xiquipiles* of warriors from all the near-by provinces in readiness. Their *xiquipiles* are made up of eight thousand men. They said

1. These were cut-glass beads.
2. Jadeite stones.

that they were all well aware that we had killed and wounded more than two hundred men only a few days before at Champoton, but that they were not such weaklings as those others, and for this reason had come to talk to us and find out what we wanted. Whatever we said would then be passed on to the *Caciques* of many towns who had assembled to decide on peace or war.

Our Captain then embraced the Indians as a sign of peace, gave them some strings of beads, and told them to go and bring an answer as soon as possible. He warned them, however, that though we did not wish to provoke them we would have to break into their town if they did not do so.

These messengers whom we sent spoke to the *Caciques* and to the *papas* – who also have a voice in their decisions – and they decided in favour of peace and gifts of food. They also decided that they and the neighbouring towns would presently look for a present of gold to give us, and so secure our friendship, in order that they should not meet with the same treatment as the people of Champoton had suffered.

From what I saw and learnt afterwards, it was the custom in that district and in other parts of New Spain to give presents when making peace, and this we shall see later on.

On the following day more than thirty Indians came to the headland of the palm trees where we were encamped, bringing roasted fish and fowls, *sapota* fruit and maize-cakes, also braziers with live coals, and incense, with which they perfumed us all. Then they spread on the ground some mats which they here call *petates*, and covered them with a cloth, and presented us with gold jewels; some in the form of diadems, some shaped like our own Spanish ducks, and others like lizards. They also gave us three necklaces of hollow beads, and other gold objects of small value. The whole lot was not worth more than two hundred pesos. They also brought some cloaks and skirts of the kind they wear, and begged us kindly to accept all this, since they had no more gold to give us, but that further on, in the direction of the sunset, there was plenty. They kept on repeating: '*Colua, Colua*', and '*Mexico, Mexico*', but we did not know what *Colua* or *Mexico* meant.

Although the present that they brought us was not worth much, we were satisfied, because we now knew for certain that they had gold. Immediately after the presentation they asked us to go on our way; and when Grijalva had thanked them and given them some more beads, we decided to go on board at once, since our two ships were in great danger. For if a northerly gale had blown it would have driven them on the lee shore. But we were also anxious to push on towards the place where they said there was gold.

Once on board, we set our course along the coast and after two days came in sight of a town and district called Ayagualulco, where many Indians marched along the sandy beach, carrying shields of turtle-shell which sparkled when the sun struck them, and which some of our soldiers swore were of low-grade gold. The Indians who carried them were cutting capers, as if mocking at the ships, for they knew that they were at a safe distance, being some way up the coast. We called this place La Rambla, and so it is named on the charts.

Sailing further up the coast, we sighted a bay into which flows the river Tonala, which we entered on our way back and named the Rio de San Antonio, as it is now marked on the charts.

Continuing on our course, we noted the position of the great river Coatzacoalcos, and decided to enter the bay, not in order to explore it but because of bad weather. Soon we came in sight of the great mountains, which are snow-covered all the year round, and we saw other mountains, nearer the sea, which are called the San Martin range. We gave them this title because the first to see them was a soldier from Havana of that name who was in our company.

As we followed up the coast, Captain Pedro de Alvarado went ahead with his ship and entered a river which is called in the Indian language Papaloapan, but which we named the Rio de Alvarado, since he was the first to enter it. Here some Indian fishermen, natives of a town called Tacotalpa, gave him some fish. We were waiting with the three other ships at the mouth of the river for him to sail down, and the General was very angry with him for having gone up without his permission. He ordered him never again to go ahead of the other ships, in case he should meet with some accident in which we could not come to his assistance.

We then sailed on, all four ships together, till we came to the mouth of another river, which we named the Rio de las Banderas,[1] because we saw a great number of Indians with long lances, from each of which hung a great cloth.

Some readers who have visited New Spain, and other interested persons who have not, may be aware that Mexico was a very large city, built in the water like Venice, and governed by a great prince called Montezuma, who was king of many neighbouring lands and ruled over the whole of New Spain, which is a country twice the size of our own. This prince was so powerful that he wished to extend his sway and information further than was possible. He had received news of our first expedition under Francisco Hernandez de Cordoba, and of the battles of Catoche and Champoton, also of the happenings at Champoton during our present voyage. He knew that our soldiers, though few, had defeated the warriors of that town and the very numerous allies who had joined them. He knew that we had entered the Tabasco river, and of our dealings with the *Caciques* of Tabasco. Moreover, he realized that our purpose was to barter the goods we had brought for gold. All this information had been presented to him painted on cloths made of sisal hemp, which is like linen. Knowing that we were sailing up the coast towards his provinces, he ordered his governors, if we brought our ships into their districts, to barter gold for our beads, especially the green ones, since they somewhat resemble their *chalchihuites*, which were valued as highly as emeralds. He also ordered them to find out more about our persons and our intentions.

Now it is a fact, as we afterwards heard, that the Indians' ancestors had prophesied that men with beards would come from the direction of the sunrise and rule over them. So, for one reason or another, many of the great Montezuma's people were posted beside that river, watching for us, and carrying long poles with a white cotton flag on the end of each, which they

1. Now called the Rio Jamapa.

waved at us, calling to us, seemingly as a sign of peace, to come and join them on the shore.

Astonished at this unusual sight, the General and his captains decided to lower two boats, ordering all our crossbowmen and musketeers, also twenty of us soldiers, the youngest and nimblest, to jump in. They sent Francisco de Montejo with us, with instructions to report immediately if the men with flags proved to be warriors, or if we saw anything else of importance.

At this time, thanks be to God, the weather was good, which it rarely is on that coast, and when we got ashore we found three *Caciques*, one of whom was Montezuma's Governor and had many of his followers with him. They had brought some of their local poultry, and of those maize cakes that they eat, and some pineapples and *sapota* fruit, which in other parts of the country are called *mameyes*. They had spread mats on the ground and were seated under the shade of some trees, and they invited us to sit down also, all by signs, because Julian, who came from Cape Catoche, did not understand their language, which was Mexican. Then they brought clay braziers with burning coals and incensed us with a sort of resin.

Captain Montejo reported all these facts to the General, and Grijalva decided to cast anchor, and go ashore with his captains and soldiers. When the *Caciques* and Governor saw him land and realized that he was the Commander of us all, they treated him ceremoniously, according to their custom, and he behaved very ingratiatingly to them. He ordered that they should be given 'blue diamonds' and green beads, and conveyed to them by signs that they should bring gold to trade with us. Then the Indian Governor sent messages to all the neighbouring towns that gold jewels must be brought to be bartered; and during the six days that we stayed there they brought more than sixteen thousand pesos'-worth of jewellery of low-grade gold, worked into a variety of shapes.

This must be the gold which the chroniclers Gomara, Illescas, and Jovio [1] say was given to us at Tabasco. They state this as the

---

1. This is the first of many refutations of statements by other historians, most of which I have omitted on account of their repetitiveness.

truth although it is well known that there is no gold in the Rio de Grijalva province or anywhere near it, and very few jewels.

We took formal possession of this country in His Majesty's name; and when we had done so, the General addressed the Indians, telling them that we intended to return to our ships, and giving them some shirts from Spain. We took one of them aboard with us, who when he understood our language became a Christian, taking the name of Francisco, and I afterwards met him with his Indian wife.

Now when we had been there six days the General saw that the Indians would bring no more gold to barter. So, the ships being in danger from a north or north-east wind, he thought it was time to embark.

As we sailed along the coast we sighted an island of white sand washed over by the sea, which lay about nine miles from the shore. This we called the Isla Blanca,[1] and it is so marked on the charts. Not far from this we sighted another island, on which were many green trees. This lay about twelve miles from the shore, and we called it Isla Verde.[2] Sailing on, we saw yet another island, larger than the others and less than five miles from the shore, and in front of it was a good roadstead in which the General ordered us to anchor.

The boats were then launched, and Juan de Grijalva with many of us soldiers landed to inspect this island, for we saw smoke rising from it. We found two stone buildings of good workmanship, each with a flight of steps leading up to a kind of altar, and on those altars were evil-looking idols, which were their gods. Here we found five Indians who had been sacrificed to them on that very night. Their chests had been struck open and their arms and thighs cut off, and the walls of these buildings were covered with blood. All this amazed us greatly, and we called this island the Isla de Sacrificios,[3] as it is now named on the charts.

We all went ashore opposite this island, and on the wide, sandy beach we set up huts and shelters made from the boughs of trees and our ships' sails. Then many Indians came down to the shore bringing various small gold articles to barter, as at

1. White Island.   2. Green Island.   3. Island of Sacrifices.

the Rio de Banderas. This they did, as we afterwards learnt, on the instructions of the great Montezuma. But the Indians who came were fearful, and brought very little. Therefore our Captain ordered the anchors to be raised, and we set sail. Our next anchorage was opposite another island about a mile and a half off shore, and this is the place where the port of Vera Cruz now stands.

We landed on a sandy beach, and to escape the many swarms of mosquitoes built our huts on the tops of the highest dunes, which are very extensive in these parts. From our boats we took careful soundings of the harbour, and discovered that there was a good bottom, also that under the shelter of the island our ships would be safe from the northerly gales.

Once this was done the General and thirty of us soldiers went to the island, fully armed, in two boats. There we found a prayer-house with a huge and ugly idol which they called Tezcatlipoca, in charge of four Indians in black cloaks and hoods, very like those of our Dominicans or canons. These were the priests or *papas*.

That day they had sacrificed two boys, cutting open their chests and offering their blood and hearts to that accursed idol. And these priests came to incense us with the same incense as they used on Tezcatlipoca, for at the time of our arrival they were burning something that smelt like incense before him. But we would not allow them to burn it over us. We were all too upset by the sight of those two dead boys, and too indignant at their cruelty. The General asked the Indian Francisco, whom we had brought from the Rio de Banderas and who seemed fairly intelligent, why they had done this; and he replied by signs – because, as I have said, we had then no interpreter, Julian and Melchior not understanding Mexican – that the people of Culua had ordered the sacrifice. But as he was slovenly in his speech he said, '*Ulua, Ulua.*' So, our Commander who was present being named Juan, and it being Saint John's day in June, we called the island San Juan de Ulua. This port is now very famous, and great sea-walls have been erected there to protect ships from the northerly gales. It is here that all merchandise from Castile is landed for Mexico and New Spain.

While we were encamped in the dunes Indians from the neighbouring towns came to barter their gold jewellery for our goods, but they brought so little and it was so nearly valueless that we took no account of it. We stayed there seven days, but found the mosquitoes unbearable, and realized that we were wasting our time. We now knew for certain that these were not islands but the mainland, and that there were large towns and great numbers of Indians. But the cassava bread we had brought was all mouldy and full of weevils, and was going sour. Moreover there were not enough soldiers in our company to found a settlement, especially as thirteen had died of their wounds and another four were still disabled. Taking all this into account, we agreed to inform Diego Velazquez of our situation, in the hope that he would send us some help. For Juan de Grijalva was most eager to found a settlement, even with the few soldiers he had with him. He was always a courageous man with all the qualities of a brave and bold leader.

It was therefore decided that Pedro de Alvarado should take the good ship *San Sebastian* and carry the message to Cuba. There were two reasons for this choice: firstly, that Grijalva and the other captains were annoyed with Alvarado for having sailed up the Rio Papaloapan, and secondly that Alvarado had come on the expedition against his will, as he was not in good health.

It was agreed that all the wounded men, and all the cloth and gold that had been gained by barter, should be sent back with him. Each of the captains then wrote to Velazquez expressing his own opinion, and the ship set sail.

No sooner had we left Cuba on our voyage with Grijalva than Velazquez began to be afraid that some disaster might befall us. In his anxiety for news, he sent a small ship with a few soldiers to look for us, under the command of Cristobal de Olid, a valuable and very resourceful captain, who was afterwards Cortes' quartermaster. Velazquez instructed him to follow Francisco Hernandez de Cordoba's route until he overtook us. His ship, however, was struck by a heavy gale while anchored off the coast of Yucatan, and his pilot ordered the cables to be cut to save it from foundering at anchor. So he returned to Santiago de Cuba, having lost his anchors.

Diego Velazquez was waiting at the port and, on hearing that Olid had no news of us, became even more anxious than before. But at this point Pedro de Alvarado arrived with the gold and cloth and the wounded men, and told the whole story of our discoveries; and when the Governor saw the gold that Alvarado brought, he greatly overestimated its value, on account of its being in the form of jewellery. With Diego Velazquez were many men from the city and other parts of the island, who were there on business; when the King's officers took the royal fifth, which is due to His Majesty, everyone was astonished at the riches of the lands we had discovered.

Pedro de Alvarado was a good story-teller, and they say that Diego Velazquez could do nothing but embrace him, and there were great rejoicings and sports for the next eight days. There had been rumours enough already about the existence of rich lands, but now, with the arrival of this gold, they were exaggerated still further throughout the islands and in Castile, as I shall tell later. But I must leave Diego Velazquez to his rejoicings, and return to our ships at San Juan de Ulua.

After Captain Pedro de Alvarado had left us for Cuba, the General, the captains, and the soldiers decided, with the approval of the pilots, that we should continue to hug the shore and discover all we could along the coast. Keeping on our course, we sighted the Sierra de Tuxtla;[1] and further on, two days later we sighted another and higher range which is now called the Sierra de Tuxpan, after a town of that name which is near by. As we followed the coast we saw many towns, apparently some six to nine miles inland, and belonging to the province of Panuco. And sailing further, we came to a great and very rapid river which we named the Rio de Canoas, at the mouth of which we anchored.

When all three ships lay at anchor and we were a little off our guard, about twenty large canoes, full of Indian warriors armed with bows, arrows, and lances, suddenly came down the

1. This is incorrect. They had already passed this range before arriving at San Juan de Ulua. The mountains they now sighted were the Sierra de Tuxpan, to be mentioned in the next sentence as a separate range.

river and made straight for the ship which seemed to them the
smallest and lay nearest the shore. It was commanded by Francisco de Montejo. The Indians then shot a flight of arrows,
which wounded five soldiers, and cast ropes about the ship, intending to tow it off. They even cut one of its cables with their
copper axes. However, the captain and soldiers put up a good
fight and overturned three of their canoes, and we hastened to
their assistance in our boats with muskets and crossbows. We
wounded more than a third of these Indians, who returned
from their unfortunate adventure to the place from which they
had come.

We then raised anchor, and sailed along the coast until we
came to a great cape which was very difficult to double, for the
currents were so strong that we could make no headway. The
pilot Alaminos told the General that it was no use trying to follow our course any further, and gave many reasons for his
opinion. A discussion was held to decide what should be done,
and it was resolved that we should return to Cuba. One reason
for this was that the winter rains were already setting in. But we
were also short of provisions, and one ship was leaking badly.
However, the captains were not of one mind. Juan de Grijalva
said that he wanted to plant a settlement, but Alonso de Avila
and Francisco de Montejo objected, saying that they would not
be able to defend it against the great number of warriors in that
country; moreover, we were all worn out by our long voyage.

So we turned round and set sail before the wind and in a few
days, with the help of the currents, reached the mouth of the
great Rio de Coatzacoalcos. But we could not enter it on account
of unfavourable weather. So, hugging the shore, we entered the
Rio de Tonala, which we had named San Antonio. There we
careened one of the ships, which was making water fast, for
as we came in it had struck the bar, where the sea was very
shallow.

While we were repairing the ship many Indians came quite
peaceably from the town of Tonala, which is about three miles
away, bringing us maize-cakes, fish, and fruit, which they gave
us freely. The Captain treated them most kindly and ordered
that they should be given green beads and 'diamonds'. He asked

them by signs to bring gold for barter and we offered them goods in exchange. So they brought jewels of inferior gold, which they exchanged for beads. Some Indians came also from Coatzacoalcos and other neighbouring towns bringing their jewellery, but this was of no value.

Besides these objects for barter, most of the Indians were in the habit of carrying brightly polished copper axes with painted wooden handles, apparently for show, or as a sign of rank; and we began to barter for these in the belief that they were made of low-quality gold. In three days we had collected more than six hundred of them, and were very well pleased. But the Indians were even more pleased with the beads. There was no profit for either party, however, since the axes were made of copper and the beads were of no value. One sailor bought seven and was quite delighted with them.

I remember that a soldier named Bartolome Pardo went to one of their temples, which stood on a hill – I have already said that these were called *cues*, which means Houses of the Gods. Here he found many idols and some copal, which is a kind of resin that they burn as incense; also some flint knives used for sacrifices and circumcision, and in a wooden chest he discovered a number of gold objects such as diadems and necklaces, and two idols and some hollow beads. This soldier kept the gold for himself, but took the idols and other objects to the Captain. However, someone reported the matter to Grijalva, who wanted to take his booty from him. But we begged that he might be allowed to keep it, since he was a decent man, and Grijalva let the poor fellow have it after deducting the royal fifth. It was worth about a hundred and fifty pesos.

I sowed some orange pips near another of these temples, and this is the story. As there were so many mosquitoes near the river, ten of us soldiers slept in a temple on a hill. It was near this that I sowed these pips, which I had brought from Cuba, for it was rumoured that we were returning to settle. The trees came up very well, for when the *papas* saw that these were different plants from any they knew, they protected them and watered them and kept them free from weeds. All the oranges in the province are descendants of these trees. I know that people will say these old stories have nothing to do with my history, and I will tell no more.[1]

We left the Indians of that province very happy when we re-embarked for Cuba, which we reached after forty-five days of variable weather, landing at the point of Santiago, where Diego Velazquez was staying. He gave us a good welcome, and was pleased with the gold we brought, which amounted to about four thousand pesos. The total, including the quantity brought by Pedro de Alvarado, came to twenty thousand pesos in all, and some said even more. The King's officers then took the royal fifth, but when the six hundred axes that we thought were inferior gold were produced, they were all tarnished, and looked like the copper they were. The officers laughed at us very heartily, and made great fun of our bargain.

The Governor was delighted at this, for he seemed to be on bad terms with his kinsman Grijalva. He had no cause, except that Francisco de Montejo and Pedro de Alvarado had quarrelled with Grijalva, and Alonso de Avila made the trouble worse. Once these squabbles were over, there began to be talk of sending another fleet, and about who should be chosen as Captain.

1. This passage is scratched out in the original manuscript. I have however restored it to its place.

The Expedition of Hernando Cortes: Preparations

DIEGO VELAZQUEZ was afraid that some court favourite would supplant him, now that it was established that the new countries were rich in gold. He therefore petitioned the Royal Council of the Indies for authority to trade with and conquer the newly discovered lands, and to settle and apportion them when peace was established; and he claimed, in his letters and report, that he had himself spent several thousand pesos on their discovery. By means of bribes, in the form of concessions in Cuba, he gained all that he wanted from the Council during the King's absence in Flanders. Before he received his answer from Spain, however, Cortes' expedition had already set out.

[At this point Bernal Díaz delivers a violent attack on his fellow chroniclers, Gomara, Illescas, and Jovio, accusing them of exaggeration, misrepresentation, and in the case of Gomara, of undue adulation of Cortes. He goes so far as to accuse Gomara of having his palm greased by Cortes' son.]

When the Governor Diego Velazquez realized that the newly discovered lands were rich, he ordered a new fleet to be sent out, much larger than Grijalva's. For this purpose he collected ten ships in the port of Santiago de Cuba, where he resided, four of them being those in which we had returned with Juan de Grijalva. These he immediately had careened, and the other six were collected from all over the island. He then loaded them with provisions, consisting of cassava bread and salt pork, for at that time there were neither sheep nor cattle in the island of Cuba, it having been only recently settled. But these provisions had only to last until we reached the port of Havana, for it was there that we were to take our stores aboard, which we duly did.

But I must leave this, and speak of the disputes that arose over the choice of a Captain to lead the expedition. There were many arguments, and much opposition. For many gentlemen said that Vasco Porcallo, a relative of the Conde de Feria, ought to be Captain. But Diego Velazquez was afraid that Porcallo would raise the fleet against him, for he was a daring man. Others said that Agustin Bermudez, or Antonio Velazquez Borrego, or Bernardino Velazquez, all kinsmen of the Governor, should have the command; and most of us soldiers who were there wanted to sail again under Juan de Grijalva, for he was a good captain, and no fault could be found with his character or his powers of command.

While all this was going on, two great favourites of Diego Velazquez, his own secretary Andres de Duero and Amador de Lares, His Majesty's accountant, made a secret compact with a gentleman called Hernando Cortes, a native of Medellin, who held an *encomienda* of Indians in the island, and had recently married a lady named Catalina Suarez, La Marcaida. She was the sister of a certain Juan Suarez who settled in Mexico after the conquest of New Spain. As far as I know, and by general report, theirs was a love-match. But some who saw it more closely have had a great deal to say about their marriage, and for that reason I will touch this delicate subject no more, but return to the compact.

These two intimates of Diego Velazquez agreed that they would get him to appoint Cortes Captain-General of the whole fleet, and that the three of them would divide the spoil of gold, silver, and jewels that fell to Cortes' share. For although Diego Velazquez announced and proclaimed that the expedition was for the purpose of settlement, his secret intention was not to settle but to trade, as was afterwards apparent from the instructions he gave.

Once this arrangement was made, Duero and the accountant went to work on Diego Velazquez. They addressed him in honeyed words, praising Cortes highly as the very man for the post of Captain, since he was not only enterprising but knew how to command and inspire fear. Moreover, they said he would carry out whatever orders he was given, in regard to the fleet and everything else. They also pointed out that since Velazquez had been his sponsor at his marriage to Doña Catalina Suarez, he was in fact the Governor's stepson. Thus they persuaded Velazquez to choose Cortes as Captain-General.

Andres de Duero, the Governor's secretary, drew up the appointment in his very best ink, as the proverb goes, and gave Cortes the ample powers he wanted. When the appointment was proclaimed some were pleased and some were angry.

One Sunday when Diego was on his way to mass – and as Governor he was escorted to church by the most distinguished men in the town – he called Hernando Cortes to walk on his right, as a sign of honour. Then a buffoon called 'the mad Cervantes' ran in front of him, making grimaces and jokes, and crying : 'Way for Don Diego, the procession of Don Diego, Don Diego, Don Diego! What a Captain you have chosen, Don Diego, a Captain from Medellin in Estremadura, a very valiant Captain! But take care, Diego, or he may run off with your fleet, for he knows how to look after himself, as everybody can tell you!' And he shouted more nonsense as well, all with a spice of malice in it. Andres de Duero, who was walking on the Governor's other side, gave him a couple of slaps to make him stop. 'Be quiet, you drunken fool,' he said, 'and stop your tricks. This so-called wit of yours is nothing but malice, and we know very well you didn't invent it yourself, either.' But the more Duero slapped him the more persistently the fool went on : 'Long live Don Diego! Way for my master Don Diego and his bold Captain! And let me tell you, friend Diego, I would rather go off with him to these new rich lands than stay behind and watch you weeping over the bad bargain you've made today.' There is no doubt that some of Velazquez' relatives had given the buffoon a gold piece or two to utter his spite in the guise of wit. Moreover, all that he said came true, as they say the utterances of fools sometimes do. Yet the choice of Hernando Cortes certainly served to exalt our holy Faith and benefit His Majesty, as I shall presently relate.

Before proceeding further, let me say that the valiant and enterprising Hernando Cortes was born a gentleman by four lines of descent. First, through his father Martin Cortes; secondly through the Pizarros; thirdly through the Monroys; and fourthly through the Altamiranos. And though he was a valiant, bold, and enterprising Captain, I will henceforth give him none of these epithets, nor speak of him as Marques del

Valle, but simply as Hernando Cortes. For the plain name Cortes
was as highly respected in Spain and throughout the Indies as
the name of Alexander in Macedonia, or those of Julius Caesar,
Pompey, and Scipio among the Romans, or Hannibal in Car-
thage, or Gonzalo Hernandez, 'the Great Captain', in our own
Castile. Indeed, the valiant Cortes himself preferred simply to
be called by this name than by any lofty titles, and so I will
call him henceforth.

As soon as Hernando Cortes was appointed General, he began
to collect arms of all kinds – guns, powder, and crossbows –
and all the munitions of war he could find, also articles for
barter, and other material for the expedition.

Moreover, he began to adorn himself and to take much more
care of his appearance than before. He wore a plume of feathers,
with a medallion and a gold chain, and a velvet cloak trimmed
with loops of gold. In fact he looked like a bold and gallant
Captain. But he had nothing with which to meet the expenses
I have described, for at that time he was very poor and in debt,
despite the fact that he owned a good *encomienda* of Indians
and was getting gold from the mines. But all this he spent on
his person, on finery for his newly married wife, and on enter-
taining guests who had come to stay with him. For he was very
friendly and a good conversationalist, and had twice been chosen
alcayde[1] of the town of Santiago de Baracoa, where he lived; and
in that country the appointment is considered a great honour.

When some merchant friends of his heard that he had been
made Captain-General, they lent him four thousand pesos in
coin, and another four thousand in goods, on the security of
his Indians and his estate. He then had two standards and
banners made, worked in gold with the royal arms and a cross
on each side and a legend that read: 'Brothers and comrades,
let us follow the sign of the Holy Cross in true faith, for under
this sign we shall conquer.' And he ordered a proclamation to
be made to the sound of trumpets and drums, in the name of
His Majesty and of Diego Velazquez as his Viceroy and of himself as his Captain-General, that anyone who wished to accompany him to the newly discovered lands, to conquer and settle,

1. Mayor.

would receive a share of the gold, silver, and riches to be gained, and an *encomienda* of Indians once the country had been pacified, and that for this enterprise Diego Velazquez held authority from His Majesty.

Now when this proclamation alleging the King's authority was made, the chaplain Benito Martinez, whom Velazquez had sent to obtain it, had not yet come back from Spain. But once the news had spread through Cuba, and Cortes had written to his friends in different towns asking them to get ready to accompany him on the expedition, some of them sold their farms to buy arms and horses, and others began to prepare cassava bread, and to salt pork for stores, and to make quilted cotton armour. They made ready all that was necessary as well as they could.

Now more than three hundred and fifty of us soldiers were collected at Santiago de Cuba, whence the fleet was to sail. From the Governor's own household came one of his stewards, Diego de Ordaz, whom he had himself sent to keep a watch on the expedition and see that Cortes did not play him a trick. For he was always afraid that Cortes might turn against him, although he concealed his fears. There was also Francisco de Morla, and one Escobar, whom we called 'the Page', and a certain Heredia, and Juan Ruano and Pedro Escudero and Martin Ramos de Lares, and many more who were friends and followers of Diego Velazquez. And I put myself last among them, for I was also a member of the Governor's household, being a relative of his.

I have put down these soldiers' names from memory. But later, in the proper time and place, I will record the names of all those who took part in the expedition, in so far as I can remember them, and will say from what part of Spain they came.

Cortes took great pains with the preparations of his fleet and hurried everything on. For malice and envy reigned among Velazquez' relatives, who were offended because their kinsman neither trusted nor listened to them, and because he had given the command to Cortes, solely on account of his marriage. For they knew that Velazquez had been very hostile to him only a few days before that. So they went about grumbling against the Governor and Cortes, and they worked on Velazquez in every possible way to induce him to revoke Cortes' commission.

Now Cortes was advised of all this, and for that reason never left the Governor's side. He was most sedulously attentive to him, and kept on telling him that, God willing, he would make him a very wealthy man in a very short time. Furthermore, Diego de Duero repeatedly advised Cortes to hasten the embarkation of himself and his soldiers since, owing to the importunities of his relatives, Velazquez was already changing his mind.

When Cortes realized this, he told his wife that all the provisions he wished to take, and such gifts as a woman will give to a husband setting out on a long voyage, were to be sent and loaded on the ships. He had already advised all the captains, pilots, and soldiers by proclamation that they must be on board by nightfall, and that no one must remain ashore. Then, when he had seen his company embarked, he went to take leave of Diego Velazquez, accompanied by his close friends and many other gentlemen, and by all the most distinguished men in the town. Then, after an exchange of gestures and embraces between himself and the Governor, he took his leave; and very early next morning, after hearing mass, we went to our ships. Diego Velazquez himself came with us; and he and Cortes again embraced, with a great exchange of compliments. We then set sail and with favourable weather reached the port of Trinidad in very few days. Here we put into harbour, and on going ashore were welcomed by most of the citizens of the town, who came to the port to meet us. I have here described all the opposition which Cortes met with, and shown that the true events entirely differ from Gomara's account of them in his history.[1]

The chief inhabitants of the town found lodgings for Cortes and the rest of us among their neighbours, and Cortes himself stayed with Juan de Grijalva. He had his standard and the royal pennant set up before his quarters, issued a proclamation, as he had done at Santiago, and ordered a search to be made for arms of all sorts, food, and other necessities, which were to be purchased.

1. They also differ from those of Las Casas in his *Brief Narration*. Here Cortes learns of Velazquez' intention to revoke his decision, raids the slaughter-houses for meat, and departs, insufficiently provisioned and defying Velazquez, who comes down to the shore to protest. Las Casas claims to have Cortes' own authority for his version of events.

From that town five brothers came to join us: Pedro de Alvarado, of whom I have already spoken, Jorge de Alvarado, Gonzalo and Gomez, and Juan de Alvarado, the eldest, who was a bastard. From here also came Alonso de Avila, who had served as a Captain in Grijalva's expedition, and Juan de Escalante, and Pedro Sanchez Farfan, and Gonzalo Mejia, who was afterwards treasurer in Mexico, and a certain Baena, and Juanes de Fuenterrabia, and Lares 'the good Horseman' (so called because there was another Lares), and Cristobal de Olid 'the valiant', who was quartermaster in the Mexican wars, and Ortiz 'the Musician', and Gaspar Sanchez, nephew of the treasurer of Cuba, and a certain Diego de Pineda or Pinedo, and Alonso Rodriguez, who owned rich gold-mines, and Bartolome Garcia, and other gentlemen whose names I do not remember, all persons of quality.

From Trinidad, Cortes wrote to Santispiritus, which is fifty-four miles away, announcing to all its citizens that he was setting out on this expedition to serve His Majesty and offering fine words and inducements to attract persons of quality who had settled in the place. Among the many who joined him were Alonso Hernandez Puertocarrero, cousin of the Conde de Medellin; Gonzalo de Sandoval, who became in course of time *alguacil mayor* [1] in Mexico, and who was for eight months Governor of New Spain; and Juan de Velazquez de Leon, who was a kinsman of Diego Velazquez. Rodrigo Rengel, Gonzalo Lopez de Jimena and his brother, and Juan Sedeño came also. This Juan Sedeño was a settler in the town, which I mention because we had two other men of that name in the fleet. All these excellent persons came from Santispiritus to Trinidad, where Cortes was, and when he heard they were coming he went out to meet them with all the soldiers in his company, receiving them most cordially, and they showed him the highest respect.

All these settlers had farms near the town, where they kept herds of swine and made cassava bread, and each one was careful to supply all the provisions he could. We continued to collect soldiers in this way, and to buy horses, which at that time were both scarce and costly. As Alonso Hernandez Puertocarrero had neither a horse nor the money to buy one, Cortes

1. Chief constable.

bought him a grey mare, which he paid for with some of the gold loops of that velvet cloak which was made for him at Santiago de Cuba.

At that very time a ship arrived in the port of Havana,[1] loaded with cassava bread and salt pork, which one Juan Sedeño of that place was taking to be sold at some gold-mines near Santiago. Immediately on landing, this man went to pay his respects to Cortes, who after a long conversation bought the ship and its cargo on credit. So we now had eleven ships and, thank God, all was going well with us.

Meanwhile, however, Diego Velazquez had sent written orders for the fleet to be held, and for Cortes to be sent to him as a prisoner.

I must go back a little and describe the events at Santiago de Cuba immediately after we had sailed. So many things were said to the Governor against Cortes that he reversed his decision. He was told that Cortes was already in rebellion and had crept silently out of port; and that he had been heard to say he intended to be Captain in spite of Diego Velazquez and all his relatives, which was the reason why he had embarked all his soldiers at night, for if any attempt had been made to detain him by force he would certainly have set sail. Velazquez was also told that he had been deceived by his secretary Andres de Duero, and by Amador de Lares the accountant, who had made a secret arrangement with Cortes. The chief participants in this plot to make Diego Velazquez revoke his authority were some members of his own family and an old man called Juan Millan, nicknamed 'the Astrologer', who some said was a little mad since he acted so impetuously. This old man kept saying to Velazquez: 'Be careful, sir, or Cortes will pay you out for putting him in prison.[2] He is cunning and determined, and he'll ruin you if you don't stop him at once.'

Velazquez listened to all this and a great deal more and, having already had his own suspicions, sent two messengers

1. This was not the present Havana, then called Puerto de Carenas, but a port on the south coast of the island.

2. This refers to an earlier incident not otherwise described by Bernal Díaz.

whom he trusted with orders and instructions to Francisco
Verdugo, the chief alcayde of Trinidad, who was his brother-in-
law, and letters to other friends and relations, all to the effect
that the fleet must on no account be allowed to sail. His orders
were that Cortes should be arrested and held prisoner, since he
was no longer Captain, his commission being now revoked and
conferred on Vasco Porcallo. Velazquez sent letters also to Diego
de Ordaz, Francisco de Morla, and others of his following, re-
questing them to prevent the sailing of the fleet.

When Cortes heard of this he spoke to Ordaz and Francisco
Verdugo, and all the soldiers and settlers of Trinidad who would,
he thought, be his enemies and would accept Velazquez' instructions, making them such speeches and promises that he brought
them over to his side. Diego de Ordaz himself immediately advised Verdugo the alcayde to say nothing about the matter and
have nothing to do with it. He pointed out that so far they had
seen no change in Cortes; on the contrary he had shown himself a faithful servant of the Governor. And he said further that
if Velazquez wanted to make any accusations against Cortes
in order to take away his command, it would be as well to remember that Cortes had many important friends who bore a
grudge against Velazquez because he had not given them good
grants of Indians. 'What is more,' he said, 'Cortes has a large
body of soldiers and is very powerful. He might well raise dissension in the town. Indeed, his soldiers might sack and plunder
it, or worse.'

So the matter was quietly dropped, and one of Velazquez'
messengers, Pedro de la Vega by name, joined our expedition.
By the other messenger Cortes sent a very friendly letter to the
Governor, expressing his astonishment at His Honour's decision,
and saying that his only desire was to serve God and His
Majesty, and to obey Velazquez as the King's representative. He
begged him to pay no more attention to what was said by the
gentlemen of his family, and not to let his decisions be affected
by an old madman like Juan Millan. He also wrote to all his
friends, and to his partners, Duero and the accountant.

Cortes then gave orders to all his soldiers to furbish up their
arms, and to the blacksmiths in the town to make helmets, and

to the crossbowmen to overhaul their stores and make arrows. He then sent for two blacksmiths and persuaded them to come with us, which they did. We were ten days in the town, and left it, as I will shortly tell, for the port of Havana.

When Cortes saw that there was nothing more to be done at Trinidad, he ordered the followers he had collected there either to come aboard the ships that were lying off the south coast, or to go overland to Havana with Pedro de Alvarado, who was going to pick up some men from the farms along the road. In his company I went. Cortes also sent a gentleman called Juan de Escalante, a great friend of his, in a ship along the north coast, and ordered the horses to be sent by land. Once these arrangements were made, he himself boarded the flagship, to set sail with all the fleet for Havana. It appears, however, that because it was night the ships of the convoy failed to see his flagship and sailed without him.

We arrived overland at Havana with Pedro de Alvarado, and the ship in which Juan de Escalante had come along the north coast was there before us, as were all the horses. But Cortes did not come, and no one could explain why. Five days passed without news of his ship, and we began to be afraid that he had been wrecked on the Jardines, near the Isla de Pinos and ten or twelve miles from Havana, where there are many shallows. We all agreed that three of the smaller vessels should go in search of him, and another two days passed in the preparation of the ships, and in discussions as to whether this man or that man should go; but still Cortes did not come. Then factions formed among us, and we began to play the game of 'who shall be Captain till we have news of Cortes?' And the man who was chiefly responsible for this was Diego de Ordaz, Velazquez' chief steward, whom he had sent merely to watch the fleet and to see that there was no rebellion against him.

To return to Cortes. He had, as I have said, embarked on the largest ship, which seems to have run aground on one of the shallows in the neighbourhood of the Isla de Pinos or the Jardines, where it remained stuck in the sand and could not be floated off. Cortes then had all the cargo that could be removed taken ashore in the boat, for there was land close by to which they could convey it, and when the ship was floating and navigable they took her into deeper water and reloaded the cargo. Thereupon they set sail and continued their voyage to Havana.

Most of us captains and gentlemen who were waiting for Cortes were delighted at his arrival, all except some who had hoped to be Captain, for the game of 'choosing the Captain' now ceased.

When we had lodged Cortes in the house of Pedro Barba, who was Velazquez' lieutenant in the town, he ordered his standards to be hung in front of his lodgings, and the same proclamation to be made as before.

From Havana there came Francisco de Montejo, a gentleman I shall mention very often, who after the conquest of Mexico became Captain and Governor of Yucatan, also Diego de Soto of Toro, who was Cortes' steward in Mexico, and a certain Angulo y Garcicaro, and Sebastian Rodriguez, and one Pacheco, and a certain Gutierrez, and one Rojas – not Rojas 'the Rich' – and a lad called Santa Clara, and the two brothers Martinez del Fregenal, and Juan de Najera – I do not mean the deaf one who played *pelota* in Mexico. All were persons of quality, and in addition there were other soldiers whose names I do not remember.

When Cortes saw all these gentlemen collected together he was greatly pleased, and immediately sent a ship to an Indian town near Cape Guaniguanico, where they made cassava bread and kept many pigs, to have her laden with salt pork. The place belonged to Diego Velazquez, and since Diego de Ordaz was steward of Velazquez' properties Cortes sent him as captain of this ship. Moreover he wanted to be rid of him, for he knew that Ordaz had not shown himself too well disposed towards him during the discussions on who should be Captain, when the flagship was aground off the Isla de Pinos. So to avoid arguments, Cortes sent him off with orders to remain at the port of Guaniguanico after taking aboard the provisions, until he should be joined by the other ship which was sailing along the north coast. Then, unless he sent Indians in a canoe to advise them of a change of plan, the two together should set out for Cozumel.

Francisco de Montejo and the other settlers at Havana put

aboard great stores of cassava bread and salt pork, the only provisions to be had, and Cortes then had all the artillery, which consisted of ten brass guns and some falconets, brought ashore and entrusted to a gunner named Mezsa, a Levantine called Arbenga, and a certain Juan Catalan, to be cleaned and tested. He told them to see that balls and powder were prepared, and gave them wine and vinegar for their cleaning, and chose one Bartolome de Usagre to help them. He also ordered that the crossbows with their cords, nuts, and other parts should be overhauled and tested at the target, to see how far each of them would carry. As there is much cotton in the country round Havana, we made ourselves well-padded armour.

It was here in Havana that Cortes began to form a household and assume the manners of a lord. The first butler he appointed was one Guzman, who very soon died, or was killed by the Indians – this was not his steward Cristobal de Guzman, who took Guatemoc prisoner in the battle for Mexico. As chamberlain he chose Rodrigo Rangel, and as steward Juan de Caceres, who became a rich man after the conquest of Mexico.

When all this was arranged Cortes ordered us to embark, and the horses to be divided among the various ships. Mangers were made for them, and a store of maize and hay put aboard.

[Bernal Díaz here lists sixteen horses, and comments on their quality. Not all were good for fighting, and some were shared between two men. The last he mentions, a chestnut mare, which was the property of Juan Sedeño of Havana, foaled on board.]

This Juan Sedeño was reputed the richest man in the fleet, for he came with the mare in his own ship, and brought a Negro, also a store of cassava bread and pork. At that time Negroes and horses were worth their weight in gold, and the reason why we had no more horses was that there were none to be bought.

To make my story clear I must now return to Diego Velazquez. When he was informed that his lieutenant and brother-in-law Francisco Verdugo had refused to drag Cortes from the fleet at Trinidad, and that both he and Diego de Ordaz had helped him get away, the Governor roared with rage and accused his secretary Andres de Duero and the treasurer Amado de Lares of making an agreement with Cortes behind his back. He swore that Cortes was mutinous, and made up his mind to send a servant with letters of instruction to Pedro Barba, his lieutenant at Havana, and others to all his relatives among the settlers in that town, also to Diego de Ordaz and Juan Velazquez de Leon, both of whom were his friends and kinsmen, urgently begging them on no account to let the fleet sail, and to arrest Cortes immediately and send him to Santiago de Cuba under a strong guard.

As soon as Garnica – for this was the messenger's name – reached Havana, the purpose of his coming became known, for this same messenger brought Cortes news of what Velazquez was doing. This is how it happened. Apparently a certain Mercedarian friar, who pretended to be one of Velazquez' followers and was at that time in his company, wrote to another friar of his Order, Bartolome del Olmedo by name, who was with us, and included in his letter a warning to Cortes of what was going on, from his two partners Andres de Duero and the treasurer.

Now as Cortes had sent Diego de Ordaz off in a ship to collect stores, there was no one likely to oppose him except Juan Velazquez de Leon. Cortes at once spoke to him, and easily won him over, since he had a grudge against his kinsman for not having given him a good grant of Indians. Of all those to whom the Governor had written not one supported him. Everyone took Cortes' part, and especially Pedro Barba, while as for us soldiers, we would all have given our lives for the Captain. So if Velazquez' orders were hushed up at Trinidad, they were totally ignored at Havana. Pedro Barba returned the Governor a letter by the same Garnica saying that he dared not arrest Cortes, since he had so strong a following that there was a danger he might sack and plunder the town, and take all the settlers away with him. The lieutenant added that from all he could learn Cortes was the Governor's faithful servant, and would not dare to be otherwise. At the same time, Cortes wrote to Velazquez in those agreeable and complimentary terms that came so easily to him, saying that he was setting sail next day and would remain his humble servant.

The Voyage

WE made no inspection of our forces till we came to the island of Cozumel. Cortes merely ordered the horses to be put on board, and directed Pedro de Alvarado to sail along the north coast in the good ship *San Sebastian*, whose pilot was to await him at Cape San Antonio, where all the ships were to collect and sail together to Cozumel. He also sent a messenger to Diego de Ordaz, who had gone along the north coast for supplies, telling him to do the same.

On 10 February 1519, after hearing mass, we set sail along the south coast with nine ships and the company of gentlemen and soldiers I have mentioned. Including the two others on the north coast we had therefore eleven ships in all. In one of these sailed Pedro de Alvarado with seventy soldiers, among them myself.

The pilot Camacho, who was in charge of our ship, paid no attention to Cortes' orders and went his own way, so that we arrived at Cozumel two days before Cortes, and we anchored in the port which I have already described in speaking of Grijalva's expedition. The reason for Cortes' failure to arrive was that the ship commanded by Francisco de Morla had lost her rudder in bad weather, and had had to be provided with another from one of the other ships. They then came on all together.

When we arrived under Pedro de Alvarado, we landed at the town of Cozumel with all our men, but found no Indians there, for they had fled. So Alvarado ordered us to go on to another town about three miles distant, whose inhabitants had also fled and taken to the bush. But they had not been able to take their possessions with them, and had left some poultry among other things, so Alvarado ordered about forty of the fowls to be commandeered. In a prayer-house too there were some old cloths hung up, and some little chests containing diadems, images, beads, and pendants of low-grade gold; and here we captured three Indians, two men and a woman, before returning to the town where we had landed.

Just as we returned, Cortes arrived with the fleet, and the first thing he did after taking up his lodging was to have the pilot Camacho put in irons for failing to obey orders and wait for him at sea. When he saw the town empty of its inhabitants and learnt that Pedro de Alvarado had been to the other place and had taken fowls and hangings and other things of small value from the idols, also some gold that was half copper, he was as angry with our captain as he had been with the pilot, and reprimanded him severely, telling him that he would never pacify the country by robbing the natives of their possessions. He sent for the two Indians and the woman we had captured, and spoke to them through the Indian Melchior, whom we had brought from Cape Catoche, and who knew their language well – his companion was dead – telling them to go and summon the *Caciques* and Indians of their town, and not to be afraid. He had the gold, hangings, and everything else restored to them, and in return for the fowls, which had already been eaten, he ordered that they should be given some beads and little bells. In addition he presented each Indian with a Spanish shirt. So they set off to summon the Chief of the town, and next day he came with all his people. Men, women, and children, they went about among us as if they had been friendly with us all their lives, and Cortes ordered us not to harm them in any way. Here in this island the Captain began to command most energetically, and Our Lord so favoured him that whatever he touched succeeded, especially the pacification of the people and towns hereabouts, as we shall see later.

When we had been at Cozumel for three days, Cortes ordered an inspection to see how many of us there were, and he discovered that there were five hundred and eight not counting the ships' captains, pilots, and sailors, who amounted to a hundred, and that there were sixteen horses or mares, the latter all fit to be used for sport or as chargers. There were eleven ships, large and small, and one that was a sort of launch, which a certain Gines Nortes had brought loaded with supplies. There were thirty-two crossbowmen and thirteen musketeers, ten brass guns and four falconets, and much powder and shot. I do not remember for certain the number of crossbowmen, but it does not matter.

After the inspection Cortes ordered Mesa, 'the Gunner' as he was called, and Bartolome de Usagre and Arbenga and Juan Catalan, all artillerymen, to see that the guns were clean and in good order, and the ammunition ready for use. He appointed Francisco de Orozco, who had served in Italy, as captain of artillery. At the same time he ordered two crossbowmen called Juan Benitez and Pedro de Guzman 'the Bowman', who were experts at repairing their weapons, to see that all the crossbows had two or three spare nuts and cords and forecords, and to keep them carefully stored, also to look after the planes and spokeshaves, and see that the men practised at the target, and the horses were kept in good condition. I do not know why I should spend so much ink on these preparations, for in fact Cortes was most careful about everything.

In his diligence, Cortes sent for me and a Basque called Martin Ramos, to ask us what we thought about the Campeche Indians' cries of *'castilan, castilan!'* that I mentioned in my account of our expedition under Francisco Hernandez de Cordoba. When we had carefully described the incident once more, Cortes said that he had often thought about it, and wondered whether there might not be some Spaniards living in that country. 'I think it would be a good thing,' he said, 'to ask these chiefs of Cozumel if they know anything about them.'

So through Melchior (the man from Cape Catoche, who now understood a little Spanish and knew the language of Cozumel very well), all the chiefs were questioned, and each one of them answered that they knew of certain Spaniards, whom they described. They said that some *Caciques* who lived two days' journey inland held them as slaves, and that here in Cozumel were some Indian traders who had spoken to them only two days before. We were all delighted with this news, and Cortes told the chiefs that letters – which in their language they call *amales* – must be sent to them at once to summon them to the island. He gave beads to the chiefs and to the Indians who carried the letters, and spoke kindly to them, telling them that when they returned he would give them some more beads. The *Cacique* advised Cortes to send a ransom to their owners, so that they might let them come; and this Cortes did, giving the messengers various sorts of beads. Then he ordered the two smallest ships to be got ready. These he sent to the coast near Cape Catoche, where the larger ship was to wait for eight days, which allowed enough time for the letters to be taken and for a reply to arrive; and when it did so the smaller vessel was to bring Cortes immediate news. Cape Catoche is only twelve miles from Cozumel, and within sight of it.

In his letter Cortes said: 'Gentlemen and brothers, here in Cozumel I have heard that you are captives in the hands of a *Cacique*. I beg you to come to this place at once, and for this purpose have sent a ship with soldiers, in case you need them, also a ransom to be given to those Indians with whom you are living. The ship will wait for you eight days. Come as quickly as you can, and you will be welcomed and looked after by me. I am staying at this island with five hundred soldiers, and eleven ships in which I am going, please God, to a town called Tabasco or Champoton.'

The two vessels were soon dispatched with the two Indian traders of Cozumel, who carried the letter on board, and in three hours they had crossed the straits. The messengers were then landed with their letters and the ransom, and in two days these were delivered to a Spaniard called Jeronimo de Aguilar. For this we discovered to be his name, and I shall call him by it henceforth. When he had read the letter and received the ransom, he carried the beads delightedly to his master the *Cacique* and begged leave to depart. The *Cacique* gave him permission to go wherever he wished, and Aguilar set out for the place some fifteen miles away where his comrade, Gonzalo Guerrero, was living. But on hearing the contents of the letter Gonzalo answered: 'Brother Aguilar, I am married and have three children, and they look on me as a *Cacique* here, and a captain in time of war. Go, and God's blessing be with you. But my face is tattooed and my ears are pierced. What would the Spaniards say if they saw me like this? And look how handsome these children of mine are! Please give me some of those

beads you have brought, and I will tell them that my brothers
have sent them from my own country.' And Gonzalo's Indian
wife spoke to Aguilar very angrily in her own language: 'Why
has this slave come here to call my husband away? Go off with
you, and let us have no more of your talk.'

Then Aguilar spoke to Gonzalo again, reminding him that he
was a Christian and should not destroy his soul for the sake of
an Indian woman. Besides, if he did not wish to desert his wife
and children, he could take them with him. But neither words
nor warnings could persuade Gonzalo to come. I believe he
was a sailor and hailed from Palos.

When Jeronimo de Aguilar saw that Gonzalo would not
come, he at once went with the two Indian messengers to the
place where their ship had been waiting for him. But when he
arrived he could see no ship. For the eight days that Ordaz had
been ordered to stay had expired; and after giving him one
more day, he had returned to Cozumel without news of the
Spanish captives. On finding no ship, Aguilar returned sadly to
his master in the town where he had been living.

When Ordaz arrived without the Spaniards, and with no
news either of them or of the Indian messengers, Cortes was
very much annoyed and told Ordaz haughtily that he had
expected better things from him, for it was certain that the
Spaniards were living in this district.

Now it happened that at this juncture some sailors from
Gibraltar, who were nicknamed the 'Men of the Rock', had
stolen some pork from a soldier called Berrio and refused to
return it. So Berrio complained to Cortes, and the sailors, when
put on oath, committed perjury. But on inquiry it was proved
that the sailors had stolen the pork and that seven of them had
divided it among them. In spite of the appeals of their captains, Cortes ordered them to be flogged.

I will now describe our stay on the island of Cozumel, to
which many Indians, both from the towns near Cape Catoche
and from other parts of Yucatan, came on pilgrimage. It seems
that a number of idols of most hideous shapes were kept in a
prayer-house in Cozumel, to which the natives of the country
habitually offered sacrifices at that season. One morning, the

courtyard of the prayer-house was crowded with men and women who were burning a resin like our incense. Presently an old Indian in a long cloak, who was the priest of these idols – I have already said that in New Spain they are called *papas* – climbed to the top of the prayer-house steps and began to preach to them. Cortes and the rest of us wondered what the outcome of this black sermon would be. He asked Melchior what the old Indian was saying; and Melchior answered that he was preaching wickedness. Cortes then sent for the *Caciques* and all the principal men, and for the *papa* himself, and told them as best he could, through our interpreter, that if they wished to be our brothers they must throw their idols out of this temple, for they were very evil and led them astray. He said that they were no gods but abominations which would bring their souls to hell. Then he spoke to them about good and holy matters, telling them to set up an image of Our Lady, which he gave them, and a cross, which would always aid them, bring them good harvests, and save their souls. He told them other things too about our holy faith and in well-chosen words.

The *papas* and the *Caciques* answered that their ancestors had worshipped these gods because they were good, and that they dared not do otherwise. They said that if we were to throw them out we should see what harm would come to us, for we should perish at sea. Then Cortes ordered us to break up the idols and roll them down the steps, which we did. Next he sent for some lime, of which there was plenty in the town, and for some Indian masons; and he set up a very fair altar, on which we placed the image of Our Lady. He also ordered two of our carpenters, Alonso Yañez and Alvaro Lopez, to make a cross of some rough timber which was there. This was placed in a sort of shrine beside the altar, and the priest Juan Diaz said mass. Meanwhile the *Cacique* and the *papa* and all the Indians stood watching us intently.

Cortes took leave of the *Caciques* and priests, consigning the image of Our Lady to their care, and telling them to worship the cross, which they must keep clean and decorate with flowers. He said they would then see what benefits they gained, and the Indians promised to obey him. Then they brought four fowls and two jars of honey, and Cortes embraced them.

We embarked and set sail on a March day, and began our voyage in fair weather. At ten o'clock that same morning loud shouts were heard from one of the ships, which lay to and fired a shot to attract the other vessels in the fleet. When Cortes observed this, he at once checked the flagship, and, seeing Juan de Escalante's ship bearing away in the direction of Cozumel, called out to the ships which were near him: 'What is the matter? What is the matter?' A soldier called Luis de Zaragoza replied that Escalante's ship was going down with all the cassava bread aboard. 'Pray God we suffer no such disaster!' he cried, and ordered the pilot Alaminos to signal to all the other ships to return to Cozumel. So this same day we returned to the port from which we had sailed, and unloaded the cassava bread. We were delighted to find the image of Our Lady and the cross well tended, and incense burning in front of them. When the *Cacique* and the *papas* came to Cortes and inquired why we had come back, he replied that one of our ships was leaking, and we wanted to caulk her. He then asked them to bring all their canoes to help our ships' boats bring the bread on shore, which they did. It took us four days to caulk the vessel.

When the Spaniard Aguilar learnt that we had returned to Cozumel with the ships, he was very joyful and gave thanks to God. He then came in all haste with the two Indians who had carried the letters and the ransom, and embarked in a canoe. Since he could pay well with the green beads we had sent him, he had soon hired one with six Indian oarsmen, who rowed so hard that, meeting no head wind, they quickly crossed the twelve-mile strait between the island and the mainland.

When they reached the coast of Cozumel and were disembarking, some soldiers who had gone out hunting – for there were wild pigs on the island – reported to Cortes that a large canoe had come from the direction of Cape Catoche and had beached near the town. Cortes sent Andres de Tapia and two other soldiers to see what was happening, since it was something new for Indians to come fearlessly into our neighbourhood in large canoes. So they set out. As soon as the Indians who had brought Aguilar saw the Spaniards, they took fright, and wanted to get back in their canoe and put out to sea. But Aguilar told them in their own language not to be afraid, for these men were his brothers. When Andres de Tapia saw that they were Indians – for Aguilar looked exactly like one – he immediately sent to tell Cortes that there were seven Cozumel Indians in the canoe. As he leapt ashore, however, Aguilar exclaimed in inarticulate and clumsy Spanish: 'God and the blessed Mary of Seville!' Then Tapia went to embrace him, and the soldier who was beside him, seeing that he was a Spaniard, ran hurriedly to Cortes to beg a reward for being the first with the news. We were all delighted when we heard it.

Tapia quickly brought the Spaniard to the place where Cortes was, but before they got there some soldiers asked Tapia: 'Where is this Spaniard?' Although they were close beside him, they could not distinguish him from an Indian, for he was naturally dark, and had his hair untidily cut like an Indian slave. He carried a paddle on his shoulder and had an old sandal on one foot, the other sandal being tied to his belt. He wore a very ragged old cloak, and a tattered loincloth to cover his private parts; and in his cloak was tied an object which proved to be a very old prayer-book.

When Cortes saw him in this condition he was as much deceived as the others, and asked Tapia where this Spaniard was. When Aguilar heard his question, he squatted down in Indian fashion and answered: 'I am he.' Cortes at once ordered him to be given a shirt and doublet and breeches, a cloak and some sandals, for he had no other clothes. Cortes asked him his name and history and when he had come to that country. The man answered, pronouncing with difficulty, that his name was Jeronimo de Aguilar, that he came from Ecija and was in holy orders. He said that eight years ago he had been wrecked with fifteen other men and two women on a voyage from Darien to the island of Santo Domingo, where he had some differences at law with a certain Enciso y Valdivia. They were carrying with them ten thousand gold pesos and the documents of the case, when the ship in which they were travelling struck the Alacranes and could not be floated off. He, his companions, and the two women had then got into the ship's boat, thinking they could reach Cuba or Jamaica. But the currents were so strong that they were thrown ashore in this country, where the *Calachiones*[1] of the district had divided them up, sacrificing many of his companions to their idols. Some too had died of disease, and the two women only recently of overwork, for they had been made to grind corn. The Indians had intended to sacrifice him, but one night he had escaped and fled to that *Cacique* with whom he had been living ever since. Now, he said, the only survivors were himself and a certain Gonzalo Guerrero, whom he had gone to summon but who had refused to come.

Aguilar thanked God for his deliverance, and Cortes promised that he would be well looked after and compensated. He then asked him about the country and the towns. Aguilar answered that, having been a slave, he only knew about hewing wood and drawing water and working in the maize-fields, and that he had only once made a journey of some twelve miles when he was sent with a load, under which he had collapsed, for it was heavier than he could carry. He understood, however, that there were many towns. When questioned about Gonzalo Guerrero, he said that he was married and had three children, that he was tattooed, and that his ears and lower lip were pierced, that he was a seaman and a native of Palos, and that the Indians considered him very brave. Aguilar also related how a little more than a year ago, when a captain and three ships arrived at Cape Catoche – this must have been our expedition under Francisco Hernandez de Cordoba – it had been at Guerrero's suggestion that the Indians had attacked them, and that he had been there himself in the company of that *Cacique* of a great town, about whom I spoke when describing that expedition. When Cortes heard this he exclaimed: 'I wish I could get my hands on him. For it will never do to leave him here.'

When the chiefs of Cozumel discovered that Aguilar could speak their language, they gave him very good food, and he advised them always to respect and revere the holy image of Our Lady, and the cross, for they would greatly benefit by it. On Aguilar's advice, the chiefs asked Cortes to give them a

1. The local name for the *Caciques*.

letter of recommendation, so that if any other Spaniards came to the port they would treat them well and do them no injury. He gave them this letter, and after bidding them a cordial farewell we set sail for the Rio de Grijalva.

On 4 March 1519, being now blessed with a useful and faithful interpreter, Cortes gave orders for us to embark in the same order we had followed before we ran back to Cozumel. We sailed along in good weather until about nightfall, when a wind struck us so fiercely that our ships were scattered and in great danger of being driven ashore. But, thank God, the wind dropped at midnight, and as dawn broke all our ships reassembled, except Velazquez de Leon's. We continued on our course until midday without seeing the missing vessel, which greatly distressed us all, as we were afraid she had been wrecked on a shoal. When the whole day had passed and she still did not appear, Cortes said to the pilot Alaminos that it would be wrong to go any further without news of her. The pilot then signalled to the rest of the fleet to lie to, in case the storm had driven her into some bay from which she could not come out against a head wind. But when she still did not arrive, the pilot said to Cortes: 'Sir, I am sure she has put in to some port or bay which we have passed, and is kept there by an adverse wind. Her pilot, Juan Alvarez, 'El manquillo',[1] was with Francisco Hernandez de Cordoba and with Grijalva, and he will know the place.'

So it was agreed that the whole fleet should go back and look for the missing ship, which, to our great relief, we found anchored in the bay of which the pilot had spoken. We stayed in that bay for a day, and lowered two boats in which the pilot and captain Francisco de Lugo went ashore. Here they found farms with maize-plantations, and places where the Indians made salt. There were four of their *cues* or temples, and many idols in them, most of them very tall female figures. We called the place therefore the Punta de las Mujeres.[2]

I remember that Aguilar said that the town where he had been held as a slave was near these farms, and it was here that he had been bringing his master's goods when he had collapsed

1. The man with one arm.
2. The Cape of the Women.

under the weight of his load. He said too that the town where Gonzalo Guerrero lived was not far away, and that there was some gold in all these places, though it did not amount to much. He suggested that we should go there, and offered to be our guide. Cortes, however, answered with a laugh that he was not after such small game but was here to serve God and the king.

Shortly afterwards Cortes ordered Captain Escobar to take his ship, which was very fast and of shallow draught, to the Boca de Terminos, to explore the place thoroughly and see if it would be a good port for a settlement, also to see if game was as plentiful there as he had been told. He did this on the pilot's advice, so that the rest of the ships should not be delayed by putting in there. Escobar's instructions were that after examining the place he should put up a sign and cut down some trees at the entrance of the harbour; or alternatively that he should write a letter and place it where it could be seen from either side of the harbour so that we should know he had been ashore; or that after inspecting the port he should beat up to windward and await the fleet at sea.

Escobar then left us, went to the Puerto de Terminos, and did all that he had been told. He found the greyhound that had been left there by Grijalva's expedition, and she was fat and sleek. He said that when she saw the ship sailing into the bay she wagged her tail with delight, then ran at once to the soldiers and jumped aboard their boat. Having made his inspection, Escobar put out from the port to await the rest of the ships. But it appears that with the south wind blowing, he was unable to lie to, and was driven far out to sea.

To return to our fleet, we stayed at the Punta de las Mujeres until the following morning, when we put to sea with a good breeze off the land, and sailed to the Boca de Terminos. On failing to find Escobar, Cortes ordered a boat to be lowered with twelve crossbowmen, who were to look for him in the Boca and see if he had left any sign or letter there. They soon found some trees that had been cut down, and a letter in which he said that the land was fertile and full of game and told the story of the greyhound. The pilot then advised Cortes to continue on our course, saying that the south wind must have driven

Escobar out to sea, but that he could not be far off, since he would lie close to the wind. Although Cortes was anxious and afraid that Escobar might have met with some accident, he ordered the sails to be raised, and we soon caught up with him. He then gave his report to Cortes, and explained why he had not been able to wait for us.

Meanwhile we arrived near Champoton, and Cortes ordered the pilot to drop anchor in the bay. But he replied that this was a bad harbour, for the tide ebbed so far that ships had to lie more than six miles from the shore. Cortes was anxious to pay the Indians out for the defeats they had inflicted on Hernandez de Cordoba and Grijalva, and many of us soldiers who had taken part in those battles begged him to go in and give them a good punishment, even if it meant staying there for two or three days. But Alaminos and the other pilots insisted that if we did go in, a head wind might keep us there for a week, whereas now the wind was fair and we could reach Tabasco in two days. So we passed on, and in three days arrived at the Rio de Grijalva, which in the Indian language is called the Tabasco river.

We reached it with all our fleet on 12 March 1519; and as we already knew from the Grijalva expedition that vessels of great draught could not enter the river, the larger ships anchored out at sea. As in Grijalva's time, all the soldiers were then landed, by the smaller vessels and the boats, on the Punta de los Palmares[1] which was about a mile from the town of Tabasco.[2] The river, its banks, and the mangrove swamps were crowded with Indian warriors, which greatly surprised us who had been here with Grijalva. In addition more than twelve thousand had gathered in the town, all prepared to attack us. For at that time the town was of considerable importance, and other large towns were subject to it. All these had prepared themselves for war, and were well supplied with the usual arms.

The reason for this was that the people of Champoton and

1. The headland with the palm-trees already described.
2. The Indian name for this place was Potonchan, and the Spaniards renamed it Santa Maria de la Victoria. Later it came to be known as Tabasco. It fell into ruins long ago.

Lazaro and other places in the neighbourhood had called the Tabascans cowards for giving Grijalva the gold jewels I mentioned. They had accused them of being too fearful to attack us, although they had more towns and warriors than their neighbours, who had attacked us and killed fifty-six of our men. It was this taunt that had decided the people of Tabasco to take up arms.

When Cortes saw the Indians drawn up for battle, he told Aguilar the interpreter, who knew their language[1] well, to ask some Indians, who appeared to be chieftains and were passing close to us in a large canoe, why they were so alarmed, since we had not come to do them any harm, but would give them some of the things we had brought with us, and treat them like brothers. He ordered him to beg them not to start a war, for which they would be sorry, and to speak to them about the advantages of remaining at peace. However, the more Aguilar talked the more defiant they became. They said they would kill us all if we entered their town, and that they had fortified it all round with barricades and fences of stout tree-trunks.

Aguilar asked them once more to keep the peace, and to let us draw water and exchange our goods for food. He also asked permission to tell their *calachiones* things that would be to their advantage, and serviceable to Our Lord. But they persisted in their threats to kill us if we advanced beyond the palm-trees.

In view of this, Cortes ordered the boats and the small ship to be made ready, and three cannon to be placed in each boat, as well as a proportion of the crossbowmen and musketeers. We remembered that in Grijalva's time we had found a narrow path that led from the palm-trees to the town, crossing some streams, and Cortes ordered three soldiers to find out that night if this path led right up to the houses, and to report back immediately. They discovered that it did. Then, after making a thorough survey, we spent the rest of the day arranging how and in what order we were to go in the boats.

Next morning we had all our arms in readiness. Then, after mass, Cortes ordered Captain Alonso de Avila and a hundred

1. These people would have been Tzendals, a branch of the Mayas, and their language would have been Mayan.

soldiers, including ten crossbowmen, to follow the path I have mentioned, and as soon as they heard shots to attack the town on one side while we attacked on the other. Meanwhile, Cortes himself and all the rest went up the river in the boats and the ships of shallow draught. When the Indian warriors who were on the banks and among the mangroves saw that we were really on the move, they came to meet us in a great many canoes, intending to prevent our getting ashore at any place where we tried to land. The whole bank was thick with Indian warriors, carrying their native arms, blowing trumpets and conches, and beating drums. When Cortes saw how things were, he ordered us to wait a little before firing our crossbows, muskets, or guns, for he wanted to be justified in all he did. Therefore he made another appeal, through Aguilar, in the presence of Diego de Godoy, the Royal Notary, asking them to let us land, take water, and speak to them about God and His Majesty. He added that if they attacked and if in self-defence we were to kill or hurt any of them, it would be their fault not ours. But they went on threatening to kill us if we landed.

Then they boldly began to shoot arrows at us and beat tattoos on their drums. With great bravery they surrounded us in their canoes, pouring such a shower of arrows on us that they kept us in the water at some places up to our waists. There was so much mud and swamp that we had difficulty in getting clear of it; and so many Indians attacked us, hurling their lances and shooting arrows, that it took us a long time to struggle ashore.

While Cortes was fighting, he lost a sandal in the mud and could not recover it. So he landed with one bare foot. However, his sandal was later picked up, and he put it on again.

In the meantime all of us captains and soldiers fell on the Indians, crying 'Santiago, Santiago!' and forced them to retire, though not very far, for they sheltered behind the barricades and fences of heavy timber that they had erected. But we wrenched them apart, and got through the small opening we made. We then attacked them again and forced them down a street to a place where other defences had been erected. Here they turned and met us face to face, fighting most valiantly and persistently. And all the time they whistled and shouted, '*Al calacheoni! Al calacheoni!'* which in their language was an incitement to kill or capture our Captain.

While we were thus surrounded, Alonso de Avila arrived with his soldiers, who, as I have already said, had come overland from the palm-trees. It seems that they could not have arrived sooner on account of the swamps and creeks. In fact their delay had been as unavoidable as our own in parleying with the Indians and breaking gaps in their barricades preparatory to our attack. Now we all joined together to drive them from their strongholds, and compelled them to retreat. But like brave warriors they went on shooting showers of arrows and fire-hardened darts, and never turned their backs until we reached a great courtyard with chambers and large halls, and three idol-houses, to which they had already carried all their possessions. Cortes ordered us to stay at these *cues*, and to pursue them no further, since they were now in flight.[1]

Then Cortes took possession of that land for the King, performing the act in His Majesty's name. He did it in this way : he drew his sword, and, as a sign of possession, made three cuts in a large silk-cotton tree which stood in that great courtyard, and cried that if any person should raise an objection he would defend the King's right with his sword and his shield, which he held in his other hand.

All of us soldiers who witnessed this act, which was performed in the presence of the Royal Notary, cried that he did right to take possession of this land in His Majesty's name, and that we would aid him against any challengers. Those of Diego Velazquez' party, however, began to grumble.[2]

I remember that in this hard-fought battle fourteen of our men were wounded. I myself received an arrow wound in the thigh, but it was not severe. We found eighteen dead Indians

1. According to Cortes' own letter, written from Vera Cruz, the Indians then sent a deputation with a small present, but still insisted that the Spaniards should leave the country. Cortes demanded food, and the Indians promised to send it. However none came. He therefore sent out foraging expeditions, as Bernal Díaz will tell us.

2. Cortes was for the first time ignoring Velazquez, whose name he did not mention, and placing himself directly under the King's protection.

lying in the water at the place where we landed. We slept in the temple square that night, with guards and sentinels on the watch.

Next morning Cortes ordered Pedro de Alvarado to set out with a company of a hundred soldiers, fifteen of them musketeers and crossbowmen, and explore the country inland for a distance of five or six miles, taking Melchior with him. But when they looked for the interpreter he could not be found, as he had fled to the people of Tabasco. It appears that on the previous night he had left his Spanish clothes hanging up in the palm-grove, and had escaped in a canoe. Cortes was much annoyed by his escape, and feared that he might tell his fellow Indians things that would be damaging to us. But let him go, and bad luck to him, and we will return to our story.

Cortes also sent Captain Francisco de Lugo in another direction with a hundred soldiers, including a dozen crossbowmen and musketeers, with instructions not to go more than six miles, and to return at nightfall to sleep in the camp. But when they had gone about three miles they met great companies of archers, and others with lances and shields, drums and standards, who immediately attacked them, surrounding them on all sides. The enemy were so numerous that when they began to shoot we could hardly stand up to them. They hurled fire-toughened darts and slung stones that fell on us like hail. Then they attacked us with their two-handed cutting swords[1]; and hard though Francisco de Lugo and his soldiers fought, they could not drive them back. When they realized this, they began to retreat towards the camp in good order, sending ahead a Cuban Indian who was a swift and daring runner, to beg Cortes for help. Meanwhile, by careful handling of his crossbowmen and musketeers, some loading while the others fired, and by occasional charges, Francisco de Lugo was able to hold off the squadrons attacking him.

Leaving him in this dangerous situation, let us return to Pedro de Alvarado who, after advancing for about three miles, came to a creek which was very difficult to cross. It pleased God, therefore, that he should return by another track, which

1. *Macanas,* or wooden swords edged with flint or obsidian.

led near the place where Francisco de Lugo was fighting. Informed of the battle by the sound of musket shots, the great din of drums and trumpets, and the shouts and whistles of the Indians, Alvarado advanced in great haste, though without breaking ranks, in the direction of the noise, and found Captain Francisco de Lugo and his men fighting with their faces to the enemy. Five Indians had already been killed when our two companies joined together, turned on the enemy, and drove them back. They were not able to put them to flight, however, for they pursued our men right back to the camp.

Other Indian bands had also attacked Cortes where he was guarding the wounded. But we soon drove them off with our guns, which brought many of them down, and with our good sword-play.

When Cortes heard of Francisco de Lugo's danger, from the Indian who came to ask him for help, we promptly went to his assistance and met the two captains with their companies about a mile and a half from the camp. Two of Francisco de Lugo's men had been killed and eight wounded, and three of Pedro de Alvarado's had been wounded. On returning to the camp we tended the wounded, buried the dead, stationed sentinels, and posted a watch.

In this skirmish fifteen Indians were killed and three captured, one of whom seemed to be a man of importance. Through Aguilar, our interpreter, we asked the prisoners why they had been so bold as to attack us, and warned them that they would be killed if they did so again. Then Cortes sent one of them with some beads to give to the *Caciques* as an overture of peace. This messenger told us that the Indian Melchior whom we had brought from Cape Catoche, who had fled to them the night before, had advised them that if they attacked us by day and night we should be beaten, for we were few in number. So it turned out that we had brought an enemy with us instead of a friend.

The Indian whom we sent as a messenger never returned, but from our two other prisoners Aguilar learnt that by next day all the *Caciques* of the neighbouring towns of that province would have come together fully armed to make war on us. Their intention was to surround our camp, as Melchior had advised.

As soon as Cortes knew that the Indians intended to attack, he ordered all the horses to be quickly landed, and the cross-bowmen, musketeers, and the rest of us soldiers, including even the wounded, to have our arms ready for use.

When the horses came ashore they were very stiff and afraid to move, for they had been on board for some time. Next day, however, they moved quite freely. Another thing that occurred at this time was that six or seven soldiers, young and healthy men, were attacked by pains in the back and could not stand but had to be carried. We could not tell the reason for this, though some said it was because of their cotton armour, which they never took off by day or night, and because they had lived comfortably in Cuba and were not used to hard work, and so were affected by the heat. Cortes decided they should not remain on shore, and had them carried back on board ship.

The best horses and riders were chosen to form the cavalry, and little bells were attached to the horses' breastplates. The horsemen were ordered not to stop and spear those who were down, but to aim their lances at the faces of the enemy.

Thirteen gentlemen were chosen to go on horseback, with Cortes as their commander. Mesa the artilleryman was ordered to have his guns ready, and Diego de Ordaz was given the command of all us footsoldiers, musketeers, and crossbowmen, for he was no horseman.

Very early next morning, which was Lady Day, after hearing Fray Bartolome de Olmedo say mass, we all formed up behind our standard-bearer, who was at that time Antonio de Villaroel, and marched to the same wide savannah,[1] about three miles from the camp, where Francisco de Lugo and Pedro de Alvarado had been attacked. This place was called Cintla, as was the near-by town, which was subject to Tabasco.

As we marched along, separated by some distance from Cortes and his horsemen, on account of swamps which the horses could not cross, we fell in with a whole force of Indian war-riors on their way to attack us in our camp. It was near this same town of Cintla that we met them on the open plain, and

1. A Carib word for a treeless plain.

if these warriors were seeking us with battle in their minds, we had the same thoughts in seeking them.

When we met the enemy bands and companies which we had marched out to find, they were, as I have said, coming in search of us. All the men wore great feather crests, they carried drums and trumpets, their faces were painted black and white, they were armed with large bows and arrows, spears and shields, swords like our two-handed swords, and slings and stones and fire-toughened darts, and all wore quilted cotton armour. Their squadrons, as they approached us, were so numerous that they covered the whole savannah. They rushed on us like mad dogs and completely surrounded us, discharging such a rain of arrows, darts, and stones upon us that more than seventy of our men were wounded at the first attack. Then, in the hand-to-hand fighting, they did us great damage with their spears. One soldier was killed outright by an arrow-wound in the ear, and they kept on shooting and wounding us. With our muskets and crossbows and good sword-play we put up a stout fight, and once they came to feel the edge of our swords they gradually fell back, but only to shoot at us from greater safety. Our artilleryman Mesa killed many of them with his cannon. For since they came in great bands and did not open out, he could fire at them as he pleased. But with all the hurts and wounds we dealt them, we could not drive them off. I said to Diego de Ordaz: 'I think we ought to close up and charge them. It's the thrust and edge of our swords that they really feel! That is why they fell back just now, out of fear of our swords, and so that they could shoot at us from out of danger.' Ordaz answered that he disagreed, for there were three hundred Indians to every one of us, and we could not hold our own against such numbers. That was why we had to endure their attack. However, we did agree to get as close as we could to them and give them a taste of our swords, which inflicted such damage on them that they retired towards a swamp. All this time Cortes and his horsemen did not come, although we very much needed them, and we were afraid that some disaster might have befallen them.

I remember that whenever we fired our guns, the Indians gave great shouts and whistles, and threw up straw and earth so that we could not see what harm we had done them. They sounded their trumpets and drums, and shouted and whistled, and cried, 'Alala! Alala!'

Just at this moment we caught sight of our horsemen. But the great host of Indians was so crazed by their attack that they did not at once see them approaching behind their backs. As the plain was bare and the horsemen were good riders, and some of the horses were very swift and nimble, they came quickly upon them and speared them as they chose. As soon as we saw the horsemen we fell on the enemy so vigorously that, caught between the horsemen and ourselves, they soon turned tail. The Indians thought at that time that the horse and rider were one creature, for they had never seen a horse before.

The savannah and fields were now full of Indians, running to take refuge in some thick woods near by, and as they fled Cortes explained to us that he had been unable to come sooner because there was a swamp in the way, and he had had to fight his way through another host of warriors before he could reach us. Three horsemen and five horses had been wounded.

After the horsemen had dismounted beneath some trees beside which some houses stood, we returned thanks to God for granting us so complete a victory. Then, as it was Lady Day, we named the town which was afterwards founded here Santa Maria de la Victoria, on account of the fact that this great victory was won on her day. This was the first battle that we fought under Cortes in New Spain.

When it was over, we bandaged our wounded with cloths, for this was all we had, and sealed the wounds of our horses with fat from the corpse of an Indian that we had cut up for this purpose. We then went to look at the dead that were lying about the field, and found more than eight hundred, most of whom had been killed by sword-thrusts, and the rest by cannon, muskets, or crossbows. And many lay groaning on the ground, half dead. For wherever the horsemen had passed there were great numbers of dead and wounded. The battle had lasted over an hour; it was now late, and we had eaten nothing. So we returned to camp, weary with fighting, bringing five prisoners whom we had taken, two of whom were captains. Then, after burying our two dead, one of whom had been fatally struck in the throat, the other in the ear, and attending to the wounds of the rest, we posted sentinels and guards, took our supper, and rested.

It is here, according to Gomara, that Francisco de Morla arrived on a dapple-grey horse in advance of Cortes and the rest of the cavalry, and the blessed apostles St James and St Peter appeared. I say that all our deeds and victories were the work of Our Lord Jesus Christ, and that in this battle there were so many Indians to every one of us that the dust they made would have blinded us, had not God of His unfailing mercy come to our aid. It may be, as Gomara says, that those glorious apostles did appear, and that I, a sinner, was unworthy to see them. However, I did see Francisco de Morla arrive on a chestnut horse at the same time as Cortes; and I seem to see that whole battle again with my sinful eyes, even as I write, with every detail as it took place. It may be I was not worthy to see either of the two apostles. But if so, since there were more than four hundred soldiers in our company, as well as Cortes himself and many other gentlemen, the miracle would have been discussed and evidence taken, and a church would have been built in their honour when the town was founded. Also the town would not have been called as it was Santa Maria de la Victoria, but Santiago or San Pedro instead.

I have said that we captured five Indians in this battle, of whom two were captains. These two were interrogated by the interpreter Aguilar, who discovered from their answers that they would be suitable as messengers. He advised Cortes to free them, therefore, so that they might go and talk to the *Caciques* of the town, and to any others they might see. They were given green and blue beads, and Aguilar addressed them in a flattering speech, telling them that they had nothing to fear, since we meant to treat them like brothers, and that the recent battle was entirely their own fault. He told them to call together the *Caciques* of all the towns, as we wished to talk to them, and he gave them gentle warnings on many other matters in order to gain their good will. The messengers went off in a good frame of mind and talked to the *Caciques* and chief men, telling them what we wished them to know about our desire for peace.

After listening to our envoys, the Indians decided that fifteen slaves, all with blackened faces and ragged cloaks and loincloths, should at once be sent to us with fowls and baked fish and maize-cakes. When these men came before Cortes he received them graciously, but Aguilar asked them rather angrily why they had come with their faces in that state, looking more as if they had come to fight than to ask for peace. He told them to go back to the *Caciques* and inform them that if they wanted the peace we offered them, they must send important men to negotiate, as was customary, and not slaves. But we treated even these black-faced slaves with consideration, and sent them off with blue beads as a sign of peace and to soothe the Indians' feelings.

Next day thirty important men came, dressed in fine cloaks and bearing fowls, fish, fruit, and maize-cakes. They asked Cortes' permission to burn and bury the bodies of those killed in the recent battle, to prevent them from smelling or being eaten by lions and tigers.[1] Permission was at once given, and they hastily brought up a number of men to burn and bury the dead according to their custom. Cortes learnt from these envoys that more than eight hundred of their men were missing, not counting those who had been carried off wounded.[2] They said, however, that they could not stay any longer discussing or negotiating with us, for the next day all the chiefs and nobles of those towns would assemble and arrange the peace.

Cortes, who was very shrewd in all matters, said with a laugh to those of us who happened to be standing with him : 'Do you know, gentlemen, I believe it is the horses that the Indians are most frightened of. They probably think that it is just they and the cannon that they have been fighting, and I've thought of a way of confirming their belief. Let us bring Juan Sedeño's mare, which foaled the other day on board ship, and tie her up here, where I am standing. Ortiz the Musician's stallion is very randy, and we can let him get a sniff of her. Then we will have both of them led off in different directions, and make sure that the

1. These would be pumas or jaguars.
2. According to Cortes' letter from Vera Cruz, only 220 were killed out of 40,000 Indians who fought in this battle.

chiefs who are coming do not hear them neighing, or see them, until they are standing and talking to me.'

Cortes' instructions were carried out exactly. The horse and the mare were brought, and he caught the scent of her in Cortes' quarters. But this was not all. Cortes ordered that the biggest cannon we had should be loaded with a large ball and plenty of powder.

It was midday by this time, and forty Indians arrived, all *Caciques* of fine appearance, dressed in their customary rich cloaks. Then, after saluting Cortes and the rest of us, and perfuming all our company with their incense, they asked our pardon for their past conduct, and promised to be friendly in future.

Cortes answered them through our interpreter somewhat sternly. He reminded them, with a show of anger, how often he had requested them to keep the peace, and said that they had committed a crime and now deserved to be put to death, together with all the inhabitants of their towns. He then pointed out that we were vassals of a great king and lord named the Emperor Charles, who had sent us to these parts with orders to help and favour those who would enter his royal service. This we would do, he continued, if they were now as well-disposed as they said, but if they were not, something would jump out of those *tepuzques* – *tepuzque* is their native name for iron – which would kill them, for some of these *tepuzques* were still angry with them for having attacked us. At this moment he secretly gave the order for the loaded cannon to be fired, and it went off with the requisite thunderous report, the ball whistling away over the hills. It was midday and very still; the *Caciques* were thoroughly terrified. Never having witnessed anything like this before, they believed Cortes' story was true. He told them through Aguilar, however, that they need not be afraid, for he had given orders that no harm should be done to them.

At that moment they brought the horse that had scented the mare, and tied him up near the place where Cortes was talking to the *Caciques*. And as the mare had been tethered at that actual spot, the horse began to paw the ground and neigh and create an uproar, looking all the time towards the Indians and the place from which the scent of the mare came. But the *Caciques* thought he was roaring at them and were terrified once more. When Cortes observed their terror he rose from his seat, went over to the horse, and told two orderlies to lead him away. He then informed the Indians that he had told the beast not to be angry, since they were friendly and had come to make peace.

While this was going on, more than thirty Indian carriers – whom they call *tamemes* – arrived with a meal of fowls and fish and fruit and other food. It appears that they had dropped behind and had not been able to reach us at the same time as the *Caciques*.

Cortes then had a long talk with the three important chieftains, who promised that they would return next day with a present and discuss other matters. After this they departed quite happily.

Early next morning, 15 March 1519,[1] many *Caciques* and important persons came from Tabasco and the neighbouring towns, and paid us great respect. They brought a present of gold, consisting of four diadems, some ornaments in the form of lizards, two shaped like little dogs and five like ducks, also some earrings, two masks of Indian faces, two gold soles for sandals, and some other things of small value. I do not know how much all this was worth. They also brought some cloaks of the kind they weave and wear, which are very rough. For, as anyone who knows this province will tell you, there is nothing there of much value.

These gifts were nothing, however, compared to the twenty women whom they gave us, among them a most excellent person who when she became a Christian took the name of Doña Marina. I will say no more about them, but speak of the pleasure with which Cortes received these overtures. He drew all the *Caciques* aside, with Aguilar the interpreter, to hold converse with them and tell them how grateful he was for what they had brought. But there was one thing he must ask of them, he said, that they should bring all their men, women, and chil-

1. This date is clearly incorrect, for the battle of Cintla was fought on 25 March.

dren back to the town, which he wished to see settled again within two days. This he would recognize as a true sign of peace. The *Caciques* then sent at once to summon all the inhabitants, and they, their wives, and their children resettled the town in the stipulated time.

Another thing that Cortes asked of them was that they should abandon their idols and sacrifices, which they promised to do. He expounded to them as best he could the principles of our holy faith, telling them that we were Christians and worshipped one true God. He then showed them a most sacred image of Our Lady with Her precious Son in her arms, and declared to them that we worshipped it because it was the image of the Mother of our Lord God, who was in heaven. The *Caciques* answered that they liked this great *tececiguata* – which is the name they give to great ladies in their country – and asked for it to be given them to keep in their town. Cortes agreed to their request, and told them to build a fine altar for it, which they did. Next morning he ordered two of our carpenters, Alonso Yañez and Alvar Lopez, to make a very tall cross.

When he had dealt with all this, Cortes asked them why they had attacked us after we had three times requested them to make peace. They replied that they had already asked and received pardon for this. The chief said that it was his brother, the chief of Champoton, who had advised him, and that he was afraid of being accused of cowardice. For he had already been reproached and dishonoured for not attacking the other captain who had come with four ships. He said too that the Indian we had brought as interpreter, who had fled in the night, had also advised them to attack us by day and night.

Cortes ordered them to bring this man before him without fail. But they answered that when he saw the battle going against them he had run away. Search had been made for him, but they did not know where he was. We discovered, however, that they had offered him as a sacrifice because his advice had cost them dear. Cortes then asked them where they procured their gold and jewels, and they answered from the direction of the sunset, saying '*Culua*' and '*Mexico*'. But as we did not know what these words meant, we did not note them.

We then brought forward another interpreter named Francisco whom we had captured, as I have mentioned, on Grijalva's expedition. But he understood nothing of the Tabascan tongue, only the word *Culua*, which is Mexican. He told Cortes by signs that Culua was far ahead, and he repeated *Mexico*, which we did not understand.

Here the conversation ended until the next day, when we set up the sacred image of Our Lady and the cross on the altar, and all paid reverence to them. Fray Bartolome de Olmedo said mass before all the *Caciques* and important persons, and we named the town Santa Maria de la Victoria. The same friar, with Aguilar as interpreter, expounded many good things about our holy faith to the twenty Indian women who had been given to us. He told them not to believe in the idols they had worshipped, since they were evil things and not gods, and to offer them no more sacrifices. He said they had been deceived, and must worship our Lord Jesus Christ, and immediately afterwards they were baptized. One of the Indian ladies was christened Doña Marina. She was a truly great princess, the daughter of *Caciques* and the mistress of vassals, as was very evident in her appearance. I will relate later how this was and in what manner she came to us. I do not clearly remember the names of all the other women, and there is no reason for naming any of them. But they were the first women in New Spain to become Christians. Cortes gave one of them to each of his captains, and Doña Marina, being good-looking, intelligent, and self-assured, went to Alonso Hernandez Puertocarrero, who, as I have already said, was a very grand gentleman, and a cousin of the Count of Medellin. And when Puertocarrero returned to Spain, Doña Marina lived with Cortes, to whom she bore a son named Don Martin Cortes.

We stayed in this town five days, to attend to the wounded and those who had been suffering from pains in the back, which now left them. Furthermore, Cortes won over all the *Caciques* with kindly words, telling them how our Lord the Emperor, whose vassals we were, ruled over many great lords, and that it would be well for them to obey him. Then, if they were in any need, either of our protection or anything else, they had only to let him know, wherever he might be, and he would come to their assistance. Hereupon all the *Caciques* thanked him most warmly and declared themselves vassals of our great Emperor. These were the first vassals in New Spain to yield their obedience to His Majesty.

Cortes then ordered the *Caciques* to come to the altar with their women and children very early next day, which was Palm Sunday, to worship the holy image of Our Lady and the cross. He also told them to send six Indian carpenters to go with our carpenters to the town of Cintla, where our lord God had granted us the victory in the battle I have described, there to cut a cross on a great tree that they call a silk-cotton tree, which grew there. This they did, and it was stood there a long time, for each time the bark is renewed the cross stands out afresh. When this was done, Cortes ordered the Indians to prepare all the canoes they owned in order to help us embark, for we wished to set sail on that holy day, since two pilots had just come in to inform Cortes that the ships were in great danger from a northerly gale which might drive them ashore.

Early next morning all the *Caciques* and important persons came in their canoes, with all their women and children, and stood in the courtyard where we had placed the church and cross, and where we had brought a pile of cut branches to be carried in the procession. The *Caciques* then saw us all, Cortes and his Captains together, marching with the greatest reverence in a devout procession, with the Mercedarian friar and the priest Juan Diaz clad in their vestments. Mass was then said, and we bowed and kissed the holy cross, while the chiefs and Indians stood watching us. When our solemn ceremony was over, the principal Indians came forward to offer Cortes ten fowls and some fish and vegetables, and we took leave of them. Cortes once more commended the blessed image and cross to their care, telling them always to keep the place well cleaned and swept and decked with branches, and to worship it if they wanted to enjoy good health and harvests.

It was already late when we got aboard, and we set sail next day, Monday morning, with a fair wind, laying our course for San Juan de Ulua and keeping close to the shore.

As we sailed along in fine weather, those of us who knew the route would say to Cortes: 'Señor, over there is La Rambla, which the Indians call Ayagualulco.' And soon afterwards we arrived off Tonala, which we call San Antonio. This we pointed out also, and further on we showed him the great river Coatzacoalcos. He saw the high snow-capped mountains, and then the Sierra de San Martin, and further on the split rock, which is a great crag that stands out to sea, with a mark on top of it that looks like a seat. Further on still we showed him the Rio de Alvarado, which Pedro de Alvarado entered during Grijalva's expedition, and then we came in sight of the Rio de Banderas where we had made sixteen thousand pesos by barter. We then showed him Isla Blanca, and told him where Isla Verde lay, and close inshore he saw the Isla de Sacrificios, where we found the altars and Indian victims in Grijalva's time. We were lucky enough to reach San Juan de Ulua soon after midday on Holy Thursday, and I remember that Alonso Hernandez Puertocarrero came up to Cortes at this point and said: 'These gentlemen who have visited this country twice before are saying to you, I think:

> Now look on France, Montesinos,
> Look on Paris, the city,
> See the waters of the Duero
> Flowing down to the sea.[1]

And I say to you: You are looking on rich lands. May you know how to govern them well!'

Cortes understood the reason why these words were said. 'God give us the same good fortune in fighting,' he replied, 'as he gave to the Paladin Roland. For the rest, with you, sir, and these other gentlemen as my captains, I shall know how to acquit myself.'

1. Lines from the ballad of Conde Montesinos.

Doña Marina's Story

BEFORE speaking of the great Montezuma, and of the famous city of Mexico and the Mexicans, I should like to give an account of Doña Marina, who had been a great lady and a *Cacique* over towns and vassals since her childhood.

Her father and mother were lords and *Caciques* of a town called Paynala, which had other towns subject to it, and lay about twenty-four miles from the town of Coatzacoalcos. Her father died while she was still very young, and her mother married another *Cacique*, a young man, to whom she bore a son. The mother and father seem to have been very fond of this son, for they agreed that he should succeed to the *Caciqueship* when they were dead. To avoid any impediment, they gave Doña Marina to some Indians from Xicalango, and this they did by night in order to be unobserved. They then spread the report that the child had died; and as the daughter of one of their Indian slaves happened to die at this time, they gave it out that this was their daughter the heiress.

The Indians of Xicalango gave the child to the people of Tabasco, and the Tabascans gave her to Cortes. I myself knew her mother and her half-brother, who was then a man and ruled the town jointly with his mother, since the old lady's second husband had died. After they became Christians, the mother was called Marta and the son Lazaro. All this I know very well, because in the year 1523, after the conquest of Mexico and the other provinces and at the time of Cristobal de Olid's revolt in Honduras, I passed through the place with Cortes, and the majority of its inhabitants accompanied him also. As Doña Marina had proved such an excellent person, and a good interpreter in all the wars of New Spain, Tlascala,[1] and Mexico – as I shall relate hereafter – Cortes always took her

1. The present spelling is Tlaxcala. The 'x', as in most Nahua words, is pronounced as 'sh'.

with him. During this expedition she married a gentleman
called Juan Jaramillo at the town of Orizaba. Doña Marina was
a person of great importance, and was obeyed without question
by all the Indians of New Spain. And while Cortes was in the
town of Coatzacoalcos, he summoned all the *Caciques* of that
province in order to address them on the subject of our holy
religion, and the good way in which they had been treated; and
Doña Marina's mother and her half-brother Lazaro were among
those who came. Doña Marina had told me some time before
that she belonged to this province, and that she was the mistress of vassals, and both Cortes and the interpreter Aguilar
knew it well. Thus it was that mother, son, and daughter came
together, and it was easy enough to see from the strong resemblance between them that Doña Marina and the old lady
were related. Both she and her son were very much afraid of
Doña Marina; they feared that she had sent for them to put
them to death, and they wept.

When Doña Marina saw her mother and half-brother in tears,
she comforted them, saying that they need have no fear. She
told her mother that when they had handed her over to the
men from Xicalango, they had not known what they were
doing. She pardoned the old woman, and gave them many
golden jewels and some clothes. Then she sent them back to
their town, saying that God had been very gracious to her in
freeing her from the worship of idols and making her a Christian, and giving her a son by her lord and master Cortes, also
in marrying her to such a gentleman as her husband Juan Jaramillo. Even if they were to make her mistress of all the provinces of New Spain, she said, she would refuse the honour, for
she would rather serve her husband and Cortes than anything
else in the world. What I have related here I know for certain
and swear to. The whole story seems very much like that of
Joseph and his brethren in Egypt, when the Egyptians came into
his power over the wheat.

To return to my subject, Doña Marina knew the language of
Coatzacoalcos, which is that of Mexico, and she knew the
Tabascan language also. This language is common to Tabasco
and Yucatan, and Jeronimo de Aguilar spoke it also. These two

understood one another well, and Aguilar translated into Castilian for Cortes.

This was the great beginning of our conquests, and thus, praise be to God, all things prospered with us. I have made a point of telling this story, because without Doña Marina we could not have understood the language of New Spain and Mexico.

A Pause on the Coast

On Holy Thursday 1519 we arrived with all the fleet at the port of San Juan de Ulua. Knowing the place well from his previous visit under Juan de Grijalva, the pilot Alaminos at once ordered the vessels to anchor where they would be safe from the northerly gales. The royal standards and pennants were raised on the flagship, and within half an hour of our anchoring two large canoes or pirogues came out to us full of Mexican Indians. Seeing the large ship with its standards flying, they knew that it was there they must go to speak with the Captain. So they made straight for the flagship, went aboard and asked who was the *Tatuan*, which in their language means the master. Doña Marina, who understood them, pointed him out; and the Indians paid Cortes great marks of respect in their fashion. They said that their lord, a servant of the great Montezuma, had sent them to find out what kind of men we were and what we were seeking, also to say that if we required anything for ourselves or our ships, we were to tell them and they would supply it.

Cortes thanked them through our interpreters, and ordered that they should be given food, wine, and some blue beads. After they had drunk the wine he told them that he had come to visit and trade with them, and that they should think of our coming to their country as fortunate rather than troublesome. The messengers went ashore very contented, and next day, which was Good Friday, we disembarked with our horses and guns on some sandhills, which were quite high. For there was no level land, nothing but sand-dunes; and the artilleryman Mesa placed his guns on them in what seemed to him the best positions. Then we set up an altar, at which mass was said at once, and built huts and shelters for Cortes and his captains. Our three hundred soldiers then brought wood, and we made huts for ourselves. We put the horses where they would be safe, and in this way we spent Good Friday.

A Pause on the Coast

On Saturday, which was Easter Eve, many Indians arrived who had been sent by a *Cacique* called Pitalpitoque, whom we afterwards named Ovandillo and who was one of Montezuma's governors.[1] They brought axes, and dressed wood for Cortes' hut and the others near it, which they covered with large cloths on account of the sun. For since it was Lent, the heat was very great. They brought fowls and maize-cakes and plums, which were then in season, and also, I think, some gold jewels; all of which they presented to Cortes, saying that next day a governor would come and bring more provisions. Cortes thanked them warmly, and ordered that they should be given certain things in exchange, with which they went away well pleased.

Next day, Easter Sunday, the governor of whom they had spoken arrived. His name was Tendile, a man of affairs, and he brought with him Pitalpitoque, who was also an important person among them. They were followed by many Indians with presents of fowls and vegetables, whom Tendile commanded to stand a little aside on a hillock, while according to their custom he bowed humbly three times, first to Cortes and then to all the other soldiers standing near by.

Cortes welcomed them through our interpreters, embraced them, and asked them to wait, as he wished to speak to them presently. Meanwhile he had had an altar set up as well as could be done in the time, and Fray Bartolome de Olmedo, who was a fine singer, chanted mass with the assistance of Padre Juan Diaz, while the two governors and the other *Caciques* who were with them looked on. After mass Cortes and some of our captains dined with the two officers of the great Montezuma, and when the tables had been removed, he took these two and our two interpreters aside, and explained to them that we were Christians, and vassals of the Emperor Don Carlos, the greatest lord on earth, who had many great princes as his vassals and servants, and that it was at his orders we had come to their country, since for many years he had heard rumours of it and of the great prince who ruled it. Cortes said that he wished to

1. Pitalpitoque or Cuitlalpitoc was the man who had been sent as ambassador to meet Grijalva.

89

be friends with this prince, and to tell him many things in the Emperor's name, which would greatly delight him when he knew and understood them. Moreover he wished to trade with their prince and his Indians in a friendly way, and to know what place this prince would appoint for their meeting.

To this Tendile replied somewhat proudly: 'You have only just arrived, and already you ask to speak with our prince. Accept now this present that we give you in our master's name, and afterwards tell me whatever you wish.'

He took out of a *petaca* – which is a sort of chest – many golden objects beautifully and richly worked, and then sent for ten bales of white cloth made of cotton and feathers – a marvellous sight. There were other things too that I do not remember, and quantities of food – fowls, fruit, and baked fish. Cortes received all this with gracious smiles, and gave them in return some beads of twisted glass and other little beads from Spain, begging them to send to their towns and summon the people to trade with us, since he had plenty of these beads to exchange for gold. They replied that they would do as he asked.

As we afterwards learnt, these two men Tendile and Pitalpitoque were the governors of the provinces called Cotustan, Tuxtepec, Guazpaltepeque, and Tatalteco, and also of some other towns recently conquered. Cortes next ordered his servants to bring an armchair, richly carved and inlaid, and some moss-agates pierced and intricately worked, and packed in cotton scented with musk to give them a good smell, also a string of twisted glass beads, and a crimson cap with a gold medal engraved with a figure of St George on horseback, lance in hand and slaying the dragon. He told Tendile that he would send the chair to his prince Montezuma – for we already knew his name – so that he could sit in it when Cortes came to visit and speak with him, and that he should wear the cap on his head. These stones, he said, and all the other things were in token of friendship from our lord the King, for he was aware that Montezuma was a great prince. Cortes then asked that a day and a place might be fixed for his meeting with Montezuma. Tendile accepted the present. Observing that his great master would be glad to know our great king, he promised to deliver it promptly and return with Montezuma's reply.

It appears that Tendile brought with him some of those skilled painters they have in Mexico, and that he gave them instructions to make realistic full-length portraits of Cortes and all his captains and soldiers, also to draw the ships, sails, and horses, Doña Marina and Aguilar, and even the two greyhounds. The cannon and cannon-balls, and indeed the whole of our army, were faithfully portrayed, and the drawings were taken to Montezuma.

Cortes ordered our gunners to load the lombards with a big charge of powder, so that they should make a great noise when fired, and told Pedro de Alvarado that all his horsemen must be ready with little bells tied to their breastplates, to gallop in front of Montezuma's servants. He too mounted his horse. 'It would be a good thing,' he said, 'if we could gallop on these dunes. But they will see that even on foot we get stuck in the sand. Let us go down to the beach when the tide is low and gallop there two by two.' And he put all the horsemen under the command of Pedro de Alvarado, whose sorrel mare was a great runner and very quick on the rein.

The display was carried out in the presence of the two ambassadors, and in order that they should see the shot leave the gun Cortes pretended that he wished to speak to them and some other *Caciques* again, just before the cannon was fired. As it was very still at that moment, the balls resounded with a great din as they went over the forest. The two governors and the rest of the Indians were frightened by this strange happening, and ordered their painters to paint it, so that Montezuma might see. It appears that one of our soldiers had a helmet that was half-gilt but somewhat rusty. This Tendile noticed, and being of a more inquiring disposition than his fellow *Cacique*, he asked if he might see it, since it was like one that they possessed which had been left them by their ancestors of the race from which they sprang and placed on the head of their god Huichilobos.[1] He said that his master Montezuma would like to see this helmet, and it was given to him. Cortes said,

1. Huitzilopochtli.

however, that as he wished to know whether the gold of their country was the same as the gold we find in our rivers, they might send it back filled with grains of gold, as a present for our great Emperor. After this Tendile took his leave of us all, and after many protestations of regard on Cortes' part, promised to return very promptly with a reply. After his departure we discovered that Tendile was not only an important man of affairs but the most active of Montezuma's servants. He went with all haste, and gave his master a complete account of events, showing him the pictures which had been painted and the present that Cortes had sent him, which is said to have astonished Montezuma, who accepted it with great satisfaction. And when he compared the helmet with that of his gold Huichilobos, he was convinced that we were of that race which, according to the prophecies of his ancestors, would come to rule the land.

When Tendile departed with Cortes' present for his lord Montezuma, the other governor Pitalpitoque stayed in our camp, occupying some huts a short distance away, to which they brought women to make maize-cakes, also fowls, fruit, and fish. This food was supplied to Cortes and his captains also, who ate with the governor. But we soldiers got nothing but the shellfish we picked up or the fish we caught.

About this time many Indians came from the towns of which these two great servants of Montezuma were governors, some of them bringing gold and jewels of little value, or fowls, to exchange with us for green beads, clear glass beads, and other articles. In this way we kept ourselves fed, for almost all the soldiers had brought goods for barter, and we had learnt in Grijalva's time that beads were a good thing to bring.

Six or seven days passed in this way. Then one morning Tendile returned with more than a hundred Indian porters, and accompanied by a great Mexican chief, who in face, features, and body was very like our Captain. The great Montezuma had chosen him on purpose. For it is said when Tendile showed him the portrait of Cortes all the princes present exclaimed that one of their number, Quintalbor,[1] looked exactly like him; and it was Quintalbor who now accompanied Tendile. On account of

1. This is not a Mexican name.

this resemblance we in the camp called them 'our Cortes' and 'the other Cortes'.

To return to my story, when these people arrived before our Captain they kissed the earth and perfumed him and all the soldiers near him with incense that they had brought in earthenware braziers. Cortes received them kindly and seated them beside him. The prince Quintalbor, who bore the presents and had been appointed joint spokesman with Tendile, welcomed us to the country and after a long speech ordered them to be brought forward. The various objects were placed on mats, which they call *petates*, on which were spread other cotton cloths. The first was a disk in the shape of the sun, as big as a cartwheel and made of very fine gold. It was a marvellous thing engraved with many sorts of figures and, as those who afterwards weighed it reported, was worth more than ten thousand pesos. There was another larger disk of brightly shining silver in the shape of the moon, with other figures on it, and this was worth a great deal for it was very heavy. Quintalbor also brought back the helmet full of small grains of gold, just as they come from the mines and worth three thousand pesos.

The gold in the helmet was worth more than twenty thousand pesos to us, because it proved to us that there were good mines in the country. Next came twenty golden ducks, of fine workmanship and very realistic, some ornaments in the shape of their native dogs, many others in the shapes of tigers, lions, and monkeys, ten necklaces of very fine workmanship, some pendants, twelve arrows and a strung bow, and two rods like staffs of justice twenty inches long, all modelled in fine gold. Next they brought crests of gold, plumes of rich green feathers, silver crests, some fans of the same material, models of deer in hollow gold, and many other things that I cannot remember, since all this was very long ago; and after this came thirty loads of beautiful cotton cloth of various patterns, decorated with feathers of many colours, and so many other things that I cannot attempt to describe them.

When the presents had been displayed these great *Caciques* Quintalbor and Tendile asked Cortes to accept them with the same grace as Montezuma had shown in sending them, and to divide them among the *Teules* [1] and men who accompanied him. Cortes accepted the gifts with delight, whereupon the ambassadors told him that they wished to repeat the message with which Montezuma had charged them. First, that he was pleased such valiant men as he had heard we were should come to his country – for he knew what we had done at Tabasco – and that he would much like to see our great Emperor, who was such a mighty prince that his fame had reached him even from the distant lands whence we came. Secondly, that he would send the Emperor a present of precious stones, and serve us in any way he could during our stay in that port. But as for a meeting, he told us not to think of it, for it was not necessary; and he put forward many objections.

Cortes thanked them with a good countenance, and with many flattering protestations gave each governor two holland shirts, some blue glass beads, and other things, and begged them to go back as his ambassadors to Mexico and inform their lord, the great Montezuma, that since we had crossed so many seas and journeyed from such distant lands solely to see and speak with him in person, our great King and lord would not give us a good reception if we were to return without doing so. Wherever their king might be, said Cortes, we should like to go and visit him and carry out his commands.

The governors replied that they would return with this message, but that they considered the requested interview superfluous. Cortes gave them to take to Montezuma as much as our poverty allowed : a cup of Florentine glass, engraved with trees and hunting-scenes and finely gilded, three holland shirts, and some other objects; and he charged them to bring him a reply.

The two governors set out, and Pitalpitoque remained in the camp; for it seems that Montezuma's other servants had given him orders to see that food was brought to us from the neighbouring towns.

After dispatching the messengers to Mexico, Cortes sent two ships to explore further along the coast. These he put under the command of Francisco de Montejo, who had served under

1. Literally gods. The Indians seem at first to have considered the Spaniards supernatural beings.

Grijalva, and instructed him to follow the course we had taken in that expedition, and look for a safe harbour and a site for settlement. For clearly we could not settle on these sand-dunes, on account of the mosquitoes and the distance from any town. Cortes chose Alaminos and Juan Alvarez 'El manquillo' as pilots, since they knew the route, and told them to sail along the coast as far as they could in ten days. Obeying his instructions, they went as far as the Rio Grande, which is close to Panuco,[1] where we had been under Grijalva, but could go no further on account of the strong currents. On discovering the difficulties of navigation, they turned round and made for San Juan de Ulua, bringing us back no other news except that some thirty-six miles on they had seen a town which looked like a fortified port and was called Quiahuitzlan, and that beside it was a harbour in which Alaminos thought our ships would be safe from the northerly gales. He gave it the ugly name of Bernal because it resembled a harbour of that name in Spain. The voyage there and back took Montejo ten to twelve days.

I must now return to the Indian Pitalpitoque, who remained behind to supply us with food. His efforts slackened to such an extent that in the end he brought nothing to the camp. Our cassava turned sour, rotted, and became infested by weevils, and we were so short of provisions that if we had not gone out to collect shellfish we should have had nothing to eat. The Indians who had been bringing gold and fowls for barter now came in smaller numbers than at first, and those who did come were very shy and fearful. We were waiting hourly for the arrival of the messengers from Mexico.

While we were in this state of expectation Tendile returned with a great company of Indians. After paying Cortes and the rest of us the usual compliment of perfuming us all with incense, he presented ten loads of fine rich feather cloth and four *chalchihuites*, and some gold articles. Not counting the *chalchihuites*, the gold alone was estimated at three thousand pesos.

Then Tendile and Pitalpitoque approached – the other great

1. Actually Cape Rojo was the furthest point reached by the Grijalva expedition.

Cacique Quintalbor was not with them, since he had fallen ill on the road – and the two governors went aside with Cortes, Doña Marina, and Aguilar to present their report. They said that their lord Montezuma had accepted our present, and was greatly pleased with it, but as for an interview that was out of the question. He wished the *chalchihuites* to be sent to the Emperor, since they were of the highest value, each of them being worth more than a great load of gold, but observed that it would be useless for us to send any further messengers to Mexico.

Cortes thanked them and gave them presents, but it certainly depressed him to be told so directly that we could not see Montezuma. 'He must surely be a great and rich prince,' he observed to some soldiers who were standing near, 'and one day, please God, we will go and see him.' And we soldiers answered: 'We only wish we were living with him now.'

It was the hour of Ave Maria, and at the sound of the camp bell we all fell on our knees, in front of a cross which we had erected on a sandhill, to say our prayers. Tendile and Pital-pitoque, being intelligent men and seeing us thus on our knees, asked us why we humbled ourselves before a log cut in that particular fashion. On hearing this question Cortes said to the Mercedarian friar who was present: 'Now, father, we have a good opportunity of explaining to them through our interpreters something about our holy faith.' He then delivered an address to the *Caciques* so apt to the occasion that no good theologian could have bettered it. After telling them that we were Christians, he explained all the relevant details of our religion, which they perfectly understood; and they replied that they would report them to their lord Montezuma. Cortes also told them that our great Emperor's purpose in sending us to their lands was to abolish human sacrifices and the other evil rites they practised, and to see that they did not rob one another and that they ceased to worship their accursed idols. He begged them to erect in their cities, in the temples where they kept these idols which they believed to be gods, a cross like the one they saw, and to set up before it an image of Our Lady, which he would give them, bearing her precious Son in her arms. He added that they would then see how well things would go with them, and what our God would do for them. He used many other arguments. But as I could not write them all down, I will leave the subject and recall how on this last occasion many Indians came with Tendile to barter gold objects which were of no great value. All the soldiers, however, set about bartering; and the gold we gained was given to the sailors who had been out fishing, in exchange for their fish.

When Diego Velazquez' friends saw some of us soldiers trading for gold, they asked Cortes why he allowed it. Protesting that Diego Velazquez had not sent out the expedition in order to enrich the soldiers, they said it would be as well if an order were issued that henceforth there should be no bartering for gold except by Cortes himself, and that what had so far been obtained should be brought out so that the royal fifth could be deducted. They further asked that some suitable person should be appointed as treasurer.

Cortes replied that they were right, and invited them to nominate the person. They chose one Gonzalo Mejia. But when they had done so he turned to them with an angry face and said, 'Observe, gentlemen, that our comrades are suffering great hardships from lack of food. For this reason we ought to overlook things, and let them all have something to eat. What is more, the amount of gold they have gained is a mere trifle, and, God willing, we are going to gain a great deal more. However, every question has two sides. As you wish, the decree has been issued that bartering for gold shall cease. Now we shall see what we get to eat.'

The historian Gomara remarks at this point that Cortes' purpose was to convince Montezuma that we attached no value to gold. But Gomara was misinformed. Ever since Grijalva's visit to the Rio de Banderas, Montezuma must have known the truth, and his opinion must have been confirmed when we sent him the helmet with a request that it should be filled with gold grains from the mines. Besides, they had seen us bartering, and the Mexicans were not the sort of people to misunderstand such things.

One morning we awoke to find not a single Indian in any of

the huts, neither those who brought us our food, nor those who came to trade, nor Pitalpitoque himself; they had all fled without a word. The reason for this, as we afterwards learned, was that Montezuma had sent orders to break off all conversations with Cortes and his company. It seems that the prince was very devoted to his idols Tezcatlipoca and Huichilobos, the god of war and the god of hell respectively, and sacrificed youths to them every day in hopes that they would tell him what to do about us. For Montezuma had formed a plan to seize us if we did not return to our ships, in order to breed from us and keep us for sacrifice. The reply that his idols gave him was that he must cease to listen to Cortes and his message about setting up a cross and an image of Our Lady, and that these objects should not be brought to the city. That is why the Indians had silently departed.

When we heard the news we thought they meant war, and put ourselves very much on the alert. One day, as I and another soldier were posted on some sand-dunes keeping a look-out, we saw five Indians coming along the beach, and so as to raise no alarm in the camp over so slight a matter allowed them to approach. They came up to us with smiles on their faces, paid us the usual respects, and asked us by signs to take them to the camp. I told my companion to stay on guard, and said I would go with them, for my feet were not as heavy at that time as they are now that I am old. And when we came to Cortes they bowed low to him and said: '*Lope luzio, lope luzio,*' which in their Totonac language means 'Prince and great lord'. The men had great holes in their lower lips, in which some carried stone disks spotted with blue, and others thin sheets of gold. They also had great holes in their ears, in which they had inserted disks of stone or gold; and they were very different in their dress and speech from the Mexicans who had been staying with us. Our interpreters did not understand these words '*Lope luzio*'; and Doña Marina inquired in Mexican if there were no *Nahuatlatos* – that is to say interpreters of the Mexican language – among them. Two of the five answered yes, that they understood it, and bade us welcome, saying that their chief had sent them to inquire who we were, and tell us that he would be glad to be of service to such valiant men. For it appears that they knew about our deeds at Tabasco and Champoton. They added that they would have come to see us before, but for their fear of the people of Culua who had been with us, but that they knew these men had run off home three days before. As this conversation went on, Cortes learnt that Montezuma had opponents and enemies, which greatly delighted him. After flattering these five messengers, Cortes dismissed them with presents, and a message to their *Cacique* that he would very soon pay him a visit. From this time on we called these Indians the *lope luzios*.

In those sand-dunes where we had camped there were always many mosquitoes, both the long-legged ones and the small ones which are called *xexenes* and are worse than the big ones; and together they gave us no sleep. We had no provisions, our cassava bread was getting short and mouldy, and some of the soldiers who owned Indians in the island of Cuba, especially the friends and servants of Diego Velazquez, were sighing to go home. When Cortes saw how things were and realized the state of opinion, he gave orders that we should go to the fortified town of Quiahuitzlan, which had been seen by Montejo and the pilot Alaminos and where the ships would be sheltered by the rock I have spoken of. But as we were preparing to depart, all Diego Velazquez' friends, relatives, and servants asked Cortes why he chose to undertake this journey without any provisions, protesting that there was no possibility of going any further, since we had lost more than thirty-five soldiers from wounds received at Tabasco, sickness, and hunger. They pointed out also that we were in a large country, that its towns were very populous, and that any day we might be attacked. Therefore, they said, it would be better to return to Cuba and render Velazquez an account of the gold gained by barter, of which the quantity was large, also of Montezuma's great presents; the sun and the silver moon, and the helmet full of golden grains from the mines, and all the jewels and cloths I have mentioned.

Cortes answered that it was bad advice to recommend our going back without reason, and that up to now we had no cause to complain of our luck. He told them we must thank God, who was helping us in all things, and that as for our losses, these were usual in war and under hardship. Moreover, it would be as well to see what this land contained, and in the meantime to live on maize and such provisions as the Indians had in the neighbouring towns, which would give us enough to eat, if our hands had not lost their cunning. Diego Velazquez' followers were somewhat though not wholly appeased by this answer, for they had already formed factions in the camp to advocate a return to Cuba.

I have already said that Diego Velazquez' friends and relatives were going about the camp protesting against our advancing any further, and demanding that we should return from San Juan de Ulua to Cuba. It appears that Cortes had already discussed the matter with Alonso Hernandez Puertocarrero, Pedro de Alvarado and his four brothers, Cristobal de Olid, Alonso de Avila, Juan de Escalante, and Francisco de Lugo, also with many other captains and gentlemen including myself, and suggested that we should elect him Captain. Francisco de Montejo was aware of all this, and on his guard. One night Puertocarrero, Escalante, and Lugo visited my hut after midnight – Lugo came from my part of the country and was my distant kinsman. 'Señor Bernal Díaz,' they said, 'arm yourself and come with us. We are going to accompany Cortes on his rounds.' Then, as soon as we were a little way from the hut, they added: 'Sir, there is something we wish to tell you which you must keep secret for a while. It is very important, and you must not let your hut companions know it, for they are partisans of Diego Velazquez.' They then went on to say: 'Sir, do you think it was right of Hernando Cortes to have brought us here by deceit? He proclaimed in Cuba that he was coming to settle, and now we discover that he has no authority to do anything but barter, and these men wish us to return to Santiago de Cuba with all the gold that has been collected. This will be the ruins of us all, for Diego Velazquez will take everything, as he did before. You, sir, have already been to this country three times, counting the present expedition, spending your own wealth and contracting debts, and have been in peril of your life many times from the wounds you have received. Many of

us gentlemen, who feel that we are your friends, wish to convince you that this state of things must end; that this land must
be settled in His Majesty's name and by Hernando Cortes on his
behalf until such time as it is possible for us to send information to our lord the King of Spain. Be sure, sir, to cast your
vote, so that he may be elected Captain by our unanimous will.
If you do so, you will be doing a service to God and our lord
the King.'

I replied that it would be a bad plan to return to Cuba, that
the land ought to be settled, and that we should elect Hernando
Cortes to be General and Chief Justice until His Majesty should
order otherwise.

This idea was passed from one soldier to another, until Diego
Velazquez' friends and relatives, who were more numerous than
we, got to know of it. Somewhat high-handedly they then
asked Cortes why he was making secret arrangements to stay
in the country, instead of returning to give an account of his
deeds to the man who had sent him as Captain. They said that
Diego Velazquez would disapprove of his conduct, and that the
sooner we embarked the better; moreover, that his subterfuges
and private meetings with us soldiers could serve no good purpose, since we had neither supplies nor men, nor any possibility
of founding a settlement.

Displaying no sign of anger, Cortes replied that he was in
agreement, and would not go against the instructions and letters
he had received from Diego Velazquez. He issued an order
that we should all embark on the following day, each in the
ship in which he had come. We who were party to the plot
protested that it was unfair to deceive us in this way. In Cuba,
we said, he had proclaimed that he was coming to make a settlement, whereas he had only come to trade. We demanded in
God's name and the King's that he should at once found a settlement and give up any other plan, because this would be of the
greatest benefit and service both to our lord God and to His
Majesty. Many other well reasoned arguments were placed
before him, to the effect that the natives would never let us
land again as they had done this time; that once the country
was settled, soldiers would arrive from all the islands to help

us; that Diego Velazquez had ruined us all by publicly proclaiming that he had His Majesty's authority to found a settlement when he had not; that he wished to found a settlement; and that those who wanted to return to Cuba should do so.

Cortes gave in, although he pretended to need much begging. It was a case of : 'Press me harder' (as the saying goes) 'but I'm very willing.' He stipulated, however, that we should make him Chief Justice and Captain-General and, worst of all, we had to concede him a fifth of all the gold we obtained, after the subtraction of the royal fifth. Then, after granting him the very fullest powers, embracing all that I have stated, in front of the King's notary Diego de Godoy, we at once set about making, founding, and settling a town which we called Villa Rica de la Vera Cruz, since we had reached the place on Maundy Thursday and landed on Good Friday. We called it *rich*, because of the gentleman's words to Cortes, which I have quoted : 'You are looking on rich lands. May you know how to govern them well.' The gentleman was Alonso Hernandez Puertocarrero, and what he meant to say was : 'May you remain here as Captain-General.'

As soon as the town was founded we appointed alcaydes and *regidores*;[1] and the first alcaydes were Puertocarrero and Francisco de Montejo. In Montejo's case, it was because he was on bad terms with him that Cortes had him appointed to this high position. I will not give the names of the *regidores*, for it is useless to name only a few of them. I will mention, however, that a pillory was placed in the square and a gallows erected outside the town. We chose Pedro de Alvarado as commander of expeditions, and Cristobal de Olid as quartermaster. Juan de Escalante was appointed high constable, Gonzalo Mejia treasurer, and Alonso de Avila accountant. A certain Corral was chosen as standard-bearer, because the former ensign Villaroel had been dismissed from his post for offending Cortes, I do not know exactly how, over some Indian woman from Cuba. A Basque called Ochoa and Alonso Romero were made *alguaciles*[2] of the camp.

It will be said that I have not mentioned Gonzalo de Sandoval,

1. A town council.   2. Storekeepers.

the famous captain second only to Cortes of whom our lord and Emperor heard such great reports. I would reply that he was still a youth, and that we did not take such account of him as of some other valiant captains until we saw him develop in such a way that we all, Cortes included, put him on a level with the Captain-General.

When Diego Velazquez' party realized that we had elected Cortes Captain and Chief Justice, and founded the town and appointed our officers, they were so furiously angry that they began to stir up factions and call meetings, and to revile Cortes and those of us who had elected him. They protested that we had no right to do so, unless all the captains and soldiers who had come on the expedition agreed; that Diego Velazquez had given Cortes no such powers, only the authority to trade; and that we of Cortes' party must take care not to be so shameless as to provoke a fight.

Then Cortes whispered to Juan de Escalante that we must ask him to produce the instructions Diego Velazquez had given him; and plucking them from his breast, he gave them to the king's scribe to read aloud. They contained the words: 'As soon as you have gained all you can by trading you are to return.' The document was signed by Diego Velazquez, and countersigned by his secretary, Andres de Duero. We begged Cortes to have this document attached to the deed which recorded the powers we had given him, and with it the proclamation that was issued in the island of Cuba. For we wished His Majesty in Spain to know that all we were doing was in his royal service, and to prevent any untruthful allegations being made against us. This proved a very good precaution in the light of our treatment in Spain by Don Juan Rodriguez de Fonseca, Bishop of Burgos and Archbishop of Rosano – for those were his titles – who according to our certain knowledge was taking steps to destroy us, as I shall afterwards relate.

Then these same friends and dependants of Diego Velazquez protested once more against our having elected Cortes without their consent, and said that they would not remain under his command but wished to return at once to Cuba. Cortes answered that he would detain nobody by force, and would willingly grant anyone who asked for it leave to return, even though he were left alone. This appeased some of them, but not Juan Velazquez de Leon, a relative of Diego's, or Diego de Ordaz, or Escobar, whom we called 'the Page' because he had been brought up by Diego Velazquez, or Pedro Escudero, or certain others of Velazquez' friends, who went so far as entirely to refuse their obedience. Cortes therefore decided to arrest them with our assistance. Taking good care that the rest should make no disturbance, we kept these men prisoners for several days in chains and under guard.

After the arrests Pedro de Alvarado was sent inland to visit some near-by towns of which we had been told, to inspect the country, and to bring back maize and other provisions, for we were extremely short of food in the camp. Alvarado took a hundred soldiers, including fifteen crossbowmen and six musketeers; more than half of them were partisans of Diego Velazquez. We of Cortes' party all remained with him for fear there should be any further disturbance or trickery or insurrection, until things became more settled.

Alvarado first visited some villages which were dependent on a larger place called Cotaxtla, where the Culua language was spoken. This language is here common to the allies of Mexico and Montezuma, just as Latin was formerly common to those of Rome. Whenever Culuan is mentioned, therefore, in connexion with this country, it must be understood to refer to the subjects and vassals of Mexico.

When Alvarado came to these villages he found that they had been deserted on that very day, and he saw in the *cues* the bodies of men and boys who had been sacrificed, the walls and altars all splashed with blood, and the victims' hearts laid out before the idols. He also found the stones on which the sacrifices had been made, and the flint with which their breasts had been opened to tear out their hearts.

Alvarado told us that most of the bodies were without arms and legs, and that some Indians had told him that these had been carried off to be eaten. Our soldiers were greatly shocked at such cruelty. I will say no more about these sacrifices, since we found them in every town we came to, but will return to

Pedro de Alvarado and mention that he found all these places well provisioned and all deserted on the very day of his arrival. Indeed we could not find more than two Indians to carry maize, and each soldier had to load himself with poultry and vegetables. Alvarado returned to camp without doing any more damage, though he had plenty of opportunity, because Cortes had given orders to the effect that there should be no repetition of the events at Cozumel. We were pleased enough in camp with the very little food they brought us, for evils and hardships vanish when there is enough to eat.

Since he was always capable of taking great pains, Cortes succeeded in making friends with Velazquez' party and bringing them round, some with presents of gold, which breaks down all opposition, and some with promises. He then released from prison all except Juan Velazquez de Leon and Diego de Ordaz, whom he kept in irons aboard ship. But he released them too after a few days, and made good and loyal friends of them, as will be seen hereafter – and all with gold, the great peacemaker!

When all was quiet we decided to visit the fortified town of which I have spoken, which was called Quiahuitzlan. The ships were to go to the rock and harbour, which was opposite the town and about three miles away. I remember that as we marched along the coast we killed a great fish which had been thrown up on the beach. When we reached the river on which Vera Cruz now stands, we found the water deep, and crossed it in some broken trough-shaped canoes, or by swimming, or on rafts. Beside the river we found some villages subject to the great town of Cempoala, from which those five Indians had come with gold rings on their lips; I mean those messengers who came to Cortes in the sand-dunes, and whom we called *lope luzios*. We found temples and places of sacrifice, and blood splashed about, and the incense they burnt, and other properties of their idols, also the stones on which they made their sacrifices, and parrots' feathers, and many of their paper books, which are folded as cloth is in Spain. But we found no Indians, because they had all fled. For never having seen men like us before, or horses, they were afraid.

We slept there that night, and went without supper; and

next day we left the coast, striking inland towards the west. Without knowing our way, we found some good meadows – which they call savannahs – on which deer were grazing. Pedro de Alvarado chased one on his sorrel mare and wounded it with a lance thrust. But it escaped into the woods and we could not catch it.

During the chase we saw twelve Indians approaching, the inhabitants of the farms in which we had slept. They had been to consult their *Cacique*, and were bringing us fowls and maize-cakes. They told Cortes, through our interpreters, that he had sent us these fowls to eat, and that he begged us to come to his town, which according to the signs they made was one sun's journey away, that is a day's march.

Cortes thanked them and made much of them, and we marched on. That night we slept in another village where many sacrifices had been made. But the reader will be tired of this constant story of sacrifices, and I will mention them no more.

In this village they gave us supper, and told us that the road to Quiahuitzlan passed through Cempoala.

The Stay at Cempoala

WE slept at the village where these twelve Indians had prepared quarters for us, and after getting good information about the road we must take to the town on the hill, we sent word to the *Caciques* of Cempoala, very early in the morning, that we were coming to their town and hoped they would be pleased. We sent six of the Indians to carry this message, and kept the other six as guides. Cortes also ordered the guns, muskets, and crossbows to be kept ready for use, and scouts to be sent ahead. The horsemen and all the rest of us kept on the alert, and thus we advanced to within three miles of the town. When we came to this point twenty Indian dignitaries came out to welcome us in the name of the *Cacique*, and brought us some cakes of their very finely scented rose-petals. These they presented to Cortes and the horsemen with every sign of friendliness, saying that their lord was awaiting us at our lodgings, since he was too fat and heavy to come out and receive us. Cortes thanked them, and we continued our march; and as we came among the houses we saw how large a town it was, larger than any we had yet seen, and were full of admiration. It was so green with vegetation that it looked like a garden; and its streets were so full of men and women who had come out to see us that we gave thanks to God for the discovery of such a country.

Our mounted scouts had come to a great square with courtyards where they had prepared our lodgings, which appeared to have been lime-coated and burnished during the last few days. The Indians are so skilful at these arts that one of the horsemen took the shining whiteness for silver, and came galloping back to tell Cortes that our quarters had silver walls. Doña Marina and Aguilar said that it must be plaster, and we laughed at his excitement. Indeed we reminded him ever afterwards that anything white looked to him like silver. But enough of this. When we came to the buildings, this fat *Cacique* came out to receive us in the courtyard. He was so fat that I must call him the fat *Cacique*. He made a deep bow to Cortes and perfumed him as is their custom, and Cortes embraced him. After leading us into our fine, large quarters, which held us all, they gave us food and brought us some baskets of plums, which were very plentiful at that season, also some of their maize-cakes. As we were hungry, and had not seen so much food for a long time, we called the town Villa Viciosa.[1] Others named it Seville.

Cortes gave orders that none of the soldiers should leave the square or annoy the inhabitants; and when the fat *Cacique* learnt that we had finished eating, he sent to tell Cortes that he wished to pay him a visit. He came with a great number of Indian dignitaries, all wearing large gold lip-rings and rich cloaks. Cortes also left his quarters to receive him, and greeted him with a great show of affection and flattery. Then the fat *Cacique* ordered a present to be brought of golden jewellery and cloth; and although it was small and of no great value, he said to Cortes: '*Lope luzio lope luzio!* Please accept this; if I had more I would give it to you.' I have already explained that in the Totonac language *lope luzio* means lord of great lords.

Cortes replied through our interpreters that he would repay this gift in services, and that if the *Cacique* would tell him what he wanted it should be done for him, since we were vassals of the Emperor Charles, a very great prince who ruled over many kingdoms and countries and had sent us to redress grievances, to punish evildoers, and to command that human sacrifices should cease. And he explained many things concerning our holy religion. On hearing all this, the fat *Cacique* heaved a deep sigh and broke into bitter complaints against the great Montezuma and his governors, saying that the Mexican prince had recently brought him into subjection, had taken away all his golden jewellery, and so grievously oppressed him and his people that they could do nothing except obey him, since he was lord over many cities and countries, and ruler over countless vassals and armies of warriors.

As Cortes knew that he could not then attend to their complaint, he answered that he would see their wrongs set right, but that he was now on the way to visit his *acales* – which is

1. The city of abundance.

the Indian word for ships – and to take up residence in the town of Quiahuitzlan, and that as soon as he was settled there he would give the matter greater consideration. To this the fat *Cacique* replied that he was quite satisfied.

Next morning we left Cempoala, and over four hundred Indian porters, here called *tamemes*, were awaiting our orders. Each can carry fifty pounds on his back and march fifteen miles with it. We rejoiced at the sight of so many porters, since hitherto those of us who had not brought servants from Cuba had had to carry our knapsacks on our backs. And only six or seven Cubans had come with the fleet, not the great number that Gomara states. Doña Marina and Aguilar told us that in time of peace the chiefs in these parts are compelled to provide *tamemes* to carry baggage as a matter of course, and from this time on, wherever we went we asked for Indians to carry our loads.

Cortes took leave of the fat *Cacique*, and next day we set out on our march, sleeping the night at a deserted village near Quiahuitzlan, where the people of Cempoala brought us supper.

On the following day, at ten o'clock, we reached the fortified town of Quiahuitzlan, which stands among great rocks and very high cliffs. If there had been any resistance it would have been very hard to capture. Expecting that there would be fighting, we moved in good formation, with the artillery in front, and marched up to the fortress prepared to do what was necessary should anything occur.

Alonso de Avila, who was then Acting Captain, was an overbearing and bad-tempered man; and when Hernando Alonso de Villanueva happened to lose his place in the ranks, he dealt him a lance thrust in the arm which maimed him, so that he was ever afterwards called Hernando Alonso de Villanueva 'El manquillo'. It will be said that I am digressing into old stories, so I must break off and go on to say that we went halfway through the town before we found a single Indian to speak to, which greatly surprised us. They had, however, fled in fear that very day, as they saw us climbing up to their houses. When we got to the top of the fortress, to the square on which their temples and great idol-houses stood, we found fifteen Indians waiting, all dressed in fine cloaks and each bearing a clay brazier full of incense. These Indians came up to Cortes, and perfumed him and all the soldiers near him. Then with deep bows they asked our pardon for not having come out to meet us, assured us that we were welcome, and asked us to rest. They said that they had kept away out of fear, until they saw what sort of creatures we were, for they had been afraid of us and our horses. They promised to recall all the inhabitants of the city that night. Cortes treated them very kindly and told them many things about our holy religion, as it was our habit to do wherever we went. He told them also that we were vassals of our Emperor Charles, and gave them some green beads and other small objects from Spain, in exchange for which they brought us poultry and maize-cakes. While we were talking someone came to tell Cortes that the fat *Cacique* was arriving in a litter borne on the shoulders of many Indian dignitaries. When he arrived he joined the *Cacique* and the principal men of that town in their complaints against Montezuma. In speaking of his great strength, they gave vent to such tears and sighs that Cortes and the rest of us were moved to pity. Before describing the way they had been brought into subjection, they told us that every year many of their sons and daughters were demanded of them for sacrifices, and others for service in the houses and plantations of their conquerors. And they made other complaints; so many that I no longer remember them. They said that if their wives and daughters were handsome, Montezuma's tax-gatherers took them away and raped them, and that they did this in all the thirty villages in which the Totonac language was spoken.

With the help of our interpreters Cortes gave them such comfort as he could. He promised to help in any way that was possible, and to prevent these thefts and crimes, since it was for this purpose that our lord the Emperor had sent us to these parts. He told them to stop being anxious, and to see what we would do. His speech seemed to give them some consolation. But their hearts were not relieved, for they were too much afraid of the Mexicans.

While these conversations were going on five Indians came in great haste from the town to tell the *Caciques* who were talking to Cortes that five of Montezuma's Mexican tax-gatherers had just arrived. The *Caciques* turned pale at the news. Trembling with fear, they left Cortes and went off to receive the Mexicans. Very quickly they decorated a room with flowers, cooked them some food, and made them quantities of chocolate, which is the best of their drinks.

When the five Mexicans entered the town, they came to the square where the *Caciques'* houses and our quarters were, and passed us by with cocksure pride, speaking not a word to Cortes or anyone else they saw. They wore richly embroidered cloaks and loincloths – for they wore loincloths at that time – and shining hair that was gathered up and seemed tied to their heads. Each one was smelling the roses he carried, and each had a crooked staff in his hand. Their Indian servants carried fly-whisks, and they were accompanied by the *Caciques* of the other Totonac towns, who did not leave them until they had shown them to their lodgings and given them a meal.

As soon as they had dined, the tax-gatherers sent for the fat *Cacique* and the other chiefs and scolded them for having entertained us in their villages, since now they would have to meet and deal with us, which would not please their lord Montezuma. For without his permission and instructions they should neither have received us nor given us golden jewels. They continued to reproach the fat *Cacique* and his nobles for their actions, and ordered them to provide twenty Indians, male and female, as a peace-offering to their gods for the wrong that had been done.

At this point Cortes asked our interpreters why the arrival of these Indians had so agitated the *Caciques*, and who they were; and Doña Marina, who understood perfectly, explained what was happening. As soon as Cortes understood what the *Caciques* were saying, he reminded them that, as he had already explained, our lord the King had sent him to chastise evil-doers and prevent sacrifices and robbery. He ordered them therefore to arrest the tax-gatherers for having made such a demand, and to hold them prisoners until their lord Montezuma was informed of the reason: namely that they had come to rob the Totonacs, to enslave their wives and children, and to do other violence.

When the *Caciques* heard this they were appalled at his

daring. To order them to manhandle Montezuma's messengers! They were far too frightened. They dared not do it. But Cortes insisted that they must arrest them at once; and they obeyed him. They secured them with long poles and collars, as is their custom, so that they could not escape, and they beat one of them who refused to be bound. Furthermore, Cortes ordered all the *Caciques* to cease paying tribute and obedience to Montezuma, and to proclaim their refusal in all the towns of their friends and allies, also to announce that if tax-gatherers came to any other towns he must be informed, and would send for them. So the news spread throughout the province. For the fat *Cacique* immediately sent messengers to proclaim it, and the chiefs who had accompanied the tax-gatherers scattered immediately after the arrest, each to his town, to convey the order and give an account of what had happened.

The act they had witnessed was so astonishing and of such importance to them that they said no human beings dared to do such a thing, and it must be the work of *Teules*. Therefore from that moment they called us *Teules*, which means gods or demons.

To return to the prisoners, all the *Caciques* were of the opinion that they ought to be sacrificed, so that none could return to Mexico to tell the tale. But Cortes said that they should not be killed, and that he would take charge of them. He set a guard over them, and at midnight summoned the soldiers of this guard to instruct them: 'Choose the two prisoners that seem to you the most intelligent, and loose them. Then bring them to my quarters. But do not let any of the village Indians see what you are doing.' When the prisoners were brought before him, he asked them, through our interpreters, why they were prisoners and from what country they came, as if he knew nothing of the matter. They answered that the *Caciques* of Cempoala had arrested them, with the aid of their followers and ours, and had held them prisoner. Cortes replied that he knew nothing about this and was very sorry. He ordered food to be brought them, and talked to them in a friendly way. He then told them to return at once to their lord Montezuma and tell him that we were all his good friends and entirely at his service. They were to explain also that he had released them for fear that harm should befall them, and had quarrelled with the *Caciques* who had arrested them; furthermore that he would do all he could to help them, and would see that their three companions were released and protected. He then told them to go off quickly and not come back to be captured and killed.

The two prisoners thanked him for his kindness, but said they were still afraid of falling into the hands of their enemies, since they could not help passing through their country. So Cortes ordered six sailors to take them in a boat during the night and put them ashore some twelve miles away on friendly territory outside the boundaries of Cempoala. When next morning the fat *Cacique* and the village chiefs saw that two prisoners were missing they were even more anxious to sacrifice the remaining three. But Cortes got these three out of their clutches. Pretending to be furious at the escape of the other two, he had a chain brought from the ships and bound them with it. Then he had them transported aboard, saying that as such a bad watch had been kept over the others he would look after them himself. Once they were aboard, he had their chains taken off and told them in a very friendly way that he would soon send them back to Montezuma.

After these events the *Caciques* of this village and of Cempoala, and all the Totonac dignitaries who had assembled, asked Cortes what was to be done, for all the forces of Mexico and of the great Montezuma would descend upon them, and they could not possibly escape death and destruction.

Cortes replied with a most cheerful smile that he and his brothers who were with him would defend them and kill anyone who tried to harm them; and the *Caciques* and their villagers one and all promised to stand by us, to obey any orders we might give them, and to join their forces with ours against Montezuma and all his allies. Then in the presence of Diego de Godoy the Notary they took the oath of obedience to His Majesty, and sent messengers to all the other towns in the province to relate what had happened. As they now paid no more tribute and the tax-gatherers had disappeared, they could not contain their delight at having thrown off the tyranny of the Mexicans.

The Foundation of Vera Cruz

As soon as we had made this treaty of alliance with the rulers of these twenty or more hill towns known as the Totonacs, who had now rebelled against the great Montezuma, sworn allegiance to His Majesty, and offered to serve us, we decided with their ready help at once to found the city of Villa Rica de la Vera Cruz on a plain a mile and a half from this fortress-like place called Quiahuitzlan. So we planned a church, a market-place, arsenals, and all the other features of a town, and built a fort. From the moment of laying the foundations till the walls were high enough to receive the woodwork, loopholes, watchtowers, and barbicans we worked very fast.

Cortes himself was the first to start carrying earth and stones and to dig the foundations; and all of us, captains and soldiers alike, followed his example. We strove hard to finish the work quickly, some of us digging and others building walls of earth-blocks, carrying water, working in the lime kilns, making bricks and tiles, and searching for food. Yet others cut the timber, and the blacksmiths, of whom we had two, made nails. In this way everyone from the highest to the lowest worked unceasingly, and the Indians helped us. So the church and the houses were soon finished, and the fortress nearly completed.

While we were at work the great Montezuma appears to have received news in Mexico of the arrest of his tax-collectors, of the rebellion of the Totonac towns, and of their withdrawal of allegiance. This enraged him against Cortes and our people. He had already called out a large army of warriors to make war on the rebels and butcher them to the last man. But now he also made preparations to attack us with a great force of many companies.

It was at this juncture that the two Indian prisoners arrived whom Cortes had set free; and when Montezuma learnt who had released them and sent them to Mexico, and when he heard the messages and promises that Cortes had entrusted to them, thanks be to God his anger died down, and he resolved to find out something about us. For this purpose he sent two of his nephews with four old men, *Caciques* of high rank, and with them a present of gold and cloth; and he told these messengers to thank Cortes for freeing his servants.

At the same time he also registered several complaints, saying that but for our protection the rebels would never have had the courage to commit the great treason of refusing him tribute and renouncing their allegiance to him. Moreover, since he was now certain we were those whose coming to their country his ancestors had foretold, and must therefore be of his own race, he failed to understand why we were living in the houses of these traitors. Still, he would not send to destroy them immediately, though the time would come when they would regret their treason.

After accepting the gold and cloth, which were worth more than two thousand pesos, Cortes embraced the envoys, offering the excuse that we were all very good friends to their lord, and that it was as Montezuma's servants that we had kept guard over the three tax-collectors. He then had them brought from the ships, where they had been well treated, and delivered them over dressed in fine clothing.

Then Cortes complained bitterly to Montezuma concerning the governor Pitalpitoque's secret nocturnal departure from our camp. He said that this was a mean action which he did not believe had been committed on the lord Montezuma's instructions, and that it was this which had caused us to come to these towns where we were staying and where we had been well received by the inhabitants; and he begged Montezuma to pardon the disrespect of which these people had been guilty. But as for that prince's protest against their refusal of tribute, he observed that they could not serve two masters, and that during the time of our residence with them they had sworn allegiance to us in the name of our lord and King. But as he, Cortes, and all his brothers were now on their way to visit Montezuma and place themselves at his service, all his commands would very shortly be attended to.

After this conversation, and several others, Cortes ordered blue and green beads to be given to the two youths, who were great *Caciques*, and to the four old men who had come in charge of them and were men of importance. He paid them every sign of honour and, as there were some good fields near by, he ordered Pedro de Alvarado, on his fine and well trained sorrel mare, and some other horsemen to gallop and skirmish in front of them, a spectacle which gave the *Caciques* much pleasure. Then they took leave of Cortes and us all in a happy frame of mind, and returned to Mexico.

About this time Cortes' horse died, and he bought or was given another called El Arriero,[1] a dark chestnut which belonged to Ortiz the Musician and Bartolome Garcia the Miner, and was one of the best horses we had brought.

Enough of this. I must now observe that since these allies of ours from the hill towns and from Cempoala had formerly been very much afraid of the Mexicans, and expected the great Montezuma to send his large armies to destroy them, the sight of his relatives coming to Cortes with presents and declaring themselves his servants and ours greatly surprised them. Their chiefs said among themselves that we must be *Teules* indeed, for Montezuma was afraid of us and had sent us presents of gold. So if we had already a reputation for valour, henceforth it was greatly increased.

After the departure of the Mexican messengers, the fat *Cacique* came with many other friendly chieftains to beg Cortes to go at once to a town called Cingapacinga, which was two days' journey – that is to say about twenty-five miles – from Cempoala, for many Culuan (that is to say Mexican) warriors had collected there, and were destroying their crops and plantations, and assaulting their vassals, and doing them other kinds of damage. They told this story with such feeling that Cortes believed them. Having already promised to help them and to kill any Culuans or other Indians who might try to harm them, Cortes could find no other answer to these urgent complaints except to say that he would willingly go, or send some soldiers under one of us to drive the Mexicans away. As he stood there, considering the matter, he said with a laugh to several of us who were with him: 'Do you know, gentlemen, I believe we

1. The Muleteer.

have now gained a reputation for bravery throughout this country. It seems to me that our treatment of Montezuma's tax-gatherers has made them think us gods, or godlike beings. So just to convince them that one of us is enough to defeat those enemy warriors who they say are occupying this fortified town, I think we'll send Heredia against them.' Heredia was an old Basque musketeer with a very ugly face covered with scars, a huge beard, and one blind eye. He was also lame in one leg.

Cortes sent for Heredia and said to him : 'Go with these chiefs as far as the river, which is less than a mile away. When you get there, stop, take a drink, wash your hands, and fire one shot from your musket. Then I will send to call you back. I'll tell you why. The people here think we are gods, or at least they have given us that name and reputation, and when they see your ugly face they'll certainly take you for one of their idols.' Heredia was an intelligent and resourceful soldier who had served in Italy, and he carried out his orders to the letter.

Then Cortes sent for the fat *Cacique* and the other dignitaries who were awaiting his help and said to them : 'I am sending this brother of mine with you to kill all the Culuans or drive them from this town of yours, and to bring me here as prisoners all who refuse to go.' The *Caciques* were mystified and did not know whether to believe him or not. But having watched Cortes' face for any change of expression and observed none, they decided that he was telling the truth. So old Heredia shouldered his musket and went off with them, firing shots in the air as he went through the forest so that the Indians should both hear and see him. And the *Caciques* sent the news to the other towns that they were bringing along a *Teule* to kill the Mexicans who were at Cingapacinga. I tell this story here merely as a joke and to show Cortes' guile. When Cortes knew that Heredia must have reached the river, he quietly sent to recall him, and the *Caciques* returned with the old musketeer. Our Captain then told them that because of the love he bore them he would go in person with some of his brothers to give them the help they needed, and visit the country and fortresses. He ordered them at once to bring a hundred porters to carry the *tepuzque* – that is to say the cannon – and they came early next morning.

So we set out on that same day with four hundred soldiers, fourteen horsemen, and some crossbowmen and musketeers, all of whom were ready.

Certain soldiers of Diego Velazquez' party were chosen to come with us, but when the officers went to warn them to prepare their arms, and those who had horses to bring them, they answered haughtily that they did not wish to go on any expedition, but to return to their farms and estates in Cuba; that they had already lost enough by having been enticed from their homes; that Cortes had promised them on the sand-dunes to give anyone who wished to depart permission and a ship and stores for the voyage, and that consequently seven soldiers were now ready to return to Cuba.

On hearing this, Cortes sent for these men, and asked them why they were behaving so shabbily. They somewhat angrily expressed their surprise that His Honour, having so few soldiers, should wish to settle in a place where there were reported to be so many thousands of Indians and such large towns. As for themselves, they said they were sick and could hardly drag themselves from one place to another. Therefore they wished to return to their homes and estates in Cuba, and now asked him for the promised leave to depart. Cortes answered them mildly that he had certainly made that promise, but they were failing in their duty by deserting their captain's flag. He then ordered them to embark immediately, assigned them a ship, and provided them with stores of cassava bread, a jar of oil, and such stocks of vegetables as we had.

When these men were ready to set sail, we soldiers and the officials of the town of Villa Rica went and begged Cortes on no account to let anyone leave the country, since in the interest of God's service and His Majesty's anyone asking for such permission must be considered by military law to have earned the death penalty as a deserter from his Captain and his flag in time of war and peril; the more so because, as they had stated, we were surrounded by so many towns peopled by Indian warriors.

Cortes pretended that he wished to give them their permission, but in the end he revoked it, and they found themselves not only tricked but shamed into the bargain.

The March to Cingapacinga
and Return to Cempoala

ONCE we had pacified the seven men who wanted to return to Cuba, we set out with the forces I have enumerated, and slept that night at Cempoala. Two thousand Indian warriors, divided into four companies, were ready to accompany us, and on the first day we marched fifteen miles in good order. The next day, shortly after dusk, we arrived at some farms close to Cingapacinga. The town's inhabitants now had news of our approach. As we were climbing towards the houses and fortress, which stood among great craggy cliffs, eight Indian chieftains and *papas* came peacefully to meet us, and to ask Cortes why, in view of our reputation for doing good to all and avenging robberies, and after our arrest of Montezuma's tax-collectors, we now wanted to kill them who had done nothing to deserve it. They said that the Cempoalan Indians who accompanied us were their enemies on account of old feuds concerning lands and boundaries, and that now, under our protection, they had come to rob and kill them. They admitted that there had been a Mexican garrison in their town, but the Mexicans had left for their own country a few days previously, on hearing that we had arrested their tax-gatherers. They begged us therefore to pursue the matter no further, and to grant them our protection.

When our interpreters had explained to Cortes what they said, he immediately ordered Captain Pedro de Alvarado, Cristobal de Olid the quartermaster, and the rest of us to prevent the Cempoalans from advancing any further; which we did. But though we acted very quickly, they had already begun to loot the farms. Then Cortes, in a fury, sent for the commanders of the Cempoalans and ordered them with angry threats to bring him the Indians, the cloth, and the poultry they had stolen from those farms. He also forbade any Cempoalan to enter the town, and said that for their lies, and for coming under our protection simply to rob and sacrifice their neighbours, they deserved execution. He repeated that our King and lord whose servants we were had sent us to prevent such enormities, and that they must be very careful that nothing of the sort happened again, or not a man of them would be left alive. The Cempoalan *Caciques* and captains surrendered everything they had seized, men, women, and poultry, and Cortes returned it all to the owners. Then he turned furiously on the Cempoalans and ordered them to retire and sleep in the fields, which they did.

On observing the justice of our behaviour and hearing the kind words that Cortes addressed to them through our interpreters, the *Caciques* and *papas* of Cingapacinga became well disposed towards us. After hearing Cortes' customary exposition of our holy faith, and his injunctions to give up human sacrifice and robbery and the foul practice of sodomy, and to cease worshipping their accursed idols, also much other good advice that he gave them, they at once called together the people of the neighbouring towns. These people then swore obedience to His Majesty, and very soon began to make the same grievous complaints against Montezuma that the Cempoalans had made when we were at Quiahuitzlan.

Next morning Cortes sent for the Cempoalan captains, who were waiting in the fields for our orders and were still very frightened of him because of the lies they had told him. When they appeared before him, he made them make friends with the people of that town, and the pact was never broken by either party. We then left for Cempoala by another road, which passed through two towns which were allied to Cingapacinga, and took a rest, for the sun was fierce and the weight of our arms made us tired. In one of these towns Cortes happened to see a soldier called de Mora from Ciudad Rodrigo take two fowls from an Indian's house. Enraged that any soldier should do such a thing in a friendly town and before his very eyes, he immediately ordered a halter to be thrown round his neck, and de Mora would have been hanged if Pedro de Alvarado, who was standing beside Cortes, had not cut the halter with his sword when the poor man was already half throttled. I record this story for the benefit not only of my interested readers, but also of those priests whose duty it is to administer the sacraments and teach the doctrine to the natives of this country.

When they see that the theft of two fowls in a friendly town almost cost a poor soldier his life, they will realize how they should behave towards the Indians today. This soldier was afterwards killed in a battle fought on a rocky height in the province of Guatemala.

But to return to our story. Having left these towns in peace and resumed our march to Cempoala, we found the fat *Cacique* and other dignitaries awaiting us at some huts with food. For although they were Indians, they saw that justice is good and sacred, and that Cortes' statement that we had come to right wrongs and abolish tyrannies was proved true by the events of that expedition. They were therefore much better disposed towards us than ever before.

We slept the night in these huts, and all the *Caciques* accompanied us to our quarters in their town. Really anxious that we should not leave their country, for they were afraid Montezuma would then send his warriors against them, they told Cortes that as we were now their friends they would like to have us for brothers and to give us their daughters to bear us children. So, to cement our friendship, they brought eight Indian girls, all the daughters of chiefs, and gave one of them, who was the niece of the fat *Cacique*, to Cortes. Another, who was the daughter of another great chief called Cuesco, was given to Alonso Hernandez Puertocarrero. All eight of them were dressed in the rich shirts that they wear, and finely adorned as is their custom. Each one of them had a gold collar round her neck and golden earrings in her ears, and with them came other girls to be their maids. As he presented them, the fat *Cacique* said to Cortes: 'Tecle' (which in their language means lord) 'these seven women are for your captains, and this one, who is my niece, is for you. She is the mistress of towns and vassals.' Cortes received them with a gracious smile, and thanked the chiefs for their gift. He said, however, that before we could accept the ladies and become their brothers, they would have to abandon their idols which they mistakenly believed in and worshipped, and sacrifice no more souls to them; and that when he saw those cursed things thrown down and the sacrifices at an end, our bonds of brotherhood would be very much firmer.

The girls, he added, must become Christians before we could receive them, and the people must give up sodomy, for they had boys dressed as women who practised that accursed vice for profit. Moreover every day they sacrificed before our eyes three, four, or five Indians, whose hearts were offered to those idols and whose blood was plastered on the walls. The feet, arms, and legs of their victims were cut off and eaten, just as we eat beef from the butcher's in our country. I even believe that they sold it in the *tianguez* or markets. Cortes told them that if they gave up these wicked practices, not only would we be their friends, but we would give them other provinces to rule. The *Caciques*, *papas*, and dignitaries all replied that it would be wrong for them to give up their idols and sacrifices, for these gods of theirs brought them health and good harvests and all that they needed; but as for sodomy, measures would be taken to see that the practice was stopped.

This insolent reply was more than Cortes or any of us who had seen all their cruelties and obscenities could stand. Reminding us of the doctrines of our holy faith, Cortes asked us: 'If we do not pay God so much honour as to stop them from making sacrifices to their idols, how can we ever accomplish anything worth doing?' He told us we must overthrow the idols that very day, and be absolutely prepared to fight if they tried to prevent us. Since we, as usual, were all armed and ready, Cortes at once told the *Caciques* that the idols must come down. Thereupon the fat *Cacique* and his captains ordered their warriors to assemble and defend them; and when they saw us preparing to ascend the many steps – I do not remember how many there were – of their *cue* or temple, which was very high, the fat *Cacique* and the rest shouted to Cortes in a great fury, inquiring why he wanted to destroy their gods, since if we desecrated and overthrew them their whole people would perish, and we with them. Cortes replied in a fierce voice that he had already told them to stop their sacrifices to these evil images and that we were going to get rid of them in order to save them from their false beliefs. He warned them that if they did not themselves remove their idols at once we would our-selves send them rolling down the steps. He said that we could no longer consider them our friends, but our mortal enemies, since we had given them good advice which they would not trust, and since he now saw their companies coming armed for battle. He added that he was angry with them, and that they would pay for their stubbornness with their lives.

When the Indians heard these threats – and Doña Marina was not only quite capable of explaining them in their language, but also threatened them with the power of Montezuma, who might fall on them any day – they replied in fear that they were unworthy to approach their gods, and that if we were to overthrow them it would not be with their consent, but that we could overthrow them or do whatever else we liked.

No sooner were the words out of their mouths than some fifty of us soldiers clambered up and overturned the idols, which rolled down the steps and were smashed to pieces. Some of them were in the form of fearsome dragons as big as calves, and others half-man half-dog and hideously ugly. When they saw their idols shattered the *Caciques* and the *papas* who were with them wept and covered their eyes; and they prayed to their gods for pardon in the Totonac language, saying that they had been overborne and were not to blame, that it was these *Teules* who had overthrown them, and that they dared not attack us for fear of the Mexicans.

After the destruction of the idols, the warriors who, as I have said, had come ready to attack us prepared to shoot their arrows. But when we saw this we seized the fat *Cacique*, six *papas*, and some other dignitaries, and Cortes shouted a warning that in case of any warlike action all these men would be killed. The fat *Cacique* commanded his men not to attack, but to retire from in front of us.

Once the *Caciques*, *papas*, and dignitaries had calmed down, Cortes ordered that the idols we had overthrown and shattered should be taken out of sight and burnt. Then the eight *papas* who were in charge of them came out of a room and carried them back to the house from which they had come, where they burnt them. These *papas* wore black cloaks like those of canons, and others smaller hoods like Dominicans. They wore their hair very long, down to their waists, and some even down to their feet; and it was all so clotted and matted with blood that it could not be pulled apart. Their ears were cut to pieces as a sacrifice, and they smelt of sulphur. But they also smelt of something worse: of decaying flesh. As they told us, and we afterwards found out for ourselves, these *papas* were the sons of chiefs and had no wives, but indulged in the foul practice of sodomy. On certain days they fasted, and what I saw them eat was the pith or seed of cotton when it was being cleaned. But they may have eaten other things that I did not see.

Cortes then spoke eloquently to the Indians through our interpreters, telling them that now we would treat them as brothers and give them all possible help against Montezuma and his Mexicans, to whom we had already sent word that they must not attack them or demand tribute of them. He said that as they would now have no more idols in their high temples he would leave them a great lady who was the Mother of our Lord Jesus Christ, whom we believe in and worship, and that they too should treat her as their lady and intercessor. On this matter and others he made them an excellent discourse, so deftly reasoned, considering the time at his disposal, that there was nothing left to say. Indeed, when he spoke of our holy faith, his explanations were as good as any priest can make today, and were listened to with good will. Then he ordered them to summon all the masons in the town, and to make them bring large quantities of lime with which to clean the *cues* and clear away the blood that encrusted them. Then next day, when the walls were cleaned and whitewashed, an altar was set up with fine altar-cloths, and some roses were sent for, of the sweet-scented kind that grow in their country, also some branches of flowers. Then Cortes picked four *papas* to look after the place, and ordered them to have their long hair cut, and to take off the clothes they wore and put on white robes. Instructing them further always to keep themselves clean, he placed them in charge of the holy image of Our Lady, with orders to keep the place swept and decorated with flowers. To see that the *papas* carried out his orders every day he left one of our soldiers, Juan de Torres of Cordoba, who was old and lame, to remain there as a hermit, and ordered our carpenters to make a cross and place it on a stone base which we had already shaped and whitewashed.

Next morning, mass was said at the altar by Fray Bartolome de Olmedo, and an order was given that the incense of their country should be burnt before the holy image and the blessed cross. They were also shown how to make candles from the local wax, and were ordered to keep them always burning on the altar. For up to that time they had not known the use of wax.

The mass was attended by the most important *Caciques* of the town and others who had gathered there. At the same time the eight Indian girls, who were still in the charge of their fathers and uncles, were brought to be made Christians. It was explained to them that they must offer no more sacrifices and no longer worship idols, but believe in our lord God. They were then instructed in our holy faith and baptized. The fat *Cacique*'s niece, who was very ugly, received the name of Doña Catalina and was led up to Cortes, who received her with a show of pleasure. The daughter of the great chief Cuesco received the name of Doña Francisca; she was very beautiful, for an Indian, and Cortes gave her to Alonso Hernandez Puertocarrero. I do not remember the names of the other six, but Cortes gave them to different soldiers. After this we took leave of all the *Caciques* and dignitaries, who were very well disposed towards us from that time forward, and particularly so when they saw that Cortes accepted their daughters, whom we took away with us. So after repeating our promises of assistance, we set out for our town of Villa Rica.

Events at Vera Cruz: The Destruction
of the Ships

AFTER the successful conclusion of this expedition we returned
to our settlement, bringing with us certain chiefs from Cempoala; and on the day of our arrival there came into port a ship
from Cuba, commanded by Francisco de Saucedo, whom we
called 'the Elegant' on account of his excessive pride in his
neatness and good looks. They say that he came from Medina
de Rio Seco, and had been chief waiter at the table of the
Admiral of Castile. With him arrived Luis Marin, a man of great
merit who was later a captain in the expedition against Mexico,
and ten soldiers. Saucedo brought a horse and Luis Marin a
mare; and they carried news from Cuba that Diego Velazquez
had received a decree from Spain empowering him to trade and
found settlements, which had greatly rejoiced his friends, who
had been even more pleased to learn that he had received his
commission appointing him *adelantado* of Cuba.

Having nothing to keep us in the town except the completion
of the fortress, on which we were still at work, the majority of
us urged Cortes to leave it unfinished as a memorial – it was
just about to be roofed. For we had already been more than
three months in that country, and we thought it would be good
to take a look at the great Montezuma – in fact to earn our livelihood and make our fortunes. Before we started on this journey,
however, we thought we should send our salutations to His
Majesty the Emperor and give him an account of what had happened since we left Cuba. We also debated whether we should
not send him all the gold we had received by barter and as a
gift from Montezuma. Cortes replied that this would be a wise
decision and that he had already talked to several gentlemen
about it; but as there might be some soldiers who wished to
keep their share of the gold, and if it was divided there would
be very little to send, he had appointed Diego de Ordaz and Francisco de Montejo, who were sound men of business, to go from
one soldier to another of those whom they suspected of want-

ing to keep their share, and to speak to them like this: 'You know, gentlemen, that we wish to make His Majesty a present of the gold we have gained here, and as it is the first to be sent from these lands it ought to be much greater than it is. We think therefore that we should all place our portions at his service. We gentlemen and soldiers have signed our names here as wishing to take nothing, but to give our shares voluntarily to His Majesty, in the hope that he may bestow favours upon us. If anyone asks for his share, it will not be refused him. But let all those who renounce theirs do as we have done and sign here.'

So they all signed to a man, and when it was settled Alonso Hernandez Puertocarrero and Francisco de Montejo – to whom Cortes had already given more than two thousand pesos to keep them on his side – were chosen as proctors to go to Spain. The best ship in the fleet was prepared for them, and two pilots appointed, one of whom was Anton de Alaminos, who knew the passage through the Bahama channel, for he had been the first to sail through it. Fifteen sailors were then chosen, and a full supply of ship's stores given to them. When everything was ready we decided to write and inform His Majesty of everything that had happened; and Cortes, so he told us, wrote a separate account of events. However we did not see his letter.

The Municipality wrote also, together with ten of us soldiers who wished to settle in the land and had appointed Cortes as our general. Our letter was completely truthful and omitted nothing; and I put my signature to it. Besides these letters and narratives we captains and soldiers jointly wrote another, the contents of which were as follows:

[The soldiers' letter summarizes the narrative that we have read, adding only the piquant detail that, in addition to the present of gold, Cortes' men also sent his Majesty a present of four Indians whom they had rescued at Cempoala from the cages in which they were being fattened for sacrifice. The captains made a bold attack on Diego Velazquez, and accused him of bribing the President of the Council of the Indies, Juan Rodriguez de Fonseca, Bishop of Burgos. They warned his Majesty that the Bishop would probably wish to appoint Velazquez governor of the new territories, which they considered too rich to be granted to any but a prince or great lord, and begged that Cortes should be confirmed in his office.

This letter was shown to Cortes, who wished his men to conceal the fact that they had promised him a fifth of the gold, and to pass over the fact that these lands had previously been visited by Hernandez de Cordoba, and by Grijalva. He was, however, over-ruled in these particulars.

The proctors sailed on 26 July 1519, and, contrary to Cortes' orders, made for Havana, from which place Montejo, or one of the sailors, sent to inform Velazquez of their mission. After a vain attempt to intercept the ships in the Bahama channel on their way from Cuba to Spain, Velazquez drew up letters of complaint against Cortes addressed to the Viceregal Court in the island of Santo Domingo, which, however, took Cortes' side. Velazquez then equipped a fleet of eighteen ships under the command of Panfilo de Narvaez, and gave them orders to take Cortes and all his men prisoners.

In the meantime the proctors reached Spain and found themselves cold-shouldered by the Bishop of Burgos, who refused to send or to let them take their present to the King, at that time in Flanders, and accused them of rebellion against Diego Velazquez. Cortes' men, however, sent a duplicate letter to the King and a memorandum of the present, and the King not only took Cortes' side against the Bishop, but announced that he would soon come to Spain to investigate the matter; which he subsequently did. The proctors kept Cortes informed of the course of events. In the meantime the march to Mexico was proceeding.]

So various are men's hearts, and so different the thoughts which sway them, that a mere four days after the departure of the proctors to lay our case before our lord the Emperor some of Diego Velazquez' friends and dependants began once more to plot against Cortes. Among them were Pedro Escudero, Juan Cermeño, a pilot called Gonzalo de Umbria, Bernardino de Coria, who afterwards settled in Chiapas, and one Juan Diaz, a priest; also certain sailors who were known as the Men of the Rock because they came from Gibraltar. All bore Cortes ill-will, some because he had refused them leave to return to Cuba after promising to do so, others because they had not received their shares of the gold that had been sent to Spain; and the 'Men of the Rock' because he had flogged them in Cozumel for stealing salt pork from the soldier Berrio. These men decided to take a small ship, to sail in her to Cuba, and on arrival to send a message to Diego Velazquez, suggesting that he would be able to seize our proctors on Francisco de Montejo's estate at Havana together with the gold and the dispatches. For they seem to have been informed by some persons in our camp that the proctors would go there, and these informers had written to Diego Velazquez also to advise him of this opportunity of catching them. Now the conspirators had already taken aboard their stores of cassava bread, oil, fish, water, and such other poor stuff as they could get, and the time being past midnight they were just going to embark, when one of their number, Bernardino de Coria, seemingly repented of his wish to go to Cuba and went to advise Cortes of the plot. On learning how many were involved, why they wished to go, and who were the persons concerned in the plot, Cortes ordered that the sails, compass, and rudder should immediately be removed from their ship and had the conspirators arrested and their confessions taken. They admitted the truth, and in their confessions implicated others of our company. But Cortes concealed his knowledge that others were involved, since no other course was possible at the time. He sentenced Pedro Escudero and Juan Cermeño to be hanged, and the pilot Gonzalo de Umbria to have his feet cut off. The Men of the Rock were each condemned to two hundred lashes, and Juan Diaz would have been punished also if he had not been a priest. As it was he received a great fright. I remember that, as Cortes signed the sentence, he exclaimed with a deep and sorrowful sigh: 'It would be better not to know how to write. Then one would not have to sign death sentences.' I think this observation is very common among judges who have to sentence men to death. It is a saying of Nero the cruel, made at the time when he showed signs of being a good emperor.

As soon as the sentence was carried out,[1] Cortes departed at a gallop for Cempoala, which was fifteen miles away, and ordered two hundred of us soldiers and all the horsemen to follow him immediately. And I remember that Pedro de Alvarado,

1. It does not appear to have been carried out, since Juan Cermeño survived to sign a letter written in the following year.

whom Cortes had sent only three days before with over two hundred soldiers into the hill towns to collect food (for in our town we were very short of supplies), was ordered to go to Cempoala also to take part in the arrangements for the march to Mexico. He was therefore not present, when, as I have described, justice was performed.

Assembled at Cempoala, we discussed with Cortes our military dispositions and the journey ahead of us. And as the conversation went on from one point to another, we who were his friends advised him (though many were of the opposite opinion) not to leave a single ship in port, but to destroy them all immediately, in order to leave no cause of trouble behind. For when we had marched inland others of our people might rebel like the last. Besides, we should be greatly reinforced by their captains, pilots, and sailors, who numbered nearly a hundred and would be better employed fighting and keeping watch than lying in port.

As far as I can judge, this plan of ours for destroying the ships had already been decided on by Cortes. But he wished it to be put forward by us, so that if we were afterwards asked to pay for the ships he could say that he had acted on our advice, and we should all have to share the cost. Juan de Escalante, the chief constable, a very brave man and a staunch friend of Cortes, who loathed Diego Velazquez because he had not given him good Indians in Cuba, was immediately sent to Villa Rica with orders to bring ashore all the anchors, cables, sails, and other things that might be useful, and then destroy the ships, preserving nothing but the boats. He was to see that the pilots, navigating officers, and sailors who were not fit to fight stayed in the town, and fished with the two nets they possessed, for there was always fish in the harbour, although not much. Juan de Escalante did as he was told, and soon returned to Cempoala with a company of sailors taken from the ships. Some of them turned out to be very good soldiers.

After his arrival Cortes sent to summon all the *Caciques* of the hill towns who were our allies and in rebellion against Montezuma, and told them to look after the Spaniards who remained in Villa Rica, and finish building the church, fortress, and houses. Taking Juan Escalante by the hand Cortes said before them all: 'This is my brother. You must do whatever he commands you.' He told them also that if they needed support against a Mexican attack he would himself come to their assistance. All the *Caciques* gladly agreed to carry out his orders, and I remember that they immediately burnt their incense before Juan de Escalante, although against his will. I have already said that he was a man well qualified for any post, and a great friend of Cortes. Our Captain could therefore appoint him to command the town and harbour with every confidence that if Diego Velazquez were to send an expedition it would be resisted.

The ships were destroyed with our full knowledge and not, as the historian Gomara alleges, in secret. Then one morning after mass, during a general discussion on military matters, after courteously begging for our attention, Cortes made a speech to the effect that we now understood what work lay before us, and with the help of our lord Jesus Christ must conquer in all battles and engagements. We must be properly prepared, he said, for each one of them, because if we were at any time defeated, which God forbid, we should not be able to raise our heads again, being so few. He added that we could look for no help or assistance except from God, for now we had no ships in which to return to Cuba. Therefore we must rely on our own good swords and stout hearts.

Cortes went on to develop some comparisons with the heroic deeds of the Romans. And we all answered to a man that we would obey his orders and that the die was cast for good fortune, as Caesar said at the Rubicon, for we were all ready to serve God and His Majesty. After this very fine speech, which was more honeyed and eloquent than I have indicated, Cortes at once sent for the fat *Cacique* and reminded him that he must deeply respect the church and cross and keep them clean. He also told him of his intention to leave at once for Mexico, where he would command Montezuma to give up robbery and human sacrifices, and said that he needed two hundred Indian carriers to transport his artillery, for as I have already mentioned they can carry fifty pounds on their backs and march fifteen miles with it. He also asked for fifty of the *Cacique's* best warriors to accompany us.

Just as we were prepared to set out, a soldier whom Cortes had sent to Villa Rica, with orders that some of the men who were still there should join him, returned with a letter from Juan de Escalante announcing that a ship was sailing along the coast. Escalante said that he had made smoke signals, raised white cloths as banners, and galloped along the shore waving a scarlet cloak to attract the attention of those on board, and that he believed they had observed all his signals but did not wish to enter the harbour. So he had sent some Spaniards to watch the ship's course, and they had reported that it had anchored near the mouth of a river about nine miles away. He now wanted to know what to do.

Immediately after reading this letter, Cortes put Pedro de Alvarado in command of the whole force at Cempoala, and with him Gonzalo de Sandoval, who was already giving proofs of the great valour which he never failed to show in later times. This, however, was his first command, and since Alonso de Avila was passed over, there arose a certain friction between these two men.

Cortes then rode quickly off with four horsemen, and ordered fifty of the swiftest soldiers to follow him; and he named those of us who were to form this company, which reached Villa Rica that same night.

On our arrival, Juan de Escalante came to Cortes and said it would be advisable to visit the ship that night, for fear it might raise sail and depart. He offered to go to do this with twenty soldiers while Cortes took a rest. But our Captain knew that he could not rest (for a lame goat never takes a nap), and said that he would go himself with the soldiers he had brought with him. So before we had time to eat a mouthful of food we set out along the coast, and on our road we met and arrested four Spaniards who had come to take possession of the land on behalf of Francisco de Garay, the governor of Jamaica. These men had been sent by a captain named Alonso Alvarez de Pineda or Pinedo, who had made a settlement on the Rio de Panuco. One who had come as a notary was called Guillen de la Loa, and the two men he had brought to witness the act of possession were Andres Nuñez, a boatbuilder, and Master Pedro 'the Harpist', from Valencia. The fourth man's name I do not remember.

When Cortes understood the reason for their coming, and realized that Garay remained in Jamaica and sent captains to do his work, he asked them by what right or title these captains had come. The four men replied that in the year 1518, when the news had spread through the islands of our discoveries under Francisco Hernandez de Cordoba and Juan de Grijalva, and of the twenty thousand gold pesos we had brought to Diego Velazquez in Cuba, Garay had been informed by Anton de Alaminos and our other pilot that he could petition His Majesty for any lands he might discover north of the Rio San Pedro y San Pablo.

Having friends at court, among them the Bishop of Burgos, Garay sent one of his stewards called Torralva to negotiate for him, and Torralva brought back a commission conferring on him the governorship of such territory as he might discover north of that river. On receiving this commission, Garay at once dispatched three ships with about two hundred and seventy soldiers, also supplies and horses, under this Captain Pineda or Pinedo, who was now founding a settlement on the Rio de Panuco, about two hundred miles away. The four men claimed that they were only carrying out their captain's orders and were themselves in no way to blame. Cortes listened to them carefully, and after ingratiating himself with them asked them blandly whether he could capture their ship. Guillen de la Loa, who was the leader of the four, said they would wave their cloaks at those on board and do what they could. But although they shouted and waved and made other signals no one would come ashore. For, as our prisoners observed, the captain knew that Cortes' soldiers were in the neighbourhood, and had warned them to avoid us.

When we saw that they would not send a boat, we realized that those aboard had seen us coming down the coast, and that unless we could induce them by a trick they would not row ashore again. Cortes asked the four men to take off their clothes so that four of our men could put them on. Then, when this was done, the rest of us went back along the coast by the way we had come, in the hope that our return would be observed from the ship, and that they would think we had really gone away. So four of our men remained behind dressed in the prisoners' clothes, and the rest of us with Cortes hid in a wood till after midnight, when the moon had set and it was dark enough for us to creep down to the mouth of the creek. Here we concealed ourselves again, leaving only the four soldiers to be seen; and when dawn broke these four began to wave their cloaks at the ship, from which a boat with six sailors quickly put off. Two of these sailors jumped ashore to fill two pitchers with water, and we who were with Cortes remained in hiding, waiting for the others to land. However they stayed in the boat, and our four men who were disguised kept their faces hidden and pretended to be washing their hands. Then the crew of the boat shouted: 'Come on board. What are you doing there? Why don't you come?' Then one of our men called back: 'Come on shore, you'll find there's a well.' As they did not recognize his voice the men in the boat rowed away, and though we went on calling no one answered us. We wanted to shoot at them with our muskets and crossbows, but Cortes would not let us. 'Let them go in peace, and report to their captain,' he said.

So six men from that ship were left with us, the four we had originally captured and the two sailors who had jumped ashore, and we returned to Villa Rica, still without having eaten any food.

When our departure for Mexico had been fully debated, we asked the *Caciques* of Cempoala what road we should take. They all agreed that the best and easiest way was through the province of Tlascala, for the Tlascalans were their friends and the deadly enemies of the Mexicans.

Forty chieftains, all fighting men, were now ready to accompany us, and they gave us great assistance on our march. The Cempoalans provided us also with the two hundred porters we needed for our artillery. But we poor soldiers had no need of help; all we then had to carry was our arms – lances, crossbows, muskets, shields, and suchlike – with which we both marched and slept. As for footwear we wore hempen shoes, and as I have often said, we were always prepared for battle.

We left Cempoala in the middle of August 1519, marching in good order, with scouts and some of our swiftest soldiers in advance; and the first day's march took us to a town called Jalapa,¹ from which we went to Socochima, a fortified place with a difficult approach, where there were many vines of the local grapes,² which grew on trellises. In both these towns we proclaimed the truths of our holy religion through Doña Marina and Jeronimo de Aguilar, and said that we were vassals of the Emperor Charles, who had sent us to put an end to human sacrifices and robbery; also certain other things that needed to be said. As the people were friends of the Cempoalans and did not pay tribute to Montezuma, we found them well disposed towards us, and they gave us food. A cross was erected in each town and its meaning explained, and they were told to treat it with great reverence.

Beyond Socochima we crossed a pass over some high mountains, and came to another town called Texutla, which we found well disposed to us also, for like the others it paid no tribute to Mexico. After we left that town we completed our ascent of the mountains and entered uninhabited country where it was very cold, and where it rained and hailed. That night we were very short of food, and a wind blew off the snowy heights on one side of us which made us shiver with cold. For as we had come from Cuba and Villa Rica, where the whole coast is very hot, into a cold country, and had nothing but our armour for covering, the difference in temperature made us feel the cold intensely.

Afterwards we entered another pass, where we found some groups of houses and large *cues* with idols, and they had great piles of firewood for the service of these idols. But we could still find nothing to eat, and the cold was fierce. Beyond the pass

---

1. Jalapa was probably a two days' journey from Cempoala. Bernal Díaz perhaps forgot to mention some intervening camping place.

2. Probably granadillas, the fruit of the passion-flower.

we came to the territory of a town called Xocotlan,[1] and sent two Cempoala Indians to announce our arrival to the *Cacique*, so that they should welcome us to their houses. This town was subject to Mexico. All the time we marched warily in perfect order, for now we were in another kind of country. When we saw the gleam of the flat roof-tops and the *Caciques'* houses, and their *cues* and idol-houses, which were very high and painted white, they seemed very much like certain towns in our native Spain. In fact we called the place Castilblanco, for some Portuguese soldiers said that it reminded them of the town of that name in Portugal, and so it is called to this day. And when the inhabitants learnt from our messengers that we were approaching, the *Cacique* came out with some other dignitaries to receive us just near their houses. The name of this *Cacique* was Olintecle. He and the others led us to some lodgings and gave us food, but very little, and it was given grudgingly.

When we had eaten, Cortes asked through our interpreters about the lord Montezuma. The chief told us of the great force of warriors that he kept in all the provinces that were tributary to him, also of the large armies that were posted on the frontiers and in the neighbouring districts. He then described the great fortress of Mexico, telling how the houses were built on the water, and one could only pass from one to another across the bridges they had built, or in canoes, and how all the houses had flat roofs and by the erection of breastworks could be transformed into fortresses. He told us that the city could be entered along three causeways, each of which had three or four openings in it through which the water flowed from one part of the lake to another, that each opening was spanned by a wooden bridge, and that if one of these bridges was raised no one could enter the city of Mexico. He then spoke of the great store of gold, silver, *chalchihuites*, and other riches that his lord Montezuma possessed. Much to the amazement of Cortes and all the rest of us, he could not stop saying what a mighty lord Montezuma was. Such is the nature of us Spaniards that the more he told us about the fortress and bridges, the more we longed to try our fortune, although to judge from Olintecle's

1. Now Zautla.

description the capture of Mexico would be an impossible enterprise. In fact the city was much stronger and more thoroughly fortified than he was capable of saying, for it is one thing to have seen the place and its strength and quite another to describe it as I do. Olintecle added that Montezuma was so great a prince that he could subdue all that he wished to his rule, and that he might be displeased when he heard that we had been received in his town and given food and lodging without his permission.

Cortes replied through our interpreters: 'I would have you know that we have come from distant lands at the bidding of our lord and King, the Emperor Charles, who has many great lords for vassals. He has sent us to command your great prince Montezuma to give up sacrifices and kill no more Indians, and not to rob his vassals, or seize any more lands, but obey our lord and King. And now I say this to you also, Olintecle, and to all the *Caciques* who are with you, that you must give up your sacrifices and cease to eat the flesh of your neighbours and practise sodomy and the other evil things you do. For such is the will of our lord God, in whom we believe and whom we worship, the giver of life and death, who will bear us up to heaven.' And he said much more about our holy religion, but they remained silent.

Then Cortes said to us soldiers who were standing by: 'Now, I think there is nothing else we can do except put up a cross.' But Fray Bartolome de Olmedo answered: 'In my opinion, sir, it is too early to leave a cross in these people's possession. They have neither shame nor fear and, being vassals of Montezuma, may either burn it or damage it in some other way. What you have told them is enough until they are better acquainted with our holy religion.' So the matter was settled and no cross was set up. To leave this subject however, we had a very large greyhound belonging to Francisco de Lugo, which barked a great deal in the night, and it seems that the *Caciques* of this town asked our friends of Cempoala whether it was a tiger or a lion or an animal we used to kill the Indians. And they answered, 'They have brought it to kill anyone who annoys them.'

They also asked what we did with the guns we carried with

us, and the Cempoalans answered that with some stones we placed inside them we could kill whomever we liked, and that the horses ran like deer and could catch anyone we told them to chase. Then Olintecle and all the chiefs exclaimed: 'Surely they must be *Teules*!' And our friends replied: 'Now that you have found this out, see that you don't do anything to annoy them, for they'll know immediately. They know what is in your thoughts. These are the *Teules* who captured your great Montezuma's tax-gatherers, and ordered that no one should pay any more tribute anywhere in the hills or in our town of Cempoala. These are the *Teules* who threw our *Teules* out of our *cues* and put their own in. They have conquered the people of Tabasco and Champoton, and such is their goodness that they have made peace between us and the people of Cingapacinga. What is more, you've seen how the great Montezuma, powerful though he is, sends them gold and cloths. Now they have come to your town, and we see you giving them nothing. Hurry up and fetch them a present.'

Apparently we had brought good persuaders. For the townspeople quickly presented us with four pendants, three necklaces, and some lizards, all of gold though it was of poor quality; and they gave us four women to grind maize for our bread, also a load of cloth. Cortes received these presents very gladly and with many expressions of thanks.

I remember that in the square where some of their *cues* stood were many piles of human skulls, so neatly arranged that we could count them, and I reckoned them at more than a hundred thousand. I repeat that there were more than a hundred thousand. And in another part of the square there were more piles made up of innumerable thigh-bones. There was also a large number of skulls and bones strung between wooden posts, and three *papas*, whom we understood to have charge of them, were guarding these skulls and bones. We saw more of such things in every town as we penetrated further inland. For the same custom was observed here and in the territory of Tlascala.

After these events at Xocotlan, we decided to set out for Tlascala, which our friends told us was not far away. In fact, they said, the boundary was quite close, and was marked by a number of boundary stones. So we asked the chief Olintecle which was the best and most level road to Mexico. He replied that it passed through a very large town called Cholula. But the Cempoalans said to Cortes: 'Don't go that way. The Cholulans are very treacherous, and Montezuma always keeps a large garrison in their town.' They advised us to go through Tlascala, which was friendly to them and hostile to the Mexicans. So we decided to take their advice, for God always guided us well.

Cortes then asked Olintecle for twenty of his best warriors to go with us, and he gave them to us at once. Then next morning we took the road to Tlascala.

The Tlascalan Campaign

So we set out from Castilblanco and began our march, with our scouts always ahead and constantly on the alert, and our musketeers and crossbowmen in regular order, and our horsemen even better placed. Each man carried his own arms, as was always our custom. But enough of this. It is a waste of words, for we were always so much on the alert both night and day that if the alarm had been given ten times we should have been found ready on each occasion.

In this order we arrived at the little town of Xalacingo, where they gave us a gold necklace and some cloth and two Indian women. And from that town we sent two Cempoalan chiefs, picking those who had most praised the Tlascalans and claimed to be their friends, as messengers to Tlascala. We gave them a letter, and a long-piled Flemish hat of the kind that was fashionable. We knew that the Tlascalans would not be able to read the letter, but we thought that when they saw paper different from their own, they would understand that it contained a message. The message that we sent them was that we were coming to their town and hoped that they would welcome us, since we did not come to harm them but to make friends. We did this because they told us in Xalacingo that the whole of Tlascala was up in arms against us. For it appears that they had already received news of our approach, and of the number of allies from Cempoala and Xocotlan and the other towns through which we had passed, who were marching with us. As all these towns habitually paid tribute to Montezuma, the Tlascalans were certain that we had come to attack them. For their territory had often been invaded by craft and cunning and then laid waste, and they thought that we were attempting a similar invasion. So as soon as our two messengers arrived with the letter and the hat and began to explain their mission, they were brusquely interrupted and made prisoner. All that day and the next we waited for an answer, and none arrived.

Cortes then addressed the chiefs of Xalacingo, repeating his usual exposition of our holy religion, and saying that we were vassals of our lord the King who had sent us to these parts to put an end to human sacrifices and the eating of human flesh, and the other beastlinesses that it was their custom to practise. He told them the many other things that we generally said in the towns through which we passed, and after making them many promises of assistance, asked for twenty good warriors to accompany us on our march. They gave them to us most willingly.

Next day, after commending ourselves to God, we set out in great confidence for Tlascala, and on our way met our two messengers who had been taken prisoner. It appears that in the turmoil of war preparations their guards had carelessly allowed them to escape; and they arrived in such a state of terror at what they had seen and heard that they could hardly manage to speak. According to their story, when they were in prison the Tlascalans had threatened them, saying: 'Now we are going to kill those whom you call *Teules* and eat their flesh. Then we shall see whether they are as brave as you proclaim. And we shall eat your flesh too, since you come here with treasons and lies from that traitor Montezuma.' For although the messengers repeatedly said that we were against the Mexicans and wanted the Tlascalans to be our brothers, they could not convince the Tlascalans that they were speaking the truth.

When we heard the Tlascalans' proud boast, and that they were preparing to fight, although it gave us matter for thought we all cried: 'If it's like that, then forward, and may fortune be on our side!' Then, commending ourselves to God, we unfurled our banner, which the ensign Corral carried before us, and marched on. For both the Cempoalans and the people of the little town where we had slept assured us that the Tlascalans would come out to meet us and resist our entry into their country.

As we marched along, we decided that the horsemen, in groups of three for mutual assistance, should charge and return at a trot, and should hold their lances rather short; and that when they broke through the Tlascalans' ranks they should aim at the enemies' faces, and give repeated thrusts, so as to prevent them from seizing their lances. If, however, a lance should be seized, the horseman must use all his strength and put spurs to his horse. Then the leverage of the lance beneath his arm and the headlong rush of the horse would either enable the rider to tear it away or drag the Indian along with him. Today one might ask why all these preparations were necessary when there was no enemy in sight to attack us? I answer in Cortes' words: 'Comrades, since we are few, we must always be as ready and as much on the alert as if we already saw our enemy coming to attack us. And we must not only act as if we saw them approaching, but as if we were already fighting them. As they frequently seize our lances with their hands, we have to be prepared for this emergency as well as for any other that may occur in battle. I know very well that in the fight you have no need of orders. I know and willingly acknowledge that you display far greater bravery without them.'

In this way we advanced about six miles till we came to a very strong fortress built of stone and mortar and some other cement so hard that it was difficult to demolish it with iron pickaxes. Indeed it was so well constructed for offence and defence that it would have been very difficult to capture. We halted to examine it, and Cortes asked the men of Xocotlan for what purpose it had been built in this way. They answered that since there was continuous war between their Lord Montezuma and the Tlascalans, the latter had built this fortress to defend their towns, this being their territory. We rested awhile, and this information gave us plenty to think about. Then Cortes said: 'Let us follow our banner, which bears the sign of the holy cross, and through it we shall conquer!' And we answered him as one man: 'May good fortune attend us, for in God lies our true strength!' So we resumed our march in the order I have described.

We had not gone far when our scouts observed about thirty Indians on the look-out. They carried two-handed swords, shields, lances, and feather plumes. Their swords, which were as long as broadswords, were made of flint which cut worse than a knife, and the blades were so set that one could neither break them nor pull them out. These spies, as I have said, wore badges and feather plumes, and when our scouts saw them they returned to give us warning, whereupon Cortes ordered them to pursue the Indians and if possible take one unwounded, and sent forward another five horsemen to help them if there was an ambush. Then our whole army hurried on in good order and in greater haste, for our allies who were with us said that there was certain to be a large number of warriors concealed in an ambush.

When the thirty Indian spies saw the horsemen approaching and beckoning to them, they would not wait for our men to catch them up and take a prisoner. Indeed they put up so good a defence that they wounded some of our horses with their swords and lances.

When our men saw them fighting so bravely and even wounding their horses, they were compelled to kill five of them. And at this moment a company of Tlascalans,[1] more than three thousand strong, who were lying in ambush, began to shower arrows on our horsemen who were now bunched together. These Indians put up a good fight with their arrows and fire-hardened darts, and did wonders with their two-handed swords. But at this moment we came up with our artillery, muskets, and crossbows, and gradually they began to give way. But they had kept their ranks and fought well for a considerable time. In this skirmish four of our men were wounded, and I think one of them died of his wounds a few days later.

As it was now late the enemy retired, and we did not pursue them. They left about seventeen dead on the field, not counting many wounded. This skirmish was fought on level ground where there were many houses and plantations of maize and *maguey* – the plant from which they make their wine.

We slept near a stream, and we dressed our wounds with the fat from a stout Indian whom we had killed and cut open, for we had no oil. We supped very well on some small dogs, which the Indians breed for food. For all the houses were deserted and the provisions had been carried away. They had even taken

1. They were probably not Tlascalans but Otomis from the town of Tecoac.

their dogs with them, but these had returned home at night, and we captured them. They proved good enough food.

We kept on the alert all night, with sentries, patrols, and scouts on the watch and our horses bitted and saddled, for fear the enemy might attack.

Next day, after commending ourselves to God, we set off with all our ranks in good order. Our cavalry had been thoroughly instructed in the art of charging, and also told to prevent the enemy from breaking our line or driving us apart. As we marched on, two armies of warriors, about six thousand strong, came to meet us with loud shouts and the noise of drums and trumpets, shooting their arrows, hurling their darts, and acting with the utmost bravery. Cortes ordered us to halt, and sent forward the three prisoners whom we had captured on the previous day to ask them not to attack for we wished to treat them as brothers. He told one of our soldiers, Diego de Godoy, the royal notary, to watch what happened so that he could bear witness if it should be necessary, in order that we should not be made responsible at some future time for the deaths and destruction that might occur, for we had begged them to keep the peace.

On being addressed by the three prisoners, the Indians became much more savage and attacked us so violently that we could not endure it. Cortes shouted: 'Saint James and at them!' And we rushed at them with such impetuosity that we killed and wounded many, including three captains. Then they began to retire towards some woods where more than forty thousand warriors under the supreme commander, Xicotenga, were lying in ambush, all wearing the red-and-white devices that were his badge and livery.

As the ground was somewhat broken we could make no use of the horses, though by careful manoeuvring we got them over it. But the passage was very difficult, for the Indians' shooting was extremely good, and they did us great damage with their spears and broadswords, also with the hail of stones from their slings. But once we had brought our horsemen and artillery on to the level ground we paid them back. We did not dare break our formations, however, for any of our soldiers who was bold enough to break ranks and pursue their swordsmen or captains was immediately wounded and in great danger. As the battle continued they surrounded us on every side, and there was little or nothing that we could do. We dared not charge them except all together for fear they might break our ranks, and when we did charge them there were more than twenty companies ready to resist us, and our lives were in great danger. For they were so numerous that they could have blinded us with clods of earth if God, of His great mercy, had not aided and protected us.

While we were at grips with this great army and their dreadful broadswords, many of the most powerful among the enemy seem to have decided to capture a horse. They began with a furious attack, and laid hands on a good mare well trained both for sport and battle. Her rider, Pedro de Moron, was a fine horseman; and as he charged with three other horsemen into the enemy ranks – they had been instructed to charge together for mutual support – some of them seized his lance so that he could not use it, and others slashed at him with their broadswords, wounding him severely. Then they slashed at his mare, cutting her head at the neck so that it only hung by the skin. The mare fell dead, and if his mounted comrades had not come to Moron's rescue, he would probably have been killed also. We might perhaps have rescued him with our whole company, but – I repeat – we hardly dared move from one place to another for fear they would finally rout us. It was all we could do to hold our own and save ourselves from defeat, for we were in great danger. However, we rushed to the battle around the mare and managed to save Moron from the enemy, who were dragging him away half-dead. We cut the mare's girths so as not to leave the saddle behind. In this act of rescue ten of our men were wounded, and I believe we killed four captains, for we advanced together in close formation, and did them great damage with our swords. After this they began to retire, taking the mare with them, and they cut her in pieces to show in all the towns of Tlascala. We learnt afterwards that they made an offering to their idols of her shoes, the red Flemish hat, and the two letters we had sent them asking for peace. The mare they killed belonged to Juan Sedeño, who had lent it to Moron, being himself incapacitated by three wounds that he had received on the previous day. As for Moron, I do not think I saw him again. He died of his wounds two days later.

The battle went on for a full hour, during which time our shots must have hit many of the enemy, for they were very numerous and in close formation. All our men fought like heroes to save their lives and do their duty. This was certainly the greatest danger we had yet faced and, as we afterwards learnt, many Indians were killed in the fighting, among them eight of their leading captains, sons of the old *Caciques* who lived in their principal town. This is why they retired, still in good order. We were not sorry, and made no attempt to follow them. Being so tired that we could hardly stand, we stayed where we were, in that little town. All the country round was thickly populated, and they even had some underground houses like caves in which many of them lived.

The site of this battle is called Tehuacingo or Tehuacacingo,[1] and it was fought on 2 September 1519. When we saw that the victory was ours we thanked God for delivering us from great danger.

We withdrew our whole force from the battlefield to some *cues* which were as strong and high as a fortress, and dressed our wounded, who numbered fifteen, with the grease of the Indian. One of them died of his wounds. We also doctored four horses that had been hurt. We rested and supped very well that night, for we found a good supply of fowls and little dogs in the houses and, having taken the precaution of posting sentries and sending out patrols, we slept well till next morning.

There was one peculiarity about the Tlascalans in this battle and all others: they carried away any of their men who were hit, and we never saw their dead.

Exhausted by the battle and by our wounds, and having to repair our crossbows and replenish our stock of arrows, we did nothing notable next day. On the following morning, however, Cortes decided to send all our fit horsemen to scour the country, so that the Tlascalans should not think that the recent

1. Probably the present-day village of San Salvador de los Comales.

battle had put an end to our fighting powers, and to show them
that although a day had passed without our coming out to pursue
them we still intended to follow them up. It was better for us to
attack them than to wait for them to come to attack us and
thus discover our weakness. As the country was flat and thickly
populated, we set out with seven horsemen, a few musketeers
and crossbowmen, about two hundred soldiers, and our Indian
allies, leaving the camp as well guarded as we could. In the
houses and towns through which we passed we captured about
twenty men and women, whom we did not harm. But our cruel
allies burnt many houses and carried off fowls and dogs, and
much other food. We soon returned to the camp, from which
we had not gone far, and Cortes set the prisoners free. But first
they were given something to eat, and Doña Marina and Aguilar
spoke kindly to them, presenting them with some beads and
telling them not to be foolish but to make peace with us, for
we wished to help them and treat them as brothers. At the same
time we released the two chieftains we had captured earlier,
and gave them a letter. We told them to inform the *Caciques* of
that town, which was the capital of the whole country, that
we had not come to harm or annoy them, but wished to pass
through their territory on our way to Mexico to speak with
Montezuma. These two messengers went to Xicotenga's camp,
which was about six miles away among some towns and houses
that I think they call Tecuacinpacingo,[1] and when they gave
him the letter and our message Xicotenga replied that we could
go to the town where his father was, and they would make
peace with us by filling themselves with our flesh and honour-
ing their gods with our hearts and blood. But as for his answer,
we should receive that early next day.

Still tired from the battles we had fought, we did not find
this haughty message encouraging. Cortes, therefore, flattered
the messengers with mild words, for they seemed to have lost all
fear. He ordered that they should be given some strings of
beads, since he wanted to send them back as envoys of peace.

Cortes learnt more from them about their captain Xicotenga
and the forces he commanded. They told him that he had more

1. The modern name for this place in Tzompantzinco.

men than when he had first attacked, having now five captains under him, each with ten thousand warriors; also that the Tlascalan banner and standard had now been brought out, a white bird like an ostrich with wings outstretched as if about to fly, and that each company could be recognized by its device and uniform, for each chief had a different one, like our own counts and dukes at home.

We knew that they were telling the truth, for some of the Indians whom we had captured and released that day had told the same story very clearly, although we had not believed them at the time. When this story was confirmed, being but men and fearful of death, many of us – indeed the majority – confessed to the Mercedarian friar and the priest Juan Diaz, who spent the whole night hearing confessions – for those who were not afraid confessed also and prayed to God that he would save us from defeat. Thus the time passed until the next day.

Next morning, 5 September 1519, we mustered the horses, and every one of the wounded joined the ranks, to give us what help he could. The crossbowmen were warned to use their supply of arrows very carefully, some of them loading while the others were shooting. The musketeers were to act in the same way, and the men with sword and shield to aim their cuts and thrusts at the enemy's bowels, so as to prevent their coming as close to us as they had done before. The artillery was ready for action and the horsemen had already been instructed to help one another, to hold their lances short, and not to stop and spear an enemy but to aim at his face and eyes, charging and returning at a trot and no man breaking away from the squadron. We left the camp with our banner unfurled and four of our company guarding its bearer, and before we had gone half a mile we saw the fields crowded with warriors, with their tall plumes and badges, and heard the blare of horns and trumpets.

What an opportunity for fine writing the events of this most perilous and uncertain battle present! We were four hundred, of whom many were sick and wounded, and we stood in the middle of a plain six miles long, and perhaps as broad, swarming with Indian warriors. Moreover we knew that they had come determined to leave none of us alive except those who were to be sacrificed to their idols. When they began to charge the stones sped like hail from their slings, and their barbed and fire-hardened darts fell like corn on the threshing-floor, each one capable of piercing any armour or penetrating the unprotected vitals. Their swordsmen and spearmen pressed us hard, and closed with us bravely, shouting and yelling as they came. The steadfastness of our artillery, musketeers, and bowmen did much to save us, and we inflicted great casualties on them. Their charging swordsmen were repelled by stout thrusts from our swords, and did not close in on us so often as in the previous battle. Our horsemen were skilful and fought so valiantly that, after God who protected us, they were our chief bulwark. Once I saw our company in such confusion that despite the shouts of Cortes and the other captains they could not hold together. The Indians were charging us in such numbers that only by a miracle of sword-play were we able to drive them back and re-form our ranks. One thing alone saved our lives: the enemy were so massed and so numerous that every shot wrought havoc among them. What is more, they were so badly led that some of their captains could not bring their men into battle.

Since the last battle, as we afterwards learnt, there had been disputes between Xicotenga and another captain, the son of the chief Chichimecatecle. The former had accused the latter of having fought badly on the first occasion, and the latter had replied that he had fought better than his accuser, as he would prove in personal combat. As a result Chichimecatecle's son had refused to bring his men to Xicotenga's aid, and had also called on the Huexotzinco men to hold back. What is more, they were now afraid of our horses and our brave fighting with musket, sword, and crossbow; and God's mercy gave us strength to hold out. So Xicotenga was refused help by two of his captains, and we inflicted great casualties on them. They endeavoured to conceal their losses, however, for whenever one of their men was wounded they bound him up and took him off on their backs. So in this battle, as in the last, we did not see any dead.

The enemy were already losing heart, and when they saw that the other two companies were not coming to their assistance, they began to give way. It seems also that at least one of their principal captains had been killed in the battle. They retired in good order, however, and our horsemen were only able to follow them for a short distance, being too weary to ride far. And when we saw we were delivered from that host we gave thanks to God.

One of our men was killed in the fighting, and sixty were wounded. All our horses were wounded also. I too was hit twice, once on the head by a stone, and once in the thigh by an arrow. But this did not prevent me from fighting, performing my watch, and helping our men. And all our wounded did the same. For unless our wounds were very dangerous, we had to fight and watch despite them, for the unwounded would not have been able to perform these duties alone.

Having returned to our camp, well contented and giving thanks to God, we buried the dead in one of the Indians' underground houses, so that they should not see we were mortal but believe that we were indeed *Teules*, as they called us. We piled a great deal of earth over this house so that they should not smell the corpses, and all our wounded were dressed with the grease of that Indian of whom I have spoken. It was a poor comfort to be without even oil and salt to dress our wounds. And there was another thing we lacked – a severe hardship. We had no clothes to protect us from the cold wind that blew off the snowy mountains and made us shiver. Our lances muskets, and crossbows made a poor covering. Still, we slept more peacefully than on the previous night, when so many of us had been on guard or patrol.

After the battle, Cortes sent the three Indian chieftains we had captured, with the two who were already in our camp and had served as messengers before, to beg the Tlascalan *Caciques* to make peace and grant us a passage through their country on our way to Mexico. The burden of this message was that we had made this request before, and would kill all their people if they did not now come to terms, and that being well disposed towards them and wishing to treat them as brothers, we should never have attempted to harm them if they had not given us cause. Cortes added other kindly assurances of a similar nature in an endeavour to gain their friendship.

The messengers willingly set out for the Tlascalan capital, and delivered their message to all the *Caciques* there, whom they found assembled with many other elders and *papas*. This whole assembly was most depressed by the outcome of the battle and the loss of those captains who were their sons and relatives. It seems therefore that they were ill-disposed to listen to the envoys, and that their decision was to summon all the soothsayers, *papas*, and those others whom they call *tacalnaguas*, who are like wizards and foretell the future, and ask them to discover by their witchcraft, charms, and lots what sort of people we were and whether if they fought us continuously by day and night we could be conquered. They also inquired of their wizards whether we were *Teules* as the Cempoalans asserted, and what things we ate; and they told them to look into these matters with the greatest care.

When the soothsayers and wizards and *papas* had got together and made their prophecies, cast their lots, and performed their usual rites, they seem to have said that they had learnt we were men of flesh and blood, and ate poultry, dogs, bread, and fruit when we had them, but did not eat the flesh or hearts of the men we killed. Apparently our Indian allies whom we had brought from Cempoala had convinced them that we were *Teules* and ate Indians' hearts, that our cannon shot lightning such as falls from heaven, that our greyhound was a tiger or lion, and that our horses were used to catch Indians when we wanted to kill them, and other nonsense of this sort.

Unfortunately their *papas* and wizards told them that we could not be conquered by day but only at night, since though we were valiant our virtues left us at sunset and in the night we had no strength at all. Believing this story, the *Caciques* sent their commander Xicotenga instructions that as soon as possible he should make a strong attack on us in the night. On receiving this command he assembled ten thousand of his bravest warriors and came to our camp,[1] which he assailed from three sides with a hail of arrows and single-pointed javelins hurled from spear-throwers. Then their swordsmen made a

1. Bernal Díaz has left out Xicotenga's earlier reconnaissance of the Spaniards' camp, described by other chroniclers.

sudden attack on the fourth side, in the positive certainty that they would be able to carry off some of our men for sacrifice. But God provided otherwise. For though they approached secretly they found us entirely prepared. As soon as our outposts and watchmen heard the noise of their movements, they rushed headlong to give the alarm. As we were all accustomed to sleep in our armour and sandals, and to keep our horses bitted and saddled, and as we kept all our arms at hand, we defended ourselves with guns, crossbows, and swords, and they quickly fled. As the ground was flat and the moon was up, our horsemen followed them a little, and in the morning we found about twenty of their dead and wounded lying on the plain. So they retired with heavy losses, and greatly regretting their night attack; and I have heard that they sacrificed two of their *papas* and wizards for offering bad advice.

One of our Cempoalan allies was killed that night, two men and a horse were seriously wounded, and we took four of the enemy. After thanking God for delivering us, and burying our dead friend and tending our wounded, we set our guard and slept for the rest of the night. But on waking next morning we realized our sad plight. We were all weary and wounded, some with two or three wounds, many of us were ragged and sick, and Xicotenga was still on our heels. We had lost forty-five men in all, in battle or from disease and chills, while another dozen were sick from fever, among them Cortes and the Mercedarian friar. What with our labours and the weight of our arms which we carried on our backs, and our sufferings from cold and lack of salt – for we could never find enough to spice our food – it is not surprising that we wondered how these battles would end, and what we should do and where we should go when they were done. We thought it would be a tough business to march into Mexico, which had great armies, and wondered what would happen to us when we had to fight Montezuma if we were reduced to such straits by the Tlascalans, whom our Cempoalan allies described as a peaceful people. Furthermore, we had heard nothing from the settlers at Villa Rica, nor had they received any news of us.

As there were several excellent and valiant gentlemen among

us who were capable of offering good advice, Cortes never acted without first consulting his soldiers. Indeed, he always bore himself like a good commander, and our Lord's crowning mercy, after our late victories, was perhaps that he gave us soldiers grace and good counsel to advise our Captain correctly. And let me say that every one of us put heart into Cortes, telling him that he must get well again, that he could count upon us, and that as with God's help we had survived these perilous battles, Our Lord Jesus Christ must be preserving us for some good purpose. We suggested that he should immediately set the prisoners free and send them to the great *Caciques* with overtures of peace and a promise to forgive everything, including the death of the mare.

But let me say that Doña Marina, although a native woman, possessed such manly valour that though she heard every day that the Indians were going to kill us and eat our flesh with *chillis*, and though she had seen us surrounded in recent battles and knew that we were all wounded and sick, yet she betrayed no weakness but a courage greater than that of a woman. She and Jeronimo de Aguilar spoke to the messengers we were now sending, telling them that the Tlascalans must make peace at once, and that if they did not come to us within two days we would go and kill them in their own city and destroy their country. With these brave words the prisoners were dispatched to the capital where Xicotenga the Elder and Mase Escasi resided.

When the messengers arrived at Tlascala they found these two principal *Caciques* in consultation. On receiving the message, they were undecided and said nothing for a few moments. Then it pleased God to inspire them with the thought of making peace with us. They sent at once to summon all the other *Caciques* and captains from their towns and those of a neighbouring province called Huexotzinco, who were their friends and allies. And when they had all gathered together in the capital, these two *Caciques*, who were wise men, made them a speech more or less to this effect, as I afterwards heard, though these are not the actual words :

'Friends and brothers, you have seen how often these *Teules* who are in our country expecting to be attacked have sent us messengers asking us to make peace, and saying that they have come to help us and adopt us as brothers. You have also seen how many of our vassals who have attacked them have been captured by them and released immediately. You well know that we have attacked them three times with all our strength both by day and night, and have failed to conquer them, and that during these attacks they have killed many of our people, our kinsmen, sons, and captains. Now they are asking us for peace once more, and the Cempoalans who have come in their company say that they are the enemies of Montezuma and his Mexicans, and have commanded the towns of the Totonac hills and Cempoala itself to pay him no more tribute. You cannot forget that the Mexicans make war on us every year, and you know that our country is so beleaguered that we dare not leave it to find salt, and therefore eat none. Nor can we look for cotton, and so we have little cotton cloth. If our people even go out to seek it, few return alive. These treacherous Mexicans and their allies kill them or make them slaves. Now our wizards and soothsayers and *papas* have told us their opinion about the nature of these *Teules*, and have spoken of their bravery. It seems to me that we should seek to be friends with them, and that whether they are men or *Teules* we should make them welcome. Therefore four of our chiefs must set out at once, taking them plenty of food, and we must offer them friendship and peace, so that they may aid us and defend us from our enemies. Let us bring them here and give them women, so that we may have kinship with their children, for, as these ambassadors of peace tell us, they have brought some women with them.'

When they had listened to this speech all the *Caciques* and principal men approved, saying that this was a wise proposal and that peace should be concluded at once. They asked that a message should be sent to young Xicotenga and his fellow captains telling them to break off hostilities and return at once, the war being now over; and messengers were immediately sent off to him. However, Xicotenga would not listen to the four chiefs, but got very angry and abusive, saying that he was against peace, for he had already killed many *Teules* and a mare, and wished to attack us once more by night and conquer and kill us all.

When his father Mase Escasi and the other *Caciques* heard his answer they were enraged, and sent immediate orders to the captains and the whole army not to join Xicotenga in an attack or accept his orders if he did not make peace. Even so Xicotenga refused to obey. Taking note of their captain's stubbornness, the *Caciques* sent the same four chieftains to our camp to carry us provisions and negotiate peace in the name of all Tlascala and Huexotzinco. But for fear of Xicotenga the Younger these four old men did not come.

As two days had passed without any happenings of note, we suggested to Cortes, who agreed to our proposal, that we should march against a town about three miles from our camp which had sent no reply when summoned to make peace, and take it by surprise. We did not intend to do it any harm – I mean to kill or wound its inhabitants or take them prisoner – but only to carry off food and frighten or talk them into making peace, according to the way they behaved. This town was called Tzompantzinco,[1] and it had several smaller towns tributary to it, among them Tecoadzumpancingo, the place where we were then encamped, and the territory all around it was thickly populated.

So one night, in the watch before the dawn, we rose up and set out for that town, leaving our camp as well guarded as we could. With us came six of our best horsemen, the soundest of our soldiers, ten crossbowmen, and eight musketeers, and Cortes led the expedition, though he was still suffering from tertian fever. We started our march two hours before dawn, with a cold wind blowing off the snowy mountains, which made us shiver and shake. The horses felt it keenly too, for two of them began to tremble and were seized by colic; which worried us a great deal, for we were afraid that they would die. So Cortes ordered their riders to lead them back to camp and doctor them.

As the town was not far off, we arrived there before daybreak; and when the inhabitants saw us they fled from their

1. See note on p. 147.

houses, shouting to one another to look out, for the *Teules* were coming to kill them. Such was their panic indeed that fathers did not stay to look after their children. On observing this, we halted in a court until daylight, to avoid doing them any harm.

On seeing us standing quietly there, some *papas*, who were in the *cues*, and a number of old chiefs came up to Cortes and asked him to pardon them for not having come to our camp and brought us food when we asked them to do so. They gave the excuse that Captain Xicotenga, who was in the neighbour-hood, had sent to tell them they must not, since his camp drew some of its supplies from their town, and he had warriors in his army from there as well as from all the rest of Tlascala. Cortes told them through our interpreters, who accompanied us on every expedition, even a night foray, that they need have no fear, but must go at once to the *Caciques* in the capital and tell them to come and make peace, since the war was disastrous for them. Cortes sent these *papas* because so far he had received no reply at all by the other messengers we had sent, and the four chiefs whom the Tlascalans had dispatched to our camp to negotiate peace had not yet arrived.

These local *papas* quickly found us forty or more cocks and hens, and two women to make us maize-cakes. Cortes thanked them for their kindness, and ordered them to send twenty men of their town to the camp at once, who brought us this food without any fear and stayed in the camp till evening. They were then given beads with which they returned home well contented, and they told all the neighbouring villages that we were good men, for we had done them no harm. But when these *papas* and elders informed Captain Xicotenga that they had given us food and women, he scolded them bitterly, whereupon they went to the capital to tell their news to the old *Caciques*, who were very pleased to learn that we were not harming their people, although we might have killed many of them that night, and that we were sending men to negotiate. They therefore ordered that we should be supplied every day with what we needed, and commanded the four chiefs whom they had orig-inally entrusted with the negotiations to leave instantly for our camp and bring us all the food that had been prepared. We then returned to our camp with these supplies and the Indian women, in a cheerful frame of mind.

On returning from Tzompantzinco with our supplies, very glad that we had left the place at peace, we found meetings and discussions going on in the camp about the great danger we were running every day in this war. On our arrival these conversations became even livelier, and the most active of the debaters were those who had houses and grants of Indians in Cuba. Seven of them – whom for their reputations' sake I will not name – met together and went to Cortes' hut; and the most eloquent of them, who spoke for the rest and was well conversant with their views, said, as though by way of advice, that Cortes ought to consider the condition we were in, wounded, thin, and harassed, and the great hardships we endured by night, as sentinels, watchmen, patrols, and scouts, and in continuous fighting both by day and night. According to their argument, we had lost more than fifty-five of our company since leaving Cuba, and we knew nothing of the settlers we had left at Villa Rica. It was true that God had given us victory in each battle, great and small, since we had left Cuba, and of His great mercy had supported us while we had been in this province, but we ought not to tempt Him so often, or our fate might be worse than that of Pedro Carbonero.[1] They said that Cortes had got us into an unexpected situation, and that one day or another, though God forbid it should happen, we should be sacrificed to the idols. They therefore advised him to lead us back to the fortified town of Villa Real, and to keep us there among our Totonac allies until we could build a ship which we could dispatch to Diego Velazquez in Cuba, and to other places and islands, to ask for assistance. They observed that the ships we had scuttled would now have been useful, and that we ought to have saved at least two of them against necessity. They protested that they had not been consulted about the scuttling or anything else, and that Cortes had listened to men who did not know how to provide for changes of fortune. They prayed God that neither he nor his advisers would have reason to

1. A proverbial figure who led his men into the land of the Moors, where they all perished.

repent of it. Now, they said, in many cases we could not carry the extra burdens we were bearing, and we were worse off than pack-horses. For when a beast had finished its day's work, its saddle was taken off and it was given food and rest, but we carried our arms and wore our sandals by both night and day. They went on to cite history, reminding Cortes that neither the Romans nor Alexander nor any other famous Captain had dared destroy their ships and attack vast populations and huge armies with a small force, as he had done. They accused him of preparing his own death and that of all his followers, and begged him to preserve us all by leading us back to Villa Rica, where the land was at peace. The reason they gave for not having said all this before was that the large armies which had attacked us every day from every side had left them no time. Although the enemy had not returned to the attack, these seven soldiers believed that they soon would, and that since Xicotenga with his great army had not come to seek us for the last three days, he must be collecting his forces for another battle like the last, for which we must not stay; and they said much more to the same effect.

Observing that they spoke somewhat haughtily for men proffering unasked advice, Cortes gave them a mild answer in which he said that he was well aware of many of the facts they had mentioned, and that to his knowledge and belief there was not another company of Spaniards in the whole world who had fought more bravely or more courageously endured excessive hardships than ours, but that if we had not marched with our arms continually on our shoulders, and watched and patrolled and suffered the cold we should have perished already, for it was to save our lives that we had endured all this and worse. 'Why gentlemen, should we talk of valorous deeds when truly Our Lord is pleased to help us? When I remember seeing us surrounded by so many companies of the enemy, and watching the play of their broadswords at such close quarters, even now I am terrified. When they killed the mare with a single sword-stroke we were defeated and lost, and at that same moment I was more aware of your matchless courage than ever before. Since God saved us from this great peril, I have every hope that He will do so again in the future. And I will say more, that in all these dangers you will find no negligence on my part; I shared every one of them with you.' And he had the right to say so, for he was indeed in the front rank in every battle.

'I wish to remind you, gentlemen,' he continued, 'that since Our Lord has been pleased to help us in the past we have hope that He may do so in the future. For ever since we entered this country we have preached the holy doctrine to the best of our ability in every town through which we have passed, and have induced the natives to destroy their idols. Now since neither Xicotenga nor his captains have returned, and we know they are afraid to do so, for we must have inflicted great losses on them in the last battles, and since they cannot reassemble their followers after their three defeats, I trust in God and our advocate St Peter that the war in this province is over. Now, as you see, the people of Tzompantzinco are bringing food and have made peace, and so have our neighbours here who have returned to live in their houses. As for scuttling the ships it was a good plan, and if some of you were not consulted about it, as other gentlemen were, it was on account of my resentment at certain events on the beach, which I do not now wish to recall. The concerted counsel which you offer me today is no more valuable than the advice which you gave me on that occasion. You will find that there are many gentlemen in the camp who will be strongly opposed to the course you advocate, and that it will be better to trust all things to God and carry on in His holy service. As for your observation, gentlemen, that the most famous Roman captains never performed deeds equal to ours, you are quite right. If God helps us, far more will be said in future history books about our exploits than has ever been said about those of the past. For, I repeat, all our labours are devoted to the service of God and our great Emperor Charles. Under his true justice and the Christian law, God in His mercy is aiding us and will turn our good fortune to better. So, gentlemen, it would clearly be wrong to take a single step backwards, for if these people we leave behind in peace were to see us retreat, the very stones would rise up against us. They who at present hold us to be gods and idols and call us so would consider us cowards and weaklings. As for what you say about our staying among our friendly allies the Totonacs, if they saw us return without visiting Mexico, they would rise up against us too. Since we told them to pay no more tribute to Montezuma, they would expect him to send his Mexican armies not only to extort the tribute and make war on them, but also to compel them to attack us; which, in order to avoid destruction and out of their great fear of the Mexicans, they would certainly do. So where we expected friends we should find enemies. And what would the great Montezuma say on hearing that we had retreated? That the whole expedition was a childish joke. What would he think of our speeches and our messages to him? So, gentlemen, if one course is bad the other is worse, and it is better to stay where we are, where the ground is level and thickly inhabited, and our camp is kept well supplied with poultry and dogs. For thank God there is now no shortage of food. But I wish we had some salt, which is our greatest lack at present, and some clothes to protect us from the cold. As for your statement, gentlemen, that we have lost fifty-five soldiers since we left the island of Cuba, from wounds, starvation, cold, sickness, and hardship, and that we are now few in number and all wounded and sick, God gives us the strength of many. It is clearly true that wars destroy men and horses and that we only sometimes eat well. We did not come here to take our ease, however, but to fight when the opportunity offered. Therefore I pray you, gentlemen, kindly to behave like gentlemen, I mean those whose habit is to encourage others whom they see displaying weakness. From now on, keep the island of Cuba and what you have left there out of your thoughts, and try to act, as you have done hitherto, like brave soldiers. For after God, who is our aid and support, we must rely on our own strong arms.'

When Cortes had delivered his reply the soldiers renewed their argument. They admitted that he had spoken well, but urged that ever since we had left Villa Rica our intention had been to go to Mexico on account of its fame as a strong city possessing a great number of warriors. The people of Cempoala said that the Tlascalans were a peaceful people, and they had no such reputation as the Mexicans. Yet we had been in great danger of our lives, and if they were to attack us on the morrow in another battle like those of the past, we should be too weary to hold our own. But even if they did not attack us again the march to Mexico seemed to them a very terrible undertaking, and they warned Cortes to reconsider his commands.

Cortes replied rather angrily that it was better, as the psalm said, to die in a good cause than to live dishonoured. And in support of these words the majority of us soldiers who had elected him Captain and advised him to scuttle the ships, cried out that he should not trouble about this chatter or listen to their tales, for with God's help we were ready to act together and do what was right. And so all the talk ended. It is true that they grumbled at Cortes and cursed him, and grumbled at us for our support of him, and at the Cempoalans for bringing us by that road. And they made other unjust accusations. But at such a time they were overlooked, and in the end everyone obeyed perfectly.

I will now go on to tell how the old chiefs of the capital of Tlascala once more sent messengers to their commander-in-chief Xicotenga, telling him without fail to pay us a peaceful visit and bring us food. This was the decree of all the *Caciques* and principal men of that country and of Huexotzinco. They also sent an order to the captains in Xicotenga's company that they must refuse him obedience if he did not go and make peace with us. They sent this order three times, because they knew for certain that Xicotenga did not intend to obey them, but was determined to make another night attack on our camp. For this purpose he had assembled twenty thousand men and, being both proud and very stubborn, now as before he refused to give in. He decided therefore to send forty men with supplies of fowls, bread, and fruit, four miserable-looking old women, much copal, and many parrot feathers; and from their appearance we supposed that these Indians came with peaceful intentions. On reaching our camp they burnt incense before Cortes, though without paying him their customary reverence. 'All this is sent to you by the Captain Xicotenga,' they said, 'so that you may eat. If you are savage *Teules*, as the Cempoalans say, and wish for a sacrifice, take these four women, sacrifice them and consume their flesh and hearts. But as we do not know in what way you do this we have not sacrificed them here before you. If you are men, however, eat these fowls and bread and fruit, and if you are gentle *Teules* here are copal' (which, as I have said, is a kind of incense) 'and parrots' feathers. Make your sacrifice with them.'

Cortes answered through our interpreters that he had already sent to tell them he desired peace and had not come to make war, and that he had come in the name of our lord Jesus Christ, and the Emperor Charles, to explain to them why they should give up their custom of killing and sacrificing, and to beg them to do so. He assured them that we were men of flesh and blood like themselves, and not *Teules* but Christians, also that it was not our custom to kill anyone; that if we had wanted to kill people, their many attacks on us by night and day had given us plenty of opportunities for cruelty. He thanked them for the food they had brought, and warned them not to repeat their foolishness, but to make peace.

It seems that these Indians whom Xicotenga sent with the food were spies sent to examine our huts and shelters, horses and artillery, and to find out how many of us were in each hut, the ways in and out, and all the other details of our camp. They stayed with us that day and the following night, and some went with messages to Xicotenga and others arrived. But our Cempoalan allies, who were watching them, observed that since it was unusual for enemies to stay in a camp all day and night for no purpose, they must be spies. Their suspicions were increased by the fact that when we had visited the little town of Tzompantzinco two old men of that place had informed them that Xicotenga was preparing to make a night attack on our camp in such a way that their approach would not be detected. At that time, the Cempoalans had taken it as a joke or boast and, not believing it, had said nothing to Cortes. As soon as Doña Marina heard this story she reported it to Cortes.

To discover the truth our Captain had two of the most honest looking of the Tlascalans taken aside, whereupon they confessed that they were spies. He then took two others, who also confessed the purpose for which Xicotenga had sent them. Cortes then ordered yet another two to be taken, and they admitted that Xicotenga was awaiting their report before attacking us that night with all his companies. On hearing this, Cortes sent instructions throughout the camp putting everyone on the alert, for he believed that they would make the assault they had planned. He then had seventeen of the spies arrested and cut off the hands of some and the thumbs of others, which he sent to Xicotenga with the message that this was a punishment for their audacity in coming to our camp to spy. He said also that Xicotenga could come by day or night, whenever he chose, during the next two days, and that if he did not do so we should give him no more time, but go and seek him in his camp. He added that we should have gone to attack and kill them already, had we not liked them, and that now they must cease their foolishness and make peace.

I have heard that these spies arrived at the very moment when Xicotenga intended to set out from his camp to deliver the night attack he had planned. But when he saw his men returning so mutilated and, having asked the reason, was informed of what had happened, he lost his courage and pride. But this was not the only cause of his discomfiture. Already one of his captains with whom he had wrangled and disagreed during the fighting had left the camp with all his men.[1]

While we were in camp, not knowing whether they would come in peace as we hoped, and busy polishing our arms, cutting arrows, and doing all that was necessary for battle, one of our scouts ran in to say that a crowd of men and women were bringing loads along the main road from Tlascala and advancing towards our camp. He said that his fellow scout, who was on horseback, was watching to see which way they went. But even as he spoke the other scout galloped in to say that they were very near and coming straight towards us, though they were

1. The actual order of events in the Tlascalan campaign is uncertain; it is very probable that Bernal Díaz places the original night attack too early, and that it actually took place after Xicotenga had sent his spies to the Spanish camp.

making short stops from time to time. We were all delighted by this news, for we believed that it meant peace, as indeed it did, and Cortes ordered us to make no display of alarm or concern but to stay hidden in our huts. Then there emerged from the crowd four important men whom the old *Caciques* had entrusted with the task of negotiation. Making their sign of peace, which was to bow the head, they came straight to the hut in which Cortes lived, and with one hand on the ground, kissed the earth, prostrating themselves three times and burning copal. They said that all the chiefs of Tlascala and their vassals, allies and friends, and confederates had come to conclude friendship and peace with Cortes, his companions and fellow *Teules*. Begging his forgiveness for their hostile actions and for the war they had fought against us, they said they had certainly believed us to be friends of Montezuma and his Mexicans, who had been their mortal enemies from very ancient times. For they had seen many of his vassals who paid him tribute, among our companions, and had believed that they were trying to enter their country with their customary guile and treachery in order to steal their women and children. They gave this as their reason for having distrusted the messengers we sent them. But they also said that the Indians who had first come out to fight us as we entered their land had not done so by their command or on their advice. They placed the blame on the Chuntales and Estomies,[1] who were savages and very stupid. As for themselves, however, when they had seen that we were few in number they had planned to capture us and carry us off as prisoners to their lords, in order to gain their gratitude, but they now came to beg our pardon for their temerity. They pointed to the food they had brought and said that they would bring more every day, and that they hoped we would accept it in the friendly spirit in which it was sent, also that within two days Captain Xicotenga would come with other *Caciques* and explain more fully how all Tlascala wished for our friendship.

When they had finished their speech, they bowed their heads, placed their hands on the ground and kissed the earth. Then

1. These were the Otomis, the descendants of earlier inhabitants of Central Mexico. The word *Chuntal* means barbarian.

Cortes addressed them gravely through our interpreters. Making a show of anger, he said that there were reasons why we should neither listen to them nor accept their friendship. For immediately on entering their country we had sent them offers of peace, and of aid against their enemies the Mexicans, but they had refused to trust us and tried to kill our ambassadors. Not content with that, they had attacked us three times, by night and day, and had spied on us and laid ambushes against us. In the attacks they had made on us, said Cortes, we might have killed many of their vassals, but had not wished to do so and we grieved for those who had died though they alone were to blame. Indeed he had made up his mind to go to the place where the old *Caciques* were and attack them. But as they had now offered peace on behalf of the whole province, he would accept it in the name of our King and lord. He thanked them for the food they had brought, and sent them back to their lords with the message that they must either come or send men with fuller powers to negotiate, and that if they did not we would go to their town and attack them. He also ordered some green beads to be given to these men which they were to hand to their *Caciques* in sign of peace, and warned them that when they came to our camp it must be by day and not by night, or we might kill them.

Then these four messengers departed, leaving the women they had brought to make our bread in some Indian huts a little way from our camp, also some fowls and everything else we needed, including twenty Indians to draw water and chop wood. From that time they brought us plenty to eat. And when we saw this and knew that they really meant peace we gave great thanks to God. For at that moment we were lean, weary, and unhappy about this war, of which we could neither see nor forecast the end.

Peace with Tlascala: Embassies from Mexico

As a result of the victories which God granted us in our battles with the Tlascalans, our fame spread through the surrounding country and reached the ears of the great Montezuma in the city of Mexico. If hitherto they had taken us for *Teules*, henceforth they respected us even more highly as valiant warriors. When the news came that so few of us had conquered such a huge force of Tlascalans and made them sue for peace, terror spread through the whole land. Now Montezuma, the great and powerful prince of Mexico, in dread that we might come to his city, sent five chieftains of the highest rank to our camp in Tlascala, to bid us welcome and congratulate us on our great victory over so many hostile bands. He sent a present of very richly worked gold and jewel ornaments worth quite a thousand pesos, and twenty loads of fine cotton, with the message that he wished to become the vassal of our great Emperor, and that he was glad we were near his city, since he felt great affection for Cortes and his brother *Teules*, who were with him. Moreover, he asked Cortes to tell him how much yearly tribute our great Emperor required, and promised to give it in gold and silver, cloth and *chalchihuites*, provided that we did not come to Mexico. This, he said, was not because he would not be very pleased to receive us, but because the land was rough and sterile, and he would not like to see us suffering hardships, which he might perhaps not be able to relieve as well as he could wish.

Cortes answered that he was most grateful to Montezuma for his good will and present, and his offer to pay tribute to His Majesty; and he begged the messengers not to depart until he had visited the Tlascalan capital, for they would then see the conclusion of the war, and he would dispatch them from there. His reason for not wishing to give them an immediate reply, however, was that, being feverish, he had purged himself the day before with some of those camomiles that grow in Cuba and are very good for anyone who knows how to take them.

While Cortes was talking to these ambassadors of Montezuma, he received a message that Captain Xicotenga was arriving with many other *Caciques* and captains, all clothed in red-and-white cloaks, a cloak half red and half white being the badge of Xicotenga's followers. They said that he was approaching in a very peaceful manner, accompanied by about fifty important men.

When Xicotenga reached Cortes' quarters he made him the most respectful obeisance, and ordered much copal to be burnt. Then Cortes seated him by his side with a great show of kindness, and Xicotenga said that he had come on behalf of his father, Mase Escasi, and all the *Caciques* and the commonwealth of Tlascala to pray Cortes to admit them to our friendship, and to ask pardon for having taken up arms against us. He said that they had only done so because they did not know who we were, and had been quite certain that we had come in the interests of their enemy Montezuma. For the Mexicans frequently used craft and cunning as a means of entering their country to rob and pillage, and they had supposed that they were doing so once more. Therefore they had endeavoured to defend themselves and their land, and had been forced to fight. He said that they were a very poor people who possessed neither gold nor silver nor precious stones, nor cotton cloth nor even salt for their food, because Montezuma never allowed them to go out to search for it; and that although their ancestors had possessed some gold and precious stones, they had long ago surrendered them to Montezuma on the various occasions when they had been forced to make peace or a truce, to save themselves from destruction. So he begged us to pardon him for having nothing left to give, pleading poverty, not lack of good will, as the reason.

Xicotenga made many complaints about Montezuma and his allies, for they were all enemies of the Tlascalans and made war on them. However, they had defended themselves very well, and had meant to do the same against us. But although they had gathered against us with all their warriors three times, this had not been possible, for we were invincible. Having discovered this, they wished to become friends with us and vassals of our lord the Emperor, for they felt certain that in our company they, their wives, and their children would be guarded and protected, and freed from the danger of surprise attacks by the treacherous Mexicans. Xicotenga said much else besides, and placed his people and his city at our disposal.

Xicotenga was tall, broad-shouldered, and well built; his face was long, pock-marked, and coarse; he was about thirty-five years old, and he carried himself with dignity.

Cortes thanked him very courteously and flatteringly, and agreed to accept the Tlascalans as friends and as vassals of our king and lord. Then Xicotenga begged us to come to his city, where all the *Caciques*, elders, and *papas* were waiting to give us a cordial welcome. Cortes promised to go there soon, saying that he would have done so at once were it not for the negotiations he was carrying on with the great Montezuma, which would delay him until the messengers were dispatched. He then spoke rather more harshly and gravely about their attacks upon us, adding however that since these could not now be remedied, he would forgive them, but that they must see the peace we were granting was firm and enduring. Otherwise he would kill them and destroy their city, and Xicotenga could expect no further talk of peace but only war.

On hearing these words Xicotenga and his companions answered as one man that peace would be firm and genuine, and that they would all stay as hostages for it.

There were then further conversations between Cortes and Xicotenga and his companions, at the end of which the visitors were given presents of blue and green beads for Xicotenga's father, for Xicotenga himself, and for the other *Caciques*, and they were sent back with the message that Cortes would very soon visit their city.

The Mexican ambassadors, who were present during all these discussions, heard all the offers that were made and were greatly depressed by the conclusion of the peace, for they realized that no good would come of it for them. So when Xicotenga had taken his leave these ambassadors of Montezuma asked Cortes half laughingly whether he believed any of the promises that had been made on behalf of Tlascala, for they were all a trick which deserved no credence, the promises of great traitors and liars who intended to attack and kill us as soon as they had us inside their city and could do so in safety. They reminded us how often the Tlascalans had tried with all their might to destroy us but had failed to do so, losing many dead and wounded in the attempt, whom they now meant to avenge by offers of a sham peace. Cortes replied with a very bold face that this idea of theirs did not trouble him in the least, for supposing it were true he would be delighted of an opportunity to punish the Tlascalans by killing them all. It did not matter to him, he said, whether they attacked him by day or night, in the fields or in the city. But he was determined to go to Tlascala to see whether their offer was genuine.

Seeing that Cortes' mind was made up, the ambassadors asked us to wait six days in our camp, as they wished to send two of their companions with a message to their lord Montezuma, who would return with a reply within that time. To this Cortes agreed, in the first place because he was, as I have said, suffering from fever, and in the second because although when the ambassadors had made their statements he had pretended to attach no importance to them, he thought that there was a chance of their being right and that until he saw a greater certainty of peace he would have to take their views into consideration.

Trusting that the peace negotiations were genuine, and seeing that all along the road we had travelled from Villa Rica de la Vera Cruz the towns were our friendly allies, Cortes wrote a dispatch to Juan de Escalante who, as I have said, had remained behind, with sixty old and sick soldiers under his command, to finish building the fort. In this dispatch Cortes spoke of our lord Jesus Christ's mercy in granting us victory in all the battles we had fought since entering the province of Tlascala, which had now sued for peace, and asked them all to thank God for it. He told them to be careful always to keep on good terms with our friends in the Totonac towns, and asked Escalante to send him immediately two jars of wine that he had left buried in a certain marked spot in his lodgings, also some wafers for mass which had been brought from Cuba, since our supplies were exhausted.

This dispatch was most welcome to Escalante, who replied with news of events at Villa Rica; and the things that Cortes asked for arrived very quickly.

About this time we set up a tall cross in our camp; and Cortes ordered the Indians of Tzompantzinco and the near-by farms to whitewash it. It was a beautifully finished work.

To return, however, to our new friends the *Caciques* of Tlascala : when they saw that we were not going to their city they came to our camp with fowls and prickly pears, which were in season. Each one brought some provisions from his own house, and gave them to us with the greatest good will, asking for nothing in return, but always begging Cortes to accompany them to their city soon. But as we had promised to wait six days for the return of the Mexicans, he put them off with fair speeches. At the end of the prescribed time, six chieftains, all men of importance, came from Mexico, bearing a rich present from the great Montezuma consisting of jewels to the value of three thousand gold pesos, wrought in various shapes, and two hundred pieces of cloth richly worked with feathers and other embellishments. On presenting these to Cortes, the chieftains said that their lord Montezuma was delighted at our great success, but that he begged Cortes most earnestly on no account to accompany the people of Tlascala to their town, or put any trust in them. For they wished to take him there in order to rob him of his gold and cloth, being themselves so poor that they did not possess a good cotton cloak among them. Moreover, the knowledge that he, Montezuma, regarded us as friends and had sent us gold, jewels, and cloth would make the Tlascalans even more eager to rob us.

Cortes accepted the present joyfully, saying that he thanked them for it, and would repay their lord Montezuma with services, and that if he found the Tlascalans planning the trick he had been warned of, they would all pay for it with their lives. He was however quite certain that they intended no such crime, and he still meant to go to see what they would do.

While these discussions were going on, many more messengers came from Tlascala to tell Cortes that all the old *Caciques* from the capital and the whole province were now coming to our huts to visit us, and take us to their city. When Cortes heard this he begged the Mexican ambassadors to wait three days for his reply to their prince, as he had now to come to a decision about the past war and the peace he was being offered. They promised to do so.

When the old *Caciques* from all Tlascala saw that we did not visit their city, they decided to come to us, some in litters, some in hammocks, some carried on men's backs, and others on foot. So they arrived at our camp with a great company of chieftains, and after making three most respectful obeisances before us they burnt copal, touched the ground with their hands, and kissed the earth. Then Xicotenga the Elder began to address Cortes in these words:

'Malinche, Malinche, we have sent many times to beg your pardon for our attack, and to offer you the excuse that it was to protect ourselves from the malice of Montezuma and his powerful forces. For we believed that you were of his party and allied to him. But if we had known what we know now, we should not only have gone out to receive you with supplies of food, but would have had the roads swept for you, and would even have gone to meet you at the sea where you keep your *acales*' (that is our ships). 'Now that you have pardoned us, I and all these *Caciques* have come to ask you to accompany us at once to our city, where we will give you of all that we possess and serve you with our persons and goods. And see, Malinche, that you do not refuse us, or we will depart at once, for we are afraid these Mexicans may have told you some of their usual wicked lies about us. Do not believe them or listen to them, for they are false in everything, and we well know that it is their fault you have not come to our city.'

Cortes answered with a cheerful smile that he had known for years, and long before we came to their country, that they were a good people, and that that was why their attack had so astonished him. As for the Mexicans, they were only awaiting a reply that he was to send to their lord Montezuma. He thanked them heartily for their invitation and for the food they were continually bringing, and for their other kindnesses, and promised to repay them by good deeds. He said that he would already have set out for their city if he had had porters to carry the *tepuzques* (that is the cannon). These words so delighted the Tlascalans that we could read the joy in their faces. 'So that is why you have delayed,' they said, 'and you have never mentioned it?' And in less than half an hour they had provided more than five hundred Indian porters.

Early next morning we began our march along the road to the Tlascalan capital, with our artillery, horsemen, musketeers, crossbowmen, and all in our customary good formation. Montezuma's messengers had already begged Cortes that they might accompany us, to see how affairs were settled at Tlascala and to be dispatched from there. They asked to be quartered in his own lodgings, however, so that they might not be insulted, for they were afraid that the Tlascalans might abuse them.

Before I proceed any further, I should like to say that in every town we passed through and in others that had only heard of us, they called Cortes Malinche, and I shall call him by this name henceforth in recording any conversations he had with Indians, both in this province and in the city of Mexico, and I shall only call him Cortes in such places as it may be proper. The reason why he received this name was that Doña Marina was always with him, especially when he was visited by ambassadors or *Caciques*, and she always spoke to them in the Mexican language. So they gave Cortes the name of 'Marina's Captain', which was shortened to Malinche.

This name was also given to a certain Juan Perez de Artiaga, a settler at Puebla, because he always went about with Doña Marina and Jeronimo de Aguilar, in order to learn the language. He was known as Juan Perez Malinche de Artiaga, as we discovered some two years later.

From the time when we entered Tlascalan territory to that of our setting out for the city was a matter of twenty-four days. We marched into Tlascala on 23 September 1519.

When the *Caciques* saw our baggage on the road to their city, they at once went ahead to have things prepared for our reception and hang our lodgings with flowers. And when we came within a mile of Tlascala these same *Caciques* who had gone ahead came out to meet us, bringing with them their sons and nephews and many of the leading inhabitants, each clan or family or party forming a separate group. There were four parties in Tlascala (not counting that of Tecapaneca, lord of Topeyanco, which made a fifth), and their subjects came from all parts of the country, wearing their different costumes which, although made of sisal, there being no cotton to be had, were very lordly, and beautifully embroidered and decorated. Then came the *papas* from all parts of the province, who were very numerous, since these peoples have large *cues* or temples. The *papas* carried braziers with live coals, and incense which they burnt over us all. Some of them wore long white cloaks in the form of surplices with hoods over them, which were, as I have said before, like those of our canons. Their hair was very long and so tangled that it could not have been parted unless they had cut it first. Moreover, it was all clotted with the blood which oozed from their ears, for they had offered them as a sacrifice that day. These *papas* lowered their heads as a sign of humility when they saw us. They wore their fingernails very long, and we were told that these were considered to be pious men who lived good lives.

Many of the chieftains drew close to Cortes and accompanied him, and when we entered the town there was no room in the streets or on the roofs, so many men and women having come out with happy faces to see us. They brought us some twenty cones made of sweet-scented native roses of various colours, which they gave to Cortes and to such other soldiers as they thought were captains, especially to the horsemen. When we arrived at some fine courts where our quarters were, Xicotenga the Elder and Mase Escasi took Cortes by the hand and led him to his lodging. For each one of us they had prepared a bed of matting such as they use for themselves, and sisal cloth sheets. They had found lodgings near us for our allies from Cempoala and Xocotlan, and Cortes asked that the great Montezuma's messengers should also be given quarters close to his own.

Although we clearly saw that we were among a people who were well and peacefully disposed towards us, we did not abandon our customary practice of vigilance. I was told that one captain whose duty it was to post scouts and sentries said to Cortes: 'They seem very peaceful, sir. We shan't need to have as many guards or be as vigilant as usual.' And Cortes answered: 'That is true enough, gentlemen, as I can see for myself. But it is a good custom always to be prepared. Though they may be a friendly people, we must not trust their peacefulness. We must be as alert as if they were going to fight us and we saw them moving up to the attack. Many captains have been defeated through over-confidence and carelessness, and it is especially needful for us to be on the alert, since we are so few. We must remember, too, that whether in good faith or bad, the great Montezuma has warned us against them.'

The great *Caciques* Xicotenga the Elder and Mase Escasi protested against our vigilance, saying to Cortes angrily: 'Malinche, either you take us for enemies or your actions do not express the confidence you feel in us or in the peace which we have concluded between us. We say this because we see that you keep watch, and because on your way here you marched ready for action, as if your companies were coming to attack us. We think we know the reason for this. It is the wicked accusations that the Mexicans have made in secret in order to turn you against us. But you must not believe them. See, you are here, and we will give you all that you want, even ourselves and our children, and we are ready to die for you. Ask for any hostages you wish.'

We were all astonished at the courtesy and mildness with which they spoke. Cortes answered that he trusted them and that there was no need of hostages; it was enough to see their good will. As to our being on the alert, he said, this was our usual custom, and they must not take it badly. He thanked them for all they had offered us, and promised to repay them in time to come.

When these conversations were over, other chiefs arrived with a great supply of poultry and maize-cakes and prickly pears and the vegetables that grew in their country. The camp was now very liberally supplied, and in the twenty days that we stayed there we always had more than enough to eat.

Early next day Cortes ordered an altar to be put up so that mass could be celebrated, for we now had wine and wafers.

This mass was said by the priest Juan Diaz, for the Mercedarian friar was sick with fever and very weak. Mase Escasi, Xicotenga the Elder, and some other *Caciques* were present, and when it was over Cortes went into his lodging, with those of us soldiers who usually accompanied him and the two old *Caciques*. Xicotenga the Elder then said that they wished to bring him a present, and Cortes answered very warmly that they could bring it whenever they wished. So, many mats were then spread and a cloth laid over them; and they brought six or seven small gold objects, some jewels of small value, and a few loads of sisal cloth. It was all very poor, not worth even twenty pesos, and as they were giving it the *Caciques* said with a laugh: 'Malinche, we know that we have too little to give for you to be grateful. Long ago we sent to tell you that we are poor, and have neither gold nor riches, and the reason is that those wicked traitors the Mexicans, and Montezuma who is now their lord, robbed us of all we used to own, on the occasions when we have had to sue for peace or a truce, in order to stave off an attack. But do not consider the small value of the gift. Accept it with a good grace, as given you by the friends and servants we shall be to you.' Then they brought separately a large supply of food.

Cortes accepted it most gladly, telling them that he valued it more as coming from their hands and being given with such good will than he would a house full of gold-dust brought by others, and that it was in this spirit he received it. He displayed much affection towards them.

It appeared that it had been decided among the *Caciques* that they would give us the most beautiful of their daughters and nieces who were ready for marriage. Therefore Xicotenga the Elder said: 'Malinche, to prove still more clearly how much we love you and wish to please you in all things, we want to give you our daughters for wives to bear you children. For you are so good and brave that we wish to be your brothers. I have one most beautiful daughter who is as yet unmarried, and I should like to give her to you.' At the same time Mase Escasi and all the other *Caciques* said they would bring their daughters and asked us to accept them as wives; and they said much else and made many other offers. Throughout the day the two old *Caciques* remained by Cortes' side; and as Xicotenga the Elder was blind from old age, he felt Cortes all over his head and face and beard, and touched his body. As for the gift of the women, Cortes answered that he and all of us were very grateful, and that we would repay them by good deeds in course of time. The Mercedarian friar was standing near, and Cortes said to him: 'Father, I think this would be a good time to try to induce these chiefs to give up their idols and stop their sacrifices, for they will do anything we tell them, because of their great fear of the Mexicans.' And the friar replied: 'Sir, that is true. But let us leave the matter until they bring their daughters. Then we shall have a pretext, for your lordship can say that you will not accept the maidens until they give up sacrifices. If that succeeds, good. If not, we shall have done our duty.' So thus the matter rested until next day.

Next day the same old *Caciques* came, bringing with them five beautiful Indian maidens, all virgins. They were very handsome for Indian women, and very richly adorned, and each one being the daughter of a chief brought a maid to serve her.

Then Xicotenga said to Cortes: 'This is my daughter. She is unmarried and a virgin. Take her for yourself' – he put the girl's hand in his – 'and give the others to your captains.'

Cortes expressed his thanks, and with a cheerful expression answered that he accepted the maidens and took them for his and ours, but that for the present they must remain in their fathers' care. The old *Caciques* then asked why he did not take them now, and Cortes replied that he wished first to do the will of our lord God, in whom we believe and whom we worship, and to perform the task for which our lord and King had sent us; which was to make them give up their idols and cease to kill and sacrifice human beings, also cease the other abominations which they practised, and believe as we believed in the one true God. He told them much more about our holy faith, and in truth he expounded it very well, for Doña Marina and Aguilar were so practised that they could explain it very clearly. Cortes showed them an image of Our Lady with her precious child in her arms, and explained to them that this image was a likeness of the Blessed Mary, who dwells in the high heavens and is the mother of Our Lord, the Child Jesus, whom she holds in her arms and whom she conceived by grace of the Holy Spirit, being a virgin before, during, and after His birth. He told them how this great Lady prays for us to her precious Son who is our Lord and God, and said other fitting things about our holy faith. He then went on to state that if they wished to be our brothers and live on terms of true friendship with us, and if they really wanted us to take their daughters for our wives, as they proposed, they must immediately give up their wicked idols and accept and worship Our Lord God, as we did. They would then see, he told them, how things would prosper for them, and when they died their souls would go to heaven to enjoy everlasting glory. But if they went on making their customary sacrifices to their idols, which were devils, they would be taken to hell, where they would burn for ever in living flames. He said no more about their forsaking their idols, since he had stressed the matter sufficiently in his previous addresses.

Their reply to his statement was as follows: 'Malinche, we have heard from you before, and certainly believe that your God and this great Lady are very good. But remember that you have only just come to our land. In the course of time we shall do what is right. But can you ask us to give up our *Teules*, whom our ancestors have held to be gods for many years, worshipping them and paying them sacrifices? Even if we old men were to do so in order to please you, would not all our *papas* and our neighbours, our youths and children throughout the province, rise against us? Especially since the *papas* have already consulted the greatest of our *Teules*, who has told them that if they omit to make human sacrifices and to perform all the customary rites, he will destroy the whole province with famine, plague, and war.' They concluded their reply by asking us to spare ourselves the trouble of making such a request again, since they would not give up sacrifices, even at the cost of their lives.

When we heard this honest and fearless reply, the Mercedarian friar, who was an intelligent man and a theologian, remarked: 'Don't attempt to press them any further on this point, sir. It would not be right to make them Christians by force. Please do not overthrow their idols, as we did in Cempoala, at least until they have some knowledge of our holy faith. And what good would it be to clear their idols from one *cue* now, if they were merely to remove them immediately to another? It will be better for them to feel the weight of our good and holy admonitions gradually, so that in future they may recognize the goodness of the advice we give them.'

Three other gentlemen, Juan Velazquez de Leon, Francisco de Lugo, and another, spoke to Cortes to the same effect: 'The father is quite right. You have fulfilled your duty by doing what you have done. Don't refer to the matter again when speaking to these *Caciques*.' And so the subject was dropped. All that our entreaties did was to persuade the chiefs to clear one *cue*, which was close by and had been newly built and, after removing the idols, to clean and whitewash it, so that we could put a cross and an image of Our Lady in it, which we promptly did. Here mass was said, and the princesses were baptized. The blind Xicotenga's daughter was named Doña Luisa. Cortes led her by the hand and gave her to Pedro de Alvarado, telling the old *Cacique* that he was giving her to his brother and Captain, and that he must be glad, since she would receive good treatment. And Xicotenga was satisfied. The beautiful daughter or niece of Mase Escasi was named Doña Elvira, and I think she was given to Juan Velazquez de Leon. The others received baptismal names too, all with the title of nobility (*Doña*), and Cortes gave them to Gonzalo de Sandoval, Cristobal de Olid, and Alonso de Avila. After this he explained to the Indians his reasons for erecting two crosses, which was to frighten off their idols. He said that wherever we camped or slept we placed them on the roads; and with all this they were quite content.

Before I go on I should like to say that when Xicotenga's daughter Doña Luisa was given to Pedro de Alvarado, the greater part of Tlascala paid her reverence, gave her presents, and looked on her as their mistress. Pedro de Alvarado, who was then a bachelor, had a son by her named Don Pedro, and a daughter, Doña Leonor, who is now the wife of Francisco de la

Cueva, a nobleman and the cousin of the Duke of Albuquerque, who has had four or five sons by her, all splendid gentlemen. I should like to add that Doña Leonor is in every way worthy of her excellent father.

Cortes took the *Caciques* aside and asked them very detailed questions about the state of Mexico. Xicotenga, being an important lord and very well-informed, took the main part in the conversations, but he was helped at times by Mase Escasi, who was a great lord also.

Xicotenga said that Montezuma had a vast host of warriors, and that if he wanted to take a great city or attack a province he could put a hundred and fifty thousand men in the field, as they knew from the experience of more than a hundred years of war.

'How is it, then,' asked Cortes, 'that with so large an army they have never entirely conquered you?'

The *Caciques* replied that although the Mexicans had several times defeated them, killing many of their subjects and taking away others to be sacrificed, they had also left many dead and prisoners on the field. Besides, the Mexicans never came so secretly that they did not get some warning; and when the Tlascalans knew that an attack was impending, they would muster their whole army, and with the aid of the Huexotzincans would both defend themselves and counter-attack. Moreover, all the towns and provinces that Montezuma had raided and subdued were very hostile to the Mexicans, and their people were forced into battle and fought against their will. Indeed, it was from them that the Tlascalans received warnings of an approaching attack, which enabled them to put up the best possible defence of their country.

The place from which the most continuous trouble had come to them, said Xicotenga, was a very large city called Cholula, which was a day's march away, and whose inhabitants were very treacherous. It was there that Montezuma secretly assembled his companies, and it was in that neighbourhood that they made their attacks by night. Mase Escasi added that in addition to the forces he brought from Mexico, Montezuma kept strong garrisons in every province, and that all the provinces paid tribute of gold and silver, feathers, precious stones, cloth, and cotton, also men and women for sacrifice and for servants. He added that Montezuma was such a great prince that he had everything he desired, and the houses in which he lived were full of riches and precious stones and *chalchihuites*, which he had taken by force from those who refused to give them to him willingly. He added that all the wealth of the country was in Montezuma's hands.

The *Caciques* then gave an account of all the servants in Montezuma's palace, which is too long for me to repeat, also of all the women he possessed, and how he married some of them off. In fact they described everything.

They then spoke of the great fortifications of the city, describing the lake, the depth of the water, and the causeways that led into the city, and the wooden bridges on each causeway, and how you could go in and out by boat through the openings in each bridge, and how when any of the bridges were raised you could be caught between them and so be unable to reach the city, and how the greater part of this city was built in the lake, and you could not get from house to house except by drawbridge or in canoes, which the Mexicans kept in readiness. They also said that all their houses were flat-roofed and all the roofs provided with parapets, so that the Mexicans could fight from them.

The *Caciques* also told us how the city was provided with water from a spring called Chapultepec, about a mile and a half from the city, and how it came by an aqueduct to a place from which they fetched it in canoes to sell in the streets. Then they described the weapons which the Mexicans used: their two-pronged javelins which they hurled with a spear-thrower and which would pierce any armour; their many good bowmen, and those who carried lances five or six feet long with flint cutting-edges, so well made that they cut better than knives; their shields and their cotton armour; their many slingers with rounded stones; their other good long lances and flint-edged two-handed swords. They brought us pictures painted on large sisal cloths showing the battles they had fought against the Mexicans, and their way of fighting.

As we had already heard all that the chiefs were telling us, Cortes stopped the conversation and, embarking on a more profound subject, asked them how they had come to inhabit this country, where they had come from, and how it was they differed so much from the Mexicans and were so hostile to them, seeing that their countries were so close together.

They said their ancestors had told them that very tall men and women with huge bones had once dwelt among them, but because they were a very bad people with wicked customs they had fought against them and killed them, and those of them who remained had died off. And to show us how big these giants had been they brought us the leg-bone of one, which was very thick and the height of an ordinary-sized man, and that was a leg-bone from the hip to the knee. I measured myself against it, and it was as tall as I am, though I am of a reasonable height. They brought other pieces of bone of the same kind, but they were all rotten and eaten away by the soil. We were all astonished by the sight of these bones and felt certain there must have been giants in that land. And Cortes said that we ought to send the leg-bone to Castile so that His Majesty might see it, which we did by the first agents who went there.

These *Caciques* also told us of a tradition they had heard from their ancestors, that one of the idols which they particularly worshipped had prophesied the coming of men from distant lands in the direction of the sunrise, who would conquer them and rule them. If we were they, said the *Caciques*, they rejoiced, since we were so brave and good. When they had made peace with us, they went on, they had remembered what their idols had said, and so had given us their daughters in order to have kinsmen to defend them against the Mexicans.

When they had concluded their speech we wondered in amazement whether what they had just said could be true. Then our Captain Cortes answered them, saying that we certainly came from the direction of the sunrise, and that our lord and King had sent us so that we might become brothers to them, for he had heard about them and prayed God to give us grace, so that by our hands and through our intercession they might be saved. And we all said Amen.

My worthy readers will be tired of listening to our discussions and conversations with the Tlascalans. But before I stop, I must mention one other thing about which they told us, and that was the volcano near Huexotzinco, which was throwing out more fire than usual while we were at Tlascala. All of us, including our Captain, were greatly astonished at this, since we had never seen a volcano before. One of our captains, Diego de Ordaz, wishing to go to see what it was, asked the general's permission to climb it. Permission was granted, and Cortes even expressly ordered him to make the ascent.[1] Diego took two of our soldiers and certain Indian chiefs from Huexotzinco, who frightened him with the information that halfway up Popocatepetl – for this was the volcano's name – the earth-tremors and the flames, stones, and ashes that were thrown out of the mountain were more than a man could bear. They said the guides would not dare to climb further than the *cues* of those idols that are called the *Teules* of Popocatepetl. Nevertheless, Diego de Ordaz and his two companions climbed on till they came to the top, leaving the Indians below too scared to make the ascent.

From what Ordaz and the two soldiers said afterwards it appears that, as they climbed, the volcano began to throw out great tongues of flame, and half-burnt stones of no great weight, and a great deal of ash, and that the whole mountain range in which it stands was so shaken that they stopped still, not daring to go forward for quite an hour, until they saw that the eruption was over and the smoke and ashes were getting less. They then climbed up to the crater, which was very round and wide and about a mile and a half across. From the summit they could see the city of Mexico and the whole lake, and all the towns on its shores. The volcano is about eighteen or twenty miles from Mexico.

Ordaz was delighted and astonished with the view of Mexico and its cities. After gazing at them for some time he went back to Tlascala with his companions, and the Indians of Huexotzinco and Tlascala regarded his climb as a very brave deed.

---

1. This account of the ascent of Popocatepetl seems to have been put in the wrong place. Cortes himself, in his second letter, says that it was climbed when the Spaniards left Cholula.

When he told his story to Captain Cortes and the rest of us, we were greatly astonished. For we had never seen or heard of Popocatepetl as we have today, when many Spaniards, including some Franciscans, have climbed to the crater.

When Diego de Ordaz went to Castile he asked His Majesty to grant him the volcano as his coat-of-arms, which his nephew, who lives at Puebla, now bears.

Since settling in this country we have never seen the volcano belch so much fire as on that first occasion, nor heard it make so much noise. Indeed it did not erupt for some years until, in 1539, it threw out great flames, stones, and ashes.

I must now tell how in this town of Tlascala we found wooden cages made of lattice-work in which men and women were imprisoned and fed until they were fat enough to be sacrificed and eaten. We broke open and destroyed these prisons, and set free the Indians who were in them. But the poor creatures did not dare to run away. However, they kept close to us and so escaped with their lives. From now on, whenever we entered a town our captain's first order was to break down the cages and release the prisoners, for these prison cages existed throughout the country. When Cortes saw such great cruelty he showed the *Caciques* of Tlascala how indignant he was and scolded them so furiously that they promised not to kill and eat any more Indians in that way. But I wondered what use all these promises were, for as soon as we turned our heads they would resume their old cruelties.

When our Captain remembered that we had been resting in Tlascala for seventeen days, and after all we had heard about Montezuma's great wealth and flourishing city, we decided to consult all our captains and soldiers whom he felt to be willing to go forward; and it was decided that we should set out without delay. But a good deal of criticism of this decision was expressed in the camp. Some soldiers said that it was very rash to start attacking this strong city when our numbers were so small, and harped on Montezuma's very great strength. But our Captain replied that we had no alternative. We had so constantly asserted and proclaimed that we were going to see Montezuma that any other course was useless.

When his opponents heard Cortes speaking with such determination, and realized from our shouts of: 'Forward, and good luck to us!' that many of us were ready to support him, there was no more opposition. The men who opposed Cortes in this debate were those who owned property in Cuba. As for me and the rest of us soldiers, we had always devoted our souls to God our Creator, and our bodies to wounds, hardships, and even death in the Lord's service and His Majesty's.

When Xicotenga and Mase Escasi saw that we were determined to go to Mexico they were sad at heart. Remaining constantly in Cortes' company, they advised him neither to embark on the expedition nor to put the least trust in Montezuma or any Mexican. He must not, they said, believe in the homage Montezuma had offered, or in his very humble and courteous words, or in all the presents he had sent, or in any of his promises, for all was treachery. They warned him that in a single hour the Mexicans would take back everything they had given him, and that he must keep careful watch by night and day, since they would most certainly attack us when we were off our guard. In fighting the Mexicans, they said, we should leave no one alive whom we were able to kill: neither the young, lest they should bear arms again, nor the old, lest they should give counsel; and they offered us a great deal more advice of this kind.

Our Captain told these counsellors that he was grateful for their warning, and treated them affectionately. He made them some promises, and gave a great part of the fine cloth which Montezuma had sent him as presents to Xicotenga the Elder and Mase Escasi and the rest. He told them also that it would be a good thing if they could make peace with the Mexicans, for once they were friends the Mexicans might bring them salt and cotton and other merchandise. But Xicotenga answered that a treaty was useless, since enmity was always deeply rooted in their hearts, and such was the Mexican character that under cover of peace they would only practise greater treachery, for they never kept their word, whatever they promised. He begged Cortes to say no more about a treaty, and implored him once more to be on his guard against falling into the hands of this wicked race.

There was some discussion about the road we should take to go to Mexico. Montezuma's ambassadors, who had stayed with us and were to be our guides, said that the best and smoothest way was through the town of Cholula, since its people were vassals of the great Montezuma and we should be well looked after. We all agreed, therefore, that we should go through Cholula. But when the Tlascalan chiefs heard that we intended to follow the way the Mexicans recommended they grew very gloomy and said once more that at all costs we ought to go by Huexotzinco, where the people were their relations and our friends, rather than by way of Cholula, where Montezuma always kept concealed ambushes.

Despite all their talk and advice not to enter Cholula, our captain, in accordance with our decision which had been well debated, still determined to take the Cholula road, in the first place because everyone agreed that it was a large town with many towers and great, high *cues* and was situated on a fine plain – indeed at that time it looked from the distance like our own city of Valladolid in Old Castile – and secondly because it had other large towns all round it and could provide ample supplies, and our friends the Tlascalans were near at hand. So we decided to stay at Cholula until we could see how to get to Mexico without having to fight, for the great Mexican army was something to be feared, and unless the Lord God by His divine mercy were to interfere on our behalf, we had no other way of entering the city of Mexico.

So after much discussion it was settled that we should take the Cholula road. Then Cortes gave orders that messengers should be sent to the town to inquire why, being so near to us, they had not come to visit us and pay us that respect which was our due as envoys of our great lord the King who had sent us to tell them of their salvation. He requested all the *Caciques* and *papas* of Cholula to come immediately to see us and offer their obedience to our lord and King; in default of which he would consider them ill-disposed towards us. While he was giving this message and talking to us and the Tlascalan *Caciques* about our departure and matters of war, news was brought to him that four ambassadors, all men of importance, had just arrived, bearing presents from Montezuma. He ordered them to be summoned; and when they came before him, after paying great reverence to him and to us who were with him, they presented their gift of rich gold jewels of varied workmanship, worth a good two thousand pesos, and ten loads of cloth finely decorated with feathers, which Cortes received most graciously.

The ambassadors then said on behalf of their lord Montezuma that he was very much surprised that we should have stayed so many days among a poor and ill-bred people, who were so wicked, so treacherous, and such thieves that they were not even fit to be slaves. He warned us that some day or night when we were off our guard they would kill us in order to rob us. He then begged us to come at once to his city, where he would give us a share of what he had, though it would not be as good as we deserved and as he would like to give us. Still, though all supplies had to be carried into the city, he would provide for us as well as he could.

Montezuma did this in order to get us out of Tlascala, for he knew that we had made friends with the people, who had clinched the friendship by giving their daughters to Malinche. The Mexicans thoroughly understood that this alliance could do them no good. Therefore they plied us with gold and presents in the hope of inducing us to come to their country, or at least to leave Tlascala. As for the ambassadors themselves, the Tlascalans knew them well, and told our captain that they were all lords over towns and vassals, and men whom Montezuma employed to negotiate matters of great importance.

Cortes thanked the ambassadors warmly, in flattering tones and with demonstrations of friendship. He answered that he would very soon visit their lord Montezuma and begged them to remain a few days with us. At that time Cortes decided that two of our captains, specially chosen for the task, should visit the great Montezuma and talk with him, and view the great city of Mexico, its large armies, and fortifications. Pedro de Alvarado and Bernardino Vazquez de Tapia therefore set out on the journey, while four of the ambassadors who had brought Montezuma's present remained behind as hostages. Some others, who had grown used to us, accompanied the two captains on their way. Because Cortes was merely trusting to luck when he sent these two gentlemen, we objected to his decision. We said that we thought it a bad plan that they should go to Mexico only to see the city[1] and its strength, and asked him to send after them and stop them. He therefore wrote, summoning them to return at once, which they did.

The ambassadors who had been escorting them gave an account of all this to Montezuma, who asked them to describe the faces and general appearance of the two *Teules* who had been travelling to Mexico, and to say whether they were captains. They seem to have told him that Pedro de Alvarado was very handsome both in his face and person, that he looked like the sun and was a captain, and in addition they brought a picture of him, with his features sketched very naturally. So they gave him the name of Tonatio, which means the Sun, or Son of the Sun, and called him by it ever afterwards. They told Montezuma also that Bernardino Vazquez de Tapia was a stout man and very friendly, and a captain as well, and Montezuma was very sorry they had turned back.

We chaffed these captains when they returned to camp, saying that it was not a very successful mission on which Cortes had sent them. But let us leave this subject, for it has not much to do with our story, and tell about the messengers whom Cortes sent to Cholula, and the reply they brought.

On receiving Cortes' summons the *Caciques* of Cholula decided to send four Indians of minor rank to present their excuses, and say that they had not come because they were ill. These messengers brought neither food nor anything else, but merely gave this curt reply. The Tlascalan chiefs, who were present when they arrived, told our Captain that the Cholulans had sent these men to make a mock of him, for they were common Indians of no importance. So Cortes sent them back

1. In a note in the original MS. Bernal Díaz says that he knows of this last incident only at second hand, since he was badly wounded at the time and was fully occupied in getting well. He also cites a different reason for the return of the two captains, saying that Bernardino Vazquez was lying ill in a Mexican city, and that it was Montezuma who sent them back, for fear they would see everything in the city.

at once with four Cempoalans to tell the men of Cholula they must send some chiefs, who must arrive within three days, the distance being only fifteen miles. Otherwise he would consider them rebels. He said that when they came he would tell them some things that were necessary for the salvation of their souls and their well-being, and receive them as friends and brothers, as he had received their neighbours the Tlascalans. But if they decided otherwise and did not want our friendship we would take measures that would both displease and anger them.

When the Cholulan chiefs had listened to this message they answered that they were not coming to Tlascala because the Tlascalans were their enemies, and they knew the latter had maligned them and their lord Montezuma. They said that it was for us to leave the territory of the Tlascalans and come to their city, and that if they then acted wrongly we could treat them as we had threatened.

Realizing that their excuse was very just, we decided to go to Cholula; and when the Tlascalan *Caciques* were informed of our decision they said to Cortes: 'So you are going to trust the Mexicans rather than us, who are your friends. We have warned you many times to beware of the Cholulans and of the might of Mexico, and to give you all possible support we have ten thousand warriors ready to accompany you.'

Cortes thanked them very warmly for their offer, but after some debate it was agreed that it would be wrong to take so many warriors into a land where we had to seek friends, and that it would be better to take only a thousand. So we asked the Tlascalans for this number, and said that the rest should remain at home.

The March to Mexico

WE started one morning on our march to Cholula, taking every possible precaution because, as I have said before, we kept much more on the alert when we expected trouble or attack, and that night we slept beside a river less than three miles from that city, where the Indians made us huts and shelters. A stone bridge has now been built at this place. That same night the *Caciques* of Cholula sent us some men of importance as messengers to welcome us to their country and bring us supplies of poultry and maize-cakes. They told us that all the *Caciques* and *papas* would come out to receive us in the morning, and asked us to forgive them for not having come immediately. Cortes told them through our interpreters that he was grateful for the food they had brought and the good will they showed.

We slept there that night after posting sentries and scouts, and as soon as dawn broke we set out towards the city. When we were on our way and already close to the town, the *Caciques* and *papas* and many other Indians came out to receive us. Most of them wore cotton garments cut like smocks, of the kind worn by the Zapotec Indians – I say this for the benefit of those who have visited that province and seen them – for this is what they wore at Cholula. They came very peaceably and willingly, and the *papas* carried braziers with which they perfumed our Captain and such of us soldiers as were near him. It seems that when these *papas* and *Caciques* saw the Tlascalans who accompanied us, they asked Doña Marina to tell the General it was wrong that their enemies should enter their city like this, with arms in their hands. When this message had been translated to Cortes, he ordered the Captains, soldiers, and baggage to halt, and having done so he addressed us: 'It seems to me, gentlemen, that before we enter Cholula we should put these *Caciques* and *papas* to the test with a friendly speech and see what it is they want. They are complaining about our friends the Tlascalans; and they have good reason for what they say.

I should like to explain to them in fair words why we have come to their city. As you gentlemen already know, the Tlascalans have told us the Cholulans are a turbulent people. It would be a good thing, therefore, if they could be brought into obedience to His Majesty in a peaceful way, which is what I think we should do.'

Cortes told Doña Marina to summon the *Caciques* and *papas* to the place where he was on his horse. We were grouped around him. The three chiefs and two priests then came forward and said : 'Malinche, forgive us for not having come to Tlascala to see you and bring you food. It was not for lack of good will but because of our enemies, Xicotenga and Mase Escasi and the rest of the Tlascalans, who have spoken a great deal of evil of us and our lord Montezuma. And not satisfied with abusing us, they now have the temerity, under your protection, to come to our city armed. We beg you as a favour to send them back to their country, or at least to tell them to stay outside in the fields and not to enter our city like this. But as for yourselves, you are very welcome.'

When our Captain saw the justice of their complaint, he at once ordered Pedro de Alvarado and the quartermaster Cristobal de Olid to ask the Tlascalans to put up their huts and shelters in the fields and not to enter the city with us, excepting those who were carrying the cannon and our friends from Cempoala. He asked them to explain to the Tlascalans that our reason for this order was that all these *Caciques* and *papas* were afraid of them, and that when we left Cholula on our way to Mexico we would send for them, and they must not be annoyed by our action. And when the Cholulans saw what Cortes had done they appeared to be much more at ease.

Then Cortes began to make them a speech, saying that our lord and King, whose vassals we were, had very great power and ruled over many great princes and chiefs, and that he had sent us to these lands to warn and command them not to worship idols, or sacrifice human beings and eat their flesh, or commit sodomy or other bestialities; and that as the road to Mexico, where we were going to speak to the great Montezuma, passed through their territory and there was no shorter way, we had come to visit their city and would treat them as brothers. Since other great *Caciques* had given their obedience to His Majesty, he concluded, it would be as well if they were to do so too.

They answered that we had hardly entered their country, yet we were already ordering them to forsake their *Teules*, which they could not do. But as for giving obedience to this King we spoke of, this they would do. And they pledged their word to it; but not before a notary. After this we at once began our march into the city, and such was the crowd that came out to see us that the streets and rooftops were full, which does not surprise me, for they had never seen men like us or horses before.

They lodged us in some large rooms, which we shared with our friends the Cempoalans and the Tlascalans who carried the baggage, and brought us food that day and the next; very good food and plenty of it.

After the Cholulans had given us this ceremonious reception, with what certainly looked like good will, Montezuma, as afterwards transpired, sent orders to his ambassadors who were still in our company to arrange with the people of the city that they should combine with an army of twenty thousand men, which he had sent and which was ready to enter Cholula, to make an attack on us by night or day. Then, when we were driven into a corner, they were to bring as many of us as they could to Mexico in bonds. He made them great promises and sent them many jewels and much cloth, also a golden drum, and he told the *papas* of the city that they could retain twenty of us to be sacrificed to their idols.

All was now prepared. The soldiers whom Montezuma had sent with such speed were hidden in shelters and thickets about a mile and a half from Cholula, while others were posted in the houses, and all had their arms ready. Breastworks had been built on the roofs, holes had been dug in the streets, barricades had been erected to impede the movements of our horses, and in some of the houses they had collected the long poles, leather collars, and ropes with which they were to secure us when they led us to Mexico.

So after taking us to our quarters they gave us food for the first two days, and appeared to be most peaceable in their conduct. Nevertheless we did not relax our usual precautions. On the third day the supplies of food stopped, and no *Cacique* or *papa* came to see us. Such Indians as we saw did not approach but stayed some way off, laughing at us as if in mockery. In view of this our Captain asked the interpreters to tell the ambassadors of the great Montezuma, who were still with us, that they must order the *Caciques* to bring us food. But all they brought was water and firewood, and the old men who brought it said they had no maize.

This same day these ambassadors were joined by others from Montezuma, who told Cortes quite shamelessly that their prince had sent them to say we must not go to his city, for he had no food to give us, and that they wished to return immediately with our reply.

When Cortes understood the unfriendliness of their speech he replied most blandly that he was surprised so great a prince as Montezuma should be of so many minds. He begged them, however, not to return to Mexico, since he intended to set out himself next day to see their prince and put himself at his service. I think he gave them some strings of beads, and the ambassadors agreed to stay.

After this our Captain called us together and said: 'I see that these people are greatly disturbed. We must keep very much on the alert, for they are up to some mischief.' He then sent for the chief *Cacique*, whose name I now forget, asking him to come himself or send some important persons. The *Cacique* replied that he was ill and could not come.

When our Captain heard this he told us to persuade two of the many *papas* who lived in the *cue* close to our lodging to come to him. We brought two of them, without doing them any disrespect, and Cortes ordered that each of them should be given a *chalchihuite*. He then asked them in the most friendly way why it was that the *Cacique* and the other chieftains and nearly all the *papas* were frightened of us, for we had sent to summon them and they had refused to come. It seems that one of these *papas* was a very important personage who had charge or command of all the *cues* in the city, like a bishop among them, and was held in great respect. He answered that the *papas* were not afraid of us, and that if the *Cacique* and the other dignitaries had refused to come he would go to summon them, for he believed they would do what he asked them.

Cortes immediately told him to go and to leave his companion with us to await his return. The *papa* went and summoned the *Cacique* and dignitaries, who returned with him immediately to Cortes' lodging. Cortes asked them through our interpreters what it was they were afraid of, and why they did not bring us anything to eat; he said that our presence in the city might inconvenience them, but we intended to leave next day to see and speak with the lord Montezuma, and he asked them to find porters to carry our baggage and the *tepuzques*, also to bring us food at once.

The *Cacique* was so confused that he could hardly speak. He said that they would search for the food, but their lord Montezuma had sent them orders not to give us any and did not want us to advance any further.

While this conversation was going on, three of our friends the Cempoalans came in, and secretly told Cortes that they had observed close to our lodgings some holes dug in the streets and covered over with wood and earth in such a way that they could not be seen without close examination. They had removed the earth from above one of these holes, however, and had found that it was full of sharp stakes to kill the horses when they charged. They also said that the roofs had breastworks of dried clay and were piled with stones, and this could be for no friendly purpose, since they had also found barricades of stout timbers in another street. At that moment eight of the Tlascalans whom we had left in the fields outside Cholula arrived and said to Cortes: 'Be careful, Malinche, for this city is hostile. We know that they sacrificed last night to their god of war. They offered him seven persons, five of them children, so that he should give them victory over you. And we have seen them moving all their baggage and women out of the city.'

When Cortes heard this he immediately sent the Tlascalans back to their captains with instructions to be fully prepared in case we sent to summon them. Then he resumed his conversation with the *Cacique* and the *papas* and dignitaries of Cholula, telling them not to be frightened or alarmed, but to remember the obedience they had sworn to him, and not violate it, or he would punish them. He reminded them that we intended to depart next morning, and that, like the Tlascalans, they must provide us with an escort of two thousand warriors from their city, for we should need them on the road. They answered that they would provide the escort, and asked his permission to go at once to prepare it.

They departed well pleased, for they thought that, trapped between the warriors they were to supply and Montezuma's companies which were hidden in the thickets and ravines, we could not escape death or capture. For the horses would be prevented from charging by the breastworks and barricades which they now instructed their garrison to build in such a way that only a narrow lane would be left, through which it would be impossible for us to pass. They also advised the Mexicans to be fully prepared, since we were setting out next day and they were providing us with an escort of two thousand men. So between the two forces our capture seemed certain. For they could catch us and bind us when we were marching off our guard, and they could be certain of this since they had sacrificed to their war-gods, who had promised them victory.

But let us leave this matter, which they looked on as a certainty, and return to our Captain. Wanting further information about this whole plot and what was going on, Cortes told Doña Marina to take more *chalchihuites* to the two *papas* who had been the first to speak, since they were not afraid, and to ask them in the friendliest way to come back with her, for Malinche wanted to speak to them again. Doña Marina returned to the *papas* and talked to them as she well knew how; and, persuaded by the presents, they came back with her at once. Cortes then asked them to tell the truth about what they knew, for they were priests of idols and chieftains, and ought not to lie. He promised them that what they said would not be revealed in any way, for we were going to depart next morning, and he offered them a large quantity of cloth. They said that their lord Montezuma had known we were coming to Cholula, and that every day he was of many minds, unable to decide what to do about it. Sometimes he sent them instructions that if we arrived they were to pay us great honour and guide us on to Mexico; and at other times he said that he did not want us to come to his city; and now recently the gods Tezcatlipoca and Huichilobos, for whom they had great devotion, had proposed to him that we should be killed at Cholula or brought bound to Mexico. The *papas* told Cortes that Montezuma had sent twenty thousand warriors on the previous day, half of whom were already inside the city walls, while the other half were hidden in some ravines near by, and that these men had already been informed that we were going to set out next day. They spoke also about the barricades that had been put up, and the escort of two thousand men that we had demanded. He said the Mexicans had agreed that twenty of us were to be left to be sacrificed to the idols of Cholula.

Cortes ordered these *papas* to be given a present of richly embroidered cloth, and told them to say nothing about their conversation with us, for if they disclosed the secret we would certainly kill them when we returned from Mexico. He said that we still intended to leave next morning, and told them to summon all the *Caciques* so that he could speak with them then.

That night Cortes discussed with us what should be done, for he had very able men who could give good advice. And as usually happens in such cases, some said that it would be better to change our route and go through Huexotzinco, and some that we must preserve the peace at all costs and return to Tlascala. Others of us, however, stated our opinion that if we let this treachery pass unpunished we should meet with worse in other places, and that since we were in this town and amply stocked with provisions, we should fight them there, for they would feel the effect of it more in their homes than in the open fields. We said that the Tlascalans should be warned at once to join us, and everyone approved this last plan.

These are the details. As Cortes had already advised them that we were leaving next day, we should make a show of tying up our baggage, which was little enough. Then, in the large courts in which we were lodged, which were surrounded by high walls, we should give the Indian warriors the beating they deserved. As for Montezuma's ambassadors, we should conceal our feelings from them, telling them that the wicked Cholulans had planned a treacherous attack and intended to throw the blame on their lord Montezuma and themselves, his ambassadors, but that we did not believe Montezuma had given any such orders, and therefore begged them to stay in their apartments and have no more communication with the people of that city, so that we should have no reason to think that they had any part in this treachery. We would then ask them to go with us as our guides to Mexico.

As things turned out, the ambassadors answered that neither they nor their lord Montezuma knew anything about what we were telling them and, little though they liked it, we put a guard on them so that they should not go away without our permission and Montezuma should not find out that we knew it was he who ordered the whole matter.

That night we were on the alert and under arms, with our horses saddled and bridled. Though it was always our custom to keep a good watch, we had more sentinels and patrols than usual, for we felt certain that all the companies, Mexican and Cholulan, would attack us that night.

Now a certain old Indian woman, a *Cacique*'s wife who knew all about the plot and the trap that had been prepared, came secretly to Doña Marina, having noticed that she was a young woman and handsome and rich, and advised her to come to her house if she wanted to escape with her life, because that night or next day we should all be killed, by command of the great Montezuma. The plan was, she said, that the Cholulans and Mexicans should join forces, and that none of us should be left alive except those who were to be taken bound to Mexico. But knowing of this, and feeling some commiseration for Doña Marina, the old woman had come to tell her she had better collect her possessions and come to her house, where she would marry her to her son, the brother of another youth who accompanied her.

When Doña Marina heard her story, she said to the old

woman, with her usual quickwittedness: 'Oh, mother, I am indeed grateful to you for telling me this! I would come with you at once, but I have no one here whom I can trust to carry my clothes and golden jewels, of which I have plenty. Wait here a little, mother, I implore you, you and your son, and we will set out tonight. For now, as you see, these *Teules* are on the watch, and would hear us.'

The old woman believed what she had said and remained chatting with her. Doña Marina asked her how they were going to kill us all, and how, when, and where the plot had been made. And the old woman told her exactly what the *papas* had told us. Then Doña Marina asked her: 'Seeing that the business is so secret, how did you come to know about it?' She answered that her husband had told her, for he was captain of one of the clans in the city, and as captain he was now out with the warriors under his command, giving them orders to join up with the great Montezuma's companies in the ravines, where she thought they were already assembling in expectation of our departure, with the intention of killing us there. As for the plot, she had known about it for three days, since they had sent her husband a gilded drum from Mexico, and rich cloaks and golden jewels to three other captains, as an inducement to bring us bound to their lord Montezuma. When Doña Marina heard this, she concealed her feelings from the old woman and said: 'I am indeed glad that this son of yours to whom you want to marry me is an important person – we have been talking a long while, and I do not want them to notice us; so wait here, mother, and I will begin to bring my possessions, because I cannot carry everything out at once. You and your son, my brother, must look after them, and then we shall be able to go.' The old woman believed all she said, and she and her son sat down to rest.

Doña Marina burst into the room where Cortes was and told him all about her conversation with the Indian woman. Our Captain ordered the old woman to be brought before him, and questioned her about these treasons and plots; and she told him exactly the same story as he had heard from the *papas*. He then put a guard on her so that she should not escape.

When dawn broke it was marvellous to see the haste with which the *Caciques* and *papas* brought in the Indian warriors. Laughing with joy, as if they had already caught us in their nets and snares, they brought us more warriors than we had asked for, and large as the courtyards are – for they still stand undemolished as a memorial of the past – they would not hold them all. Though it was early when the Cholulan warriors arrived, we were already quite prepared for what had to be done. Soldiers with swords and shields were stationed at the gate of the great court so as not to let a single armed Indian escape.

When our Captain, mounted on his horse, with many soldiers round him for a guard, saw that the *Caciques, papas,* and warriors had assembled, he said: 'How anxious these traitors are to see us among the ravines so that they can gorge themselves on our flesh. But Our Lord will prevent it.' He then asked for the two *papas* who had revealed the plot, and was told that they were at the gate of the courtyard with some other *Caciques* who were about to enter; and he sent the interpreter Aguilar to tell them to go home, since we had no need of their presence now. For they had done us a good turn and he did not want to repay it by killing them. Still on his horse, with Doña Marina beside him, Cortes then asked the *Caciques* why they had turned traitors and decided the night before that they would kill us, seeing that we had done them no harm but had merely warned them against certain things as we had warned every town through which we had passed: against wickedness and human sacrifice, and the worship of idols, and eating their neighbours' flesh, and sodomy. All we had done was to tell them to lead good lives and inform them of certain matters concerning our holy faith, and this without compulsion of any kind. For what purpose, he asked, had they recently prepared long, stout poles, with collars and many ropes, and stored them in a house near their large *cue*? And why three days ago had they raised barricades and dug holes in the streets, and built breastworks on the roofs of their houses? And why had they sent their wives and children and goods out of the city? Their hostility was plain to see, and their treachery also, which they could not conceal, for they had not even brought us food, but only water and firewood as a mockery, and had said they had no maize. He was well aware, he said, that they had many companies of warriors lying in wait for us in some ravines near by ready to carry out the treacherous attack they had planned, with many other bands of warriors who had joined them the night before in the belief that we should be passing that way on our march to Mexico. So in return for our coming to treat them like brothers, and tell them the commands of our lord God and the King, they were planning to kill us and eat our flesh, and had already prepared the pots with salt and peppers and tomatoes. If this was what they wanted, he said, it would have been better if they had made war on us in the field like good, brave warriors, as their neighbours the Tlascalans had done. He knew very well all that they had planned in the city, and even that they had promised their god, the god of war, to sacrifice twenty of us before his idol, also that three nights ago they had sacrificed seven Indians to him so that he might give them victory, which he had promised them. But being both wicked and false, he neither had nor would have any power over us, and all the crimes and treacheries they had planned and carried out were about to recoil on themselves.

Doña Marina translated this speech and made it perfectly clear to them. When they heard it the *Caciques* and *papas* and captains said that what she stated was true but it was not their fault, since Montezuma's ambassadors had commanded them to do it, by order of their master.

Then Cortes told them that the King's laws decreed such treachery should not go unpunished, and that they must die for their crime. Then he ordered a musket to be fired, which was the signal we had agreed on; and they received a blow they will remember for ever, for we killed many of them, and the promises of their false idols were of no avail.

In less than two hours our Tlascalan allies, who as I have said had remained in the fields, arrived after fighting a tough battle in the streets, where the Cholulans had posted other companies to defend the town and prevent their entrance, which had been quickly defeated however. The Tlascalans went about the place plundering and taking prisoners, and we could not stop them. Next day more bands arrived from the Tlascalan towns, and did great damage too, for they hated the Cholulans. The sight of this destruction aroused compassion in Cortes and his soldiers, and we stopped the Tlascalans from doing any more harm. Cortes ordered Cristobal de Olid to summon all their captains so that he could talk to them, and they very promptly came. He told them to collect their people together and camp in the fields, which they did and only the Cempoalans remained with us.

Just then certain *Caciques* and *papas* of Cholula who belonged to other districts and claimed to have taken no part in the plot – for it is a large city and they were a separate party or faction – came and asked Cortes to pardon the treachery that had been plotted against us now that the traitors had paid for it with their lives. Then the two friendly *papas* who had revealed the plot and the old captain's wife who had wanted Doña Marina for her daughter-in-law, also came; and they all begged Cortes to pardon the people.

When they spoke to him Cortes made a great display of anger, and ordered Montezuma's ambassadors, who had been kept with us, to be summoned. He said that the whole city deserved destruction, but that out of respect for the lord Montezuma, whose vassals they were, he would pardon them. Thenceforth, however, they must be of good behaviour, for if there were any repetition of the recent happenings they would pay for it with their lives.

Then he summoned the Tlascalans from the fields and told them to return the men and women they had taken prisoner, since the damage they had done was enough. The Tlascalans, however, protested, saying that the Cholulans deserved far worse punishment for the many treacherous attacks they had made on them. Nevertheless, on Cortes' instructions they surrendered many persons, but they kept a rich store of gold and robes, cotton, salt, and slaves. Cortes went further, however. He persuaded the two peoples to make friends; and from what I have heard I believe their friendship remains unbroken.

Furthermore, Cortes ordered the *papas* and *Caciques* of Cholula to bring the people back to the city, to hold their markets and fairs, and have no fear, for no harm would be done them. They answered that the city would be entirely peopled again within five days, since most of the inhabitants were at present hiding in the hills. They said that Cortes would have to choose a *Cacique* for them since their former *Cacique* was among those who had been killed in the courtyard. He asked them who should succeed to the office, and they said the brother of the old *Cacique*. So Cortes at once appointed him governor till further orders.

Afterwards, when he saw that the inhabitants had returned confidently and were holding their markets, he summoned the *papas* and captains and other dignitaries of the town and gave them a clear exposition of the principles of our holy faith. He told them to give up worshipping their idols, to stop sacrificing and eating human flesh, to give up robbery and their customary bestialities. He pointed out that their idols were wicked and had deceived them, and reminded them of the lying promises of victory they had made five days before, when seven persons had been sacrificed. All that they told the *papas* and the people being evil, he begged the Cholulans to throw them down and smash them to pieces. But if they were unwilling, he said we would do it for them. He also ordered them to whitewash a place rather like a shrine, so that we could put up a cross there.

In the matter of the cross, they immediately did what we asked, and they promised to pull down the idols. But although we told them to do so many times they put it off. Then the Mercedarian friar said that it was too much to expect the chiefs to destroy their idols until they had a better understanding of our faith, and until they saw the outcome of our visit to Mexico. He added that time would show what we ought to do, and that our exhortations and the setting up of the cross were enough.

Cholula is situated on a plain with many other towns around it; Tepeaca, Tlascala, Chalco, Tecamachalco, Huexotzinco, and a great many more. It is a land rich in maize and other vegetables, and in peppers, and in the *maguey* from which they brew their wine. They make very good pottery in this district, of red and black and white clay painted in various designs, and they supply Mexico and all the neighbouring provinces with it, as Talavera or Placencia do in Castile. At that time the city had many lofty towers, which were the temples and shrines in which they kept their idols, in particular the great *cue* which was higher than that of Mexico, although the *cue* at Mexico was very grand and tall. They had courts also for the service of the *cues*. We heard that they had a very great idol, the name of which I forget, but they were very devoted to it and came from many places to sacrifice to it and hold services like *novenas*. They gave it offerings of part of their property.

Let us now turn to those companies sent by the great Montezuma which were posted in the ravines beside Cholula and in pursuance of the plot had constructed barricades and narrow lanes to prevent our horses from charging. When they heard what had happened they returned to Mexico at a quick pace and gave Montezuma an account of the way things had gone. But though they went fast the news had already reached him through the *Caciques* who had been with us and who ran to him post-haste. We learnt on trustworthy authority that when the prince heard the news he was deeply grieved and angry, and that he immediately sacrificed some Indians to his idol Huichilobos, the god of war, in order that the god might tell them what would be the outcome of our journey to Mexico and whether he should admit us into the city. We even heard that for two days he remained shut in at his devotions and sacrifices with his ten principal priests, and that the idol advised him to send messengers to us disclaiming all responsibility for the Cholula affair, and to admit us to Mexico with demonstrations of friendship. For once we were inside he could either cut off our food and water or raise one of the bridges and then kill us. If he were to attack us, he would put an end to us all in a single day, and he could then offer his sacrifices to Huichilobos, who had made this reply, and to Tezcatlipoca, the god of hell; and they could feast on our thighs, legs, and arms, and the snakes, serpents, and tigers that they kept in wooden cages, as I shall relate in due course, could gorge on our entrails and bodies and all that was left.

The news of the plot and of the Cholulans' punishment

spread through all the provinces of New Spain. If we had a reputation for bravery before – for they had heard of the battles of Champoton and Tabasco, and of Cingapacinga and the affair of Tlascala, and called us *Teules* after their gods or evil things – from now on they took us for magicians and said that no plot against us could be so secret as to escape discovery. On this account they showed good will towards us.

I think that my readers must have heard enough of this tale of Cholula, and I wish that I were finished with it. But I cannot omit to mention the cages of stout wooden bars that we found in the city, full of men and boys who were being fattened for the sacrifice at which their flesh would be eaten. We destroyed these cages, and Cortes ordered the prisoners who were confined in them to return to their native districts. Then, with threats, he ordered the *Caciques* and captains and *papas* of the city to imprison no more Indians in that way and to eat no more human flesh. They promised to obey him. But since they were not kept, of what use were their promises?

Let us anticipate a little and say that these were the great cruelties about which the bishop of Chiapas, Fray Bartolome de las Casas, wrote, and was never tired of talking. He insisted that we punished the Cholulans for no reason at all, or just to amuse ourselves and because we had a fancy to. He writes so persuasively that he would convince anyone who had not witnessed the event, or had no knowledge of it, that these and the other cruelties of which he writes took place as he says, whereas the reverse is true. Let the Dominicans beware of this book of his, because they will find it contradicts the facts. I should like to say also that some good Franciscans, who were the first friars His Majesty sent to New Spain after the capture of Mexico, went to Cholula to inquire into the details of this punishment and the reason for it, and examined the actual *papas* and elders of the city. After questioning them thoroughly they found the facts to conform exactly with the account I have written, and not with the bishop's. If we had not inflicted that punishment, our lives would have been in great danger from the companies of Mexican warriors and Cholulans, and their barricades and breastworks. And if we had been so unfortunate as to be killed, this New Spain of ours would not have been conquered so rapidly, nor would another *armada* have dared to set out, or if it had done so it would have met with greater difficulties, because the Mexicans would have defended the ports. And they would still have remained in a state of idolatry.

We had been at Cholula for fourteen days and there was nothing more for us to do. We saw the city full of people again and the markets being held; we had made peace between the Cholulans and the Tlascalans, we had erected a cross, and we had instructed them in the tenets of our holy faith. But realizing that the great Montezuma was sending spies into our camp to inquire secretly into our plans and learn whether we intended to press on to his capital – for he succeeded in getting a very thorough knowledge of everything from the two ambassadors who were with us – Cortes decided to consult certain captains and soldiers whom he knew to be favourably disposed towards him – and who were not only brave but sound advisers – for he never did anything without first inquiring our opinion.

It was agreed that we should send a mild and friendly message to the great Montezuma, saying that in order to fulfil the purpose for which our lord the King had sent us we had crossed many seas and distant lands, and all this for the sole purpose of visiting him and telling him certain things which would be very profitable to him when he understood them. Furthermore, that on our way to his city his ambassadors had guided us to Cholula, which they said was tributary to him, and that for the first two days we spent there the inhabitants had treated us well, but that on the third day they had treacherously plotted to kill us. But since we were men against whom no trickery or double-dealing or wickedness could be plotted without our immediately discovering it, we had punished some of them who had hatched this design against us; and since our Captain knew they were his subjects, out of respect for his person and because of our great friendship for him, we had refrained from destroying and killing all those who had shared in the planning of this treachery. However, the worst of it was that the *papas* and *Caciques* said it was by his advice and at his command and his ambassadors' that the Cholulans had decided on this action. We had refused to believe that so great a prince would give such commands, especially as he had declared himself our friend; and we had inferred from his character that if his idols had put such an evil thought into his head as to make war on us he would do it in the open field. However, we did not care whether we were attacked in the open country or in the town, by day or by night, for we would kill anyone who ventured to do so. But as we felt quite certain that he was our great friend, and wished to see and speak with him, we would set out for his city immediately, to give him a very complete account of what our lord the King had commanded us to do.

When Montezuma received this message and learnt that we did not blame him alone for the affair at Cholula, he and his *papas* resumed, as we heard, the fasts and sacrifices to see whether their gods would now give him different advice about allowing us to enter the city or would repeat their previous commands. The gods gave them the same advice as before, that he should certainly let us in and then he could kill us when he chose. Montezuma's captains and *papas* also advised him that if he tried to prevent our entry we would fight him in his subject towns, seeing that we had the Tlascalans and all the Totonacs of the hills as our friends and other towns also had accepted our alliance. The best way to avoid these evils, they said, was to follow the advice which his god Huichilobos had given.

When the great Montezuma had once more taken counsel with his god and his *papas* and captains and they had all advised him to let us enter the city where he could safely kill us; and when he had received our protestations of friendship and our boast that we were not the sort of men against whom plots could be hatched in secret, and that we did not care whether we were attacked in town or country, by night or day, or by any sort of craft; and when, in addition, he had reflected on our wars with Tlascala and the affairs of Champoton, Tabasco, and Tzompantzinco and the recent events in Cholula, he was not only dazed, but he was also afraid. After much deliberation, therefore, he sent six chieftains with a present of gold and jewels of various sorts which were estimated to be worth more than two thousand pesos, and also some loads of very rich cloaks, beautifully worked.

When these chiefs came before Cortes with the present they touched the ground with their hands, and addressed him after the usual prostrations: 'Malinche, our lord the great Montezuma sends you this present, and begs you to accept it with the great love he has for you and all your brothers. He says that the wrong which the people of Cholula did you grieves him greatly, and that he wishes to visit further punishment upon them, for they are a wicked and lying people, in that they tried to lay the blame on him and his ambassadors for the crime they attempted to commit.' Montezuma then assured us that he was truly our friend, and that we could come to his city whenever we liked, for he wished to do us great honour as very valiant men and messengers of one whom we proclaimed to be so great a king. But because he had no food to give us, everything having to be brought into the city by porters since it was built on a lake, he could not give us a very adequate reception. Still, he would endeavour to do us all the honour he could, and had ordered the towns through which we had to pass to give us everything we might need.

When this speech was explained to Cortes he received the present very graciously and, embracing the messengers, ordered them to be given some twisted glass beads. We captains and soldiers were all delighted with the good news that Montezuma had invited us to the city, for most of us had been fervently desiring this every day, especially those who had left no estates behind us in Cuba, and had come on two voyages of exploration before joining Cortes.

Let us leave this subject and say that the Captain gave the ambassadors a good and cordial reply, and ordered three of those who had come with the present to remain behind and act as our guides, while the other three returned to their lord with our answer and the news that we were already on the way.

When the Tlascalan *Caciques*, Xicotenga the Elder and Mase Escasi, heard that we were going they were sad at heart. Reminding Cortes of their frequent warnings, they begged him once more to be cautious, and not to enter this strong city in which the Mexicans had so many warriors. For one day or another, we would be attacked, and they were afraid that we could not escape with our lives. However, out of their good will for us, they offered to send ten thousand men under valiant captains to accompany us and carry the provisions for our journey.

Cortes thanked them warmly for their friendly offer, but answered that it would be wrong to enter Mexico with such a host of warriors, especially as they and the Mexicans were on such bad terms. He said that he only needed a thousand men, to carry the *tepuzques* and the baggage and clear some of the roads, and they immediately sent the thousand Indians, very well equipped.

Just as we were about to set out, the *Caciques* and all the principal warriors whom we had brought from Cempoala, who had marched with us and served us very well and faithfully, came to Cortes and said that they wished to go no nearer to Mexico than Cholula, but to return since they felt sure that to go to that city would mean certain death both for them and for us. For the great Montezuma would order them to be killed, since they were the leading men of Cempoala and had violated their obedience to him by refusing to pay tribute and imprisoning his tax-collectors.

When Cortes saw their determination, he replied through our interpreters that they need have no fear of coming to any harm. For as they would march in our company, who would dare to molest either them or us? He asked them to change their minds and stay with us, and promised to make them rich. But although Cortes urged them, and Doña Marina addressed them in the most warm-hearted manner, they still insisted on returning. Seeing that they were resolved, Cortes observed: 'God forbid that we should take these Indians by force, who have served us so well!' And he called for many loads of rich cloaks, which he divided among them, setting aside two loads each for our friend the fat *Cacique* who was lord of Cempoala and the other great *Cacique*, his nephew. He also wrote to Juan de Escalante whom we had left behind as Captain, giving him news of all that had happened to us and saying that we were on our way to Mexico. He told him to look after the settlers well and keep a good watch and be alert by day and night, also to finish building the fortress and to support the natives of those parts against the Mexicans and see that none of the soldiers under his command molested them.

When he had written this letter and the Cempoalans had departed we set out on our journey, keeping well on the alert.

We left Cholula in our usual strict formation, with our mounted scouts and most active foot-soldiers prospecting the country ahead, and arrived that same day at some huts which stand on a sort of hill six miles from Cholula. I think the place is called Iscalpan; and it is a settlement from Huexotzinco. Here we were soon visited by the *Caciques* and *papas* of the near-by towns of Huexotzinco, who were friends and allies of the Tlascalans, also by men from other small places on the slopes of the volcano near the border. These dignitaries brought us food and a present of gold jewellery of little value, which they asked Cortes to accept, considering not the paltriness of the gift but the good will with which it was given. Then they advised him not to go to Mexico, since it was a very strong city and full of warriors, and we should be running a great risk. But if we decided to go, they said, we must look out when we had climbed the pass, for we should find two wide roads, one leading to a town called Chalco and the second to another called Tlamanalco,[1] both subject to Mexico. One of the roads had been swept and cleared so that we might be tempted to take it, and the other was blocked by great pines and other stout trees to make it impassable for horses. They said that a little way down the mountain, along the road which had been cleared, and which the Mexicans thought we must choose, they had cut away a piece of the hillside and made ditches and barricades, and that some bands of Mexicans were waiting there to kill us. They advised us, therefore, not to take the swept road

1. Bernal Díaz' memory is inaccurate. The right-hand road led by way of Tlamanalco to Chalco, and the other, which was more direct, went to Amecameca. According to Cortes' second letter, it was this road that the expedition took.

but the one which had been blocked by trees, and promised to send us plenty of men who, together with the Tlascalans, would find it quite easy to remove these obstacles and clear the way which would take us to Tlamanalco.

Cortes accepted their present very graciously, and thanked them for their counsel. With God's aid, he said, he intended to go on; and he would take the road they advised. Early next morning we began our march, and it was nearly midday when we reached the ridge of the mountain, where we found the roads exactly as the people from Huexotzinco had described them. Here we rested a little and began to think of the Mexican bands and the cut in the hillside and those barricades about which we had been warned.

Then Cortes summoned the ambassadors of the great Montezuma who accompanied us, and asked them how it was that those two roads were in that condition, one very clean and swept and the other blocked by newly felled trees. They answered that this was in order that we should go by the cleared road, which led to a town called Chalco, where we would be well received since it belonged to their lord Montezuma, and that they had felled the trees and blocked the other road so that we should not use it, for there were bad places on it and it took a rather roundabout way to Mexico by way of another town which was not so big as Chalco. Cortes then said that he wished to go by the blocked road, and we began to climb the mountain with the greatest caution, our allies shifting the stout tree trunks with great efforts to let us pass; some of them still lie by the roadside to this day. As we came to the top it began to snow, and the snow caked on the ground. We then marched down the pass. We slept the night in some shacks that are used as a sort of inn or lodging for Indian traders. We supped well, but the cold was intense. Then we posted our sentries, organized our patrols, manned some listening-posts, and sent out scouting parties. Next day we started on our march, and at about the hour of high mass we reached a town which, as I have already said, was called Tlamanalco.[1] Here we were well received and there was no scarcity of food.

1. According to Cortes this must have been Amecameca.

When the other towns heard of our arrival people quickly came from Chalco and joined those of Tlamanalco. Some came also from Chimaluacan and Amecameca and Ayotzingo, which is their harbour where they keep the canoes, also from some other little towns whose names I cannot now remember. All of them together brought us a present of gold, two loads of mantles, and eight Indian women. The gold was worth more than a hundred and fifty pesos. 'Malinche,' they said, 'accept these presents and think of us henceforth as your friends!' Cortes accepted them with great good will, offered to assist the givers in every way and, seeing them all collected together, told the Mercedarian friar to speak to them about our holy faith and counsel them to give up their idols. The friar spoke to them in the same way as we had spoken to the people in every town through which we had passed, and they replied that what he said was good and they would remember it. He also spoke to them of the great power of our lord the Emperor, and of his purpose in sending us to the country, which was that we should right wrongs and put an end to robbery.

On hearing this, all these towns complained about Montezuma and his tax-collectors, speaking in private so that the Mexican ambassadors should not hear them, however. They said these officials robbed them of all they possessed, and that if their wives and daughters were pretty they would violate them in front of their fathers and husbands and carry them away. They also said that the Mexicans made the men work like slaves, compelling them to carry pine-trunks and stone and firewood and maize overland and in canoes, and to perform other tasks, such as planting maize-fields, and that they took away the people's lands as well for the service of their idols. They complained of many other things too, which with the passage of time I have forgotten.

Cortes comforted them with kind words, which he did not find difficult, but added that at present he had not time to see justice done. If they would be patient for a while, however, he said he would free them from Mexican rule. He then secretly asked two of their chiefs to go with four of our Tlascalan allies and inspect the cleared road which the people of Huexotzinco had told us not to follow, and see what breastworks and barricades there were, and whether there were any armed bands. The chiefs answered: 'Malinche, there is no point in going to see, because they are all cleared away and levelled now. But you should know they cut away the hillside at a narrow place, and posted so many warriors there that you would not have got by. But we have been told that Huichilobos, their god of war, has now counselled them to let you pass, and kill you when you enter the city of Mexico. Therefore we think you should stay here with us, and accept a share of what we have, and that you should give up your journey to Mexico, which is so strong and so full of warriors that you will certainly not escape with your lives.'

Cortes answered with a cheerful smile that neither the Mexicans nor any other nation had the power to kill us, only God in whom we believed, and that we were going to explain to Montezuma himself and all his *Caciques* and *papas* what God had commanded. As he wished to set out immediately, he asked them to give him twenty of their leading men to accompany him, and he promised that as soon as we arrived in Mexico he would do them great service and see that they received justice. Montezuma and his tax-collectors would then cease to perpetrate the violent abuses of which they complained. The townspeople smilingly accepted his promise, and brought him the twenty men he asked for.

Just as we were starting on our march four Mexicans arrived, bringing a present of gold and cloaks from the great Montezuma. After making their customary prostrations they addressed Cortes to this effect: 'Malinche, this present is sent to you by our lord the great Montezuma, who says that he is sorry you have endured so many hardships in travelling from far distant lands to see him, and that he has already sent to tell you that he will give you much gold and silver and many *chalchihuites*, as a tribute for your Emperor and yourself and the *Teules* of your company, provided you do not come to Mexico. Now he begs you once more kindly not to advance any further, but to return whence you came, and he will send to the port a great quantity of gold and silver and precious stones for your king, and to you he will give four loads of gold, and to each of your brothers one load. Your entry into Mexico, however, is forbidden. All his vassals are in arms to prevent it. What is more, there is only the narrowest of roads, and no food there for you to eat.' And he cited many other difficulties in this message, in the hope that we should advance no further.

Although their message grieved him, Cortes most graciously embraced each of the messengers and accepted the present. I do not know how much it was worth, but in my experience, as I have said before, Montezuma unfailingly sent some gold whenever he sent messengers. But to return to our story, Cortes expressed his amazement that the lord Montezuma, who had proclaimed himself our friend and was such a great prince, should be so changeable that he said one thing at one time and sent contrary orders at another. As for his promise to send gold for our lord the Emperor and ourselves, Cortes thanked him for it, saying that any he sent now would be paid for in good deeds in course of time. Yet how could Montezuma think it right that being so near the city, we should turn back without fulfilling our prince's commands? If Montezuma had sent his messengers and ambassadors to some great lord like himself, and if after nearly reaching his house these messengers should turn back without delivering the message they carried, what sort of reception would he give them when they returned into his presence with such a tale? He would consider them a pack of worthless cowards, and our lord the Emperor would undoubtedly think the same of us. So we were determined at all costs to visit his city, and he must make no more attempts to put us off, since Cortes intended to see and speak with him, and to explain the whole purpose for which we had come; which he could do only in person. Once Montezuma had heard him we would return whence we came, if our presence displeased him. As for his excuse that he had not enough food to feed us, we were men who could exist on very little, and we were already on our way to Mexico. Therefore we expected him to welcome us.

After dispatching the messengers we set out. But having been told that Montezuma had consulted his *papas* and idols as to

whether he should allow us to enter or attack us on the road,
and that Huichilobos' reply had been that he must let us in and
kill us afterwards, we could not get this prospect out of our
thoughts, being men who feared death. Since the country is
thickly populated we made very short marches. Commending
ourselves to God and Our Lady, we discussed ways and means
of entering the city, and it put courage into our hearts to think
that since our lord Jesus Christ had vouchsafed to guard us in
past perils, He would also protect us from the power of Mexico.

We spent the night at a town called Itzapalatengo,[1] where
half the houses are in the water and half on dry land, and
where there is a low mountain – there is an inn there now –
and there we had a good supper.

Let us leave this and return to the great Montezuma. When
his messengers returned with Cortes' reply, he immediately
decided to send one of his nephews, Cacamatzin, the lord of
Texcoco, with great pomp to welcome us. So, it being our usual
custom to post sentinels and scouts, one of our scouts came to
tell us that a large crowd of friendly Mexicans was advancing
along the road, and that they appeared to be dressed in rich
cloaks. It was very early in the morning when this occurred,
and we were just ready to start. But Cortes ordered us to remain in our quarters until we saw what this was about. At that
moment four dignitaries arrived, bowed deeply to Cortes, and
announced the imminent approach of Cacamatzin, the great
lord of Texcoco, a nephew of the mighty Montezuma, who
begged us kindly to await his visit.

We had not long to wait. Cacamatzin soon arrived, with
greater pomp and splendour than we had ever beheld in any
Mexican prince. He came borne on a litter, most richly worked
in green feathers with much silver decoration and precious
stones set in tree designs that were worked in the finest gold.
His litter was carried by chieftains, each of whom, as they told
us, was ruler of a town. When they came near the house where
Cortes was lodged, they helped the prince out of his litter,
swept the ground, and removed the straws from his way. Then,
as they came before our Captain they made a deep bow, and

1. A mistake for Ayotzingo.

Cacamatzin said: 'Malinche, we have come here, I and these chieftains, to place ourselves at your service, and to see that you receive everything you require for yourself and your companions, and to install you in your home, which is our city. For so we have been commanded by our lord the great Montezuma, who asks you to pardon him for not coming with us himself. It is on account of ill-health and not from lack of very good will towards you that he has not done so.'

When we beheld such pomp and majesty in these chiefs, and even more in Montezuma's nephew, we were greatly impressed. If this *Cacique* is so magnificent, we said to one another, how grand will the great Montezuma himself be?

When Cacamatzin had made his speech, Cortes embraced him, and was very attentive to him and the other chieftains. He gave them three beads called *margaritas*, which are streaked with different coloured veins, and to the rest of the chiefs he gave blue glass beads; and he expressed his thanks to them, saying that when he was able he would repay the lord Montezuma for his daily favours to us.

When this conversation was over we immediately set out; and as these chiefs had brought many followers with them, and people had come out to see us from the many towns in the district, all the roads were full.

Next morning, we came to a broad causeway [1] and continued our march towards Iztapalapa. And when we saw all those cities and villages built in the water, and other great towns on dry land, and that straight and level causeway leading to Mexico, we were astounded. These great towns and *cues* and buildings rising from the water, all made of stone, seemed like an enchanted vision from the tale of Amadis. Indeed, some of our soldiers asked whether it was not all a dream. It is not surprising therefore that I should write in this vein. It was all so wonderful that I do not know how to describe this first glimpse of things never heard of, seen or dreamed of before.

When we arrived near Iztapalapa we beheld the splendour of the other *Caciques* who came out to meet us, the lord of that

1. The causeway of Cuitlahuac, which separated the lakes of Chalco and Xochimilco.

city whose name was Cuitlahuac, and the lord of Culuacan, both of them close relations of Montezuma. And when we entered the city of Iztapalapa, the sight of the palaces in which they lodged us! They were very spacious and well built, of magnificent stone, cedar wood, and the wood of other sweet-smelling trees, with great rooms and courts, which were a wonderful sight, and all covered with awnings of woven cotton.

When we had taken a good look at all this, we went to the orchard and garden, which was a marvellous place both to see and walk in. I was never tired of noticing the diversity of trees and the various scents given off by each, and the paths choked with roses and other flowers, and the many local fruit-trees and rose-bushes, and the pond of fresh water. Another remarkable thing was that large canoes could come into the garden from the lake, through a channel they had cut, and their crews did not have to disembark. Everything was shining with lime and decorated with different kinds of stonework and paintings which were a marvel to gaze on. Then there were birds of many breeds and varieties which came to the pond. I say again that I stood looking at it, and thought that no land like it would ever be discovered in the whole world, because at that time Peru was neither known nor thought of. But today all that I then saw is overthrown and destroyed; nothing is left standing.

The *Caciques* of that town and of Coyoacan brought us a present of gold worth more than two thousand pesos; and Cortes thanked them heartily for it, and he showed them great kindness, telling them through our interpreters something about our holy faith, and declaring to them the great power of our lord the Emperor. But there were too many conversations for me to describe them all.

The Entrance into Mexico

EARLY next day we left Iztapalapa with a large escort of these great *Caciques*, and followed the causeway, which is eight yards wide and goes so straight to the city of Mexico that I do not think it curves at all. Wide though it was, it was so crowded with people that there was hardly room for them all. Some were going to Mexico and others coming away, besides those who had come out to see us, and we could hardly get through the crowds that were there. For the towers and the *cues* were full, and they came in canoes from all parts of the lake. No wonder, since they had never seen horses or men like us before!

With such wonderful sights to gaze on we did not know what to say, or if this was real that we saw before our eyes. On the land side there were great cities, and on the lake many more. The lake was crowded with canoes. At intervals along the causeway there were many bridges, and before us was the great city of Mexico. As for us, we were scarcely four hundred strong, and we well remembered the words and warnings of the people of Huexotzinco and Tlascala and Tlamanalco, and the many other warnings we had received to beware of entering the city of Mexico, since they would kill us as soon as they had us inside. Let the interested reader consider whether there is not much to ponder in this narrative of mine. What men in all the world have shown such daring? But let us go on.

We marched along our causeway to a point where another small causeway branches off to another city called Coyoacan, and there, beside some towerlike buildings, which were their shrines, we were met by many more *Caciques* and dignitaries in very rich cloaks. The different chieftains wore different brilliant liveries, and the causeways were full of them. Montezuma had sent these great *Caciques* in advance to receive us, and as soon as they came before Cortes they told him in their language that we were welcome, and as a sign of peace they touched the ground with their hands and kissed it.

There we halted for some time while Cacamatzin, the lord of Texcoco, and the lords of Iztapalapa, Tacuba, and Coyoacan went ahead to meet the great Montezuma, who approached in a rich litter, accompanied by other great lords and feudal *Caciques* who owned vassals. When we came near to Mexico, at a place where there were some other small towers, the great Montezuma descended from his litter, and these other great *Caciques* supported him beneath a marvellously rich canopy of green feathers, decorated with gold work, silver, pearls, and *chalchihuites*, which hung from a sort of border. It was a marvellous sight. The great Montezuma was magnificently clad, in their fashion, and wore sandals of a kind for which their name is *cotaras*,[1] the soles of which are of gold and the upper parts ornamented with precious stones. And the four lords who supported him were richly clad also in garments that seem to have been kept ready for them on the road so that they could accompany their master. For they had not worn clothes like this when they came out to receive us. There were four other great *Caciques* who carried the canopy above their heads, and many more lords who walked before the great Montezuma, sweeping the ground on which he was to tread, and laying down cloaks so that his feet should not touch the earth. Not one of these chieftains dared to look him in the face. All kept their eyes lowered most reverently except those four lords, his nephews, who were supporting him.

When Cortes saw, heard, and was told that the great Montezuma was approaching, he dismounted from his horse, and when he came near to Montezuma each bowed deeply to the other. Montezuma welcomed our Captain, and Cortes, speaking through Doña Marina, answered by wishing him very good health. Cortes, I think, offered Montezuma his right hand, but Montezuma refused it and extended his own. Then Cortes brought out a necklace which he had been holding. It was made of those elaborately worked and coloured glass beads called *margaritas*, of which I have spoken, and was strung on a gold cord and dipped in musk to give it a good odour. This he hung round the great Montezuma's neck, and as he did so attempted

1. Actually a Cuban word; the Mexican word was *cactli*.

to embrace him. But the great princes who stood round Montezuma grasped Cortes' arm to prevent him, for they considered this an indignity.

Then Cortes told Montezuma that it rejoiced his heart to have seen such a great prince, and that he took his coming in person to receive him and the repeated favours he had done him as a high honour. After this Montezuma made him another complimentary speech, and ordered two of his nephews who were supporting him, the lords of Texcoco and Coyoacan, to go with us and show us our quarters. Montezuma returned to the city with the other two kinsmen of his escort, the lords of Cuitlahuac and Tacuba; and all those grand companies of *Caciques* and dignitaries who had come with him returned also in his train. And as they accompanied their lord we observed them marching with their eyes downcast so that they should not see him, and keeping close to the wall as they followed him with great reverence. Thus space was made for us to enter the streets of Mexico without being pressed by the crowd.

Who could now count the multitude of men, women, and boys in the streets, on the roof-tops and in canoes on the waterways, who had come out to see us? It was a wonderful sight and, as I write, it all comes before my eyes as if it had happened only yesterday.

They led us to our quarters, which were in some large houses capable of accommodating us all and had formerly belonged to the great Montezuma's father, who was called Axayacatl. Here Montezuma now kept the great shrines of his gods, and a secret chamber containing gold bars and jewels. This was the treasure he had inherited from his father, which he never touched. Perhaps their reason for lodging us here was that, since they called us *Teules* and considered us as such, they wished to have us near their idols. In any case they took us to this place, where there were many great halls, and a dais hung with the cloth of their country for our Captain, and matting beds with canopies over them for each of us.

On our arrival we entered the large court, where the great Montezuma was awaiting our Captain. Taking him by the hand, the prince led him to his apartment in the hall where he was to

lodge, which was very richly furnished in their manner. Montezuma had ready for him a very rich necklace, made of golden
crabs, a marvellous piece of work, which he hung round Cortes'
neck. His captains were greatly astonished at this sign of honour.

After this ceremony, for which Cortes thanked him through
our interpreters, Montezuma said: 'Malinche, you and your
brothers are in your own house. Rest awhile.' He then returned
to his palace, which was not far off.

We divided our lodgings by companies, and placed our artillery in a convenient spot. Then the order we were to keep was
clearly explained to us, and we were warned to be very much
on the alert, both the horsemen and the rest of us soldiers. We
then ate a sumptuous dinner which they had prepared for us in
their native style.

So, with luck on our side, we boldly entered the city of
Tenochtitlan or Mexico on 8 November in the year of our Lord
1519.

The Stay in Mexico

WHEN the great Montezuma had dined and was told that our Captain and all of us had finished our meal some time ago, he came to our quarters in the grandest state with a great number of princes, all of them his kinsmen. On being told of his approach, Cortes came into the middle of the hall to receive him. Montezuma then took him by the hand, and they brought chairs made in their fashion and very richly decorated in various ways with gold. Montezuma requested our Captain to sit down, and both of them sat, each on his own chair.

Then Montezuma began a very good speech, saying that he was delighted to have such valiant gentlemen as Cortes and the rest of us in his house and his kingdom. That two years ago he had received news of a Captain who had come to Champoton, and that last year also he had received a report of another Captain who had come with four ships. Each time he had wished to see them, and now that he had us with him he was not only at our service but would share all that he possessed with us. He ended by saying that we must truly be the men about whom his ancestors had long ago prophesied, saying that they would come from the direction of the sunrise to rule over these lands, and that he was confirmed in this belief by the valour with which we had fought at Champoton and Tabasco and against the Tlascalans, for lifelike pictures of these battles had been brought to him.

Cortes replied through our interpreters that we did not know how to repay the daily favours we received from him, and that indeed we did come from the direction of the sunrise, and were vassals and servants of a great king called the Emperor Charles, who was ruler over many great princes. Having heard news of Montezuma and what a great prince he was, the Emperor, he said, had sent us to this country to visit him, and to beg them to become Christians, like our Emperor and all of us, so that his soul and those of all his vassals might be saved. Cortes promised to explain to him later how this could be, and how we worship the one true God and who He is, also many other good things which he had already communicated to his ambassadors Tendile, Pitalpitoque, and Quintalbor.

The great Montezuma had some fine gold jewels of various shapes in readiness which he gave to Cortes after this conversation. And to each of our captains he presented small gold objects and three loads of cloaks of rich feather work; and to us soldiers he gave two loads of cloaks each, all with a princely air. For in every way he was like a great prince. After the distribution of presents, he asked Cortes if we were all brothers and vassals of our great Emperor; and Cortes answered that we were brothers in love and friendship, persons of great distinction, and servants of our great king and lord. Further polite speeches passed between Montezuma and Cortes, but as this was the first time he had visited us and we did not want to tire him, the conversation ended.

Montezuma had ordered his stewards to provide us with everything we needed for our way of living: maize, grindstones, women to make our bread, fowls, fruit, and plenty of fodder for the horses. He then took leave of us all with the greatest courtesy, and we accompanied him to the street. However, Cortes ordered us not to go far from our quarters for the present until we knew better what conduct to observe.

Next day Cortes decided to go to Montezuma's palace. But first he sent to know whether the prince was busy and to inform him of our coming. He took four captains with him: Pedro de Alvarado, Juan Velazquez de Leon, Diego de Ordaz, and Gonzalo de Sandoval, and five of us soldiers.

When Montezuma was informed of our coming, he advanced into the middle of the hall to receive us, closely surrounded by his nephews, for no other chiefs were allowed to enter his palace or communicate with him except upon important business. Cortes and Montezuma exchanged bows, and clasped hands. Then Montezuma led Cortes to his own dais, and setting him down on his right, called for more seats, on which he ordered us all to sit also.

Cortes began to make a speech through our interpreters,

saying that we were all now rested, and that in coming to see and speak with such a great prince we had fulfilled the purpose of our voyage and the orders of our lord the King. The principal things he had come to say on behalf of our Lord God had already been communicated to Montezuma through his three ambassadors, on that occasion in the sandhills when he did us the favour of sending us the golden moon and sun. We had then told him that we were Christians and worshipped one God alone, named Jesus Christ, who had suffered His passion and death to save us; and that what they worshipped as gods were not gods but devils, which were evil things, and if they were ugly to look at, their deeds were uglier. But he had proved to them how evil and ineffectual their gods were, as both the prince and his people would observe in the course of time, since, where we had put up crosses such as their ambassadors had seen, they had been too frightened to appear before them.

The favour he now begged of the great Montezuma was that he should listen to the words he now wished to speak. Then he very carefully expounded the creation of the world, how we are all brothers, the children of one mother and father called Adam and Eve; and how such a brother as our great Emperor, grieving for the perdition of so many souls as their idols were leading to hell, where they burnt in living flame, had sent us to tell him this, so that he might put a stop to it, and so that they might give up the worship of idols and make no more human sacrifices – for all men are brothers – and commit no more robbery or sodomy. He also promised that in the course of time the King would send some men who lead holy lives among us, much better than our own, to explain this more fully, for we had only come to give them warning. Therefore he begged Montezuma to do as he was asked.

As Montezuma seemed about to reply, Cortes broke off his speech, saying to those of us who were with him : 'Since this is only the first attempt, we have now done our duty.'

'My lord Malinche,' Montezuma replied, 'these arguments of yours have been familiar to me for some time. I understand what you said to my ambassadors on the sandhills about the three gods and the cross, also what you preached in the various towns through which you passed. We have given you no answer, since we have worshipped our own gods here from the beginning and know them to be good. No doubt yours are good also, but do not trouble to tell us any more about them at present. Regarding the creation of the world, we have held the same belief for many ages, and for this reason are certain that you are those who our ancestors predicted would come from the direction of the sunrise. As for your great King, I am in his debt and will give him of what I possess. For, as I have already said, two years ago I had news of the Captains who came in ships, by the road that you came, and said they were servants of this great king of yours. I should like to know if you are all the same people.'

Cortes answered that we were all brothers and servants of the Emperor, and that they had come to discover a route and explore the seas and ports, so that when they knew them well we could follow, as we had done. Montezuma was referring to the expeditions of Francisco Hernandez de Cordoba and of Grijalva, the first voyages of discovery. He said that ever since that time he had wanted to invite some of these men to visit the cities of his kingdom, where he would receive them and do them honour, and that now his gods had fulfilled his desire, for we were in his house, which we might call our own. Here we might rest and enjoy ourselves, for we should receive good treatment. If on other occasions he had sent to forbid our entrance into his city, it was not of his own free will, but because his vassals were afraid. For they told him we shot out flashes of lightning, and killed many Indians with our horses, and that we were angry *Teules*, and other such childish stories. But now that he had seen us, he knew that we were of flesh and blood and very intelligent, also very brave. Therefore he had a far greater esteem for us than these reports had given him, and would share with us what he had.

We all thanked him heartily for his signal good will, and Montezuma replied with a laugh, because in his princely manner he spoke very gaily: 'Malinche, I know that these people of Tlascala with whom you are so friendly have told you that I am a sort of god or *Teule*, and keep nothing in any of my houses that is not made of silver and gold and precious stones. But I know very well that you are too intelligent to believe this and will take it as a joke. See now, Malinche, my body is made of flesh and blood like yours, and my houses and palaces are of stone, wood, and plaster. It is true that I am a great king, and have inherited the riches of my ancestors, but the lies and non-sense you have heard of us are not true. You must take them as a joke, as I take the story of your thunders and lightnings.'

Cortes answered also with a laugh that enemies always speak evil and tell lies about the people they hate, but he knew he could not hope to find a more magnificent prince in that land, and there was good reason why his fame should have reached our Emperor.

While this conversation was going on, Montezuma quietly sent one of his nephews, a great *Cacique*, to order his stewards to bring certain pieces of gold, which had apparently been set aside as a gift for Cortes, and ten loads of fine cloaks which he divided: the gold and cloaks between Cortes and the four captains, and for each of us soldiers two gold necklaces, each worth ten pesos, and two loads of cloaks. The gold that he then gave us was worth in all more than a thousand pesos, and he gave it all cheerfully, like a great and valiant prince.

As it was now past midday and he did not wish to be importunate, Cortes said to Montezuma: 'My lord, the favours you do us increase, load by load, every day, and it is now the hour of your dinner.' Montezuma answered that he thanked us for visiting him. We then took our leave with the greatest courtesy, and returned to our quarters, talking as we went of the prince's fine breeding and manners and deciding to show him the greatest respect in every way, and to remove our quilted caps in his presence, which we always did.

The great Montezuma was about forty years old, of good height, well proportioned, spare and slight, and not very dark, though of the usual Indian complexion. He did not wear his hair long but just over his ears, and he had a short black beard, well-shaped and thin. His face was rather long and cheerful, he had fine eyes, and in his appearance and manner could express geniality or, when necessary, a serious composure. He was very neat and clean, and took a bath every afternoon. He had many women as his mistresses, the daughters of chieftains, but two legitimate wives who were *Caciques* in their own right, and when he had intercourse with any of them it was so secret that only some of his servants knew of it. He was quite free from sodomy. The clothes he wore one day he did not wear again till three or four days later. He had a guard of two hundred chieftains lodged in rooms beside his own, only some of whom were permitted to speak to him. When they entered his presence they were compelled to take off their rich cloaks and put on others of little value. They had to be clean and walk barefoot, with their eyes downcast, for they were not allowed to look him in the face, and as they approached they had to make three obeisances, saying as they did so, 'Lord, my lord, my great lord!' Then, when they had said what they had come to say, he would dismiss them with a few words. They did not turn their backs on him as they went out, but kept their faces towards him and their eyes downcast, only turning round when they had left the room. Another thing I noticed was that when other great chiefs came from distant lands about disputes or on business, they too had to take off their shoes and put on poor cloaks before entering Montezuma's apartments; and they were not allowed to enter the palace immediately but had to linger for a while near the door, since to enter hurriedly was considered disrespectful.

For each meal his servants prepared him more than thirty dishes cooked in their native style, which they put over small earthenware braziers to prevent them from getting cold. They cooked more than three hundred plates of the food the great Montezuma was going to eat, and more than a thousand more for the guard. I have heard that they used to cook him the flesh of young boys. But as he had such a variety of dishes, made of so many different ingredients, we could not tell whether a dish was of human flesh or anything else, since every day they cooked fowls, turkeys, pheasants, local partridges, quail, tame and wild duck, venison, wild boar, marsh birds, pigeons, hares and rabbits, also many other kinds of birds and beasts native to their country, so numerous that I cannot quickly name them all. I know for certain, however, that after our Captain spoke against the sacrifice of human beings and the eating of their flesh, Montezuma ordered that it should no longer be served to him.

Let us now turn to the way his meals were served, which was like this. If it was cold, they built a large fire of live coals made by burning the bark of a tree which gave off no smoke. The smell of the bark from which they made these coals was very sweet. In order that he should get no more heat than he wanted, they placed a sort of screen in front of it adorned with the figures of idols worked in gold. He would sit on a soft low stool, which was richly worked. His table, which was also low and decorated in the same way, was covered with white tablecloths and rather long napkins of the same material. Then four very clean and beautiful girls brought water for his hands in one of those deep basins that they call *xicales*.[1] They held others like plates beneath it to catch the water, and brought him towels. Two other women brought him maize-cakes.

When he began his meal they placed in front of him a sort of wooden screen, richly decorated with gold, so that no one should see him eat. Then the four women retired, and four great chieftains, all old men, stood beside him. He talked with them every now and then and asked them questions, and as a great favour he would sometimes offer one of them a dish of whatever tasted best. They say that these were his closest relations and advisers and judges of lawsuits, and if he gave them anything to eat they ate it standing, with deep reverence and without looking in his face.

Montezuma's food was served on Cholula ware, some red and some black. While he was dining, the guards in the adjoining rooms did not dare to speak or make a noise above a whisper. His servants brought him some of every kind of fruit that grew in the country, but he ate very little of it. Sometimes they brought him in cups of pure gold a drink made from the cocoa-plant, which they said he took before visiting his wives. We did not take much notice of this at the time, though I saw them bring in a good fifty large jugs of this chocolate, all frothed up, of

1. Gourds.

which he would drink a little. They always served it with great reverence. Sometimes some little humpbacked dwarfs would be present at his meals, whose bodies seemed almost to be broken in the middle. These were his jesters. There were other Indians who told him jokes and must have been his clowns, and others who sang and danced, for Montezuma was very fond of music and entertainment and would reward his entertainers with the leavings of the food and chocolate. The same four women removed the tablecloths and again most reverently brought him water for his hands. Then Montezuma would talk to these four old chieftains about matters that interested him, and they would take their leave with great ceremony. He stayed behind to rest.

As soon as the great Montezuma had dined, all the guards and many more of his household servants ate in their turn. I think more than a thousand plates of food must have been brought in for them, and more than two thousand jugs of chocolate frothed up in the Mexican style, and infinite quantities of fruit, so that with his women and serving-maids and bread-makers and chocolate-makers his expenses must have been considerable.

One thing I had forgotten to say is that two more very handsome women served Montezuma when he was at table with maize-cakes kneaded with eggs and other nourishing ingredients. These maize-cakes were very white, and were brought in on plates covered with clean napkins. They brought him a different kind of bread also, in a long ball kneaded with other kinds of nourishing food, and *pachol* cake, as they call it in that country, which is a kind of wafer. They also placed on the table three tubes, much painted and gilded, in which they put liquidamber[1] mixed with some herbs which are called tobacco. When Montezuma had finished his dinner, and the singing and dancing were over and the cloths had been removed, he would inhale the smoke from one of these tubes. He took very little of it, and then fell asleep.

I remember that at that time his steward was a great *Cacique* whom we nicknamed Tapia, and he kept an account of all the revenue that was brought to Montezuma in his books, which

1. The gum of a native tree.

were made of paper – their name for which is *amal* – and he had a great house full of these books. But they have nothing to do with our story.

Montezuma had two houses stocked with every sort of weapon; many of them were richly adorned with gold and precious stones. There were shields large and small, and a sort of broadsword, and two-handed swords set with flint blades that cut much better than our swords, and lances longer than ours, with five-foot blades consisting of many knives. Even when these are driven at a buckler or a shield they are not deflected. In fact they cut like razors, and the Indians can shave their heads with them. They had very good bows and arrows, and double and single-pointed javelins as well as their throwing-sticks and many slings and round stones shaped by hand, and another sort of shield that can be rolled up when they are not fighting, so that it does not get in the way, but which can be opened when they need it in battle and covers their bodies from head to foot. There was also a great deal of cotton armour richly worked on the outside with different coloured feathers, which they used as devices and distinguishing marks, and they had casques and helmets made of wood and bone which were also highly decorated with feathers on the outside. They had other arms of different kinds which I will not mention through fear of prolixity, and workmen skilled in the manufacture of such things, and stewards who were in charge of these arms.

Let us pass on to the aviary. I cannot possibly enumerate every kind of bird that was in it or describe its characteristics. There was everything from the royal eagle, smaller kinds of eagles, and other large birds, down to multi-coloured little birds, and those from which they take the fine green feathers they use in their feather-work. These last birds are about the size of our magpies, and here they are called *quetzals*. There were other birds too which have feathers of five colours : green, red, white, yellow, and blue, but I do not know what they are called. Then there were parrots with different coloured plumage, so many of them that I have forgotten their names. There were also beautifully marked ducks, and bigger ones like them. At the proper season they plucked the feathers of all these birds, which then grew again. All of them were bred in this aviary, and at hatching time the men and women who looked after them would place them on their eggs and clean their nests and feed them, giving each breed of birds its proper food.

In the aviary there was a large tank of fresh water, and in it was another type of bird on long stilt-like legs with a red body, wings, and tail. I do not know its name, but in Cuba birds rather like them are called *ypiris*. Also in this tank there were many other kinds of water birds.

Let us go on to another large house where they kept many idols whom they called their fierce gods, and with them all kinds of beasts of prey, tigers and two sorts of lion, and beasts rather like wolves which they call *adives*,[1] and foxes and other small animals, all of them carnivores, and most of them bred there. They were fed on deer, fowls, little dogs, and other creatures which they hunt and also on the bodies of the Indians they sacrificed, as I was told.

I have already described the manner of their sacrifices. They strike open the wretched Indian's chest with flint knives and hastily tear out the palpitating heart which, with the blood, they present to the idols in whose name they have performed the sacrifice. Then they cut off the arms, thighs, and head, eating the arms and thighs at their ceremonial banquets. The head they hang up on a beam, and the body of the sacrificed man is not eaten but given to the beasts of prey. They also had many vipers in this accursed house, and poisonous snakes which have something that sounds like a bell in their tails. These, which are the deadliest snakes of all, they kept in jars and great pottery vessels full of feathers, in which they laid their eggs and reared their young. They were fed on the bodies of sacrificed Indians and the flesh of the dogs that they bred. We know for certain, too, that when they drove us out of Mexico and killed over eight hundred and fifty of our soldiers, they fed those beasts and snakes on their bodies for many days, as I shall relate in due course. These snakes and wild beasts were dedicated to their fierce idols, and kept them company. As for the horrible

1. Bernal Díaz is mistaken here. This is an Arabic word for jackal, quite commonly used in Spain.

noise when the lions and tigers roared, and the jackals and foxes howled, and the serpents hissed, it was so appalling that one seemed to be in hell.

I must now speak of the skilled workmen whom Montezuma employed in all the crafts they practised, beginning with the jewellers and workers in silver and gold and various kinds of hollowed objects, which excited the admiration of our great silversmiths at home. Many of the best of them lived in a town called Atzcapotzalco, three miles from Mexico. There were other skilled craftsmen who worked with precious stones and *chalchihuites*, and specialists in feather-work, and very fine painters and carvers. We can form some judgement of what they did then from what we can see of their work today. There are three Indians now living in the city of Mexico, named Marcos de Aquino, Juan de la Cruz, and El Crespillo, who are such magnificent painters and carvers that, had they lived in the age of the Apelles of old, or of Michael Angelo, or Berruguete in our own day, they would be counted in the same rank.

Let us go on to the women, the weavers and sempstresses, who made such a huge quantity of fine robes with very elaborate feather designs. These things were generally brought from some towns in the province of Cotaxtla, which is on the north coast, quite near San Juan de Ulua. In Montezuma's own palaces very fine cloths were woven by those chieftains' daughters whom he kept as mistresses; and the daughters of other dignitaries, who lived in a kind of retirement like nuns in some houses close to the great *cue* of Huichilobos, wore robes entirely of feather-work. Out of devotion for that god and a female deity who was said to preside over marriage, their fathers would place them in religious retirement until they found husbands. They would then take them out to be married.

Now to speak of the great number of performers whom Montezuma kept to entertain him. There were dancers and stilt-walkers, and some who seemed to fly as they leapt through the air, and men rather like clowns to make him laugh. There was a whole quarter full of these people who had no other occupation. He had as many workmen as he needed, too, stonecutters, masons, and carpenters, to keep his houses in repair.

We must not forget the gardens with their many varieties of flowers and sweet-scented trees planted in order, and their ponds and tanks of fresh water into which a stream flowed at one end and out of which it flowed at the other, and the baths he had there, and the variety of small birds that nested in the branches, and the medicinal and useful herbs that grew there. His gardens were a wonderful sight, and required many gardeners to take care of them. Everything was built of stone and plastered; baths and walks and closets and rooms like summerhouses where they danced and sang. There was so much to see in these gardens, as everywhere else, that we could not tire of contemplating his great riches and the large number of skilled Indians employed in the many crafts they practised.

When we had already been in Mexico for four days, and neither our Captain nor anyone else had left our quarters except to visit these houses and gardens, Cortes said it would be a good thing to visit the large square of Tlatelolco and see the great *cue* of Huichilobos. So he sent Aguilar, Doña Marina, and his own young page Orteguilla, who by now knew something of the language, to ask for Montezuma's approval of this plan. On receiving his request, the prince replied that we were welcome to go, but for fear that we might offer some offence to his idols he would himself accompany us with many of his chieftains. Leaving the palace in his fine litter, when he had gone about half way, he dismounted beside some shrines, since he considered it an insult to his gods to visit their dwelling in a litter. Some of the great chieftains then supported him by the arms, and his principal vassals walked before him, carrying two staves, like sceptres raised on high as a sign that the great Montezuma was approaching. When riding in his litter he had carried a rod, partly of gold and partly of wood, held up like a wand of justice. The prince now climbed the steps of the great *cue*, escorted by many *papas*, and began to burn incense and perform other ceremonies for Huichilobos.

Let us leave Montezuma, who had gone ahead as I have said, and return to Cortes and our soldiers. We carried our weapons, as was our custom, both by night and day. Indeed, Montezuma was so used to our visiting him armed that he did not think it strange. I say this because our Captain and those of us who had horses went to Tlatelolco mounted, and the majority of our men were fully equipped. On reaching the market-place, escorted by the many *Caciques* whom Montezuma had assigned to us, we were astounded at the great number of people and the quantities of merchandise, and at the orderliness and good arrangements that prevailed, for we had never seen such a thing before. The chieftains who accompanied us pointed everything out. Every kind of merchandise was kept separate and had its fixed place marked for it.

Let us begin with the dealers in gold, silver, and precious stones, feathers, cloaks, and embroidered goods, and male and female slaves who are also sold there. They bring as many slaves to be sold in that market as the Portuguese bring Negroes from Guinea. Some are brought there attached to long poles by means of collars round their necks to prevent them from escaping, but others are left loose. Next there were those who sold coarser cloth, and cotton goods and fabrics made of twisted thread, and there were chocolate merchants with their chocolate. In this way you could see every kind of merchandise to be found anywhere in New Spain, laid out in the same way as goods are laid out in my own district of Medina del Campo, a centre for fairs, where each line of stalls has its own particular sort. So it was in this great market. There were those who sold sisal cloth and ropes and the sandals they wear on their feet, which are made from the same plant. All these were kept in one part of the market, in the place assigned to them, and in another part were skins of tigers and lions, otters, jackals, and deer, badgers, mountain cats, and other wild animals, some tanned and some untanned, and other classes of merchandise.

There were sellers of kidney-beans and sage and other vegetables and herbs in another place, and in yet another they were selling fowls, and birds with great dewlaps,[1] also rabbits, hares, deer, young ducks, little dogs, and other such creatures. Then there were the fruiterers; and the women who sold cooked food, flour and honey çake, and tripe, had their part of the market. Then came pottery of all kinds, from big water-jars to little

1. Turkeys.

jugs, displayed in its own place, also honey, honey-paste, and other sweets like nougat. Elsewhere they sold timber too, boards, cradles, beams, blocks, and benches, all in a quarter of their own.

Then there were the sellers of pitch-pine for torches, and other things of that kind, and I must also mention, with all apologies, that they sold many canoe-loads of human excrement, which they kept in the creeks near the market. This was for the manufacture of salt and the curing of skins, which they say cannot be done without it. I know that many gentlemen will laugh at this, but I assure them it is true. I may add that on all the roads they have shelters made of reeds or straw or grass so that they can retire when they wish to do so, and purge their bowels unseen by passers-by, and also in order that their excrement shall not be lost.

But why waste so many words on the goods in their great market? If I describe everything in detail I shall never be done. Paper, which in Mexico they call *amal*, and some reeds that smell of liquidamber, and are full of tobacco, and yellow ointments and other such things, are sold in a separate part. Much cochineal is for sale too, under the arcades of that market, and there are many sellers of herbs and other such things. They have a building there also in which three judges sit, and there are officials like constables who examine the merchandise. I am forgetting the sellers of salt and the makers of flint knives, and how they split them off the stone itself, and the fisherwomen and the men who sell small cakes made from a sort of weed which they get out of the great lake, which curdles and forms a kind of bread which tastes rather like cheese. They sell axes too, made of bronze and copper and tin, and gourds and brightly painted wooden jars.

We went on to the great *cue*, and as we approached its wide courts, before leaving the market-place itself, we saw many more merchants who, so I was told, brought gold to sell in grains, just as they extract it from the mines. This gold is placed in the thin quills of the large geese of that country, which are so white as to be transparent. They used to reckon their accounts with one another by the length and thickness of these little quills, how much so many cloaks or so many gourds of chocolate or so many slaves were worth, or anything else they were bartering.

Now let us leave the market, having given it a final glance, and come to the courts and enclosures in which their great *cue* stood. Before reaching it you passed through a series of large courts, bigger I think than the Plaza at Salamanca. These courts were surrounded by a double masonry wall and paved, like the whole place, with very large smooth white flagstones. Where these stones were absent everything was whitened and polished, indeed the whole place was so clean that there was not a straw or a grain of dust to be found there.

When we arrived near the great temple and before we had climbed a single step, the great Montezuma sent six *papas* and two chieftains down from the top, where he was making his sacrifices, to escort our Captain; and as he climbed the steps, of which there were one hundred and fourteen, they tried to take him by the arms to help him up in the same way as they helped Montezuma, thinking he might be tired, but he would not let them near him.

The top of the *cue* formed an open square on which stood something like a platform, and it was here that the great stones stood on which they placed the poor Indians for sacrifice. Here also was a massive image like a dragon, and other hideous figures, and a great deal of blood that had been spilled that day. Emerging in the company of two *papas* from the shrine which houses his accursed images, Montezuma made a deep bow to us all and said : 'My lord Malinche, you must be tired after climbing this great *cue* of ours.' And Cortes replied that none of us was ever exhausted by anything. Then Montezuma took him by the hand, and told him to look at his great city and all the other cities standing in the water, and the many others on the land round the lake; and he said that if Cortes had not had a good view of the great market-place he could see it better from where he now was. So we stood there looking, because that huge accursed *cue* stood so high that it dominated everything. We saw the three causeways that led into Mexico: the causeway of Iztapalapa by which we had entered four days before, and that of Tacuba along which we were afterwards to flee on the night of our great defeat, when the new prince Cuitlahuac drove us out of the city (as I shall tell in due course), and that of Tepeaquilla.[1] We saw the fresh water which came from Chapultepec to supply the city, and the bridges that were constructed at intervals on the causeways so that the water could flow in and out from one part of the lake to another. We saw a great number of canoes, some coming with provisions and others returning with cargo and merchandise; and we saw too that one could not pass from one house to another of that great city and the other cities that were built on the water except over wooden drawbridges or by canoe. We saw *cues* and shrines in these cities that looked like gleaming white towers and castles: a marvellous sight. All the houses had flat roofs, and on the causeways were other small towers and shrines built like fortresses.

Having examined and considered all that we had seen, we turned back to the great market and the swarm of people buying and selling. The mere murmur of their voices talking was loud enough to be heard more than three miles away. Some of our soldiers who had been in many parts of the world, in Constantinople, in Rome, and all over Italy, said that they had never seen a market so well laid out, so large, so orderly, and so full of people.

But to return to our Captain, he observed to Father Bartolome de Olmedo, whom I have often mentioned and who happened to be standing near him: 'It would be a good thing, I think, Father, if we were to sound Montezuma as to whether he would let us build our church here.' Father Bartolome answered that it would be a good thing if it were successful, but he did not think this a proper time to speak of it, for Montezuma did not look as if he would allow such a thing.

Cortes, however, addressed Montezuma through Doña Marina: 'Your lordship is a great prince and worthy of even greater things. We have enjoyed the sight of your cities, and since we are now here in your temple, I beg of you to show us your gods and *Teules*.' Montezuma answered that first he

1. Guadalupe.

235

would consult his chief *papas*; and when he had spoken to them he said that we might enter a small tower, an apartment like a sort of hall, in which there were two altars with very rich wooden carvings over the roof. On each altar was a giant figure, very tall and very fat. They said that the one on the right was Huichilobos, their war-god. He had a very broad face and huge terrible eyes. And there were so many precious stones, so much gold, so many pearls and seed-pearls stuck to him with a paste which the natives made from a sort of root, that his whole body and head were covered with them. He was girdled with huge snakes made of gold and precious stones, and in one hand he held a bow, in the other some arrows. Another smaller idol beside him, which they said was his page, carried a short lance and a very rich shield of gold and precious stones. Around Huichilobos' neck hung some Indian faces and other objects in the shape of hearts, the former made of gold and the latter of silver, with many precious blue stones.

There were some smoking braziers of their incense, which they call copal, in which they were burning the hearts of three Indians whom they had sacrificed that day; and all the walls of that shrine were so splashed and caked with blood that they and the floor too were black. Indeed, the whole place stank abominably. We then looked to the left and saw another great image of the same height as Huichilobos, with a face like a bear and eyes that glittered, being made of their mirror-glass, which they call *tezcat*. Its body, like that of Huichilobos, was encrusted with precious stones, for they said that the two were brothers. This Tezcatlipoca, the god of hell, had charge of the Mexicans' souls, and his body was surrounded by figures of little devils with snakes' tails. The walls of this shrine also were so caked with blood and the floor so bathed in it that the stench was worse than that of any slaughter-house in Spain. They had offered that idol five hearts from the day's sacrifices.

At the very top of the *cue* there was another alcove, the woodwork of which was very finely carved, and here there was another image, half man and half lizard, encrusted with precious stones, with half its body covered in a cloak. They said that the body of this creature contained all the seeds in the world, and that he was the god of seedtime and harvest. I do not remember his name.[1] Here too all was covered with blood, both walls and altar, and the stench was such that we could hardly wait to get out. They kept a very large drum there, and when they beat it the sound was most dismal, like some music from the infernal regions, as you might say, and it could be heard six miles away. This drum was said to be covered with the skins of huge serpents. In that small platform were many more diabolical objects, trumpets great and small, and large knives, and many hearts that had been burnt with incense before their idols; and everything was caked with blood. The stench here too was like a slaughter-house, and we could scarcely stay in the place.

Our Captain said to Montezuma, through our interpreters, with something like a laugh: 'Lord Montezuma, I cannot imagine how a prince as great and wise as your Majesty can have failed to realize that these idols of yours are not gods but evil things, the proper name for which is devils. But so that I may prove this to you, and make it clear to all your *papas*, grant me one favour. Allow us to erect a cross here on the top of this tower, and let us divide off a part of this sanctuary where your Huichilobos and Tezcatlipoca stand, as a place where we can put an image of Our Lady' – which image Montezuma had already seen – 'and then you will see, by the fear that your idols have of her, how grievously they have deceived you.'

Montezuma, however, replied in some temper (and the two *papas* beside him showed real anger): 'Lord Malinche, if I had known that you were going to utter these insults I should not have shown you my gods. We hold them to be very good. They give us health and rain and crops and weather, and all the victories we desire. So we are bound to worship them and sacrifice to them, and I beg you to say nothing more against them.'

On hearing this and seeing Montezuma's fury, our Captain said no more on the subject but observed cheerfully: 'It is time for your Majesty and ourselves to depart.' Montezuma replied that this was so, but that he had to pray and offer certain sacrifices on account of the great *tatacul* – that is to say sin – which he had committed in allowing us to climb his great *cue*

1. This was probably Tlaltecuhtli.

and in being instrumental in letting us see his gods and in the dishonour we had done them by our abuse. Therefore before he left he must pray and worship.

'If that is so, my lord,' Cortes answered, 'I ask your pardon.' And we went down the steps, of which there were a hundred and fourteen, as I said. As some of our soldiers were suffering from pustules or running sores, their thighs pained them as they went down.

I will now give my impression of the *cue*'s surroundings. Do not be surprised, however, if I do not describe them as accurately as I might, for I had other thoughts in my head at the time than that of telling a story. I was more concerned with my military duties and the orders my Captain had given me. But to come to the facts, I think the site of the great *cue* was equal to the plots of six large town houses at home. It tapered from the base to the top of the small tower where they kept their idols. Between the middle of this tall *cue* and its highest point there were five holes like loopholes for cannon, but open and unprotected. But as there are many *cues* painted on the banners of the conquerors, including my own, anyone who has seen them can gather what a *cue* looked like from the outside. I heard a report that, at the time when this great *cue* was built, all the inhabitants of that mighty city placed offerings of gold and silver and pearls and precious stones in the foundations, and bathed them in the blood of prisoners of war whom they had sacrificed. They also put there every kind of seed that grew in their country, so that their idols should give them victories and riches and great crops. Some curious readers may ask how we came to know that they had thrown gold and silver and precious *chalchihuites* and seeds into the foundation of the *cue*, and watered them with the blood of Indian victims, seeing that the building was erected a thousand years ago. My answer is that after we conquered that great and strong city and divided the ground we decided to build a church to our patron and guide St James in place of Huichilobos' *cue*, and a great part of the site was taken for the purpose. When the ground was excavated to lay a foundation, gold and silver and *chalchihuites*, and pearls, seed-pearls, and other precious stones were found in great quantities; and a settler in Mexico who built on another part of the site found the same. The officers of His Majesty's Treasury demanded this find as rightfully belonging to the King, and there was a lawsuit about it. I do not remember what the outcome was, only that they asked for information from the *Caciques* and dignitaries of Mexico, and from Guatemoc who was then alive, and they affirmed that all the inhabitants of Mexico had thrown jewels and other things into the foundations, as was recorded in their pictures and records of ancient times. The treasure was therefore preserved for the building of St James's church.

Let me go on to describe the great and splendid courts in front of Huichilobos, on the site where that church now stands, which was called at that time Tlatelolco. I have already said that there were two masonry walls before the entrance to the *cue*, and the court was paved with white stones like flagstones, and all was whitened, burnished and clean. A little apart from the *cue* stood another small tower which was also an idol-house or true hell, for one of its doors was in the shape of a terrible mouth, such as they paint to depict the jaws of hell. This mouth was open and contained great fangs to devour souls. Beside this door were groups of devils and the shapes of serpents, and a little way off was a place of sacrifice, all blood-stained and black with smoke. There were many great pots and jars and pitchers in this house, full of water. For it was here that they cooked the flesh of the wretched Indians who were sacrificed and eaten by the *papas*. Near this place of sacrifice there were many large knives and chopping-blocks like those on which men cut up meat in slaughter-houses; and behind that dreadful house, some distance away, were great piles of brushwood, beside which was a tank of water that was filled and emptied through a pipe from the covered channel that comes into the city from Chapultepec. I always called that building Hell.

Crossing the court you came to another *cue*, where the great Mexican princes were buried. This also contained many idols and was full of blood and smoke. It too had doorways with hellish figures; and beside it was another *cue*, full of skulls and large bones arranged in an orderly pattern, and so numerous that you could not count them however long you looked. The skulls were in one place and the bones in separate piles. Here there were more idols, and in every building or *cue* or shrine were *papas* in long black cloth robes and long hoods.

To proceed, there were other *cues*, a short distance away from that of the skulls, which contained other idols and sacrificial altars decorated with horrible paintings. These idols were said to preside over the marriages of men. But I will waste no more time on the subject of idols. I will only say that all round that great court there were many low houses, used and occupied by the *papas* and other Indians who were in charge of them. On one side of the great *cue* there was another, much bigger pond or tank of very clean water which was solely devoted to the service of Huichilobos and Tezcatlipoca, and the water for this tank was also supplied by covered pipes that came from Chapultepec. Near by were the large buildings of a kind of nunnery where many of the daughters of the inhabitants of Mexico dwelt in retirement until the time of their marriage. Here there were two massive female idols who presided over the marriages of women, and to which they offered sacrifices and feasts in order that they should get good husbands.

I have spent a long time talking about the great *cue* of Tlatelolco and its courts. I will conclude by saying that it was the biggest temple in Mexico, though there were many other fine ones, for every four or five parishes or districts supported a shrine with idols; and since there were many districts I cannot keep a count of them all. I must say, however, that the great *cue* in Cholula was higher than that in Mexico, for it had a hundred and twenty steps. The idol at Cholula, as I heard, had a great reputation, and people made pilgrimages to it from all over New Spain to obtain pardons. This was the reason why they had built it such a magnificent *cue*. It was differently planned from that of Mexico, but also had great courts and a double wall. The *cue* of the city of Texcoco was very high too, having a hundred and seventeen steps, and fine wide courtyards, again of a different shape from the others. Absurd though it was, every province had its own idols, and those of one province or city were of no help in another. Therefore they had infinite numbers of idols and sacrificed to them all.

When we were all tired of walking about and seeing such a diversity of idols and sacrifices, we returned to our quarters, still accompanied by the many *Caciques* and dignitaries whom Montezuma had sent with us.

When our Captain and the Mercedarian friar realized that Montezuma would not allow us to set up a cross at Huichilobos' *cue* or build a church there, it was decided that we should ask his stewards for masons so that we could put up a church in our own quarters. For every time we had said mass since entering the city of Mexico we had had to erect an altar on tables and dismantle it again.

The stewards promised to tell Montezuma of our wishes, and Cortes also sent our interpreters to ask him in person. Montezuma granted our request and ordered that we should be supplied with all the necessary material. We had our church finished in two days, and a cross erected in front of our lodgings, and mass was said there each day until the wine gave out. For as Cortes and some other captains and a friar had been ill during the Tlascalan campaign, there had been a run on the wine that we kept for mass. Still, though it was finished, we still went to church every day and prayed on our knees before the altar and images, firstly because it was our obligation as Christians and a good habit, and secondly so that Montezuma and all his captains should observe us and, seeing us worshipping on our knees before the cross – especially when we intoned the Ave Maria – might be inclined to imitate us.

It being our habit to examine and inquire into everything, when we were all assembled in our lodging and considering which was the best place for an altar, two of our men, one of whom was the carpenter Alonso Yañez, called attention to some marks on one of the walls which showed that there had once been a door, though it had been well plastered up and painted. Now as we had heard that Montezuma kept his father's treasure in this building, we immediately suspected that it must be in this room, which had been closed up only a few days before. Yañez made the suggestion to Juan Velazquez de Leon and

Francisco de Lugo, both relatives of mine, to whom he had attached himself as a servant; and they mentioned the matter to Cortes. So the door was secretly opened, and Cortes went in first with certain captains. When they saw the quantity of golden objects – jewels and plates and ingots – which lay in that chamber they were quite transported. They did not know what to think of such riches. The news soon spread to the other captains and soldiers, and very secretly we all went in to see. The sight of all that wealth dumbfounded me. Being only a youth at the time and never having seen such riches before, I felt certain that there could not be a store like it in the whole world. We unanimously decided that we could not think of touching a particle of it, and that the stones should immediately be replaced in the doorway, which should be blocked again and cemented just as we had found it. We resolved also that not a word should be said about this until times changed, for fear Montezuma might hear of our discovery.

Let us leave this subject of the treasure and tell how four of our most valiant captains took Cortes aside in the church, with a dozen soldiers who were in his trust and confidence, myself among them, and asked him to consider the net or trap in which we were caught, to look at the great strength of the city and observe the causeways and bridges, and remember the warnings we had received in every town we had passed through that Huichilobos had counselled Montezuma to let us into the city and kill us there. We reminded him that the hearts of men are very fickle, especially among the Indians, and begged him not to trust the good will and affection that Montezuma was showing us, because from one hour to another it might change. If he should take it into his head to attack us, we said, the stoppage of our supplies of food and water, or the raising of any of the bridges, would render us helpless. Then, considering the vast army of warriors he possessed, we should be incapable of attacking or defending ourselves. And since all the houses stood in the water, how could our Tlascalan allies come in to help us? We asked him to think over all that we had said, for if we wanted to preserve our lives we must seize Montezuma immediately, without even a day's delay. We pointed out that all the gold Montezuma had given us, and all that we had seen in the treasury of his father Axayacatl, and all the food we ate was turning to poison in our bodies, for we could not sleep by night or day or take any rest while these thoughts were in our minds. If any of our soldiers gave him less drastic advice, we concluded, they would be senseless beasts charmed by the gold and incapable of looking death in the eye.

When he had heard our opinion, Cortes answered: 'Do not imagine, gentlemen, that I am asleep or that I do not share your anxiety. You must have seen that I do. But what strength have we got for so bold a course as to take this great lord in his own palace, surrounded as he is by warriors and guards? What scheme or trick can we devise to prevent him from summoning his soldiers to attack us at once?'

Our captains (Juan Velazquez de Leon, Diego de Ordaz, Gonzalo de Sandoval, and Pedro de Alvarado) replied that Montezuma must be got out of his palace by smooth words and brought to our quarters. Once there, he must be told that he must remain as a prisoner, and that if he called out or made any disturbance he would pay for it with his life. If Cortes was unwilling to take this course at once, they begged him for permission to do it themselves. With two very dangerous alternatives before us, the better and more profitable thing, they said, would be to seize Montezuma rather than wait for him to attack us. Once he did so, what chance would we have? Some of us soldiers also remarked that Montezuma's stewards who brought us our food seemed to be growing insolent, and did not serve us as politely as they had at first. Two of our Tlascalan allies had, moreover, secretly observed to Jeronimo de Aguilar that for the last two days the Mexicans had appeared less well disposed to us. We spent a good hour discussing whether or not to take Montezuma prisoner, and how it should be done. But our final advice, that at all costs we should take him prisoner, was approved by our Captain, and we then left the matter till next day. All night we prayed God to direct events in the interests of His holy service.

Next morning two Tlascalan Indians arrived very secretly with letters from Villa Rica containing the news of an attack by the Mexicans at a place called Almeria, in which one of our men and the Constable's horse had been killed, as well as many Totonacs. Moreover the Constable Escalante himself and six more men had died of their wounds after returning to Villa Rica. Now all the hill towns and Cempoala and its dependencies were in revolt. They refused to bring food or serve in the fort; whereas hitherto our men had been respected as *Teules*, now after this disaster Mexicans and Totonacs alike were behaving like wild beasts. They could not control the Indians in any way, and did not know what measures to take.

God knows the distress this news caused us. It was the first defeat we had suffered in New Spain, and misfortunes, as the reader will see, were now descending upon us.

Montezuma's Captivity

HAVING decided on the previous day that we would seize Montezuma, we prayed to God all night that His service would profit by the turn of events, and next morning we decided on our course of action.

Cortes took with him five captains, Pedro de Alvarado, Gonzalo de Sandoval, Juan Velazquez de Leon, Francisco de Lugo, Alonso de Avila, and myself, together with Doña Marina and Aguilar. He warned us all to keep very alert, and the horsemen to have their mounts saddled and bridled. I need not say that we were armed, since we went about armed by day and night, with our sandals always on our feet – for at that time we always wore sandals – and Montezuma was used to seeing us like this whenever we went to speak with him. He was neither surprised nor alarmed, therefore, when Cortes and the captains who had come to seize him approached him fully armed.

When we were all prepared, our captains sent to inform the prince that we were coming to his palace. This had always been our practice, and we did not wish to frighten him by making a sudden appearance. Montezuma guessed that the reason for Cortes' visit was his indignation about the attack on Escalante. But although apprehensive, he sent him a message of welcome.

On entering, Cortes made his usual salutations, and said to Montezuma through our interpreters: 'Lord Montezuma, I am greatly astonished that you, a valiant prince who have declared yourself our friend, should have ordered your captains stationed on the coast near Tuxpan to take up arms against my Spaniards. I am astonished also at their boldness in robbing towns which are in the keeping and under the protection of our King and master, and demanding of them Indian men and women for sacrifice, also that they should have killed a Spaniard, who was my brother, and a horse.'

Cortes did not wish to mention Escalante and the six soldiers who had died on reaching Villa Rica, since Montezuma did not know of their deaths, nor did the Indian captains who had attacked them. Therefore he continued: 'Being so much your friend, I ordered my captains to help and serve you in every possible way. But Your Majesty has acted in quite the opposite fashion towards us. In the affray at Cholula your captains and a host of your warriors received your express commands to kill us. Because of my great affection for you I overlooked this at the time. But now your captains and vassals have once more lost all shame and are secretly debating whether you do not again wish to have us killed. I have no desire to start a war on this account, or to destroy this city. Everything will be forgiven, provided you will now come quietly with us to our quarters, and make no protest. You will be as well served and attended there as in your own palace. But if you cry out, or raise any commotion, you will immediately be killed by these captains of mine, whom I have brought for this sole purpose.'

This speech dumbfounded Montezuma. In reply he said that he had never ordered his people to take up arms against us, and that he would at once send to summon his captains so that the truth should be known and they be punished. Thereupon he immediately took the sign and seal of Huichilobos from his wrist, which he never did except when giving some order of the first importance that had to be carried out at once. As to being made a prisoner and leaving his palace against his will, he said that he was not a person to whom such orders could be given, and that it was not his wish to go. Cortes answered him with excellent arguments, which Montezuma countered with even better, to the effect that he refused to leave his palace. More than half an hour passed in these discussions. But when Juan Velazquez de Leon and the other captains saw that time was being wasted, they became impatient to remove Montezuma from his palace and make him a prisoner. Turning to Cortes, Velazquez observed somewhat angrily: 'What is the use of all these words? Either we take him or we knife him. If we do not look after ourselves now we shall be dead men.'

Juan Velazquez spoke in his usual high and terrifying voice;

and Montezuma, realizing that our captains were angry, asked Doña Marina what they were saying so loudly, and she, being very quickwitted, replied: 'Lord Montezuma, I advise you to accompany them immediately to their quarters and make no protest. I know they will treat you very honourably as the great prince you are. But if you stay here, you will be a dead man. In their quarters the truth will be discovered.'

Then Montezuma said to Cortes: 'Lord Malinche, I see what is in your mind. But I have a son and two legitimate daughters. Take them as hostages and spare me this disgrace. What will my chieftains say if they see me carried off a prisoner?'

Cortes replied that there was no alternative, he must come with us himself; and after a good deal of argument Montezuma agreed to go. Then Cortes and our captains addressed him most ingratiatingly, saying that they begged him humbly not to be angry, and to tell his captains and his guard that he was going of his own free will, since on consulting his idol Huichilobos and the *papas* who served him he had learnt that for the sake of his health and the safety of his life he must stay with us. Then his fine litter was brought, in which he used to go out attended by all his captains, and he was taken to our quarters, where guards and a watch were put over him.

Cortes and the rest of us did our best to provide him with all possible attentions and amusements, and he was put under no restraint. Soon his nephews and all the principal Mexican chieftains visited him to inquire the reasons for his imprisonment, and to ask whether he wished them to make war on us. Montezuma replied that he was spending some days with us of his own free will and under no constraint, that he was happy and would tell them when he wanted anything of them. He told them not to disturb either themselves or the city, and not to be distressed, since his visit was agreeable to Huichilobos, as he had learnt from certain *papas* who had consulted that idol.

This is the way in which the great Montezuma was made prisoner; and there in his lodging he had his servants, his women, and the baths in which he bathed; and twenty good lords, captains, and counsellers remained continuously with him as before. He showed no resentment at being detained.

Ambassadors from distant lands came to him where he was, bringing their suits or tribute, and important business was conducted there.

I remember that when important *Caciques* came from far away to discuss boundaries or the ownership of towns or other such business, however great they might be, they would take off their rich robes and put on poor ones of sisal cloth. They had to appear before him barefoot, and on entering his apartments did not pass straight in but up one side. When a *Cacique* came before the great Montezuma he gazed on the ground; and before approaching him he made three bows, saying as he did so: 'Lord, my lord, my great lord!' Then he presented a drawing or painting upon sisal cloth, representing the suit or question upon which he had come, and pointed out the grounds for his claim with a thin polished stick. Beside Montezuma stood two old men, who were great *Caciques*; and when they thoroughly understood the pleadings, these judges told Montezuma the rights of the case, which he then settled in a few words, by which the ownership of the land or villages in question was decided. Thereupon the litigants said no more, but retired without turning their backs, and after making the customary three bows went out into the hall. On leaving Montezuma's presence, they put on other rich robes, and took a walk through the city of Mexico.

Leaving the subject of Montezuma's imprisonment, I will now tell how the messengers whom he sent with his sign and seal to summon the captains who had killed our soldiers brought them before him as prisoners. What he said to them I do not know, but he sent them to Cortes for judgement. Montezuma was not present when their confession was taken, in which they admitted the facts and agreed that their prince had ordered them to wage war, to recover tribute and, should any *Teules* take part in the defence of the towns, to fight and kill them.

When Cortes was shown this confession, he sent to inform Montezuma that he was deeply implicated, and the prince made such excuses as he could. Cortes answered that he himself believed the confession and that, since our King's ordinances prescribed that anyone causing others to be killed, whether they were guilty or innocent, should himself die, Montezuma deserved punishment. But such, he protested, was his affection and concern for Montezuma, that, even if he were guilty, he would rather pay with his own life than allow the prince to forfeit his. Montezuma was alarmed by this message; and without further discussion Cortes sentenced the captains to be burned to death before the royal palace. This sentence was immediately carried out and, to prevent any interference, Cortes had Montezuma put in chains while they were being burned. The prince roared with anger at this indignity, and became even more alarmed than before. After the burning, Cortes went to Montezuma's apartment with five of his captains, and himself removed the chains; and so affectionately did he speak to the prince that his anger soon passed away. For Cortes told him that he looked on him as more than a brother and that though Montezuma was lord and master of so many towns and provinces, yet he, Cortes, would in time, if it were possible, give him domination over even more lands, which he had not been able to conquer and which did not obey him. He said that if Montezuma now wished to go to his palace he would allow him to do so. This he said through our interpreters, and while he was speaking the tears were seen to spring to Montezuma's eyes. The prince replied most courteously that he was grateful for this kindness. But he well knew that Cortes' speech was mere words, and that for the present it would be better for him to remain a prisoner. For his chieftains being numerous, and his nephews and relations coming every day to suggest they should attack us and set him free, there was a danger that once they found him at liberty they would force him to fight us. He did not want to see a rebellion in his city, he said, and feared that if he did not give in to their wishes they might try to set up another prince in his place. So he had put these thoughts out of their heads, he concluded, by informing them that his god Huichilobos had told him he must remain a prisoner. From what we understood, however, there seemed little doubt that Aguilar had said to Montezuma privately, on Cortes' instructions, that though Malinche might order his release the rest of us captains and soldiers would never agree to it.

On hearing this reply, Cortes threw his arms round the prince and embraced him, saying: 'How right I am, Lord Montezuma, to love you as dearly as I love myself!' Then Montezuma asked Cortes that the page called Orteguilla, who already knew the language, might attend him, and this was of great benefit both to him and to us. For from this page, of whom he asked many questions, Montezuma learnt a great deal about Spain, and we learnt what his captains said to him. So useful was Orteguilla to the prince that he became very fond of him.

Montezuma was quite delighted by the great flattery and attention he received and the conversations he had with us all. Whenever we came into his presence, all of us – even Cortes himself – would take off our mailed caps or helmets – for we always went armed – and he treated us with great civility and honour.

Now when the news of the captains' execution spread through the provinces of New Spain, there was great fear; and the towns on the coast, where our soldiers had been killed, resumed the services they had previously rendered to the settlers who remained at Villa Rica.

Those readers who are interested by this history must wonder at the great deeds we did in those days: first in destroying our ships; then in daring to enter that strong city despite many warnings that they would kill us once they had us inside; then in having the temerity to seize the great Montezuma, king of that country, in his own city and inside his very palace, and to throw him in chains while the execution was carried out. Now that I am old, I often pause to consider the heroic actions of that time. I seem to see them present before my eyes; and I believe that we performed them not of our own volition but by the guidance of God. For what soldiers in the world, numbering only four hundred – and we were even fewer – would have dared to enter a city as strong as Mexico, which is larger than Venice and more than four thousand five hundred miles away from our own Castile and, having seized so great a prince, execute his captains before his eyes? There is much here to ponder on, and not in the matter-of-fact way in which I presented it. But I will go on to tell how Cortes sent another captain to be stationed at Villa Rica in place of Juan de Escalante, who had been killed.

After justice had been done on Quetzalpopoca and his captains, and the great Montezuma had been tamed, our Captain decided to send, as his lieutenant at Villa Rica, a soldier named Alonso de Grado, a very intelligent man of good speech and presence, a musician and a great writer. This Alonso de Grado was one of those who had been in constant opposition to Cortes about the march to Mexico. At the time of the Tlascala affair, when factions had gathered in opposition, Alonso de Grado had been the chief agitator. If his prowess as a soldier had been as remarkable as his good manners, he would have been a great help to our enterprise. I mention his manners because of Cortes' remarks to him when offering him the appointment. Knowing that he was not a man to take offence, he said to him jokingly: 'Here, Señor Alonso de Grado, you have your wish fulfilled. Now you are going to Villa Rica as you wanted to, and you will take charge of the fortress. See that you don't go out on expeditions and get yourself killed, as Juan de Escalante did.' And as he was speaking Cortes winked at those of us who were standing near, and we well understood the reason for his remarks. For everyone knew that Alonso de Grado would never go on such an expedition even if he were threatened with penalties for refusing.

[Alonso de Grado played the great man at Villa Rica, collecting jewels and pretty women, and neglecting the fortress. He also began to plot an intervention by Diego Velazquez. Cortes therefore sent Gonzalo de Sandoval to relieve him, and brought him back as a prisoner. But after two days' confinement in some newly constructed stocks, 'the wood of which smelt of onions and garlic', Alonso made his peace with Cortes and afterwards received civilian employment as auditor. Bernal Díaz concludes this chapter on political intrigue with a note on some instructions given to Sandoval when he departed for Villa Rica.

When Cortes sent Gonzalo de Sandoval to Villa Rica, as his lieutenant and as captain and chief constable, he ordered him immediately on arrival to send two blacksmiths with all their equipment of bellows and tools and plenty of iron from the ships we had destroyed, also two iron chains [forged on instructions sent with Alonso de Grado] which were already made. He instructed his lieutenant to send also sails and tackle and pitch and tow and a mariner's compass, and everything else that was needed for the construction of two sloops to sail on the lake of Mexico. Sandoval sent all these things at once exactly as he had been told.

Our Captain was very thorough in every way. Fearing that Montezuma might be depressed by his imprisonment, he endeavoured every day after prayers – for we had no wine for mass – to go to pay him court in his captivity. He went accompanied by four captains, and usually Pedro de Alvarado, Juan Velazquez de Leon, and Diego de Ordaz were of that number. They would ask Montezuma most deferentially how he was, and request him to issue his orders, which would be carried out, and beg him not to be distressed by his imprisonment. He would reply that, on the contrary, he was glad to be a prisoner, since either our gods gave us power to confine him or Huichilobos permitted it. In one conversation after another they offered him a fuller explanation of the tenets of our holy faith and of the great power of our lord the Emperor.

Then sometimes Montezuma would play Cortes at *totoloque*, a game played with small, very smooth gold pellets specially made for it. They would throw these pellets a considerable distance, and some little slabs as well which were also of gold, and in five throws they either gained or lost certain pieces of gold or rich jewels that they had staked. I remember that Pedro de Alvarado was once keeping the score for Cortes, and one of Montezuma's nephews, a great chief, was doing the same for Montezuma; and Pedro de Alvarado was always marking one point more than Cortes gained. Montezuma saw this and observed with a courteous smile that he did not like Tonatio – which was their name for Pedro de Alvarado – marking for Cortes, because he made too much *ixoxol* in the score, which means in their language that he cheated by always adding an extra point. We who were on guard at the time could not help laughing at Montezuma's remark, nor could Cortes himself. You may ask why the remark amused us. It was because Pedro de

Alvarado, though handsome and good-mannered, had the bad habit of talking too much. Knowing his character so well we were overcome by laughter. But to return to the game. If Cortes won he gave the jewels to those nephews and favourites of Montezuma who attended him, and if Montezuma won he divided them among us soldiers of the guard. In addition to what we gained from the game, he unfailingly gave presents of gold and cloth every day to us and the captain on guard, at that time Juan Velazquez de Leon, who in every way showed himself Montezuma's true friend and servant.

I also remember that there was once on guard a certain Trujillo, a very tall and strong man of excellent health. He was a sailor, and when it was his turn for the night watch he was so inconsiderate – I apologize for mentioning it – as to commit a nuisance within Montezuma's hearing. As the valiant king of that country, Montezuma considered it both insulting and ill-mannered that this guard should do such a thing within his hearing and without consideration for his person. He asked the page Orteguilla who this dirty and ill-bred person was; and Orteguilla replied that he was a man used to travelling on the seas, with no knowledge of politeness or good breeding. He also told him something about the quality of each of us soldiers there, who was a gentleman and who was not. He was always telling Montezuma things that he wanted to know.

To return to the soldier Trujillo, as soon as it was day Montezuma sent for him and asked him why he was so ill-bred that he had no consideration for his presence and paid him no proper respect. He begged him never to do such a thing again, and then ordered him to be given a gold jewel worth five pesos. Trujillo took no notice of what he said, but next night deliberately did the same thing, believing that Montezuma would give him another present. But Montezuma reported the matter to Juan Velazquez, the captain of the guard, and the captain ordered that Trujillo should never again be put on guard and should be severely reprimanded.

There was another soldier called Pedro Lopez, a great cross-bowman, who was put on guard over Montezuma. He was a decent man, though difficult to understand, and in the night he had some words with the officer of the watch about whether it was time to go on duty. 'To hell with this dog!' he shouted. 'I'm sick to death of always guarding him!' Montezuma overheard this and brooded on it; and when Cortes came to visit him he told him about it. Cortes was so furious that, good soldier though Lopez was, he ordered him to be flogged in our quarters; and after that all soldiers of the guard performed their watch silently and with good manners. However, it was not necessary to instruct most of us who did guard duty about the civility that was due to this great chief. He knew us all, and our names and characters too. Indeed he was so kind that he gave us all jewels and to some of us he gave cloaks and beautiful girls. I was a young man in those days and I used to doff my helmet very respectfully every time I went on guard or entered his presence; and the page Orteguilla had told him that I had been on two voyages of discovery in New Spain before coming with Cortes. I talked to Orteguilla and asked him to beg Montezuma kindly to give me a very pretty Indian girl. When Montezuma received this message, he sent for me and said: 'Bernal Díaz del Castillo, they say that you are short of clothes and gold. But today I will tell them to give you a fine girl. Treat her well, for she is the daughter of an important man, and they will give you gold and cloaks as well.' I answered him most deferentially that I kissed his hands for the favour, and hoped that our lord God might prosper him.

Montezuma seems to have asked the page what I answered and, when Orteguilla told him, I believe he replied: 'Bernal Díaz seems to me to be a gentleman' – for he knew all our names, as I have said. He told them to give me three small slabs of gold and two loads of cloaks. We had discovered that from among the ladies he kept as his mistresses he would marry some to his captains or intimate favourites, or even give some to us soldiers. The girl whom he gave to me was one of these, and her bearing showed her distinction. We gave her the name of Doña Francisca.

When all the material for the two sloops had arrived, Cortes at once sent to inform Montezuma that he wanted to build two little boats in which we could take pleasure trips on the lake.

He asked him to send his carpenters to cut the wood and work with our master boat-builders, Martin Lopez and Andres Nuñez. And as there was oak about twelve miles away, the wood was quickly brought and the shapes constructed. As there were many Indian carpenters the boats were soon built and caulked and tarred, and their rigging was set up and their sails cut to the right shape and measurement, and an awning was provided for each one. They turned out as good and fast as if a month had been spent in making the shapes. For Martin Lopez was a very fine craftsman, and it was he who afterwards built the thirteen sloops that helped in the capture of Mexico, as I shall relate in due course. He was also a good soldier in battle.

Let us now go on to say that Montezuma told Cortes he wished to go to visit his temple, and make sacrifices, and pay the necessary devotion to his gods. He said that this must be done so that his captains and chiefs might observe it, especially certain nephews of his who came every day to tell him that they wished to free him and make war on us. He answered them that he was glad to stay with us, in the hopes of convincing them that what he had said before was true and his god Huichilobos had really commanded him to stay.

Cortes replied that, as for this request, he must take care not to do anything that would cost him his life. To prevent any disorders, or any commands to his captains or *papas* to release him to make war on us, he would send captains and soldiers with him who would immediately stab him to death if they detected any change in his bearing. Cortes said that Montezuma was welcome to go, but must not sacrifice any human beings, for this was a great sin against the true God, about whom we had preached to him, and that here were our altars and the image of Our Lady before which he could pray. Montezuma said that he would not sacrifice a single human being, and went off in his grand litter, in his usual great state, accompanied by his *Caciques*. They carried his insignia in front of him, a sort of staff or rod which denoted that his royal person was going that way, and the custom is still followed today by the viceroys of New Spain. With him as guard went four of our captains, Juan Velazquez de Leon, Pedro de Alvarado, Alonso de Avila, and Francisco de Lugo, with a hundred and fifty soldiers; and the Mercedarian friar also went with us to stop any attempt at human sacrifice. So we went to the *cue* of Huichilobos; and as we approached that accursed temple, Montezuma ordered them to lift him from his litter. He was then supported on the arms of his nephews and other *Caciques* up to the *cue* itself. As I have already stated, all the chiefs had to keep their eyes downcast while he passed through the streets, and could never look him in the face. When we reached the foot of the steps that lead to the shrine, there were many *papas* waiting to support him as he climbed.

Four Indians had already been sacrificed there the night before and, despite our Captain's protest and the discussions of the Mercedarian friar, Montezuma insisted on killing some more men and boys for his own sacrifice. We could do nothing at the time except pretend to overlook it, for Mexico and the other great cities were on the point of rebelling under Montezuma's nephews, as I shall in due course relate. When Montezuma had completed his sacrifices, which he did very quickly, we returned with him to our quarters. He was very cheerful and gave presents of jewels to us soldiers who had escorted him.

As soon as the two sloops were built and launched, and their masts and rigging set up and adorned with the royal and imperial banners, and when sailors had been chosen to navigate them, our men went out rowing and sailing in them, and found that they sailed very well. When Montezuma heard about this, he told Cortes he would like to go hunting on a rocky island in the lake, which was reserved for him, not even the greatest chieftains daring to hunt there, on pain of death. Cortes answered that he was very welcome to go, but that he must remember what had been said to him before, when he went to visit his idols, that if he raised any disturbance it would cost him his life. Moreover he could go in one of our sloops, for they sailed better than even the biggest of his canoes or pirogues.

Montezuma was delighted to sail in the faster of the two sloops, and took many lords and chieftains with him. The other sloop was filled with *Caciques* also, including one of Montezuma's sons, and the huntsmen were instructed to follow in canoes and *pirogues*. Cortes commanded Juan Velazquez de Leon, the captain of the guard, and Pedro de Alvarado, Cristobal de Olid, and Alonso de Avila, with two hundred soldiers, to accompany Montezuma and to be very vigilant in their duty of watching him. All these captains, being most scrupulous men, took the soldiers aboard, also four brass cannon with all the powder we possessed, and our two gunners, Mesa and Arbenga; and because of the weather they put up a highly decorated awning, under which Montezuma and his chieftains sat. As at that season there was a very strong breeze, and the sailors not only enjoyed working the sails, but were delighted to give Montezuma pleasure, the sloop went scudding along, leaving the canoes that contained his huntsmen and chieftains far behind, despite their large number of oarsmen. Montezuma was charmed and said it was a great art to combine sails and oars together. So he arrived at the island, which was not very far off, and after killing all the game he wanted, deer, hares, and rabbits, returned very contented to the city.

As we approached Mexico, Pedro de Alvarado and Juan Velazquez de Leon and the other captains ordered the cannon to be fired, and this too delighted Montezuma. Finding him so frank and pleasant, we treated him with the respect habitually paid to kings in those parts, and he treated us in the same way.

Meanwhile, however, the nephews and kindred of the great Montezuma agreed with other *Caciques* throughout the country that we should be attacked and Montezuma released, and that some of them should proclaim themselves kings of Mexico.

When Cacamatzin, lord of the largest and most important city in New Spain except Mexico, heard that his uncle Montezuma had been imprisoned for some days and that we were taking control in every way we could, and when he got news also that we had opened the chamber where the great treasure of his grandfather Axayacatl was kept, but had so far left it untouched, he decided that before we actually took possession of it something must be done. He called together all the lords of Texcoco, who were his vassals, and the lord of Coyoacan, who was his cousin and Montezuma's nephew, and the lord of

Tacuba, and the lord of Iztapalapa, and another great chief who was lord of Matalcingo, a very close relative of Montezuma of whom it was even said that he was the rightful heir to the Caciqueship and kingdom of Mexico. He was a chieftain well known among the Indians for his personal bravery.

While Cacamatzin was arranging with them and other Mexican chieftains that on a given day they should come with all their forces and attack us, it appears that this chief, who was noted for his personal bravery but whose name I cannot remember, said that if Cacamatzin would assure him the kingdom of Mexico, which was rightfully his, he and all his relations, and the chiefs of the province of Matalcingo would be the first to take up arms and either expel us from Mexico or kill us to the last man. Cacamatzin appears, however, to have said that the Caciqueship of Mexico rightfully belonged to him, and that he himself must be king, since he was the nephew of Montezuma, also that if the lord of Matalcingo did not wish to take part he would attack us without him and his people. For Cacamatzin had already won over all the other towns and chiefs I have named, and had arranged the day on which they were to come to Mexico, where they would be admitted by the chieftains of his faction inside the city.

While these negotiations were going on Montezuma learnt all about them from his great relative who was refusing to give in to Cacamatzin's wishes. And to get further information, he sent for all the *Caciques* and chieftains of Texcoco, who told him how Cacamatzin was trying to persuade them all with promises and gifts to help him fight us and release his uncle. As Montezuma was cautious and did not want to see his city rise in armed insurrection, he told Cortes everything that was happening. We and our Captain already knew something about this unrest, but not so much as Montezuma now told us. The advice that Cortes gave him was to give us his Mexican soldiers, and we would then fall on Texcoco and take or destroy both the city and its surroundings. This plan, however, did not suit Montezuma. Cortes then sent a message to Cacamatzin that he must cease his war preparations, which would lead him to destruction, and offered him his friendship, saying that he would do all he could for him and paying him many other compliments.

Now Cacamatzin was a young man and found many others who shared his viewpoint and were eager for war. So he sent Cortes a message, that he understood his flatteries and wished to hear no more from him until they came face to face, when Cortes could say whatever he liked. Cortes then sent Cacamatzin a second message, warning him not to do a disservice to our lord and King, for he would pay for it in person and it would cost him his life. But Cacamatzin replied that he knew no king and wished he had never known Cortes, who by fair words had imprisoned his uncle.

On receiving this answer Cortes implored Montezuma, as he was a great prince, to arrange with the people of Texcoco for Cacamatzin's arrest. For Montezuma had great *Caciques* and kinsmen among his captains in Texcoco who were on bad terms with Cacamatzin and disliked him for his pride. In Mexico itself Montezuma had a young prince in his household, a brother of Cacamatzin and a good-natured lad, who had fled to avoid being killed by him, since he was the next heir to the kingdom of Texcoco. Cortes begged Montezuma either to organize Cacamatzin's arrest with the help of his people in Texcoco, or to send him a secret summons to Mexico and, should he come, to seize him and keep him under restraint until he calmed down. Cortes suggested further that since his other nephew was obedient to him and a member of his household, he should make him lord over Texcoco and take the title away from Cacamatzin, who was working against him and stirring up all the *Caciques* and cities in the land so that he might usurp Montezuma's city and kingdom.

Montezuma promised to send him a summons immediately, and to organize his arrest with his captains and relations should he refuse to come, as he feared he would. Cortes thanked him warmly for this and went so far as to say : 'My lord Montezuma, believe me, you are free to go to your palace if you wish. I see how well disposed you are towards me, and I myself feel great love for you. Were our position not so difficult, indeed, I should not insist on accompanying you, were you and all your nobles to return there. If I have kept you here till now it has been on account of my captains, who contrived your arrest and do not want me to release you, and because Your Majesty says that you prefer to remain in confinement in order to prevent the revolt by which your nephews would attempt to obtain control over your city and deprive you of your authority.'

Montezuma replied by expressing his thanks. But he was getting to understand Cortes' flattering speeches, and saw that his intention was not to release him but to test his good will. Moreover the page Orteguilla had told him that it was really our captains who had advised his arrest, and he must not expect Cortes to release him without their consent. Montezuma said therefore that it would be as well for him to remain a prisoner until he saw what his nephews' plots would lead to, and promised to send messengers to Cacamatzin immediately, asking him to come to Mexico, ás he wished to speak to him about making friends with us. As for his imprisonment, he would tell Cacamatzin that he need not worry about it, since had he wanted to free himself many opportunities had been offered, and Malinche had already told him twice that he might return to his palace. However, he did not wish to do so, but to obey the commands of his gods, who had told him that he must remain a prisoner, for if he did not he would soon be dead. This he had learnt some days ago from the priests who ministered to his idols, and for this reason it would be as well to keep friendly with Malinche and his brothers. Montezuma sent the same message to the captains of Texcoco, telling them that he was summoning his nephew to make friends with us, and that they must be careful not to let this youth turn their heads and persuade them to attack us.

Let us return to Cacamatzin, who understood this message perfectly, and held a consultation with his chiefs as to what should be done. Here he began to brag that he would kill us all within four days, and to call his uncle chicken-hearted for not having attacked us when he was advised to do so, as we came down the mountain towards Chalco where he had his troops all posted and everything prepared. Instead of this, he protested, Montezuma had received us into his city in person as if he supposed we had come to confer some benefit on him, and had given us all the gold that had been brought to him as tribute. What was more, we had broken into the treasure-house of his grandfather Axayacatl, and taken Montezuma himself prisoner, and now we were telling him that he must remove the idols of the great Huichilobos so that we could set up our own in their places. Cacamatzin begged his chieftains to help him prevent bad from becoming worse, and to punish these acts and insults. For all that he had described to them they had seen with ir own eyes, and they had even seen us burn Montezuma's own captains. Now, he said, the people had reached the end of their endurance. They must all unite and make war on us.

Cacamatzin promised his hearers then and there that if the lordship of Mexico fell to him he would make them great chieftains, and he gave them many gold jewels as well. He told them also that he had already arranged with his cousins, the lords of Coyoacan and Iztapalapa and Tacuba, and with his other relations, that they should assist him, and there were other chieftains in Mexico itself who would both help him and admit him to the city at any hour he might choose. Some of them could go along the causeways and all the rest across the lake in their pirogues and small canoes, and they would enter the city without opposition. For his uncle was a prisoner, and they need have no fear of us, since, as they well knew, in the affair at Almeria only a few days ago his uncle's captains had killed many *Teules* and a horse, and they had themselves seen the head of the *Teule* and the body of the horse.[1] He said they could finish us all off in an hour, and feast on our bodies till they were full.

They say the captains looked at one another after this speech, and waited for those who usually spoke first at councils of war to begin, and that four or five of them replied by asking how they could possibly go without their lord Montezuma's permission and make war in his own palace and city. First, they said, he must be informed of the proposal. If he consented they would accompany Cacamatzin very gladly indeed; but if he did not they did not wish to act as traitors. It seems that Cacamatzin

1. This had been sent round the towns after the attack on Escalante.

got angry with these captains and ordered that three of them who had given this reply should be imprisoned. There were other captains present at this debate, however, who were relatives of his, and anxious for trouble, and they promised to support him to the death. So he decided to send his uncle the great Montezuma a message that he ought to be ashamed of himself for commanding him to make friends with men who had done him so much harm and dishonour as to keep him a prisoner, and that such a thing was only possible because we were wizards and had robbed him of his great strength and courage with our witchcraft, or because our gods and the great woman of Castile whom we spoke of as our advocate gave us strength to do what we did. And in this last remark he was not wrong. The long and the short of it was that Cacamatzin was coming, in spite of us and in spite of his uncle, to talk to us and kill us.

When the great Montezuma heard this insolent reply, he was greatly annoyed, and at once sent to summon six of his most trusted captains, to whom he gave his seal, also some golden jewels, ordering them to go to Texcoco immediately and secretly show the seal to certain captains and relations of his who resented Cacamatzin's pride and were on bad terms with him. They were then to arrange for the arrest of Cacamatzin and those in his confidence, and to bring them before him at once. The captains departed and explained Montezuma's orders in Texcoco, and Cacamatzin, who was extremely unpopular, was arrested in his own palace while discussing war-preparations with his confederates, five of whom were arrested with him.

As Texcoco lies beside the great lake, Montezuma's captains prepared a large pirogue with awnings, put Cacamatzin and the five others aboard, and with a numerous crew of oarsmen rowed them to Mexico. Then, when he had disembarked, they put him on a rich litter befitting his kingly rank, and most respectfully brought him before Montezuma.

It seems that when conversing with his uncle, Cacamatzin was more insolent than ever. Montezuma already knew of the plots he had hatched to make himself lord of Mexico, but learnt further details about them from the other prisoners. If he had been angry with his nephew before, he was now doubly so. So he sent him to our Captain to be kept as a prisoner, and released the other captains.

Cortes went at once to Montezuma's chamber in the palace to thank him for this great favour, and orders were given that the young brother of Cacamatzin, who was in Montezuma's company, should be made king of Texcoco. To solemnize the appointment and win the city's approval, Montezuma summoned the principal chieftains of the whole province before him, and after a long discussion they elected the youth king and lord of that great city. He was afterwards named Don Carlos.

When the *Caciques* and petty kings who were lords of Coyoacan, Iztapalapa, and Tacuba, heard of Cacamatzin's imprisonment, and learnt that the great Montezuma knew of their share in the plot to deprive him of his kingdom in favour of Cacamatzin, they were frightened and ceased to make their customary visits to the palace. Meanwhile Cortes was urging and persuading Montezuma to order their arrest and, at the end of a week, to the considerable relief of ourselves and our Captain, they were all in prison secured to a great chain.

When Cortes heard that these three kinglets were in prison and all the cities peaceful, he reminded Montezuma that before we entered Mexico he had twice sent word that he wished to pay tribute to His Majesty, and that since he now knew how powerful our King was and how many lands paid him tribute as their overlord, and how many kings were his subjects, it would be well for him and all his vassals to offer him their obedience, for it is customary first to offer obedience and then to pay tribute. Montezuma answered that he would call his vassals together and discuss the matter with them, and within ten days all the many princes of that territory assembled. But the *Cacique* who was most closely related to Montezuma did not come. He had, as I have already said, a reputation for great valour, which his bearing, body, limbs, and face confirmed. He was also somewhat rash, and at that time he was at one of his towns called Tula. It was said that he would succeed to the kingdom of Mexico on Montezuma's death.

On receiving his summons, this prince replied that he would neither come nor pay tribute, for the income from his provinces was not enough for him to live on. This answer infuriated Montezuma, who sent some captains to arrest him. But as he was a great lord and had many relatives, he received warning in advance and retired to his province, where they could not then lay hands on him.

Montezuma's discussion with the *Caciques* of all the territory was attended by none of us except the page Orteguilla. The prince is said to have asked them to reflect how for many years past they had known for certain from their ancestral tradition, set down in their books of records, that men would come from the direction of the sunrise to rule these lands, and that the rule and domination of Mexico would then come to an end. He believed from what his gods had told him that we were these men. The *papas* had consulted Huichilobos about it and offered up sacrifices, but the gods no longer replied as of old. All that Huichilobos vouchsafed to them was that he could only reply as he had done before and they were not to ask him again. They took this to mean that they should offer their obedience to the King of Spain, whose vassals these *Teules* proclaimed themselves to be.

'For the present,' Montezuma continued, 'this implies nothing. In the future we will see if we get another reply from our gods, and then we will act accordingly. What I command and implore you to do now is to give some voluntary contribution as a sign of vassalage. Soon I will tell you what is the most suitable course, but now I am being pressed for this tribute by Malinche. I beg therefore that no one will refuse. Remember that during the eighteen years that I have been your prince you have always been most loyal to me, and I have enriched you, extended your lands, and given you power and wealth. At present our gods permit me to be held a prisoner here, and this would not have happened, as I have often told you, except at the command of the great Huichilobos.'

On hearing these arguments, they all replied with many tears and sighs that they would obey, and Montezuma was more tearful than any of them. However, he sent a chieftain to us at once to say that next day they would give their obedience to His Majesty.

After this talk Montezuma discussed the matter once more with his *Caciques*, and in the presence of Cortes, our captains, many of our soldiers, and Cortes' secretary Pedro Hernandez, they swore fealty to His Majesty, showing much grief in doing so. Indeed, Montezuma himself could not restrain his tears.

When Cortes and his captains were paying court to Montezuma they asked him among other things where the mines lay, and from which rivers they collected the gold they brought him in grains, also how and by what means they got it. For Cortes wanted to send two of our soldiers, both experienced miners, to inspect the place. Montezuma answered that there were three places, and that the district from which they got most gold was the province of Zacatula, which is on the south coast about ten or twelve days' journey from Mexico. He said they collected it in gourds by washing away the earth, and that when the earth was washed away some small grains remained. He added that at present they also brought it from another province called Tuxtepec, where it was gathered from two rivers, near the place where we disembarked on the north coast. Near that province also there were other good mines in the country of the Chinantecs and Zapotecs, who were not his subjects and did not obey him, and that if Cortes wanted to send his soldiers there he would give him chieftains to escort him.

Cortes thanked Montezuma for the offer and immediately sent a pilot called Gonzalo de Umbria with two other soldiers experienced in mining to the mines of Zacatula.[1] This Gonzalo de Umbria was the man whose feet Cortes had ordered to be cut off when he hanged Pedro Escudero and Juan Cermeño and had the 'Men of the Rock' flogged for their attempt to steal a ship at San Juan de Ulua. These men then set out, and Cortes allowed them forty days for their journey there and back.

To examine the mines on the north coast Cortes sent a captain called Pizarro, a lad of twenty-five, whom he treated as a relative. At that time there was no rumour of Peru, and the name Pizarro was unknown in these lands. He set out with four

1. On the Pacific coast.

soldiers and was also given forty days for his journey, for these mines were about two hundred and fifty miles away. He received four Mexican chiefs as an escort.

After these expeditions had departed Montezuma gave our Captain a sisal cloth on which all the rivers and bays on the north coast from Panuco to Tabasco – about four hundred miles – were faithfully painted. Among the rivers marked was the Coatzacoalcos, which was said to be very strong and deep. This was the only river on this cloth that we did not know from the time of our expedition under Grijalva, so Cortes decided to send and explore it, and take soundings of the harbour and the entrance. That very prudent and valiant captain Diego de Ordaz, whom I have so often mentioned, volunteered to make this journey and investigate the nature of the country and people, and he asked for Indian chieftains to accompany him. Cortes at first refused his offer, since he was a man of sound sense and Cortes preferred to have him at his side. However, so as not to displease him, in the end he gave him leave to go.

Montezuma told Ordaz that his authority did not extend over Coatzacoalcos, and that the people there were very unruly and he must be careful what he did. He said that if anything happened to Ordaz, he would not be to blame. However, on his way to the province he would find a garrison of Mexican warriors stationed on the border, whom he might take with him if he needed them. And Montezuma paid Ordaz many other compliments.

The first to return to Mexico and give an account of his mission was Gonzalo de Umbria. He and his companions brought three hundred pesos' weight of grains which the inhabitants of Zacatula had extracted before their eyes. According to Umbria's account, the *Caciques* of that province took many Indians to the rivers, who washed the earth in vessels like small troughs, and collected the gold. They said there were two rivers, and that if good miners were to wash the earth as they did in Santo Domingo and Cuba they would be a rich source of gold. They also brought back with them two chiefs sent by the province who brought a present of gold jewels worth about two hundred pesos, and freely offered themselves as servants of His

Majesty. Cortes was as delighted with the gold as if it had been thirty thousand pesos, for he was now certain that there were good mines. He treated the chieftains who brought the present very cordially, and ordered them to be given some green beads from Castile. Then after friendly speeches they returned to their country well pleased.

Umbria said that not far from Mexico there were some large towns with a civilized population, which must have been those that belonged to the aforementioned relative of Montezuma's, and that there was another province there called Matalcingo. As we all saw, Umbria and his companions came back with plenty of gold and riches, which was the purpose for which Cortes had sent him. For he wanted to make him a friend, on account of what had happened in the past.

Diego de Ordaz in his turn reported that he had passed through very large towns, whose names he gave, on his three-hundred-and-sixty-mile journey. He said that all the inhabitants paid him honour, and that on the way, near Coatzacoalcos itself, he had found Montezuma's frontier garrisons, and the whole neighbourhood complained of them for their robberies and for taking their women and demanding other tributes. Ordaz and the Mexican chiefs with him had reprimanded the captains who commanded this garrison and threatened that if they committed any more robbery they would inform Montezuma, who would then send for them and punish them as he had punished Quetzalpopoca and his companions for robbing our allies' towns. These speeches had frightened the commander of the garrison.

Then Ordaz continued his journey to Coatzacoalcos, taking only one Mexican chief with him, and when the *Cacique* of that province, whose name was Tochel, heard he was coming, he sent his chieftains out to receive him and made him very welcome. For they knew a good deal about us from the time of the Grijalva expedition. So when the *Caciques* of Coatzacoalcos heard Ordaz' purpose they gave him many big canoes, and the *Cacique* Tochel himself with many other chieftains took soundings of the river mouth. They found the depth at ebb tide in the shallowest place to be three full fathoms, and a little higher up the river there was room for large ships to navigate. Indeed the higher up they went the deeper it became, and just near what was at that time an inhabited town carracks could ride at anchor.

After Ordaz had taken the soundings and visited this place with the *Caciques*, they gave him some gold jewels and a very beautiful Indian girl, and offered themselves as servants of His Majesty. They too complained of Montezuma and his garrison, saying that recently they had fought a battle with them, near a small town where many Mexicans had been killed. For that reason they now call this place Cuylonemiquis, which in their language means Where-the-Mexican-swine-were-killed.

Ordaz thanked them heartily for their reception and presented them with some beads from Castile which he had brought for the purpose. He then returned to Mexico, where he was joyfully welcomed by Cortes and the rest of us. He said there was good farming and grazing land there, and the port was convenient for Cuba, Santo Domingo, and Jamaica, but it was far from Mexico and there were great swamps close by. For this reason we never made much use of it as a port for trading with Mexico.

Let us now turn to Captain Pizarro and his companions, who had gone in the direction of Tuxtepec to look for gold and examine the mines. Pizarro returned to make his report accompanied by a single soldier, and brought with him over a thousand pesos in gold grains. They said that in the provinces of Tuxtepec and Malinaltepec[1] and other neighbouring districts they had visited the rivers accompanied by many people who were sent with them, and there they had gathered a third part of the gold they brought. They had then gone up into the hills of another province, that of the Chinantecs, and when they got there many Indians had come to meet them fully armed, carrying lances longer than ours and bows and arrows and small shields. These men had said that not a single Mexican should enter their country, for they would kill him if he did, but the *Teules* were very welcome. So they went on, but the Mexicans were left behind and proceeded no further. When the *Caciques* of

1. In the present State of Oaxaca.

Chinanta understood the purpose of their journey they assembled a lot of people to wash gold, and took them to some rivers where they gathered all the rest of what they brought, which was in curly grains. The miners said that this source would have the longest life because the gold originated there. Pizarro also brought two *Caciques* from that country who came to offer themselves as vassals to His Majesty and make friends with us. They too gave us a present of gold, and all these *Caciques* abused the Mexicans, who were so heartily loathed in those provinces for the robberies they committed that no one could bear to see them or mention them by name.

Cortes welcomed Pizarro and the chiefs he brought, and accepted the present they gave him – I cannot remember what it was worth, since it is long ago. He made the Chinantecs a generous speech offering to help them and be their friend. He then told them to go back to their country, and, to save them from being molested by the Mexicans on the road, commanded two Mexican chiefs to escort them and not to leave them till they reached safety. So they went away well contented.

Cortes asked about the other soldiers whom Pizarro had taken with him, namely Barrientos and the elder Heredia, the younger Escalona, and Cervantes the jester, and Pizarro answered that as it seemed a very good country, and rich in mines, and as the towns through which they passed had been very peaceful, he had ordered them to plant a large farm of cocoa and maize and to make cotton plantations, and collect plenty of the local birds, also to examine all the rivers and see what mines there were.

Although Cortes said nothing at the time, he was displeased with his kinsman for thus exceeding his instructions. We heard privately that he gave him a good scolding, telling him that it showed a weak character to spend your time breeding birds and planting cocoa. He at once sent a soldier with a peremptory order to the soldiers whom Pizarro had left behind, calling on them to return immediately. What actually happened I will relate in due course.

When Diego de Ordaz and the other soldiers arrived with samples of gold and reports that the whole land was rich,

Cortes, on the advice of Ordaz and others, decided to demand
from Montezuma that all the *Caciques* and people of the land
should pay tribute to His Majesty, and that he himself, as the
greatest chieftain, should also give some of his treasures. Montezuma replied that he would send to all his towns to ask for
gold, but that many of them possessed nothing more than
some jewels of small value that they had inherited from their
ancestors. He at once dispatched chieftains to the places where
there were mines and ordered each town to give so many ingots
of fine gold of the same size and thickness as they usually paid
in tribute, and the messengers carried two ingots as samples.
Some places, however, only contributed jewels of small value.

Montezuma also sent to the province whose *Cacique* and
ruler was that close kinsman who refused to obey him, which
was about thirty-five miles from Mexico; and the messengers
returned with the answer that he would give neither gold nor
obedience to Montezuma, that he too was lord of Mexico and
had as much right to the title as Montezuma himself who was
sending to ask him for tribute.

This answer so enraged Montezuma that he immediately dispatched some loyal captains with his seal and insignia to bring
his kinsman back as a prisoner. Even when he came into the
royal presence, however, this prince spoke boldly and dis-
respectfully, without the least sign of fear. They said that he
suffered from attacks of mania, and he certainly seemed quite
uncontrolled. On hearing of his behaviour, Cortes sent a request
to Montezuma that he should hand the prisoner over to him
for safe keeping, for he had heard that Montezuma meant to
kill him. When the *Cacique* came before Cortes, our Captain
spoke to him most amicably, telling him not to act like a madman against his prince, and wanted to set him free. However,
when this came to Montezuma's ears he said that the *Cacique*
must not be freed, but must be attached to the same stout chain
as the other imprisoned kinglets.

Within twenty days all the chieftains whom Montezuma had
dispatched to collect the gold tribute returned, and as soon as
they arrived Montezuma sent for Cortes and our captains, also
for certain of us soldiers whom he knew, because we belonged

to his guard, and made us a formal address in words like these:

'I wish you to know, my lord Malinche and my lords Captains and soldiers, that I am indebted to your great King and bear him good will, both for being such a great king, and for having sent from such distant lands to make inquiries about me. But what impresses me most is the thought that he must be the one who is destined to rule over us, as our ancestors have told us and even our gods have indicated in the answers they have given us. Take this gold which has been collected; only haste prevents there being more. What I myself have got ready for the Emperor is the whole of the treasure I received from my father, which is under your hand in your own apartments. I know very well that as soon as you came here you opened the door and inspected it all, and then sealed it up again as it was before. When you send it to him, tell him in your papers and letter: "This is sent by your loyal vassal Montezuma." I will also give you some very precious stones to be sent to him in my name. They are *chalchihuites* and must not be given to anyone else but your great prince, for each one of them is worth two loads of gold. I also wish to send him three blowpipes with their pellet-bags and moulds, since they have such beautiful jewel-work that he will be pleased to see them. And I should also like to give him some of my own possessions, though they are small. For all the gold and jewels I had I have given you at one time or another.'

On hearing this speech we were all amazed at the great Montezuma's goodness and liberality. Doffing our helmets most respectfully, we expressed our deep thanks, and in a most cordial speech Cortes promised that we would write to His Majesty of the magnificence and liberality with which he had given us this gold in his own royal name. After a further exchange of compliments Montezuma dispatched his stewards to hand over all the gold and treasure in the sealed chamber. It took us three days to examine it and remove all the embellishments with which it was decorated; and to help us take it to pieces Montezuma sent us silversmiths from Atzcapotzalco. There was so much of it that after it was broken up it made three heaps of gold weighing over six hundred thousand pesos in all, not counting the silver and many other valuables, or the ingots and slabs of gold, or the grains of gold from the mines. With the help of the Indian goldsmiths from Atzcapotzalco we began to melt this down into broad bars a little more than two inches across, and no sooner was this done than they brought another present, the one which Montezuma had promised to give for himself. It was marvellous to behold so much gold, and the richness of the jewels he gave us. Some of the *chalchihuites* were so fine that among these *Caciques* they were worth a vast quantity of gold. The three blowpipes and their pellet-moulds, all encrusted with pearls and precious stones, and the feather-pictures of little birds set with mother-of-pearl and even smaller birds, were things of very great value. I will not mention the plumes and feathers and other valuables or I shall never bring my recollections to an end. Let me say that all this gold was stamped with an iron die made by order of Cortes and the King's officers appointed by him in His Majesty's name, and with our general consent, to act until further orders. These were at this time Gonzalo Mejia, treasurer, and Alonso de Avila, accountant, and the die was the royal coat of arms as it appears on a *real* and the size of a four-*real* piece. The rich jewellery, however, was not stamped, since we did not think it ought to be broken up.

For weighing all these bars of gold and silver and the jewels which were not broken up, we had neither weights nor scales. Cortes and these same officers of the King's treasury thought it would be proper, therefore, to make some iron weights, some as heavy as twenty-five pounds, and others of twelve and a half, two, one and a half, and a pound, also of four ounces and other ounce weights. In this way we could not hope to be very exact, but would not be more than half an ounce out in each weighing.

After the weight was taken the King's officers said that the bars and grains and ingots and jewels, all together, came to more than six hundred thousand pesos, and this did not include the silver and the many other jewels which were not yet valued. Some soldiers said there was more. All that remained to be done was to take out the royal fifth, and then give each captain and soldier his share, preserving their shares for those who had remained at Villa Rica. It seems, however, that Cortes attempted to postpone the division until we had more gold, good weights, and a proper account of the total. But most of us said that the division must be made at once. For we had noticed that when the pieces taken from Montezuma's treasury were broken up there had been much more gold in the piles, and that a third of it was now missing, having been taken away and hidden for the benefit of Cortes, the captains, and the Mercedarian friar. We also saw that the gold was still diminishing. After a good deal of argument what was left was weighed out. It amounted to six hundred thousand pesos without the jewels and bars, and it was agreed that the division should be made next day.

First of all the royal fifth was taken. Then Cortes said that another fifth must be taken for him, a share equal to His Majesty's, which we had promised him in the sand-dunes when we made him Captain-General. After that he said that he had been put to certain expenses in Cuba and that what he had spent on the fleet should be deducted from the pile, and in addition the cost to Diego Velazquez of the ships we had destroyed. We all agreed to this and also to pay the expenses of the advocates we had sent to Spain. Then there were the shares of the seventy settlers who had remained at Villa Rica, and the cost of the horse that died, and of Juan Sedeño's mare, which the Tlascalans had killed with a knife-thrust. Then there were double shares for the Mercedarian friar and the priest Juan Diaz and the captains and those who had brought horses, and the same for the musketeers and crossbowmen, and other trickeries, so that in the end very little was left, so little indeed that many of us soldiers did not want to touch it, and Cortes was left with it all. At that time we could do nothing but hold our tongues; to demand justice in the matter was useless. There were other soldiers who took their shares of a hundred pesos and clamoured for the rest. To satisfy them, Cortes secretly gave a bit to one and another as a kind of favour and by means of smooth speeches made them accept the situation.

At that time many of the captains ordered very large golden chains to be made by Montezuma's goldsmiths from Atzcapotzalco, and Cortes too ordered various jewels and a great service of plate. Some soldiers too had laid hands on so much that ingots marked and unmarked and a great variety of jewels were in public circulation. Heavy gambling was always going on with some cards which Pedro Valenciano had manufactured out of drum-skins, and which were as well made and painted as the real thing. Such was the state we were in.

It reached Cortes' ears, however, that many of the soldiers were dissatisfied with their share of the gold and said that the heaps had been robbed, so he decided to make them a speech that was all honeyed words. He said that what he had was for us, and that he did not want his fifth but only the share that came to him as Captain-General, and that if anyone needed anything he would give it to him. He said that the gold we had got so far was only a trifle, and that they could see what great cities there were, and what rich mines, and that we should be lords of them all and very rich and prosperous. He used other arguments too, well couched in the manner of which he was a master. In addition he secretly gave golden jewels to some soldiers and made great promises to others, and he ordered that the food brought by Montezuma's stewards should be divided equally among all the soldiers, receiving no greater share himself than the rest.

Now all men alike covet gold, and the more we have the more we want, and several recognizable pieces were missing from the heaps. At the same time Juan Velazquez de Leon was employing the Atzcapotzalco goldsmiths to make him some large gold chains and pieces of plate for his table. Gonzalo Mejia, the treasurer, privately requested him to deliver this gold to him, since it had not paid the royal fifth and was known to belong to the treasure Montezuma had given us. Juan Velazquez, being Cortes' favourite, refused to give up anything, on the plea that he had not taken any share of what had been collected or anything else, but only what Cortes had given him before the bars were cast.

Gonzalo Mejia answered that what Cortes himself had taken and hidden from his companions was enough, and that as treasurer he demanded all the gold that had not paid the royal fifth. One thing followed another, till both men lost their tempers and drew their swords. Indeed if we had not quickly separated them they would have killed one another, for they were men of great character and brave fighters. As it was they emerged from the battle with two wounds apiece.

When news of this came to Cortes he ordered them both to be put in prison, and each to be attached to a heavy chain. But, as many soldiers reported, he privately told his friend Juan Velazquez that he would only be imprisoned for two days and that Gonzalo Mejia, as treasurer, would be released at once. Cortes arrested them to prove to us that justice would be done and Velazquez imprisoned, even though he was hand in glove with him.

The affair of Gonzalo Mejia was rather more complicated. For the treasurer accused Cortes of having secretly taken much of the missing gold. He said that all the soldiers were complaining to him about it, and asking him why as treasurer he did not demand restitution. But this is a long story and I will not pursue it.

Juan Velazquez was imprisoned in a room not far from Montezuma's apartments. Being a large man and very strong, he dragged the chain after him as he moved about the hall, which made a great noise; and when Montezuma heard it he asked the page Orteguilla who it was that Cortes had bound in chains. The page answered that it was Juan Velazquez, who had once been Montezuma's personal guard – and had now been replaced by Cristobal de Olid. Montezuma then asked the reason, and the page answered, on account of some missing gold.

Later in the day, when Cortes was paying him a visit, Montezuma asked him, after the usual civilities and a little preliminary conversation, why he had imprisoned Juan Velazquez, for he was a good and valiant captain. As I have already said, Montezuma knew us all very well, even to our personal characteristics. Cortes answered him half laughingly that it was because he was a bit touched, by which he meant out of his senses, and because, not having received much gold, he wanted to go to Montezuma's towns and cities and demand it of the

Caciques. For this reason, and to prevent him from killing anyone, he had been put in prison.

Montezuma begged Cortes to release Juan Velazquez and send him to look for more gold, promising that he would give him some of his own, and Cortes pretended that it went against the grain to release him. But at last he said that he would do so to please Montezuma. I believe he sentenced him to be banished from the camp and sent to Cholula with some of Montezuma's messengers to demand gold. Before this, however, he and Gonzalo Mejia were reconciled. Velazquez returned from his banishment, as I observed, within six days, bringing more gold with him, and I observed also that from that time Gonzalo Mejia and Cortes were no longer good friends. I have recorded this although it is outside my story, to show that, under colour of doing justice and striking fear into all, Cortes was capable of great cunning.

One day Montezuma said to Cortes: 'See, Malinche, how much I love you. I should like to give you one of my daughters, a very beautiful girl, to marry and have as your legal wife.' Cortes doffed his helmet in gratitude, and said that this was a great favour Montezuma was conferring on him, but he was already married, and that among us it was not permissible to have more than one wife. He would however treat her with the honour to which the daughter of so great a prince was entitled, but first of all he desired her to become a Christian, as other ladies, the daughters of chieftains, had done. To this the prince consented.

The great Montezuma continued to show his accustomed good will towards us, but never ceased his daily sacrifices of human beings. Cortes tried to dissuade him but met with no success. He therefore consulted his captains as to what we should do in the matter, since he did not dare to put a stop to this practice for fear of arousing the city and the *papas* of Huichilobos. The advice he received was that he should announce his intention of overthrowing the great images of that god. Then if we saw they were prepared to defend them or rise in revolt, he should merely ask permission to set up an altar in one part of the high *cue* with a crucifix and an image of Our

Lady. When this plan was agreed Cortes went to the palace where Montezuma was imprisoned, taking seven captains and soldiers with him, and said to him : 'My lord, I have often asked you to give up sacrificing human beings to your gods, who are false gods, but you have never done so. Now I must tell you that all my companions, and these captains who have come with me, beg you for permission to remove the gods from your temple and put Our Lady and a cross in their place. But if you refuse they will go and remove them just the same, and I should not like them to kill any *papas*.'

When Montezuma heard these words and saw that the captains were somewhat excited, he said : 'Malinche, how can you wish to destroy our whole city? Our gods would be enraged against us, and I do not know that they would even spare your lives. I pray you to be patient for the present, and I will summon all the *papas* and see what they reply.'

On hearing this, Cortes made a sign to Montezuma that he wished to speak with him in private, without the presence of the captains he had brought with him, and ordered them to depart and leave him alone. When they had gone he told the prince that, to prevent this matter from becoming public and causing a disturbance, and so as not to offend the *papas* by overthrowing their idols, he would persuade our people to refrain from action, provided they were given a room in the great *cue* where they could set up an altar on which they could put an image of Our Lady and a cross. Then, in course of time, his people would see how good and advantageous it was for their souls, and for their health, prosperity, and good harvests. Sighing deeply and with a very sad face, Montezuma promised to consult his *papas*; and after a good deal of discussion our altar was set up some distance from their accursed idols, with great reverence and thanks to God from us all. Thereupon mass was sung. Cortes picked an old soldier to remain there as a guard, and begged Montezuma to order his *papas* not to touch the altar, but to sweep the floor and burn incense, and keep wax candles burning, night and day, and to decorate the place with flowers and branches.

Cortes in Difficulties

THERE was never a time when we were not subject to surprises so dangerous that but for God's help they would have cost us our lives. No sooner had we set up the image of Our Lady on the altar, and said mass, than Huichilobos and Tezcatlipoca seem to have spoken to their *papas*, telling them that they intended to leave their country, since they were so ill-treated by the *Teules*. They said that they did not wish to stay where these figures and the cross had been placed, nor would they stay unless we were killed. This, they said, was their answer, and the *papas* need expect no other, but must convey it to Montezuma and all his captains, so that they might at once attack us and kill us. Their gods also observed that they had seen us break up the gold that was once kept in their honour and forge it into ingots, and warned the Mexicans that not only had we imprisoned five great *Caciques* but were now making ourselves masters of their country. They recited many more of our misdeeds in order to incite their people to war.

Wishing us to hear what his gods had said, Montezuma sent Orteguilla to our Captain with the message that he wished to speak to him on very serious business. The page said that Montezuma was very sad and agitated, and that on the previous night and during much of the day many *papas* and important captains had been with him, holding secret discussions which he could not overhear.

On receiving this message Cortes hurried to the palace where Montezuma was, taking with him Cristobal de Olid, the captain of the guard, and four other captains, also Doña Marina and Jeronimo de Aguilar. All paid great respect to the great Montezuma, who addressed them in these words: 'My lord Malinche and captains, I am indeed distressed at the answer which our *Teules* have given to our *papas*, to me, and to all my captains. They have commanded us to make war on you and kill you and drive you back across the sea. I have reflected on this command,

and think it would be best that you should at once leave this city before you are attacked, and leave no one behind. This, my lord Malinche, you must certainly do, for it is in your own interest. Otherwise you will be killed. Remember that your lives are at stake.'

Cortes and our captains were distressed and even somewhat alarmed; which was not surprising, for the news was so sudden and Montezuma was so insistent that our lives were in the greatest and immediate danger. The matter was clearly urgent. Cortes replied by thanking him for the warning, and saying that at the moment he was troubled by two things : that he had no ships in which to depart, since he had ordered those in which we came to be broken up, and that Montezuma would have to accompany us so that our great Emperor might see him. He begged him as a favour therefore to restrain his *papas* and captains until three ships could be built in the sand-dunes. This course, he argued, would be to their advantage, for if they began a war they would all be killed. And to show that he really meant to build these ships without delay, he asked Montezuma to tell his carpenters to go with two of our soldiers who were expert shipbuilders, and cut wood near the coast.

On hearing Cortes say that he would have to come with us and visit the Emperor, Montezuma was even sadder than before. He said he would let us have the carpenters, and urged Cortes to hurry up and not waste time in talk but get to work. In the meantime he promised to tell his *papas* and captains not to foment disturbances in the city, and to see that Huichilobos was appeased with sacrifices, though not of human lives. After this excited conversation Cortes and our captain took their leave of Montezuma and we were all left in great anxiety wondering when the fighting would begin.

Cortes immediately sent for Martin Lopez, the ship's carpenter, and Andres Nuñez, and the Indian carpenters whom Montezuma had lent us, and after some discussion about the size of the three vessels to be built, he ordered Lopez to start work at once and get them ready. For all that was necessary in the way of iron and blacksmith's tackle, tow, caulkers, and tar was to be found at Villa Rica. So they set out and cut the wood near the coast, and after making calculations and templates hastily began to build the ships.

Meanwhile we in Mexico went about in great depression, fearing that at any moment we might be attacked. Our Tlascalan auxiliaries and Doña Marina told Cortes that this was imminent, and the page Orteguilla was always in tears. We all kept on the alert and placed a strong guard on Montezuma. I say that we were on the alert, but I do not have to repeat this so often, since we never took off our armour, gorgets, or leggings by night or day. Some may ask when we slept, and what our beds were like. They were nothing but a little straw and a mat, and anyone who had a curtain put it underneath him. We slept in our armour and sandals with our weapons close beside us. The horses stood saddled and bridled all day, and everything was so fully prepared that at a call to arms we were already at our posts, and waiting. We posted sentinels every night, and every soldier did his guard-duty. There is something else I would say, though I do not like to boast: I grew so accustomed to going about armed and sleeping in the way I have described that after the conquest of New Spain I kept the habit of sleeping in my clothes and without a bed. I slept better that way than on a mattress.

Even when I go to the villages of my *encomienda* I do not take a bed or, if I sometimes do, it is not because I want it, but because some gentlemen are travelling with me, and I do not wish them to think I do not possess a good bed. But I always lie down fully dressed. What is more, I can only sleep for a short time at night. I have to get up and look at the sky and stars and walk about for a bit in the dew; and this without putting a cap or a handkerchief on my head. I am so used to it that, thank God, it does me no harm. I have said all this so that my readers shall know how we, the true conquistadors, lived, and how accustomed we became to our arms and to keeping watch.

[Meanwhile, with backing from Spain, Diego Velazquez went about organizing a fleet which was to follow Cortes and either kill or capture him and his soldiers. The fleet was nineteen ships strong and carried fourteen hundred soldiers, under the command of Panfilo Narvaez. Narvaez met and was joined by the three soldiers whom Pizarro had left behind to farm and prospect, and was then visited by some secret envoys of Montezuma's, who were impressed by the size of his expedition. Montezuma sent presents to Narvaez, and for three days Cortes knew nothing at all about it.]

One day when our Captain went to make his usual state visit to Montezuma, he noticed, after the usual civilities, that Montezuma appeared more cheerful and happy. He asked him how it was, and Montezuma replied that his health was better. But when Cortes paid him a second visit on the same day the prince was afraid that he had learnt about Narvaez' ships. So to get the advantage of our Captain and to avoid suspicion, he said: 'Lord Malinche, just a moment ago some messengers came to tell me that eighteen or more ships with a great many men and horses have arrived at the port where you disembarked. They brought me a picture of it all painted on cloths; and seeing you visiting me for a second time today I thought you had come to bring me the same news, for now you will not need to build ships. But you have told me nothing about it. So I have been annoyed with you, on the one hand, for keeping me in ignorance, and delighted, on the other hand, at the arrival of your brothers. For now you can all return to Spain without more discussion.'

When Cortes heard about the ships and saw the painting on the cloth, he rejoiced greatly. 'Thank God, who provides for us at the right time,' he said. And we soldiers were so pleased that we could not keep quiet. The horsemen rode skirmishing round, and musket shots were fired. But Cortes grew very thoughtful, for he knew quite well that the fleet had been sent against him and us by the Governor Diego Velazquez. Being a wise man, he told us soldiers and captains what he felt, and by great gifts of gold and promises to make us rich persuaded us to stand by him. He did not yet know who was in command of the fleet, but we were highly delighted with the news, and with the gold he had given us by way of gratuity, since it came from his own property and not from what should have fallen to our share. Our Lord Jesus Christ was indeed sending us help and assistance.

[Having learnt all Cortes' dispositions from Pizarro's three followers who had joined him, Narvaez demanded the surrender of Villa Rica.

Sandoval, however, sent away his old and crippled soldiers in preparation for a fight, and arrested Narvaez' three envoys when they threatened him. He then bundled these three, the priest Guevara, the notary Vergara, and a relative of Diego Velazquez called Amaya, off to Mexico under escort. Dazzled by the richness of the country they passed through, they were even more overwhelmed by the gracious reception which Cortes gave them and the sight of Mexico itself. Wheedled by bribes and flattery, on their return to Narvaez' camp they began to persuade Narvaez' men to come over to Cortes' side. At the same time Cortes wrote putting himself at Narvaez' disposition and begging him not to let the Indians see any divergence of view among the Spaniards. Bribes and presents of gold soon produced dissension among Narvaez' followers, but the captain himself obstinately persisted in his hostility to Cortes. A few of his men deserted to Sandoval. Narvaez then moved on to Cempoala, where he extracted from the fat chief all the treasure that Cortes had left in his charge, and from there began to march on Mexico. Cortes then decided to attack him, leaving Pedro de Alvarado and the least reliable soldiers to guard Montezuma. The Mexican prince, who was playing a double game, sent gold and supplies to Narvaez and attempted to dissuade Cortes from attacking him. After an argument with a notary who attempted to serve writs on him, Cortes sent first the Mercedarian friar and then Juan Velazquez to win him friends in Narvaez' camp. His guile succeeded. But at the same time he bought a number of long copper-tipped lances from the Chinantecs to be used against Narvaez' horsemen, and trained his men to handle them. He then made a surprise attack on Narvaez, whose men quickly lost their artillery. The night was wet and they were not used to the country. Narvaez himself was wounded and lost an eye, and his men failed to defend the *cues* at Cempoala which seemed to offer them a natural stronghold. Five men were killed on Narvaez' side and four on Cortes'. Narvaez' men then passed with greater or less willingness to Cortes' side, and many of them were permitted to settle in the country. Cortes insisted that his men should return the horses and other valuables which they had captured, a demand which provoked some resistance on his own side. One of Narvaez' followers, a black man, was suffering from smallpox, and a severe epidemic spread among the Indians, who did not know this disease. The victory of Cempoala, however, was quickly followed by very bad news from Mexico.]

Just at the moment of victory news came from Mexico that

Pedro de Alvarado was besieged in his quarters, which the Mexicans had set alight in two places, killing seven of his men and wounding many others. He sent to demand assistance in great urgency and haste, and entrusted the message to two Tlascalans who brought no letter. The letter, however, was brought shortly afterwards by two other Tlascalans. God knows how this bad news depressed us!

We began our journey back to Mexico by forced marches, leaving Narvaez and his captain Salvatierra as prisoners at Villa Rica, in charge of Rodrigo Rangel, who was made commander of the place and was left to look after not only the prisoners but many of Narvaez' followers who were recovering from their wounds.

As we were about to start four important chieftains arrived whom the great Montezuma had sent to Cortes to complain about Pedro de Alvarado. With tears streaming from their eyes, they said that Alvarado had come out of his quarters with all the soldiers whom Cortes had left him, and for no reason at all had fallen on their *Caciques* and dignitaries, who were dancing and celebrating a festival in honour of their idols Huichilobos and Tezcatlipoca, for which they had Alvarado's permission. Many Mexicans had been killed and wounded, and in defending themselves they had killed six of our soldiers. In reply to their bitter complaints against Alvarado, Cortes merely said in some disgust that he would go straight to Mexico and put things right. When the messengers brought their answer to the great Montezuma, he is said to have taken it very badly and flown into a great rage.

Cortes also promptly sent letters to Pedro de Alvarado, advising him to make sure that Montezuma did not escape, and telling him that we were coming by forced marches. At the same time he informed him of our victory over Narvaez, about which Montezuma knew already.

The Flight from Mexico

WHEN the news came that Pedro de Alvarado was besieged and Mexico in revolt the captaincies that had been given to Juan Velazquez de Leon and Diego de Ordaz over settlements to be formed at Panuco and Coatzacoalcos were revoked. Neither of them went, everyone stayed with us. Feeling that Narvaez' followers would not willingly assist us in the relief of Alvarado's garrison, Cortes implored them to forget their hostility, and promised to make them rich and give them commands. Since they had come to seek a livelihood, he told them, and were in a country where they could both serve God and His Majesty and enrich themselves, now was the chance. He was so persuasive in fact, that every one of them offered to come with us. But if they had known the Mexicans' strength, not one of them would have volunteered.

We quickly set out for Tlascala by forced marches, and on getting there learnt that Montezuma and his captains had attacked continuously until the news came that we had defeated Narvaez, and had killed seven of Alvarado's men as well as setting fire to his quarters. The messengers added that Alvarado's men were exhausted through want of food and water, for Montezuma had ceased to send them supplies.

This news was brought to us by Tlascalan Indians at the very moment of our arrival, and Cortes immediately ordered a parade to be held of the men who had come with him. There were over thirteen hundred soldiers, counting Narvaez' people and his own, also some ninety-six horses, eighty crossbowmen, and as many musketeers. This force seemed to him sufficient for us to make a safe entry into Mexico, and in addition the Tlascalan chiefs gave us two thousand warriors. So we set out at once for Texcoco by forced marches, but when we came to that great city we received no welcome. Not a single chieftain was to be seen. They were all hostile and in hiding.

We arrived at Mexico on St John's Day in June 1520. No

Caciques or captains or Indians whom we recognized appeared in the streets, and all the houses were empty. When we reached the quarters where we had formerly lodged, the great Montezuma came out into the courtyard to embrace and speak to Cortes. He welcomed him and congratulated him on his victory over Narvaez. But Cortes, arriving as the victor, refused to listen to him, and Montezuma returned to his lodging very sad and thoughtful.

Cortes was anxious to find out the cause of the Mexican revolt. It was quite clear to us that Montezuma was distressed about it. Many of those who had been with Pedro de Alvarado through the critical time said that if the uprising had been desired by Montezuma or started on his advice, or if Montezuma had had any hand in it, they would all have been killed. Montezuma had pacified his people and made them give up the attack.

Pedro de Alvarado's account of events was that the Mexicans had revolted in order to free Montezuma, and at the command of Huichilobos, who was angry because we had placed the image of Our Lady and the cross in his house. He said that a crowd of Indians had come to remove the image from the altar, but had been unable to do so. They had looked on this as a great miracle, and had reported it to Montezuma; and he had told them to leave it on the altar and do nothing more about it. It was therefore left in place.

Pedro de Alvarado gave other reasons for the revolt also : the fact that Narvaez' message to Montezuma that he was coming to release him and capture us had turned out untrue; and a similar disillusionment in the matter of Cortes' specious promise to Montezuma that as soon as we possessed ships we would go aboard and leave the country entirely. For not only were we not going, but many more *Teules* were arriving. The Mexicans thought, therefore, that they had better kill Pedro de Alvarado and his soldiers and release Montezuma before we returned to Mexico with all Narvaez' followers. After this they would turn on Cortes' forces and kill us to the last man. For they had taken it for granted that Narvaez' men would conquer us, but now all their hopes had proved vain.

When Pedro de Alvarado had told his story, Cortes asked him

why he had attacked the Mexicans while they were dancing and holding their festival. He said he had received positive information that when the feasts and dancing were over and the sacrifices had been made to Huichilobos and Tezcatlipoca, they would attack us at once. This and all the rest he had learnt from a *papa* and two chieftains and certain other Mexicans. 'But they told me,' said Cortes, 'that they asked your permission to hold their feast and dances.' Alvarado agreed that this was so, and said that, to surprise and scare them and prevent them from attacking us, he had got his attack in first.

On hearing this Cortes exclaimed very angrily that it was a bad thing and a great mistake, and that he wished to God Montezuma had escaped and he had never had to listen to this story. He then turned away and said no more on the subject.

When Cortes found that we were no better received than we had been in Texcoco, and that no market was being held and the whole place was in revolt, and when he heard Pedro de Alvarado's account of his uncontrolled attack on the Mexicans, he was very sad. Moreover, it seems that on the march he had boasted to Narvaez' captains of the great respect and authority he enjoyed among the Indians, saying that they would come out on the road to meet him and welcome him with presents of gold, as they always did. When nothing turned out as he had promised, therefore, and they did not even bring him food to eat, he was greatly irritated, and most haughty in his behaviour to the many Spaniards in his company.

Soon after the discussion with Alvarado, Montezuma sent two chieftains to beg Cortes to pay him a visit, since he wanted to speak to him. The reply they received was: 'Visit him? Why, the dog doesn't even keep a market open for us, or see that they send us food to eat!'

When our captains, Juan Velazquez de Leon, Cristobal de Olid, Alonso de Avila, and Francisco de Lugo, heard Cortes speak in this way, they protested: 'Calm yourself, sir. Do not be so angry. Remember how well and honourably the king of this country has treated us. He is a good man. If it had not been for him we should all of us be dead by now, and they would have eaten us. Remember he has even given us his daughters.'

This infuriated Cortes more than ever, for he took it as a reproof. 'Why should I be civil,' he exclaimed, 'to a dog who was holding secret negotiations with Narvaez, and now, as you can see, does not even give us any food?' 'That he certainly should do,' replied the captains, 'you are quite right.' Having so many Spaniards with him in the city, our own men and Narvaez' followers, Cortes did not restrain himself at all. Turning to the chieftains, he told them to tell their master to have the fair and markets opened immediately, or he would not answer for the consequences.

The chieftains understood Cortes' insulting remarks, and the captains' reproof of their commander. Knowing all our captains well from the time when they had guarded Montezuma, and thinking of them as good friends to the prince, they repeated the conversation to Montezuma, in so far as they understood it. Perhaps their report infuriated the Mexicans. Perhaps, on the other hand, the attack was already planned. Be that as it may, within a quarter of an hour a soldier appeared, in great haste and severely wounded, saying that he had come from the town of Tacuba, not far away, and had been escorting some Indian women who belonged to Cortes, among them a daughter of Montezuma. It seems that Cortes had left them in charge of the lord of Tacuba, whose relations they were, when we went on the expedition against Narvaez. This soldier said that the whole city and the road by which he had come was crowded with warriors, carrying arms of every kind, and that they had taken the Indian women from him and wounded him twice. If he had not let the women go, he said, they would already have had him in a canoe and taken him off to be sacrificed. They had laid hands on him, in fact, and had broken down a bridge.

This news greatly distressed Cortes and those of us who heard it. We who were used to campaigning against the Indians knew very well what great hosts they always collected, and that however hard we fought, even with our numbers we should be in great hazard of our lives, and of hunger and hardships, since the city around us was so strong.

Cortes immediately ordered Diego de Ordaz to go with four hundred soldiers, among them most of the crossbowmen and musketeers and some horsemen, to examine the situation described by the wounded soldier, and if he found he could pacify the Indians without fighting or disturbance, to do so. He set out to obey these instructions, but had hardly reached the middle of the street down which he was to march when he was attacked by a great number of Mexican bands, while an equal number shot at him from the roofs. The attack was so fierce that at the first assault eight of our soldiers were killed and all the rest wounded, including Diego de Ordaz himself, who received three wounds. They could not advance a single yard, but had to retreat step by step to their quarters. On the way back another good soldier called Lezcano was killed, after doing valiant deeds with his broadsword.

While many bands were attacking, even more came to our quarters, and discharged so many javelins and sling-stones and arrows that in the single attack they wounded forty-six of our men, twelve of whom died of their wounds. So many warriors assailed us that Diego de Ordaz was unable to retire into our quarters because of the fierce attacks made on him from front and rear and from the rooftops. Our cannon, muskets, crossbows, and lances were of little use; our stout sword-thrusts and our brave fighting were in vain. Though we killed and wounded many of them, they pushed forward over the points of our swords and lances and, closing their ranks, continued to fight as bravely as before. We could not drive them off.

At last, thanks to our cannon, muskets, and crossbows and the damage we did them with our swords, Ordaz was able to enter our quarters. Not till then, hard though he tried, could he force a passage with his badly wounded soldiers, who were reduced by fourteen. Still many bands continued to attack us, crying that we were like women, and calling us rogues and other abusive names, and the damage they had done us till then was as nothing to what was to come. They were so bold that, attacking from different directions, they forced a way into our quarters and set them on fire, and we could not stand up to the smoke and flames till we found the remedy of throwing heaps of earth on top of them and cutting off those rooms from which the fire was coming. Indeed, they believed they would burn us alive in there. These battles lasted all day, and during the night, too, many bands attacked us, hurling javelins, sling-stones, arrows, and stray stones in such numbers that they covered the court-yard and the surrounding ground like corn on a threshing floor.

We spent the night dressing our wounds, repairing the breaches the enemy had made in the walls, and preparing for next day. As soon as dawn broke our Captain decided that we and Narvaez' men combined should sally out and fight them, taking our cannon, muskets, and crossbows, and endeavouring to defeat them, or at least to make them feel our strength and valour better than the day before. I may say that when we were forming this plan the enemy was deciding on similar measures. We fought very well, but they were so strong and had so many bands which relieved one another by turns, that if we had had ten thousand Trojan Hectors and as many Rolands, even then we should not have been able to break through.

I will describe the whole of the battle. We were struck by the tenacity of their fighting, which was beyond description. Neither cannon, muskets, nor crossbows were of any avail, nor hand-to-hand combat, nor the slaughter of thirty or forty of them every time we charged. They still fought on bravely and with more vigour than before. If at times we were gaining a little ground or clearing part of a street, they would pretend to make a re-treat, in order to lure us into following them. By thus attacking at less risk, they believed they would prevent us from struggling back alive, for they did us most damage when we were retiring.

Then, as to going out and burning their houses, I have already described the drawbridges between them, which they now raised so that we could only get across through deep water. Then we could not stand up to the rocks and stones which they hurled from the roofs in such numbers that many of our men were hurt or wounded. I do not know why I am writing so calmly, for some three or four soldiers of our company who had served in Italy swore to God many times that they had never seen such fierce fighting, not even in Christian wars, or against the French king's artillery, or the Great Turk; nor had they ever seen men so courageous as those Indians at charging with closed ranks.

With great difficulty we withdrew to our quarters, hard pressed by many bands of yelling and whistling warriors, who blew their trumpets and beat their drums, calling us rogues and cowards who did not dare to meet them in a day's battle but turned away in flight.

Ten or twelve more soldiers were killed that day, and we all returned badly wounded. We spent the night coming to the decision that in two days' time every able-bodied soldier in the camp would sally forth under the protection of four engines, which we would construct. These were to take the form of strong timber towers, each capable of sheltering twenty-five men, and provided with apertures and loopholes which were to be manned by musketeers and crossbowmen; and close beside them were to march the other soldiers, musketeers and cross-bowmen, and the artillery and all the rest; and the horsemen were to make charges.

After settling on this plan, we spent the next day building the machines and strengthening the many breaches they had made in the walls. We did not go out to fight that day. I cannot describe the bands of warriors who came to attack us in our quarters, not just at ten or twelve points but at more than twenty. We were divided among them all, and stationed in many other places too. While we bricked ourselves in and strengthened our fortifications, many other bands openly endeavoured to break into our quarters, and neither guns, cross-bows, nor muskets, neither frequent charges nor sword-thrusts, were enough to drive them back. Not one of us, they shouted, would remain alive that day. They would sacrifice our hearts and blood to their gods, and with our legs and arms they would have enough to glut themselves at their feasts. They would throw our bodies for the tigers, lions, vipers, and serpents to gorge on; and for that reason orders had been given that for the last two days the beasts in their cages should be given no food. As for the gold we had, we would get little pleasure from that, or from all our cloth; and as for the Tlascalans who were with us, they would put them into cages to fatten, so that their bodies could be offered one by one as sacrifices. They shouted also, in less violent language, that we must surrender their great lord Montezuma, and they shouted other things as well. At night too, they went on yelling and whistling in the same way, and discharging showers of darts, stones, and arrows.

When dawn broke we commended ourselves to God and sallied forth with our towers. The cannon, muskets, and cross-bows went ahead, and the horsemen made charges. But, as I have said, it was to no purpose. Although we killed many of them we could not drive them back. Bravely though they had fought on the previous two days, they were much more vigor-ous on this occasion and brought up even greater forces. Never-theless we were determined, even at the cost of our lives, to advance with our towers as far as the great *cue* of Huichilobos.

I will not give a full account of the fighting in one fortified house, or tell how they wounded our horses, which were use-less to us. For though they charged the enemy bands, they re-ceived so many arrows, darts, and stones that, well-armoured though they were, they could not break the enemy's ranks. If they caught up with any Mexicans, these warriors would quickly jump for safety into the canals or the lake, beside which they had raised fresh walls against the horsemen. There many other Indians were stationed with very long lances to finish them off. If our horses were useless, it was equally useless to turn aside and burn or demolish a house. For, as I have said, they all stood in the water with drawbridges between them. To swim across the gap was very dangerous, for they had so many rocks and stones on their fortified flat roofs that it meant certain destruc-tion to attempt it. In addition to this, when we did set fire to some houses, a single one would take all day to burn, and one did not catch light from the other, because their roofs were flat and because of the water between. It was no good our risking our lives in this direction, therefore, so we made for the great *cue*.

Suddenly more than four thousand warriors ascended it, to reinforce the bands already posted there with long lances and stones and darts. Then all of them together took up a defensive position, and for a long time prevented our ascending the steps. Neither our towers, nor our cannon or crossbows, nor our mus-kets were of any avail; and although our horsemen tried to charge, the horses lost their foothold and fell down on the great slippery flagstones with which the whole courtyard was paved. While those on the steps of the *cue* prevented our advance, we had so many of the enemy also on both our flanks that although ten or fifteen of them might fall to one cannon-shot, and many others were killed by sword-thrusts and charges, the hosts against us were overwhelming. For a long time we could not ascend the *cue*, although we most persistently pressed home our attacks. We did not take the towers, for they were already destroyed, but in the end we reached the top.

Here Cortes showed himself the brave man he was! The battle was fierce and the fighting intense. It was a memorable sight to see us all streaming with blood and covered with wounds; and some of us were slain. It pleased Our Lord that we should reach the place where the image of Our Lady used to stand, but we did not find it there. It appears, as we afterwards learnt, that the great Montezuma paid devotion to it, and he had ordered it to be kept safe. We set fire to their idols, and a large part of the hall in which Huichilobos and Tezcatlipoca stood was burnt down. In all this we received great help from the Tlascalans. And when we reached the top, some of us fighting and some of us lighting the fire, the *papas* who belonged to that great *cue* were a sight to see! As we retired, however, four or five thousand Indians, every one a leading warrior, tumbled us down the steps, six or ten at a time. Then there were some enemy bands posted on the battlements and in the embrasures of the *cue*, who shot so many darts and arrows at us that we could face neither one group of squadrons nor the other. So we resolved, with much toil and risk of our lives, to return to our quarters. Our towers had been destroyed, all of us were wounded, we had lost sixteen men, and the Indians constantly pressed on our flanks and rear. We captured two of their chief *papas* in this battle, whom Cortes told us to bring back with great care.

The Mexican bands continued to attack our quarters most obstinately and tenaciously all the time we were fighting outside. On our laborious return, indeed, we found as many of the enemy in the fortress as in the force that was pursuing us. They had already demolished some walls to force an entry, but they broke off their attacks when we arrived. Nevertheless during what remained of the day they never ceased to fire darts, stones, and arrows, and during the night they not only fired them but yelled also.

We spent the night dressing the wounded and burying the dead, preparing for going out to fight next day, strengthening and adding parapets to the walls they had pulled down and the breaches they had made, and discussing some method of fighting which would cost us less in dead and wounded. But much though we talked we found no remedy at all.

I must mention the abuse which Narvaez' followers hurled at Cortes. They cursed him and the country, and Diego Velazquez too, who had sent them here when they were peacefully settled in their homes in Cuba. They were quite crazy and uncontrolled.

To return to our story, we came to the conclusion that we must ask for peace, in order that we might retire from Mexico. As soon as it was dawn many more bands of warriors arrived and very effectually surrounded our quarters on every side. The stones and arrows fell even thicker than before, the howls and whistles were even louder, and new bands endeavoured to force an entrance in new places. Cannon and muskets were of no avail, though we did them plenty of damage.

In view of this situation, Cortes decided that the great Montezuma must speak to them from the roof and tell them that the attacks must cease, since we wished to leave the city. When they went to give this message to the prince, it is reported that he said in great grief: 'What more does Malinche want of me? Fate has brought me to such a pass because of him that I do not wish to live or hear his voice again.' He refused to come, and he is even reported to have said that he would not see Cortes again, or listen to any more of his false speeches, promises, and lies. Then the Mercedarian friar and Cristobal de Olid went and talked to him most respectfully and tenderly, and Montezuma answered: 'I do not believe that I can do anything towards ending this war, because they have already chosen another lord, and made up their minds not to let you leave this place alive. I believe therefore that all of you will be killed.'

While the fighting continued, Montezuma was lifted to a battlement of the roof with many of us soldiers guarding him, and began to speak very lovingly to his people, telling them that if they stopped their attacks we would leave Mexico. Many of the Mexican chiefs and captains recognized him and ordered their people to be silent and shoot no more darts, stones, or arrows, and four of them, coming to a place where Montezuma could speak to them and they to him, addressed him in tears: 'Oh lord, our great lord, we are indeed sorry for your misfortune and the disaster that has overtaken you and your family. But we must tell you that we have chosen a kinsman of yours as our new lord.' And they named Cuitlahuac, the lord of Iztapalapa – for it was not Guatemoc, who was lord soon after. They said moreover that the war must be carried on, and that they had promised their idols not to give up until we were all dead. They said they prayed every day to Huichilobos and Tezcatlipoca to keep him free and safe from our power, and that if things ended as they hoped, they would undoubtedly hold him in greater regard as their lord than they had done before. And they begged for his forgiveness.

Barely was this speech finished when a sudden shower of stones and darts descended. Our men who had been shielding Montezuma had momentarily neglected their duty when they saw the attack cease while he spoke to his chiefs. Montezuma was hit by three stones, one on the head, one on the arm, and one on the leg; and though they begged him to have his wounds dressed and eat some food and spoke very kindly to him, he refused. Then quite unexpectedly we were told that he was dead.

Cortes and all of us captains and soldiers wept for him, and there was no one among us that knew him and had dealings with him who did not mourn him as if he were our father, which was not surprising, since he was so good. It was stated that he had reigned for seventeen years, and was the best king they ever had in Mexico, and that he had personally triumphed in three wars against countries he had subjugated.

I have spoken of the sorrow we all felt when we saw that Montezuma was dead. We even blamed the Mercedarian friar for not having persuaded him to become a Christian, but he excused himself by saying that he had not supposed that Montezuma would die of these wounds, though he ought to have ordered them to give him something to deaden the pain. After much discussion Cortes ordered a *papa* and a chief from among our prisoners to go to tell the chief Cuitlahuac and his captains that the great Montezuma was dead, and that they had seen him die, and of the manner of his death and the wounds he had received from his own people. They were to say how grieved we all were, and that they must bury him like the great king that he was, and raise his cousin who was with us to be king in his place, since the inheritance was rightfully his; or else one of his sons, for the prince they had chosen had no right to the succession; and that they should negotiate a peace, so that we could leave the city. Failing that, our messengers were to say that we would sally out to fight them and burn all their houses and do them great damage, since only our respect for Montezuma had prevented us from destroying their city, and he was now dead.

To convince them of Montezuma's death, Cortes ordered six Mexicans, all important men, and the rest of the *papas* whom we held prisoner, to carry him out on their shoulders and hand him over to the Mexican captains, to whom they were to convey Montezuma's orders at the time of his death. For those who carried him out had been present at his deathbed, and they told Cuitlahuac the whole truth, that his own people had killed the prince with three stones.

When they saw Montezuma dead they wept, as we could see, very bitterly, and we clearly heard their shrieks and lamentations. But for all this their fierce attack did not cease; darts, stones, and arrows continued to fly, and they came on again with greater force and fury, crying: 'Now you shall indeed pay for the death of our king and lord, and for your insults to our gods. As for the peace you ask for, come out here and we will settle the terms!'

They said much else that I cannot now remember, about how they had chosen a brave king, who would not be so faint-hearted as to be deceived by false speeches like their good Montezuma. As for his burial, we need not trouble about that, but about our own lives, for in two days not one of us would be left to send them any more messages. With these words came loud yells and whistles and showers of stones, darts, and arrows; and other bands continued their attempts to set fire to our quarters in many places.

In face of all this, Cortes and the rest of us agreed that we would all come out of our camp next day and attack in another direction, where there were many houses on dry land. Then, doing them all the damage we could, we would make for the causeway. First, however, our horsemen would break through their bands, and spear them or drive them into the lake, even at the cost of losing the horses. This plan was made in the hope that the death and wounds we should inflict on them might make them abandon their attack, and arrange some sort of peace that would let us go free without more destruction. But though we all fought bravely next day and killed many of the enemy, and burnt some twenty houses and almost reached the mainland, it was all to no purpose because of the heavy casualties we suffered. We could not hold a single bridge, for they were all half broken down. Many Mexicans charged down on us, and they had set up walls and barricades in the places which they knew our horses could reach. Great though our trials had been before, we found much greater ones ahead of us.

But let us turn from the subject and repeat that we decided to get out of Mexico.

Now we saw our forces diminishing every day, and the Mexicans increasing in numbers. Many of our men had died, and all the rest were wounded. Though we fought most valiantly, we could not drive back the many bands which attacked us by night and day, or force them to a standstill. We became short of powder, and then of food and water. We had sent to ask them for a truce, but because of Montezuma's death they would not leave us in peace. In fact we stared death in the face, and the bridges had been raised. It was therefore decided by Cortes and all of us captains and soldiers that we should depart during the night, choosing the moment when their warriors were most careless. And to put them off their guard, on that very afternoon we sent one of their *papas* whom we had captured, a man of great importance among them, with some other prisoners, to propose that they should let us retire within eight days, leaving them all the gold. But this was only in order to distract their attention, so that we could get out that night.

In our company was a soldier called Botello, who seemed a very decent man and knew Latin and had been in Rome. He was reputed, however, to be a sorcerer. Some said that he had a familiar spirit, others called him an astrologer. Now, four days before, this Botello had claimed to have learnt, by casting lots or by astrology, that if we did not leave Mexico on that particular night, but delayed our departure, not one of us would escape with his life. He had said also, on other occasions, that Cortes was to suffer many hardships and lose both position and honour, but that he would afterwards become a great lord, rich in wealth and reputation. He made other prophecies as well. But enough of Botello, whom I shall mention again later on.

An order was now given that a bridge should be made of very strong beams and planks. This we were to carry with us and use in the places where the bridges had been broken. Four hundred Tlascalans and a hundred and fifty soldiers were chosen to carry this bridge and place it in position, and to guard the passage until the army and all the baggage had crossed. Two hundred Tlascalans and fifty soldiers were chosen to carry the cannon, and Gonzalo de Sandoval and Diego de Ordaz to lead the men and do the fighting, while a company of a hundred picked and valiant young soldiers under Francisco de Saucedo and Francisco de Lugo were to march in two equal companies and rush to any place where there was a heavy attack. Cortes himself, Alonso de Avila, Cristobal de Olid, and other captains were to go in the middle, and Pedro de Alvarado and Juan Velazquez de Leon in the rear, behind two of Narvaez' captains and their soldiers. Finally the three hundred Tlascalans and thirty soldiers were ordered to guard the prisoners and Doña Marina and Doña Luisa. By the time these dispositions had been made it was already night, and the gold could be divided among those who were to carry it.

Cortes ordered Cristobal de Guzman his steward, and other soldiers who were his servants, to have all the gold and jewels and silver brought out. He gave them many Tlascalans to do the work, and it was all placed in the hall. Cortes then told the

King's officials, Alonso de Avila and Gonzalo Mejia, to take charge of the royal portion. He gave them seven wounded and lame horses and one mare and more than eighty of our Tlascalan allies, and they loaded men and animals alike with as much as each could carry. It was, as I have said, made up into very broad ingots, but much gold still remained piled up in the hall. Then Cortes called his secretary, and others who were the King's notaries, and said : 'Bear witness for me that I can do no more with this gold. Here in this hall we have more than seven hundred thousand pesos' worth, and as you have seen, it cannot be weighed or brought to safety. I now give it over to any soldiers who care to take it. Otherwise we shall lose it to these dogs.'

On hearing this, many of Narvaez' men and some of ours loaded themselves with it. I had no desire, I assure you, but to save my life. Nevertheless I picked up four *chalchihuites* from the little boxes in which they lay, and quickly stowed them in my bosom, under my armour. The price of them afterwards served to cure my wounds and buy me food.

As soon as we knew Cortes' plan that we should escape during the night, we prepared to move towards the bridges. Since it was rather dark and there was some mist and drizzle, we began before midnight to transport the bridge and the baggage; and the horses, the mare, and the Tlascalans who were carrying the gold started on their way. The bridge was quickly put in place, and Cortes crossed over with those of the leading detachment and many of the horses. While this was happening the shouts and cries and whistles of the Mexicans rang out, and they called in their language to the people of Tlatelolco : 'Bring out your canoes at once. The *Teules* are departing. You must cut them off, so that not one remains alive.' Then all of a sudden we saw many bands of warriors descending on us, and the whole lake so thick with canoes that we could not defend ourselves, since many of our men had already crossed the bridge. While we were in this position, a great crowd of Mexicans charged down on us to remove the bridge and kill and wound our men, who could not help one another. And since misfortune is cruel at such times, one disaster followed another. Because of the rain two of the horses slipped and fell in the lake. Just as we saw this, I and some others of Cortes' detachment struggled to the other side of the bridge, but we were borne down on by so many warriors that, hard though we fought, no further use could be made of it. The channel, or water-gap, was soon filled up with dead horses, Indians of both sexes, servants, bundles, and boxes.

Fearing that we should inevitably be killed, we pushed ahead along the causeway, where we found many bands with long spears awaiting us. They shouted abuse at us. 'Villains,' they cried, 'are you still alive?' Although six of my companions were wounded, we cut and hacked our way through. They seemed to have concocted some accursed plan, just as we had. For though Cortes and the captains and soldiers who rode first spurred along the causeway, and did not fail to reach dry land and save their lives, and the horses with the gold and the Tlascalans reached safety also, I declare that if the horsemen had waited for the soldiers at each bridge, it would have been the end of us all: not one of us would have survived. For as we passed along the causeway, charging the Mexican bands, the water was on one side of us and flat roofs on the other, and the lake was full of canoes. There was nothing we could do. Moreover all the muskets and crossbows had been left behind at the bridge, and it was night. What more could we have attempted than we did, which was to charge and deal swordthrusts at those who tried to seize us, and push ahead till we were off the causeway?

Had it been day-time things would have been even worse. Those of us who escaped only did so by the grace of God. It must be terrifying merely to read of the hosts of warriors who descended on us that night, and the canoes that bore down to seize our soldiers. As we advanced along the causeway towards the town of Tacuba, which Cortes had already reached with Gonzalo de Sandoval, Cristobal de Olid, and the other horsemen who had gone ahead, there were cries of: 'My lord Captain, let us halt here. They say that we are running away and leaving them to die at the bridges. Let us go back and help them, if any of them survive and cannot get away.' But Cortes replied that it was a miracle any of us had escaped. He turned back, however, with the horsemen and those soldiers who were unwounded. But they did not go far, for Pedro de Alvarado soon met them, badly wounded, on foot and with a spear in his hand, since they had killed his sorrel mare. With him he brought four soldiers as badly wounded as himself and eight Tlascalans, all of them pouring blood from many wounds.

While Cortes was on the causeway with the other captains, we took refuge in the square at Tacuba. Many bands had already reached there from Mexico and were shouting orders to the people of that town and another called Atzcapotzalco. Then they began to hurl darts, stones, and arrows at us, and to attack us with their long lances. We engaged them several times, attacking them and defending ourselves.

To return to Pedro de Alvarado. When Cortes and the other captains met him and saw that no more soldiers were coming down the causeway, tears sprang to their eyes. Pedro de Alvarado told them that Juan Velazquez de Leon lay dead at a bridge, with many other gentlemen both of Narvaez' company and our own, more than eighty in all. He said that he and the four soldiers had crossed the bridge in great peril after their horses had been killed, treading on the dead men, horses, and boxes with which the approach to it was choked. He said also that all the bridges and causeways were crowded with warriors. That unhappy bridge was afterwards called Alvarado's Leap. But no soldier stopped at the time, I assure you, to see whether his leap was long or short. We had enough to do to save our lives, for so many Mexicans were charging down on us that we were in great danger of death. I never heard anything about the leap of Alvarado's until after the capture of Mexico, and then it was in some satirical verses by a certain Gonzalo Ocampo, which I will not print here, since they are somewhat scurrilous. In one line he says: 'You should remember the leap which you took from the bridge.' But I will dwell no more on this delicate subject.

While we remained in Tacuba, many Mexican warriors from the lakeside towns gathered and killed three of our soldiers. So we decided to leave the place as quickly as possible, and five Tlascalans, who found a path to Tlascala without following the road, guided us with great precautions until we reached some small houses built on a hill, and beside them a fortress-like *cue* that was their shrine. Here we halted.

During our retreat we were followed by the Mexicans, who hurled arrows and darts at us, and stones from their slings. The way they surrounded us and continually attacked us was most terrifying. I have already said this many times, and am tired of repeating myself, but my readers must not think me prolix, for each time they attacked and wounded us I am forced to speak of it again.

Let us tell how we defended ourselves. We took refuge in that fortified *cue* and attended to our wounded, and made many fires, but there was not so much as a morsel to eat. Later on, after the great city of Mexico was finally captured, we built a church on the site of that *cue*, which is called Nuestra Señora de los Remedios,[1] and is now much visited. Many citizens and ladies of Mexico go there on pilgrimages, and to make *novenas*.

Let me now say that it was pitiable to see our wounds dressed and bandaged with cotton cloths, for being both chilled and swollen they were very painful. But more deplorable was the loss of the gentlemen and brave soldiers who were missing, namely Juan Velazquez de Leon, Francisco de Saucedo, Francisco de Morla, Lares 'the good rider', and many others of Cortes' followers. I mention these few only, since it would be a long business to write down the names of our many missing comrades. Of Narvaez' company, the majority fell at the bridge, weighed down with gold.

I will now speak of Botello the astrologer. His astrology did not help him, for he too died there with his horse. But let me go on to say that after we got to safety some papers, bound together like a book, were found in his box, marked with figures, lines, notes, and symbols; and beside them were the words: 'Whether I shall die in this wretched war, murdered by the Indians.' And further on there were other lines and figures, beside which it said: 'You will die.' But beside others it said: 'You will not die.' In another place were the words. 'Whether they will kill my horse,' and a little further on it said: 'They

1. Our Lady of Succours.

will kill him.' There were other figures in these papers, apparently for fortune-telling, and other pairs of contradictory statements. Also in the box was an object four inches long and made of leather, in the shape of a man's genitals. The resemblance was remarkable, and it was stuffed with flock.

Among those who perished at the bridge were the sons and daughter of Montezuma, the prisoners we were bringing with us, and Cacamatzin, lord of Texcoco, also some other provincial rulers. But enough of our disasters. We were thinking of the prospect before us. We were all wounded, only twenty-three horses survived, we had saved no muskets, cannon, or powder, and had very few crossbows. These we promptly mended with cord, however, and we made new arrows. But the worst thing of all was that we did not know in what state of mind we should find our Tlascalan allies. Moreover, once darkness fell we were continuously surrounded by shouting Mexicans who fell on us with their darts, arrows, and slings. So we decided to leave the place at midnight, with the Tlascalans as guides, and taking every precaution. We then placed the wounded in the middle and provided the lame with staffs; and those who were very ill and could not walk went on the croups of such horses as were lame and unfit for fighting. Those horsemen who were not wounded went ahead, or in bands on one flank or the other. The wounded Tlascalans walked in the middle of our squadron, and the rest of them who were unwounded faced the enemy with us.

The Mexicans continually harassed us with loud shouts and cries and whistlings. 'You are going to a place where you will perish to a man,' they shouted. We did not understand why, but it will be seen later on. I have forgotten to record how glad we were to see our Doña Marina, and Doña Luisa, Xicotenga's daughter, still alive. They had been rescued at the bridge by some Tlascalans, as had also the only Spanish woman in Mexico, Maria de Estrada. Some of Xicotenga's sons, the brothers of Doña Luisa, had been the first to escape across the bridges. But most of the women servants we had been given in Tlascala and in Mexico were left behind.

To continue the story of our march, that day we reached

some farms and isolated houses belonging to a large town named Cuauhtitlan[1] (after the capture of Mexico these were awarded to Alonso de Avila), and though the Mexicans yelled and shouted at us, hurling stones, darts, and arrows, we withstood it all. From there we went past some houses and shacks with the Mexicans still following us, and, as many of them had now collected, they endeavoured to slaughter us. Beginning to surround us, they hurled stones from their slings and darts and arrows; and at a difficult pass they attacked us with their broadswords, killing two of our soldiers and one horse, and wounding almost all the rest. But with cut and thrust we killed several of them, and our horsemen accounted for several more. Having slept in these houses and eaten the horse they killed, we resumed our march early next morning, sending half the horsemen ahead. But when we reached a plain about three miles further on and were beginning to think we could march on in safety, our scouts rode back from the country they had reconnoitred to tell us that the fields were full of Mexican warriors who were lying in wait for us. Alarmed though we were by this news, we were not dismayed. Ready to meet them and fight them to the death, we halted for a little, while orders were given to the cavalry that they must charge and return rapidly, aiming at the enemies' faces until they had broken their ranks, and to us soldiers that we must drive our swords into their bellies and so most thoroughly avenge our dead and wounded comrades. Then, if God willed it, we should escape with our lives.

We saw them beginning to surround us. Our horsemen, charging in bands of five, broke their ranks. And then, commending ourselves most heartily to God and the Blessed Mary, and calling on the name of our patron St James, we charged them, all together.

It was a destructive battle, and a fearful sight to behold. We moved through the midst of them at the closest quarters, slashing and thrusting at them with our swords. And the dogs fought back furiously, dealing us wounds and death with their lances and their two-handed swords. And, the field being level, our

1. Possibly a slip of memory. The location is uncertain.

horsemen speared them at their pleasure, charging and retiring and charging again. Although both they and their horses were wounded, they never stopped fighting, like the brave men they were. As for the rest of us who had no horses, we seemed all to be given double strength. For although we were wounded and now received fresh wounds, we did not stop to bind them up, for there was no time, but most courageously closed with the enemy, to stab them with our swords. I should like to describe the actions of Cortes, Cristobal de Olid, Gonzalo de Sandoval, Gonzalo Dominguez, and a certain Juan de Salamanca, who rode from one part of the field to the other breaking the enemy's ranks, although themselves badly wounded, and to record Cortes' instructions to us who were in the thick of the enemy that we must aim our cuts and thrusts at distinguished chieftains, who all wore great golden plumes and rich armour and devices.

We were marvellously encouraged also by the brave and bold Sandoval, who cried: 'Today gentlemen, is the day on which we are certain to win. Trust in God, and we shall come out of this alive, and to some purpose!' I must say once more that they killed and wounded many of our soldiers.

Now by God's grace, Cortes and the captains who rode with him came to the place where the commander-in-chief of the Mexicans marched with his banner displayed, in rich golden armour and high silver plumes, followed by his great band of warriors. And when Cortes saw him and other Mexican chieftains, all with high plumes, he said to his captains: 'Now gentlemen, let us cut our way through them, and leave none of them without a wound!' Then, commending themselves to God, our horsemen charged, and Cortes, riding straight for the Mexican commander, made him drop his banner, while the other captains succeeded in breaking the large bands of Indians who followed him. Cortes' charge had not thrown the Mexican down, but Juan de Salamanca, who rode beside our Captain on a piebald mare, dealt him a lance-thrust and snatched his rich plume. This he afterwards gave to Cortes, saying that it was his by right, since he had charged him first and made him drop his banner, thus depriving his followers of the courage to fight.

However, three years afterwards His Majesty gave it to Salamanca as his coat of arms, and his descendants carry it on their
saddle-cloths.

Let us return to the battle. When the Mexican commander
and many other chiefs had been killed, it pleased the Lord that
their attack should slacken. Then all our horsemen followed
them, and we felt neither hunger nor thirst. It was as if we had
suffered no disaster and undergone no hardships; we followed
up our victory, dealing death and wounds, and our allies the
Tlascalans became like very lions. With their swords, their two-
handed blades, and other weapons which they had just captured, they fought most valiantly and well.

When our horsemen returned from following up our victory,
we all gave great thanks to God for our escape from this mighty
host. For never had there been seen throughout the Indies so
many warriors assembled for any battle. All the flower of
Mexico, of Texcoco, of all the towns around the lake, and of
many others in the neighbourhood, was present, and the men
of Otumba, Tepetezcuco, and Saltocan, who all came in the
belief that this time we should be totally destroyed. Their
armour moreover was extremely rich, and decorated with much
gold and many plumes and devices, and nearly all of them
were chieftains or important persons. Near the spot where this
famous and sternly contested battle was fought – for indeed
it can be so described, since only by God's grace did we escape
with our lives – stood the town of Otumba.

Interested readers will remember that when we went to the
relief of Pedro de Alvarado in Mexico, we numbered in all
thirteen hundred soldiers, including ninety-seven horsemen,
eighty crossbowmen, and as many musketeers. In addition we
had more than two thousand Tlascalans and we brought in
many cannon. Now the day of our entry into Mexico was
Midsummer Day 1520, and we escaped on 10 July of the same
year; the battle of Otumba, as it was called, being fought on
14 July. But now, within a matter of days, in the battle of
Mexico and on the bridges and causeways, and all the engagements, including that of Otumba and those on the road, more
than eight hundred and sixty soldiers were killed and sacrificed,

and seventy-two more, together with five Spanish women – all belonging to Narvaez' company – at the town of Tuxtepec, also a thousand Tlascalans. And if we come to consider it, none of us had much luck with his share of the gold we received, for if more of Narvaez' men than those of Cortes fell at the bridges it was because they were so weighed down by the stuff that they could neither run nor swim.

We marched along very cheerfully towards Tlascala, eating some gourds that they call *ayotes*, and the Mexican bands did not dare to collect and attack us from the small towns, although they still shouted at us from places where we could not get at them, and hurled stones, darts, and arrows at us, until we took refuge first in some farm buildings and then in a small town, where there was a good *cue* and a strong house in which we could spend the night. Here we dressed our wounds and got some rest. We were still followed by Mexican bands, however. But they dared not draw close, and those who came nearest seemed to say: 'There you go, out of our country!' From this small town where we rested we could see the hills above Tlascala, and the sight was as welcome to our eyes as if we had seen home. But how could we be sure that the Tlascalans would be loyal to us? What did we know of their attitude, or of the fate of the settlers at Villa Rica, whether they were alive or dead? Cortes said to us that although we were so few, only four hundred and forty of us surviving, with twenty horses, twelve crossbowmen, and seven musketeers – almost the same number as had followed him into Mexico in the first place – and though we had no powder and were all wounded, lamed, and maimed, we could clearly see that it had been Jesus Christ's pleasure to spare our lives, and that we must always give Him great thanks and honour.

With our scouts riding ahead of us, we reached a spring on the hillside where there were some walls and defences from ancient times, and our Tlascalan allies said that this was the boundary between them and the Mexicans. There, in welcome peace after the hardships we had gone through, we halted to wash and eat. Then quickly resuming our march, we reached the Tlascalan town of Hueyotlipan, where they received us and gave us food, though only a little, and this had to be paid for with some small pieces of gold and *chalchihuites* which some of us carried. Here we rested for a day.

When the news of our coming reached the capital of Tlascala, Mase Escasi, Xicotenga the Elder, Chichimecatecle, and many other *Caciques* and chieftains promptly came to us, accompanied by nearly all the inhabitants of Huexotzinco. On reaching the town where we were they advanced to embrace Cortes and the rest of us, and some of them were in tears. 'Oh Malinche, Malinche!' they cried. 'How grieved we are at your misfortunes and those of all your brothers, and at the number of our own people who have been killed with you! We told you so often not to trust the Mexicans, for one day they were sure to attack you, but you would not believe us. Now that it has happened all we can do is to tend your wounds and give you food. Consider yourselves at home. Rest, and we will return to our town and prepare quarters for you. Do not think it a small thing that you have escaped with your lives from that strong city and its bridges. If we thought of you as brave men before, we consider you much braver now. Many women in our towns will be mourning the death of sons, husbands, brothers, and kinsmen, but do not be disturbed by that. You owe much to your gods, who have brought you here and delivered you from the host of warriors who were waiting for you at Otumba. I knew four days before that they had gathered there to kill you. I wanted to go to your rescue with thirty thousand of our warriors, but I could not start because they had not yet assembled and were still being collected.'

Cortes and all our men embraced and thanked them. Cortes gave all the chieftains golden jewels and precious stones, and as every soldier had brought away all that he could, some of us gave presents out of what we had to the Indians we knew. How they rejoiced and how happy they seemed when they saw that Doña Luisa and Doña Marina were safe! And how sorrowfully they wept for the others who were absent and dead, especially Mase Escasi, who bewailed his daughter Doña Elvira and the death of Juan Velazquez de Leon, to whom he had given her.

Cortes Collects Fresh Strength

[THE Spaniards spent twenty-two days at Tlascala, where a further disaster had befallen them. The gold that had been stored there, which was the Villa Rica settlers' share of the booty, had been recaptured by the Mexicans, who had killed the three settlers sent to fetch it away. The Tlascalans, however, remained fervently loyal. Indeed, their chiefs claimed that things had never been so good before the arrival of these *Teules* whom their gods had prophesied. Though Xicotenga the Younger had been stirring up mischief and advocating an alliance with Mexico and an attack on the Spaniards, his success had been so small that, but for his father, he would have been slain by the other chiefs. Nevertheless he remained at liberty.

Cortes cast around him for reinforcements. He sent letters to Villa Rica in which he concealed the truth, and merely asked for powder and crossbows for a campaign in the neighbourhood of Mexico. He also asked for the crews of Narvaez' two ships to be sent to him, and that the ships should be destroyed if unseaworthy. Only seven thin sickly individuals arrived, led by a soldier called Lencero, and they were the joke of the camp.

Cortes decided to lead his forces to Tepeaca, a town garrisoned by the Mexicans, where sixteen Spanish soldiers had been killed, and he started to train Narvaez' undisciplined band for a campaign. But Narvaez' men, led by Andres de Duero, demanded to go home. They drew up a petition asking for a return to Villa Rica and the abandonment of the war, pointing out that everyone was wounded and that all weapons and stores were exhausted. On seeing, however, that Cortes' men stood behind him, they grudgingly gave in, promising to follow him on his expedition, on condition that they were allowed to return home as soon as possible.

The expedition approached Tepeaca, and found the inhabitants defiant. They threatened the Spaniards with a greater slaughter than they had suffered in the battles at the bridges and at Otumba. Cortes then drew up before a notary a decree condemning to slavery all the allies of Mexicans who had revolted after giving their obedience to His Majesty. Thus the enslavement of the Mexicans was legally begun.

The Tepeacans and their Mexican garrison were easily routed in a battle among the maize-fields in which the Spanish horsemen were able to deploy. The Tepeacans then gave in and swore obedience to His Majesty, and their town was refounded under the name of La Villa Segura de la Frontera, which became a base for the raiding of the countryside, where slaves were freely taken and branded with a special brand.

Meanwhile, in Mexico Montezuma's successor had died of small-pox, and Guatemoc – whom Bernal Díaz describes as 'a young man of about twenty-five, very much of a gentleman, for an Indian, and very valiant' – was chosen in his place. His wife was one of Monte-zuma's daughters. After the defeat of Tepeaca and the enslavement of a large part of the local population, Guatemoc feared that the Spaniards would attack other provinces of his empire and sent out reinforcements. His Mexican troops, however, ill-treated the people of Guacachula and Izucar, the two chief towns reinforced, and the population turned against them. Realizing that the Spaniards were putting an end to the rape and robbery that the Mexicans practised in subject territory, they betrayed the Mexicans' dispositions to Cristobal de Olid, the leader of a large Spanish expedition in the region. Olid was irresolute, and the Narvaez' men among his follow-ers at one moment persuaded him to retreat. The Tlascalans, how-ever, having captured booty and slaves from the Tepeacans, were enthusiasts for battle, and the Mexicans were defeated.

Meanwhile two small ships had come to Villa Rica, bearing sup-plies from the governor of Cuba which were intended for Narvaez. For the news of his defeat and imprisonment had not yet reached Cuba. The crews of these ships were cleverly inveigled ashore, and persuaded to carry their stores up-country to Cortes. A further contingent of sixty sick men also joined him at Segura de la Fron-tera after failing to make a settlement at the Panuco river. Many of these men died, and the rest were nicknamed 'green-bellies', for they were the colour of death and their bellies were swollen. A further group of fifty-three soldiers and seven horses under Miguel Diaz de Auz, who had been sent to reinforce the Panuco settlement but had found it deserted, arrived in a healthier condition and were more welcome. They received the nickname of the 'tough-backs', and another group of forty who wore heavy cotton armour, and brought ten horses and some crossbows, were called the 'pack-saddles'. These last two contingents came from Jamaica. Thus un-wittingly the governors of Cuba and Jamaica were enabling Cortes to rebuild his depleted forces. He now had a hundred and fifty more soldiers and twenty more horses at his disposal.

Cortes now learnt that it was in the towns of Cacatami and Xalacingo that the Villa Rica settlers had been murdered and their load of gold stolen. Some of Narvaez' men also had been killed there on their way up to Mexico. He sent Gonzalo de Sandoval, therefore, with two hundred of his men and a large force of Tlascalans, to deal with these towns. A preliminary request for the return of the gold was refused. Once more the battle was in open country, and so the Indians were routed. In the *cues* the Spaniards found clothes, armour, and bridles that had belonged to horsemen who had been sacrificed to the Indian gods. They did not, however, find the missing gold, which had been transported to Mexico.

The chiefs of the captured towns sued for peace, and Sandoval sent them to Cortes, who had by now achieved a great reputation among the Indians for bravery and fairness. Smallpox was spreading through the country, and many *Caciques* died. Consequently, various disputes as to the succession and ownership of property were brought to Cortes for settlement. Sandoval returned from his expedition with a great haul of women and boys, who were branded as slaves.

When the expeditions were successfully completed and the country pacified Cortes proceeded with the aid of the King's officials to the division of the slaves. Only women and boys were considered valuable, since the Tlascalan allies provided enough men to perform the necessary labour and act as auxiliaries. Cortes decided that all should be branded, so that the king's fifth and afterwards his own could be taken. For this purpose all the soldiers were told to bring the women whom they were 'sheltering', and to do so by the end of the day following that of the proclamation. They found, however, that not only were the two-fifths taken, but all the best-looking women disappeared. There was not a pretty one left. Accusations were broadcast, especially by Narvaez' men, and references were made to Cortes' inaccurate estimates of the gold and treasure they had won in Mexico. Now 'the poor soldier, who had done all the hard work and was covered with wounds' had not only lost his share of the gold but was robbed of the woman he had chosen for himself.

Cortes tried as usual the effect of smooth words. He promised that all the women should be sold by auction, when the best-looking would fetch the highest price. Then the soldiers would have no grievance against him.

A further quarrel broke out, on the subject of the gold saved on the flight from Mexico. At the last moment Cortes had offered the ingots that could not be taken by horses or porters to anyone who cared to carry them away. A number of soldiers had loaded themselves with this treasure, and some had paid for it with their lives. Cortes now proclaimed that a third of it must be returned to him, and that if it was not brought in it would be seized. Cortes gained some of it by force. But as nearly all the captains and the King's officials themselves had secret hoards, the proclamation was largely ignored.

Now that Cortes had received reinforcements, Narvaez' men once more requested permission to return home. This time it was granted, and a ship was set aside to carry them. Cortes sent Diego de Ordaz to represent him in Spain, where he and his men were still considered to be traitors, and Alonso de Avila to put his case to the Royal courts in Santo Domingo. In addition he sent a ship to Jamaica to buy horses. All this was paid for with the gold ingots which had been kept out of sight.

Cortes now decided to transfer his army to Tlascala and to concentrate on the building of thirteen sloops with which to master the lake and protect his flanks while they marched up the causeways to recapture Mexico. In all this the Tlascalans cooperated, and at Mase Escasi's death from smallpox Cortes was instrumental in the choice of his son as the next ruler. The older chiefs now became Christians.

The timber was cut; anchors, sails, rigging, cables, and tow were brought from Villa Rica, blacksmiths were sent for, and pitch was made in the pine-woods. It was then debated whether the army should move on to Texcoco or to Ayotzingo, so that the sloops could be assembled and launched in the creeks which ran into the lake. The decision was for Texcoco, and almost as soon as it was taken news reached the army that a ship had arrived from Spain and the Canaries, loaded with arms and powder and a great variety of merchandise. These supplies were purchased, and the men aboard came up to Cortes' camp, where they offered timely assistance.]

When Cortes found himself in possession of a good supply of muskets and powder, crossbows, and horses, and realized how eager we were, soldiers and captains alike, to make a fresh attack on the great city of Mexico, he decided to ask the rulers of Tlascala for ten thousand warriors to join us on an expedition against Texcoco, one of the biggest cities in New Spain. In answer to his request, Xicotenga the Elder (who, as I have said, had now become a Christian and had taken the name of

Don Lorenzo de Vargas) agreed to give him not only ten thousand but as many more as he would take, and to send another brave chief, our great friend Chichimecatecle, as their captain. Cortes thanked him, and after we had made our muster, on the day after Christmas 1520, we began the march in our usual excellent order. We slept that night in a town that was subject to Tlascala, where they gave us everything we needed.

From there onwards it was Mexican territory, and we proceeded more cautiously, with our artillery, musketeers, and crossbowmen drawn up in careful order, and with four mounted scouts and four very active soldiers with swords and shields going ahead to look out for bad places and see if they were practicable for horses. For we had been warned on the road that a dangerous pass had that day been blocked by newly felled trees, news of our advance having already reached Mexico and Texcoco.

That day we met with no obstacles and camped at the foot of the Sierra, a march of about nine miles. The night was very cold, and when dawn broke we began to climb a small pass. In some difficult ravine-like places the hillside had been cut away so that we could not get by, and many pine-trees and other timber had been placed across the track. But thanks to our many Tlascalan allies a way was soon cleared. Sending a company of musketeers and crossbowmen in advance, we marched on with the utmost caution, our allies cutting and pushing aside the trees to let our horsemen past. Thus we got to the top of the Sierra, from which we dropped a little to a place where the whole lake of Mexico lay before us, with its great cities standing in the water. And when we saw it we gave God great thanks for allowing us to look on it again. Then, remembering our great defeat and expulsion from Mexico, we vowed that, God willing, we would now adopt a different method of fighting, and blockade the city.

As we came down the Sierra, we saw great smoke-signals which were being sent up by the people of Texcoco and their subject cities. Advancing further, we came upon a large band of Mexican and Texcocan warriors who were waiting for us at a bad spot, where the track ran through a thicket and there was a wooden bridge, which seemed to be broken, with a deep gulf and a waterfall below it. However, we soon beat these bands and crossed over in safety. Then how they shouted at us from the farms and the ravines! But that was all they did, and they only called out from places where the horses could not reach them. Our friends the Tlascalans carried off fowls and anything else they could steal, despite the fact that Cortes had ordered them not to make war on the people unless they were attacked. But the Tlascalans answered that if the people were well disposed and peaceful, they would not have come to attack us at the bridge over the ravine.

We spent that night at a deserted town belonging to Texcoco, posting our sentries, sending out patrols, and taking every precaution against a night attack. For we had heard from five Mexicans whom we had captured at the bridge that many bands of warriors were waiting for us at another dangerous spot. But as we afterwards learnt, they had not the courage to attack us or even to await our coming. For there seem to have been disputes and enmity between the Texcocans and the Mexicans, and they had not yet fully recovered from the smallpox which had swept through the country. Moreover, they had heard of our victories over the various Mexican garrisons.

When dawn broke we began our march on Texcoco, which was about six miles from the place where we had slept. Before we had gone much more than a mile, however, we saw our scouts returning at a breakneck gallop, and looking very cheerful. They told Cortes that ten Indians were approaching unarmed and carrying golden devices and banners, and that there was no more yelling and shouting from the farms they had passed, as there had been on the day before. To all appearances everything was peaceful, and we rejoiced at it. Then Cortes ordered a halt to await the approach of seven chieftains from Texcoco, who carried a golden banner and a long lance. Before coming up to us they lowered the banner and knelt down, which is their sign of peace. When they came before Cortes, who had Doña Marina and Jeronimo de Aguilar standing beside him, they said: 'Malinche, Coanacotzin, our lord and the lord of Texcoco, sends to beg for your friendship. He is peacefully awaiting you in his city of Texcoco, as a proof of which please be so good as to accept this banner of gold. He humbly begs you to order your Tlascalans and your own brothers not to harm his country, but to come and lodge in his city, where he will give you all you need.' They also said that the bands stationed in the ravines and rough places were not Texcocans but Mexicans sent by Guatemoc.

We were all delighted to hear this offer of peace, and Cortes immediately embraced the messengers, especially those three who were related to Montezuma and whom we all recognized as his former captains. After a brief discussion, Cortes hastily sent for the Tlascalan captains, and ordered them in a friendly way not to do more harm and take no property anywhere in the country, since peace had now been made. They obeyed his instructions, but he did not ask them to take no food, for all the houses were well stocked.

Cortes then consulted his captains, and our general opinion was that these negotiations for peace were a trick. For if they had been genuine, these chieftains would not have come so precipitately, and they would have brought some provisions. Nevertheless Cortes accepted the banner, which was worth eighty pesos, and thanked the messengers, saying that he was not in the habit of harming His Majesty's vassals, but on the contrary would favour and protect them against the Mexicans so long as they kept the peace they proffered. He pointed out also that he had already restrained the Tlascalans. On the other hand, he knew that forty Spaniards and about two hundred Tlascalans had been killed in their city during our retreat from Mexico, and many loads of gold and other spoil belonging to them had been stolen. He asked the messengers therefore to request their lord and the other *Caciques* and captains of Texcoco to return the gold and the cloth, though for the death of the Spaniards there was no remedy and he would not ask for one.

The messengers replied that they would convey his request to their lord, but that the killing of the Spaniards and the taking of the spoil had been ordered by the chieftain Cuitlahuac, who had been chosen king of Mexico after Montezuma's death. Most of the *Teules*, they said, had been taken to Mexico and there sacrificed to Huichilobos. On hearing this reply Cortes gave no answer for fear his indignation would frighten them, but merely bade them farewell. One of them remained in our company.

We then went on to a suburb of Texcoco whose name I have forgotten, where they gave us plenty to eat and everything that we needed. After throwing down some idols in the houses where we were lodged, we went on early next morning to Texcoco itself. Here we saw no women, boys, or children in any of the streets or houses, and all the men looked frightened and hostile.

We took up our quarters in some great rooms and halls, and Cortes at once summoned his captains and most of us soldiers. He then told us not to leave the precincts of the great courts, and to keep well on our guard until we saw how things were going, for he did not think the city looked very peaceful. He ordered Pedro de Alvarado, Cristobal de Olid, and some other soldiers, myself among them, to ascend the great *cue*, which was very high, taking some twenty musketeers with us as a guard, and to look over the lake and city, for everything could be seen from there. On reaching the top, we saw all the inhabitants of these towns moving off with their goods and possessions, and their women and children, some to the hills and others to the reed-thickets in the lake, which was swarming with canoes of every size.

On receiving this news, Cortes decided to arrest the chieftain who had sent him the golden banner. But the *papas* whom he sent to summon him found that the man had already fled for safety with a number of other chiefs, who had been the first to leave for Mexico. That night we were very careful in our posting of sentinels and scouts, and very early next morning Cortes commanded that all the chieftains who had remained in Texcoco should be summoned before him. For the city being a large one, there were many who belonged to factions opposing the chief who had fled. Indeed there had been discussions and disputes as to who should be captain and ruler of the place. On coming before Cortes, they told him the story of Coanacotzin's

seizure of control, saying that in his lust for power he had in-
famously murdered his elder brother Cuicuitzcatzin with the
help of that prince Cuitlahuac who had attacked us when we
were fleeing from Mexico. They also told Cortes that there
were other chiefs with a better right to their kingdom, and that
it should rightfully go to a certain youth, who was promptly
baptized a Christian with great religious pomp, and assumed
the name of Don Hernando Cortes, our Captain standing as his
godfather. This youth, they said, was the legitimate son of
Nezahualpilli, lord of Texcoco, and they appointed him their
natural king and lord with all the ceremonies they perform in
such cases, and to the accompaniment of great festivities and
rejoicings throughout Texcoco. The new king governed absolutely, in complete peace and with the love of all his vassals
there and in the neighbouring towns; and for his better instruction in our Christian faith, also to guide his behaviour and teach
him our language, Cortes appointed as his tutors Antonio de
Villa Real and a bachelor of arts called Escobar.

Cortes asked the new chief for a large force of Indian labour-
ers to broaden and deepen the ditches and canals along which
we were to tow our launches to the lake when they were completed and ready to sail. He also explained to Don Hernando
and the other chiefs the reason and purpose for which they
had been built, and how we were going to blockade Mexico.

[Don Hernando helped the Spaniards in every way, and used his
good offices to persuade some other towns to make peace. Work
proceeded on the canals, and the Mexicans watched the Spaniards
from their canoes, hoping to take them by surprise.]

When we had been twelve days in Texcoco the Tlascalans
ran out of supplies, for the Texcocans could not feed them
because they were so many. Since we did not want our allies
to become a burden, and since they were most eager to fight
the Mexicans and avenge their comrades who had been killed
and sacrificed after their past defeats, Cortes decided that we
should now set out on our march to Iztapalapa, which is about
twelve miles from Texcoco. We had passed through the place
on our way to Mexico. It is, as I have said before, a fine town,

with more than half its houses built on the water and the rest on dry land. Cortes himself was in command, and with him went Andres de Tapia, Cristobal de Olid, thirteen horsemen, twenty crossbowmen, six musketeers, two hundred and twenty soldiers, our Tlascalan allies, and some twenty chiefs from Texcoco, whom Don Hernando had given us and whom we knew to be his relatives and the enemies of Guatemoc, the present king in Mexico.

We advanced in our customary good order, and the Mexicans, who always kept a careful watch on us, and held garrisons and bands of warriors in readiness to reinforce any of their towns as soon as they knew we were going to attack them, sent a warning to Iztapalapa, together with a contingent of more than eight thousand men. Like good warriors, they awaited our arrival on dry land, and for a while both the Iztapalapans and the Mexicans who had come to help them fought bravely against us. But our horsemen broke their ranks, and were followed by the crossbowmen and musketeers and by all our Tlascalan allies, who charged them like mad dogs. The enemy then suddenly quitted the plain and took refuge in the town. This was a preconcerted stratagem which would have cost us dear if we had not quickly retired. In pursuance of their plan they made a show of flight, some getting into their canoes which lay ready on the water, and others entering the houses, while yet others concealed themselves in the reed-beds. The night being dark, we were able to take up our positions noiselessly, and with no armed display, in some houses by the lakeside; we stayed there, pleased with the spoil we had captured, and still more pleased with our supposed victory. We placed our sentinels and watchmen, we sent out patrols and scouts. But when we were off our guard, such a flood of water swept through the town that if the chiefs we had brought from Texcoco had not shouted to us to get out of the houses as quickly as we could and make for dry land, we should all have been drowned. For the enemy had emptied the fresh- and salt-water canals, and cut through a causeway, which caused the level of the water to rise suddenly. Since our Tlascalan allies were not used to the water, and could not swim, two of them perished.

As for us, we managed to escape, without our belongings and at great risk of our lives. We were all soaked, our powder was spoilt, and we were very cold. In this sorry condition we spent a bad and supperless night, which was rendered even more unpleasant by the jeers and catcalls and whistling of the Iztapalapans and the Mexicans, who were safe in their houses and canoes. However, there was still worse to come. For news having reached Mexico of this plan to drown us, many battalions of warriors were waiting to receive us on land. As soon as day dawned, these Mexicans attacked us and pressed us so hard that we could scarcely withstand them. But although they killed two soldiers and a horse, and wounded many others, they did not defeat us. Little by little their attack slackened, and we returned to Texcoco, somewhat ashamed of having been taken in by their trick with the water, and annoyed at having gained so little glory in the subsequent battle because we had run out of powder.

Nevertheless the enemy were frightened, and had enough to do to bury or burn their dead, and cure their wounded and repair their houses.

When we had been in Texcoco for two days, after our return from the expedition to Iztapalapa, three towns – Tepetezcuco, Otumba (the scene of our great battle), and another the name of which I forget – came peaceably to Cortes to ask pardon for recent attacks and for the deaths of the Spaniards they had killed. The excuse they offered was that they had acted on the orders of Montezuma's successor, Cuitlahuac, and had merely attacked with his other vassals, also that the gold, horses, and cloth they had captured had been taken to Mexico, as had also the *Teules*, who had been sacrificed there. Seeing this to be the only possible course at the time, Cortes rebuked them severely and pardoned them. And they promised, with repeated protestations, that they would always be enemies to the Mexicans, and serve His Majesty as his loyal vassals, which they did.

At the same time the inhabitants of a lakeside town named Mizquic, which is also called Venezuela, came to ask for peace and friendship. It seems that they had never been on good terms with the Mexicans and heartily loathed them. We were all very pleased at this people's coming, because of their position on the water, and because through them we hoped to be able to approach their neighbours further along the lake. Cortes thanked them, therefore, and dispatched them with promises and kind words.

While these conversations were taking place, a message was brought to him that great bands of Mexicans were advancing on the four towns which had been the first to seek our friendship, Guatinchan and Guaxuntlan[1] and two others the names of which escape me. They told Cortes that the inhabitants were afraid to stay in their houses and wanted to take to the hills or come to Texcoco, and they begged him so insistently to help them that he immediately assembled twenty horsemen, two hundred soldiers, thirteen crossbowmen, and ten musketeers, and taking Pedro de Alvarado, Cristobal de Olid, the camp commandant, and myself with him, went to the towns from which these complaints came.

It seemed to be true that the Mexicans had threatened them with destruction for accepting our friendship, but the chief subjects of dispute were some large maize plantations beside the lake, which were ready for harvesting and from which the Texcocans and their neighbours were provisioning our camp. The Mexicans wanted to take this maize, which they said was rightfully theirs since it was the custom of these four towns to sow and harvest the plantations for the benefit of the *papas* of Mexico.

When he understood the situation, Cortes told them to have no fear and to stay in their houses, and promised that when they had to go out and gather maize either for our camp or for their own needs, he would send a captain with many horsemen and soldiers to protect those who brought it in. This offer contented them and we returned to Texcoco. After that, whenever we needed maize for our camp we mustered warriors from all these towns, and with our Tlascalan allies, ten horsemen, and a hundred soldiers, also a few crossbowmen and musketeers, went to the fields to fetch it. I mention this because I twice went for it myself, and on one occasion we had a fine skirmish with

1. Huexotla.

great bands of Mexicans, who had come in more than a thousand canoes and were lying in wait in the maize-fields. But as we had our allies with us, we drove the Mexicans back to their canoes, bravely though they fought. One of our soldiers was killed and a dozen wounded, as were also a few Tlascalans. The enemy, however, had nothing much to boast of, for they left ten or fifteen corpses behind them, and another five who were taken prisoner.

Next day we heard news that the people of Chalco and Tlamanalco and their dependencies wished to make peace, but could not do so on account of the garrisons stationed in their towns. They complained that these Mexicans took their women, especially those who were beautiful, and violated them in front of their fathers, mothers, or husbands.

We had received news that the timber for the launches had been cut and prepared at Tlascala. But though the time was passing, none of it had been brought to Texcoco, and this very much perturbed us. Moreover people were coming from Mizquic and other friendly towns to tell Cortes that the Mexicans were about to attack them for making friends with us.

Cortes realized that if we helped some of the towns that were calling for our protection, and supported the people of Chalco too so that they could come to make peace with us, we could offer adequate security to neither, for we had to be constantly on the alert in Texcoco itself. So he decided to go first to Chalco and Tlamanalco, and therefore sent Gonzalo de Sandoval and Francisco de Lugo with fifteen horsemen and two hundred soldiers, also some musketeers and bowmen and our Tlascalan allies, with orders to break up and completely disperse the Mexican garrisons and drive them out of Chalco and Tlamanalco. This would leave the road to Tlascala quite clear and allow us to travel to and from Villa Rica without interference from Mexican warriors. As soon as this was decided, he sent some Texcocan Indians very secretly to Chalco to advise the people, so that they might be prepared to fall on the Mexican garrisons either by day or night, and the people of Chalco, who could have asked for nothing better, made thorough preparations.

When Gonzalo de Sandoval advanced with his army, he considered it advisable to leave a rearguard of five horsemen and as many crossbowmen, to protect the large number of Tlascalans who were laden with the spoils they had captured. Now, as the Mexicans always kept spies on the watch, they knew that our men were marching on Chalco. So, to reinforce the garrison, they had recently collected many squadrons of warriors, who now fell on the rearguard in which the Tlascalans were marching with their baggage, and punished them severely. Our horsemen and crossbowmen could not resist them, for two of the crossbowmen were killed and the others were wounded. Although Gonzalo de Sandoval very quickly turned on the enemy and drove them off, killing ten Mexicans, the lake was so close that they were able to leap into the canoes in which they had come and get away. For all that territory is thick with dependencies of Mexico.

When the enemy had been driven off, Sandoval saw that all the five horsemen whom he had left in the rearguard were wounded, and their horses too, also that the two crossbowmen were dead and the others wounded. Nevertheless he could not prevent himself from saying to the rest of those whom he had left to defend the rear that he despised them for their inability to resist the enemy and defend themselves and our allies. In fact he was very much enraged with them. They were some of the recent arrivals from Spain, and as he told them, quite obviously did not know what war was. He then marched the Tlascalans with their spoil to safety, and dispatched some letters which Cortes had directed to Villa Rica, in which he informed the commander there of our intention to blockade Mexico, warned him to keep a good look-out, and requested him to send any soldiers who were disposed to fight as far as Tlascala, but no further until the roads were safer.

Having dispatched the messengers and sent the Tlascalans home, Sandoval turned back to Chalco, which was close by, marching with the utmost caution and sending his scouts out ahead, for he knew well that a surprise attack might come from any of the towns and homesteads he passed. As he drew near to Chalco, he saw many bands of Mexicans coming against him.

On some level ground, where there was a large plantation of maize and *magueys*, they attacked him stoutly with darts, arrows, and stones from slings, and with long lances which they directed against the horses. Seeing this great host approaching, Sandoval cheered his men on and twice broke the enemy's ranks; and with the aid of the muskets and crossbows and the few allies who had stayed with us, he defeated them, although they wounded five soldiers and six horses and many of our allies. However, he fell on them so quickly and so furiously that he thoroughly avenged the damage they had done at the outset. When the people of Chalco knew of his approach, they came out along the road to receive him with great rejoicing and honour.

After their meeting, Sandoval said that he intended to return to Texcoco next day, and the people of Chalco wished to go with him to see and speak to Malinche, and bring with them the two sons of the ruler of that province, who had died a few days before of smallpox. On his deathbed he had charged his chieftains and elders to take these lads to the Captain, so that he might install them as lords of Chalco, adding that all must endeavour to become subjects of the great king of the *Teules*, for his ancestors had assuredly prophesied that their lands would be ruled by bearded men who came from the direction of the sunrise, and his own eyes told him we were those men. Then Sandoval returned to Texcoco with all his army, taking the sons of the lord of Chalco and the other chiefs and eight Mexican prisoners.

Cortes was overjoyed by the news of Sandoval's arrival. After hearing his lieutenant's account of his journey, he went to his lodgings, where the chiefs immediately appeared before him. After paying him great respect and explaining the wishes of their late ruler, they presented him with rich jewels worth two hundred gold pesos; and when he had listened to the translation of their speeches, our Captain treated them very kindly and embraced them. He then conferred the lordship of Chalco on the elder brother, with more than half the subject towns, reserving Tlamanalco and Chimaluacan with Ayotzingo and some other places, for the younger; and he proffered much advice to the principal elders and the newly appointed *Caciques*. These then expressed the wish to return to their own country. But Cortes begged them to stay two days, as he was about to send a captain to Tlascala for logs and planks, who would take them in his company and protect them from Mexican attacks on their homeward road.

After this interview, Cortes decided to send the eight prisoners whom Sandoval had captured to Mexico to tell the prince Guatemoc how reluctant we should be to bring ruin on him and his great city. Having advised the Mexicans to sue for peace, in which case he would forgive them for the losses and deaths we had suffered in their city and would ask nothing from them, he warned them that war is easy to stop at the beginning, but very difficult towards the middle and end, and that finally they would be destroyed. He told them that he knew of all their preparations against us, but they were useless, since the Lord we worship always helped us, and all the towns in the neighbourhood were now on our side, as well as the Tlascalans, whose only wish was for a war in which they could take revenge for the Mexicans' treachery and murder.

Our eight messengers came before Guatemoc, who refused to give any answer, but went on building defences and gathering equipment. He sent an order round all his provinces that if any isolated Spaniards were captured they should be brought to Mexico to be sacrificed, and that when he sent to summon them all his vassals should come at once with their arms. Furthermore, he remitted much of their tribute, and made them great promises.

As we were always longing to get the launches finished and begin the blockade of Mexico, our Captain Cortes decided to waste no more time. He ordered Gonzalo de Sandoval to go for the timber, with two hundred soldiers, twenty musketeers and crossbowmen, fifteen horsemen, and a large company of Tlascalans, also twenty chieftains from Texcoco, and instructed him to take with him the youths and elders from Chalco, and see them safely home. Before they set out, Cortes made peace between the Tlascalans and the people of Chalco. For the people of Chalco had formerly been members of the Mexican confederation, and when the Mexicans went to war with Tlascala they had taken people from Chalco to help them, because they lived close at hand, and from that time the Tlascalans had hated the people of Chalco and treated them as enemies.

[On his way Sandoval visited the town of Pueblo Morisco, where Narvaez' men had been murdered on the way up from Villa Rica. They found the remains of men and horses in the *cue*, but pardoned the inhabitants on condition that they joined them against the Mexicans.]

On his way towards Tlascala, when he was near the principal place where the *Caciques* reside, Sandoval met eight thousand men carrying all the logs and planks for the launches, and as many more followed as a guard with their arms and plumes, and two thousand others who brought food and relieved the porters. Everything was in charge of Martin Lopez, the master carpenter, who had cut the timber and made the shapes and calculations for the planks, and there were other Spaniards with him whose names I forget. When Sandoval saw them coming he was overjoyed, for he had expected to be delayed some time in Tlascala waiting until they were ready. For two days they marched with us in this same order, until we entered Mexican territory. The Mexicans whistled and shouted at us from the farms and ravines, where neither our muskets nor our horsemen could harm them.

Then Martin Lopez said that we ought to change our order of march, for the Tlascalans told him that they feared the great armies of Mexico might make a surprise attack at that point on the road and defeat them, since they were so hampered by their heavy loads of timber and provisions. Sandoval at once split up the horsemen, crossbowmen, and musketeers, so that some should go in advance and others on the flanks, and he ordered Chichimecatecle, who was in command of all the Tlascalans, to drop behind and march with him in the rearguard. The *Cacique*, however, took this as a reflection on his bravery and was offended. But they then spoke to him so persuasively that he became reconciled, especially as Sandoval marched behind with him and it was explained to him that the Mexicans always made their attacks on the baggage in the rear.

Another two days' march brought the Tlascalans to Texcoco. Before entering they put on very fine cloaks and plumes, and marched in good order to the music of drums and trumpets. They took half a day marching into the city in an unbroken line, shouting, whistling and crying out: 'Long live our Lord and Emperor!' and : 'Castile! Castile!', and: 'Tlascala! Tlascala!'

On their arrival at Texcoco, Cortes and some of his captains came out to meet them, and Cortes made great protestations of friendship to Chichimecatecle and his captains. The logs and planks and the rest of the material for the launches were placed beside the canals and creeks where they were to be built, and from that moment the construction of thirteen launches proceeded swiftly. Martin Lopez and some other Spaniards, also certain Indian carpenters and two smiths with their forges, all worked with the greatest speed until the craft were assembled. After that they had only to be caulked and to have their masts, rigging, and sails set up.

I must not fail to describe the great precautions that we took in the camp in the matter of spies and scouts and guards for the launches during their construction. For they lay near the lake, and three times the Mexicans tried to set them on fire. We captured fifteen of these would-be incendiaries, and Cortes obtained from them full knowledge of what was going on in Mexico and of Guatemoc's intentions, which were that they would never make peace, but either kill us or die to the last man.

I must now speak of the messengers and summonses sent by the Mexicans to all their subject towns, letting them off their tribute, and of the work they did by night and day digging ditches and deepening the channels beneath the bridges, and building stronger barricades, and preparing their darts and slings, and making very long lances to kill our horses.

Lastly, let me describe the ditch and channel along which our launches were to pass to the great lake. It was now very wide, and deep enough to carry ships of reasonable draught, because, as I have already said, eight thousand Indians were continuously at work on it.

Expeditions around the Lake

[As there was not enough food in Texcoco to feed fifteen thousand Tlascalans, and Chichimecatecle was anxious to revenge himself on the Mexicans, Cortes led an expedition consisting chiefly of Tlascalans, but with two hundred and fifty Spanish soldiers, to Saltocan, a lakeside town sixteen or so miles from Texcoco. The people had broken down the bridge connecting their houses with the mainland, but the Spaniards found a way across, burnt much of the place, and took booty. They did not however succeed in defeating the Mexican army, since the warriors could always get away in their canoes when the fighting went against them. Once at Tacuba, they lured the Spaniards on to a causeway and broke a bridge behind them, thus almost gaining a victory, but the Spaniards fought their way out. On their return they were summoned by some towns in the north which were hard pressed by the Mexicans, but Cortes knew that too many of his men were sick or wounded for him to be able to help them, and advised them to call on their neighbours, taking care always to fight the Mexicans in the open. They were heartened by this advice and by his letters, to which they ascribed a magical power. Meanwhile Chalco and Tlamanalco were hard pressed also, and it was necessary to help them in order to keep the road to Villa Rica open.

Sandoval was given two hundred men and instructions to relieve these two cities.]

On 12 March 1521, Sandoval set out after hearing mass, and they slept at some farms belonging to Chalco. Next morning they arrived at Tlamanalco, where the *Caciques* and captains welcomed them with gifts of food, and advised Sandoval to go at once in the direction of a large place called Huaxtepec, for he would find the whole Mexican army assembled either there or on the road towards it. They said that all the warriors from the province of Chalco would accompany him.

Sandoval accepted their advice, and commanded his force to set out immediately and keep good order. They slept that night at Chimaluacan, another dependency of Chalco. For the spies whom the people of Chalco had posted to watch the Culuas came to report that enemy warriors were lying in wait for them in some rocky defiles not far from that town. Sandoval was a very cunning and good tactician. He sent his musketeers and crossbowmen in advance, and ordered the horsemen to ride together in groups of three, and when the musketeers and crossbowmen had fired their shots to charge the enemy at an easy gallop with their lances held short, and put them to flight by thrusting at their faces, taking care always to preserve their own formation. He commanded the foot soldiers always to keep in close order and not to charge the enemy until he gave the word. For the Mexicans were reported to be very numerous, and this report proved true. They were posted in rough ground, and it was not known whether they had dug pits or raised barricades. So Sandoval was anxious to keep his soldiers well in hand, for fear of a disaster.

As he came down the road he saw the Mexican bands approaching him in three divisions, whistling and shouting, and sounding trumpets and drums. They came on to meet us like fierce lions, and when Sandoval saw their daring, he abandoned his plan. He told the horsemen to charge them immediately, before they could reach our army, and cheering his men on with 'Santiago and at them!' he himself led the charge, which almost but not quite routed some of the Mexican bands. They soon turned and faced us, the bad and broken ground being in their favour, since it prevented our horsemen from galloping in pursuit of them. For this reason Sandoval ordered his musketeers and crossbowmen to go forward once more in good order, with the shield-bearers on their flanks. Then, when they could see that they were inflicting damage on the enemy, they could expect to hear a shot fired from the other side of the ravine, which would be the signal for all the horsemen to charge together and hurl the Mexicans from their position, for he thought they could be driven on to the level ground near by. He also warned his allies that they must then come to the Spaniards' help. Sandoval's commands were obeyed, though many of our men were wounded in this violent action, and after many engagements the Mexicans were forced to retreat. They fled, however, into another rough place, and so, though Sandoval and his horsemen pursued them, they only caught three or four. During this pursuit, owing to the bad ground, the horse of one of our cavalrymen named Gonzalo Dominguez fell with his rider beneath him, and the man died from his fall a few days later.

Sandoval and his army pursued the enemy almost as far as the town of Huaxtepec. But before they could reach it, more than fifteen thousand Mexicans came out to meet them and began to encircle them, wounding many soldiers and five horses. However, the ground being level in some places, with a concerted effort our horsemen broke up two of their bands, and the rest fled towards the town to take up fresh posts again on some barricades they had raised. But our soldiers and allies followed so closely that they had no time to defend themselves, and our horsemen kept up the pursuit from other directions until they had enclosed the enemy in a part of the town where they could not be reached. Thinking that the enemy would not renew the attack that day Sandoval ordered his men to rest, and they dressed their wounds and began to eat, for they had taken much spoil in that town. Just then, however, two horsemen and two soldiers who had been placed on guard ran in, crying: 'To arms! To arms! Here come many more Mexicans!' As our men always kept their arms ready, the horsemen were quickly mounted and rode out into the great square. The Mexicans were immediately upon them, and there was another successful battle. For some time the enemy resisted us behind some barricades, from which they wounded some of our men. But Sandoval fell on them so suddenly with his horsemen that with the help of the muskets and crossbows, and the sword-play of the soldiers, he drove them out of the town into some ravines, from which they did not emerge again that day.

When Captain Sandoval saw that the struggle was over, he gave hearty thanks to God, and went to rest and sleep in an orchard within the town, which was most beautiful and had many fine buildings. In fact it was the finest town we had seen in New Spain.

I did not myself go on this expedition, and did not see the

orchard until I went there some twenty days later with Cortes, when we were making a circuit of the great towns on the lake. The reason for my absence was that, during the affray at Iztapalapa when they tried to drown us I had been badly wounded by a spear-thrust in the throat, and was in danger of death.

Next morning, hearing no more sound of Mexican warriors, Sandoval sent to summon the *Caciques* of the town, dispatching as his messengers five natives of the place whom he had captured, two of them chieftains. The burden of their message was that the *Caciques* need have no fear, and that if they came to make peace the past would be forgiven. The messengers who were sent made pacific proposals, but the *Caciques* did not dare to come in for fear of the Mexicans.

The same day Sandoval sent to another large place called Yecapixtla, about six miles from Huaxtepec, asking the people to consider the benefits of peace, and not to seek war. Reminding them of what had happened to the bands of Culuas stationed at Huaxtepec, he asked them to treat for peace and expel the Mexican guards and garrison from their country, and warned them that if they did not he would make war on them and punish them. Their answer was that the Spaniards could come when they liked, for they were looking forward to feasting on their flesh and sacrificing them to their idols.

On hearing this, the *Caciques* from Chalco who were with Sandoval knew that there must be a very large Mexican force garrisoned at Yecapixtla and ready to attack Chalco as soon as they knew Sandoval had retired. For this reason they begged him to go to Yecapixtla and hurl the Mexicans out. Sandoval was unwilling to go, however, firstly because he had himself been wounded and so had many soldiers and horses, and secondly because he had already fought three battles and did not wish to undertake more than Cortes had commanded him to do. Also several gentlemen in his company who belonged to Narvaez' party advised him to return to Texcoco and not go to Yecapixtla, which was strongly fortified, lest some disaster might befall him. However, Captain Luis Marin counselled him to press on to the fortress at all costs and do what he could. For the *Caciques* from Chalco said that if he turned back without defeating the forces gathered there, the enemy would attack Chalco as soon as they heard that Sandoval had departed.

Since it was only six miles from one town to the other, Sandoval decided to go. As soon as he came within sight of the place, however, a host of warriors emerged, and before he could approach they fired a hail of darts and arrows and stones which wounded three horses and many soldiers. Our men were unable to inflict any harm on the enemy, who climbed up among their crags and strongholds, from which they shouted and whistled at us, and sounded their trumpets and drums. Sandoval then ordered some of his horsemen to dismount, and the rest to stay in the field where the ground was level, and see that no Mexican reinforcements reached Yecapixtla while we were attacking the town. On observing that the *Caciques* from Chalco and their captains and many of the Indian warriors were eddying round but dared not attack the enemy, Sandoval decided to try them and see how they would answer. 'What are you doing?' he asked. 'Why don't you begin to fight, and break into the city, seeing that we are here to defend you?' The reply was that they did not dare, for the enemy was in a stronghold, which was why Sandoval and his brother *Teules* had come with them. Having marched from Chalco under his protection, they relied on his help to expel the Mexicans.

So Sandoval began the attack with all his soldiers, musketeers, and crossbowmen, and many of them were wounded as they climbed up to the fortress. Sandoval himself received another wound in the head, and many of the allies were wounded also. For they too entered the town, where they did great damage. Indeed, it was the men from Chalco and our Tlascalan allies who wrought most havoc among the enemy. Once our soldiers had broken the enemy's ranks and put them to flight they would not stab another Indian: it seemed to them mere cruelty. What chiefly concerned them was to look for a pretty woman or find some spoil. Frequently they reproached our allies for their cruelty, and took Indian men and women away from them to save their lives.

When all this was over Sandoval and his army returned to Texcoco with much spoil, especially of good-looking Indian women.

Now when Guatemoc, lord of Mexico, heard of the defeat of his armies, it is said that he was very angry and even angrier that the people of Chalco, who were his subjects and vassals, should have been so bold as to fight three actions against him. He was so much incensed, indeed, that he decided to send a great force of warriors against Chalco as soon as Sandoval was back in camp at Texcoco. Hastily collecting this force in the city of Mexico, and adding to it other warriors who were on the lakeside, he armed them with every sort of weapon. Twenty thousand of them in all were ordered to make a sudden descent on Chalco in more than two thousand canoes, and to destroy everything they could.

All was so skilfully and rapidly done that Sandoval had no sooner returned to Texcoco and spoken to Cortes than messengers came once more in canoes across the lake to tell the Captain that more than two thousand canoes carrying over twenty thousand Mexicans had come to Chalco, and to implore his immediate assistance. This was at the very moment when Sandoval had come to give Cortes a report of the expedition he had just made. Cortes was so furious that he refused to listen, for he supposed it was through some fault or carelessness on Sandoval's part that our friends at Chalco were in such trouble. He immediately commanded his lieutenant, therefore, to leave his wounded in the camp and to return in haste with all those who were sound. Sandoval was much distressed by this treatment and by Cortes' refusal to hear him, but set out immediately for Chalco, where his men arrived tired out by the weight of their arms and their long march.

It appears that the people of Chalco had learnt from their spies that Guatemoc intended to make this sudden attack on them, and had sent to summon aid from the near-by province of Huexotzinco. The Huexotzincans arrived that same night fully armed and joined them, so that they were more than twenty thousand strong in all. The men of Chalco had by now lost their fear of the Mexicans, and calmly awaited them in the open fields. Here they fought valiantly, and though the Mexicans killed and captured many of them, the men of Chalco killed many more Mexicans, and captured fifteen chieftains and captains and many other warriors of less importance. The Mexicans considered this battle in which they were beaten by the people of Chalco far more disgraceful than any defeat by us.

On arriving at Chalco, Sandoval found that there was nothing for him to do, for the danger was over and the Mexicans would not return. He therefore returned to Texcoco, bringing the Mexican prisoners. Cortes was highly delighted, but Sandoval showed great resentment at what had happened, and did not go to see or speak to Cortes until Cortes sent to tell him that he had misunderstood the affair and had supposed that it was through some carelessness on Sandoval's part that things had gone wrong, for though he had set out with a large force of soldiers and horsemen he appeared to have come back without defeating the Mexicans. But enough of this, for Cortes and Sandoval soon became friends again, and there was nothing our Captain would not do to please his lieutenant.

[Fresh trouble arose over the branding and distribution of slaves. Some men again tried to keep back the prettiest women, and there was some difficulty in extracting the king's fifth from the soldiers, who were heavily in debt.

Another ship arrived from Spain carrying arms and a number of gentlemen who joined the expedition, also a certain Franciscan who brought Bulls from the new Pope offering dispensation for any sins committed during the fighting. He returned to Spain a few months later 'rich and well set up'. News came with this ship that the Bishop of Burgos had fallen out of favour, and that the Emperor no longer believed the stories which were told him against Cortes and in Diego Velazquez' favour.]

As Cortes had promised the people of Chalco that he was coming to protect them from further Mexican attacks, and we had been going every week to their assistance, he ordered three hundred soldiers and thirty horsemen, twenty crossbowmen, and fifteen musketeers to be assembled, and the treasurer Julian de

Alderete,[1] Pedro de Alvarado, Andres de Tapia, Cristobal de Olid, and the Friar Pedro Melgarejo[1] to go back with them, also myself and many Tlascalans and allies from Texcoco. To guard Texcoco and the launches, he left Gonzalo de Sandoval with a good force of soldiers and horsemen.

On the morning of Friday 5 April 1521, after hearing mass, we set out for Tlamanalco, where we were well received and where we slept. Next day we went on to Chalco, which was very near; and there Cortes ordered all the *Caciques* of the province to be called together, and made them a speech through our interpreters in which he explained that we were now going to try to bring peace to some towns on the lake, and to inspect the land and the general situation with a view to the blockading of Mexico. He also told them that we were going to put thirteen launches on the lake, and asked them to have all their warriors ready next day so that they could accompany us. When they understood his message they all said with one voice that they would gladly do so.

Next night we slept at another town that was tributary to Chalco, called Chimaluacan, where we met twenty thousand allies from Chalco, Texcoco, Huexotzingo, Tlascala, and other towns. I had never known us to be joined by such a host of allied warriors in any expedition in which I had taken part. Many of them came, as I have said before, in the hopes of gathering spoil and, of course, of gorging themselves on human flesh, if there should be fighting, as they knew there certainly would be.

About that time we received news that many squadrons and companies of Mexicans with all their allies from that district had gathered on a plain close by and were waiting to attack us. So Cortes warned us to be very vigilant.

After hearing mass, we set out from Chimaluacan very early in the morning, and marched in good formation through a rocky place between two hills, on which were strong fortifications and stockades in which many Indians, both men and women, had gathered. From these strongholds they yelled and shouted

1. His Majesty's Treasurer, and the Franciscan with the Bulls, who had arrived on the recent ship.

at us, but we did not care to attack them. So we advanced quietly towards a large place called Yautepec, which we afterwards found to be deserted. Arriving at a plain, we discovered some springs with very little water, and a great crag on one side crowned with a fortress extremely difficult to capture, as the attempt soon proved.

When we came up to this crag, we found it swarming with warriors who shouted at us from the summit and threw stones, and shot darts and arrows, which wounded three of our men. Then Cortes ordered us to halt, and said: 'It seems that all these Mexicans who shut themselves up in fortresses make fun of us so long as we don't attack them.' He was thinking, as he spoke, of those we had left behind us on the lower hills. He then commanded some horsemen and a few crossbowmen to go to the other side of the crag and see if there was an easier way up. On their return they reported that the best approach was where we were, for there was no other route. Everywhere else the rock was sheer. Cortes then ordered us to make an attack. Corral the standard-bearer led the ascent with other ensigns, and we all followed, while the horsemen kept guard on the plain in case other bands of Mexicans should fall on our baggage, or on our rear as we attacked the fortress.

When we began to climb the hill, the Indians stationed above us threw so many stones and rocks that merely to see them hurtling down was terrifying. It was a miracle that we were not all killed. One soldier fell dead at my feet. He was wearing a helmet, and he fell without uttering a word. We kept on climbing, and as the *galgas* – which is our name for big rocks in this country – came rolling and bouncing and falling they killed two more good soldiers, but we kept on. Then another brave soldier was killed, and yet another, and two more were wounded in the head, and nearly all the rest of us were hit on the legs. But still we persevered and pushed on.

As I was nimble in those days, I kept on behind the standard-bearer Corral, and we got into the safety of some hollows or cavities in the crag. But as I struggled from hollow to hollow a stray rock might easily have hit me, and I was indeed very lucky not to be killed. The standard-bearer Corral was sheltering behind some thick trees which were very thorny and grew in these cavities. But he was hit on the head. His face was streaming with blood and his banner was broken. 'Oh, Bernal Díaz,' he cried out, 'it is impossible to go any further. Mind one of those stones or boulders doesn't catch you. Come into this hole.' For now there were no more hand-holds, let alone any possibility of climbing.

Just then I saw Pedro Barba, a captain of crossbowmen, and two other soldiers climbing up in the same way that Corral and I had done. 'Don't come any further, Captain,' I shouted down. 'There's no hold for your hands and feet. You'll just roll down.' But he called back very bravely, or in lordly affectation: 'Why say that? Just go on.' I took his answer as an insult. 'Well, let's see you come where I am,' I called back, and went on higher. At that moment a quantity of stones rolled down on us from the place where they had been piled. Pedro Barba was hurt and one of the soldiers killed, and they could not climb a step higher. Then Corral cried out that word must be passed down to Cortes that we could not get any higher, and to retire was equally dangerous.

When the message reached him Cortes realized what was happening. For there below, where he stood on the level ground, three soldiers had been killed and seven wounded by the great hail of boulders that were hurled down on them. Indeed, he felt certain that most of us who had climbed must have been killed or badly wounded, for from where he stood he could not see the hollows in the hill. So from signs and shouts and musket-shots we on the crag understood that the order had gone out to retire; and we descended in good formation from hollow to hollow, carrying the bodies of the dead. Our heads were cracked and running with blood, our banners were torn, and eight men had been killed. When Cortes saw us he thanked God for our escape. Pedro Barba himself told him of our dispute, and Corral described the great difficulty of the hill, saying what a marvel it was that the boulders had not carried us down with them, and the story soon spread right through the camp.

Let us leave these vain matters, and speak of the many companies of Mexicans concealed in places where we could neither see nor find them, in expectation of the moment when they could bring help and relief to the men posted on the crag. They knew very well that we should not be able to storm their stronghold, and decided that in the midst of the fighting, the warriors on the crag on one side and they on the other should deliver a fierce attack. They came to their comrades' assistance according to their plan, and when Cortes observed their approach he ordered the horsemen and all of us on foot to go and attack them; which we did. The ground being very flat, like a sort of field lying between more large hills, we pursued the enemy for a while until they came to another very strong crag. But we killed very few Indians during the pursuit, for they took refuge in places where we could not reach them.

Returning to the fortress we had attempted to scale, we could find no water. Neither we nor the horses had drunk all day, for the springs that I have spoken of contained nothing but mud : the many allies we had brought had descended on them and churned them up. For this reason, orders were given to move our camp, and we went down through some fields to another hill about four and a half miles away, thinking that we should find water there. But there was very little. Near this hill were some native mulberry trees, beside which we halted, and beneath it stood some twelve or thirteen houses. As soon as we arrived before their stronghold, the Indians began to throw darts and boulders and shoot arrows from the top. There were far more men in this fortress, as we afterwards learnt, than on the other crag, and it was even stronger. Our musketeers and crossbowmen fired at the enemy. But they were so high up and their ramparts were so stout that we could not harm them, and there was no way of climbing up and storming the place. We made two attempts, for there were some steps beside the houses by which we could climb. But after one or two bends in the path we could go no further, for this crag, as I have said, was worse than the last. So here we did not increase our reputation any more than at the fortress. The Mexicans and their allies had the victory.

We slept that night in the mulberry grove, half dead with thirst, and planned that next day all the musketeers and crossbowmen should climb another crag close to the large one (for there was a way up it, though it was not an easy one) to see if their weapons would carry from there to the other fortress, so that they could attack it. Cortes commanded Francisco Verdugo and the treasurer Julian de Alderete, who claimed to be a good bowman, and Pedro Barba to be leaders, and all the rest of us soldiers to attack from the steps that rose above the houses, as if we intended to climb. So we began the ascent. But so many stones were hurled down, great and small, that many men were wounded. Moreover we could not in fact climb, for the way was too difficult, and even using both hands and feet we could get no further. While we were making this attempt, however, the musketeers and bowmen from the other hill just succeeded in hitting the enemy, killing a few and wounding others. When we had been attacking like this for about half an hour, by God's grace they decided to ask for peace. The reason was that they had no water, and there were many of them on the crag. For on the flat ground at the top people from the whole neighbourhood had taken refuge: men, women, children, and servants. To inform us down below that they wanted peace, the women waved their cloaks and clapped their hands together as a sign that they would make us maize-cakes or bread, and the warriors threw no more darts or stones or arrows.

When Cortes understood their meaning he ordered a cessation of hostilities, and informed them by signs that five chieftains must come down to arrange for peace. On arrival these five most humbly begged Cortes to pardon them, since they had only taken refuge in their stronghold for their own protection. Cortes replied somewhat angrily through our interpreters that they deserved death for having started the fighting, but as they had come to make peace they must go immediately to the other crag and summon the *Caciques* and leading men who were there, and bring in the dead bodies. If they made peace he promised to forgive the past; if not, he would attack them and blockade them till they died of thirst, for we knew very well they had no water, since there is very little in that part of the country. So they went off obediently to summon the other Caciques.

[Cortes sent Pedro de Ircio and Bernal Díaz to inspect the strong-hold, with instructions 'not to take a grain of maize'. They went up over the sheer rock, and found the Indians camped in a flat field at the top, with twenty dead and not a drop of water. Bernal Díaz wanted to take the bundles of robes which they were preserving as a tribute for Guatemoc. But Pedro de Ircio, as his senior officer, forbade him. On their return Cortes took Bernal Díaz' part, and made the Captain look a fool.]

The *Caciques* came down from the other crag, and after much discussion about forgiveness for the past, all swore obedience to His Majesty. Then, as there was no water in those parts, we went immediately to the town of Huaxtepec, where the garden is that I have described, the finest garden I have ever seen in my life. We all camped in it that night, and the *Caciques* of the town came to speak to Cortes, and offered to serve him. For Gonzalo de Sandoval had already made peace with them when he entered the town.

After spending the night there, we set out early next morning on the road to Cuernavaca.[1] Here we met some Mexican bands who had come out of that town, and followed them for almost two miles till they took refuge in another large place called Tepoztlan, where the inhabitants were so completely off their guard that we attacked before the spies they had posted to watch us could reach them.

Here we found some very pretty Indian women and much spoil, but no Mexicans and none of the male inhabitants of the place. Cortes sent three or four times to summon the *Caciques* to make peace, and threatened that if they did not come we would burn the town and go to find them. But they refused. So, to strike fear into the neighbouring towns, Cortes ordered that half the houses in the district should be set on fire. At this moment the *Caciques* of the town through which we had passed that day, which was called Yautepec, came and swore obedience to His Majesty. And next day we went to a finer and larger place called Coadlavaca – a name that we generally corrupt today into Cuernavaca. Here there were many warriors, both

1. Actually, according to Cortes' third letter, they took the road to Yautepec.

Mexicans and natives of the town, which was rendered very strong by some ravines, more than fifty feet deep, with streams at the bottom. These streams did not carry much water. Nevertheless they transformed the place into a fortress, into which there was no approach for horses except over two bridges which were broken down. But though it was too strong for us to force an entrance we fought with them from across the stream and the ravine, and their darts and arrows and the stones from their slings fell on us like hail.

During this fighting, Cortes received information that a little over a mile further on there was a place where horses could cross. He at once set off with all the horsemen and Narvaez' people, leaving us to find a way where we were. We saw that with the help of some trees that grew near the edge the deep ravine could be crossed, and although three soldiers fell down into the water and one of them broke his leg we made the passage. For myself I must truly confess that the danger and difficulty of the crossing made me turn quite giddy. But I struggled across with some more of our soldiers and many Tlascalans, and we fell on the rear of the Mexicans who were shooting across the ravine. When they saw us they could hardly believe their eyes, and supposed that we were more numerous than we were. At that moment Cristobal de Olid and Andres de Tapia arrived on the scene with some other horsemen who had made almost as dangerous a crossing over a broken bridge, and we attacked the enemy so hard that they turned and fled to the hills or to other parts of the deep ravine where we could not reach them. Soon afterwards Cortes himself arrived with the rest of the horsemen.

Our scouts then arrived with the report that about twenty Indians were approaching, whose appearance and bearing indicated that they were *Caciques* and chieftains, and who appeared to be carrying a message or suing for peace. They proved to be the *Caciques* of the town; and when they came before Cortes they ceremoniously presented him with gold jewels, and begged his pardon for not having made peace. They said that the Lord of Mexico had sent them orders to stay in their stronghold and attack us from there, and that he had sent them a large force of Mexicans to help them. But they now saw there was no place so strong that we could not attack and capture it, and humbly begged Cortes to make peace with them. Cortes received them graciously, and they swore obedience to His Majesty.

So we set out for Xochimilco, a great city about seven and a half miles from Mexico, in which most of the houses were built in a fresh-water lake. Advancing most cautiously and in our usual close order, we passed through some pine-woods, but could find no water anywhere on the road. As we were wearing our armour and the afternoon sun was very hot, we suffered terribly from thirst. Nor did we know if there was any water ahead. We had advanced eight or nine miles, and had no idea how far we were from a well which we had been told was on the road.

When Cortes saw that our whole army was tired, and our Tlascalan allies dispirited – one of them had died of thirst, and one of our men too, I think, who was old and ailing – he ordered a halt to be made in the shade of the pine-trees, and sent six of the horsemen ahead towards Xochimilco to see how far off the nearest village or farm might be, or where this well was that we had been told about, for we wanted to encamp beside it for the night.

When the horsemen set out I decided to step aside so that neither they nor Cortes should see me and then to follow them with my three strong and nimble Tlascalan servants. But they saw me behind them and stopped to turn me back, for fear I might be attacked by Mexican warriors and be unable to defend myself. But I insisted on going with them; and as Cristobal de Olid was a friend of mine he agreed on condition that I kept my hands ready to fight and my feet ready to run for safety if we met any more Mexicans. But I was thirsty enough to risk my life for a drink of water. About a mile and a half ahead there were a number of farms and huts on the hillsides belonging to the people of Xochimilco, and the horsemen went across to the houses to look for water, which they found and drank. One of my Tlascalans brought me a great pitcher of very cold water out of a house – they have very large pitchers in that country – and I and my servants quenched our thirst.

Then I decided to return to where Cortes was resting, because the inhabitants of these farms were already giving the call to arms, and shouting and whistling at us. I told my servants to carry the pitcher, and met Cortes, who had resumed his march with his army. I told him that there was water in the near-by farms, and that I had drunk, and was bringing him some in a pitcher. The Tlascalans were carrying it very cautiously so that it should not be taken from me. For thirst knows no laws. Then Cortes and some other gentlemen drank, and he was well satisfied. They all rejoiced and hastened on their march, so that we arrived at the farms before sunset, where they found water in the houses, but not very much; and because of their hunger and thirst a few soldiers ate some thistle-like plants, which hurt their tongues and their throats.

At this moment the horsemen came back to say that the well was far off, and that as the whole country was being called to arms they thought it advisable for us to sleep where we were. Scouts, sentinels, and look-outs were posted, and I was one of the watch. I think it rained a little that night, or else it was very windy.

Next morning we resumed our march very early, and reached Xochimilco at about eight o'clock. I cannot compute the great number of warriors who were awaiting us, some on land and some at the approach to a bridge that they had broken, or the number of ramparts and barricades they had thrown up. Some of their captains carried scythe-like lances made from the swords they had captured from us during the slaughter on the causeway; others had long straight gleaming lances, which were also made from captured swords. Then there were archers and warriors with double-headed javelins, and with slings and stones, and their two-handed swords. The whole mainland was thick with them, and we fought with them for more than half an hour at the approach to the bridge. But we could not get through. Neither muskets nor crossbows nor our repeated charges were of any avail, and the worst of it was that many more bands of them were coming to attack us on the flank. When we saw this we rushed through the water and over the bridge, some half-swimming and others jumping. And here some of our soldiers involuntarily drank so much water that when they had passed the bridge their bellies swelled up with it.

To return to our battle, many of our soldiers were wounded at the passage of the bridge. But we managed to get at the enemy with our swords in some streets where there was solid ground in front of us. Cortes and the horsemen turned in another direction on the mainland, where they met more than ten thousand Indians, all Mexicans, who had come to help the people in the town. Their method of fighting was to await our horsemen with their lances, and they wounded four of them. Cortes was in the midst of the fray, mounted on a very good dark chestnut called *El Romo* [1] because he was either fat or worn-out (for he was a pampered beast), when the animal faltered, and the enemy, who were in great numbers, laid hands on Cortes and dragged him from his back. Others say that they brought him down by main force. In any case, many more Mexicans came up to try to carry him off alive. At the sight of this some Tlascalans and a very brave soldier called Cristobal de Olea, of Medina del Campo in Old Castile, rushed to the spot and with good cuts and thrusts cleared a space, which enabled Cortes to remount his horse, although badly wounded in the head. Olea also had received three very severe knife-wounds. But by this time all of us soldiers who were anywhere near had come to their assistance, for we had failed to keep close together, since every street in the city was choked with bands of warriors and we had been unable to follow our banners. Some of us were attacking here and some there, as Cortes had commanded. However, we all knew from the shrieks and shouts and whistling that the fighting was hottest where Cortes and the horsemen were engaged. So with no more ado, although surrounded by hosts of warriors, we forced our way at peril of our lives to stand at Cortes' side. He had been joined by fifteen horsemen, and they were battling with the enemy beside some canals, along which they had built ramparts and barricades. When we arrived we routed the Mexicans, though not all of them ran away. The soldier Olea had been badly wounded by three sword-cuts and was losing blood, and the streets of

1. Pudgy.

this town were full of warriors. We therefore advised Cortes to retire to some barricades so that he and Olea and the horse could have their wounds attended to. So we turned back, but not without anxiety, on account of the missiles that fell on us from the ramparts. For, thinking that we were retreating, the Mexicans assailed us most furiously.

Now Andres de Tapia and Cristobal de Olid came up, with the rest of the horsemen who had gone off in other directions. Olid's face was streaming with blood and so was his horse, and every one of them was wounded. They said they had been fighting so many Mexicans in the open country that they could make no headway against them. It seems that once we had crossed the bridge Cortes had divided them into two halves, each following different enemy bands.

While we were treating our wounds by searing them with oil, a noise of yells, trumpets, conches, and drums arose in some streets on the mainland, and a host of Mexicans burst into the courtyard where we were, throwing such a volley of darts and stones that several of our men were quickly wounded. They did not get much advantage from this onslaught, however, for we immediately attacked them, and with good cuts and thrusts left plenty of them stretched on the ground. The horsemen too were not slow in riding out to the attack, and they killed many, though two of their horses were wounded. Still, we drove them out of the courtyard; and when Cortes saw that they had all gone we went to rest in another court which contained the great temples of that place. Many of our soldiers climbed up the taller *cue* in which they kept their idols, and looked over the city of Mexico and the whole lake, all of which could be viewed from the top; and from there they saw more than two thousand canoes full of warriors approaching from Mexico, and making for just where we stood. We learnt afterwards that Guatemoc, Prince of Mexico, had sent them with orders to attack us that night or next day, and had also sent ten thousand warriors by land to do so from another direction, so that, caught between the two, none of us would escape from the town alive. (He had also prepared another ten thousand men as a reinforcement, to be thrown in when the attack was made. All this we found out next day from five Mexican captains whom we captured in the battle.)

However, our Lord ordained otherwise. For on seeing this great fleet of canoes and realizing that they were coming to attack us, we set a very good watch throughout the camp, especially at the landing-places and along the canals, where they would have to disembark. The horsemen waited all night very much on the alert, with their horses saddled and bridled, both on the causeway and on the mainland, and Cortes with his captains also watched and patrolled through the night. I with two other soldiers kept guard on various canals.

While I and my companions were on the watch, we heard the sound of many canoes approaching with muffled paddles, to disembark at the landing-place where we were posted. With our lances and volleys of stones we prevented their coming ashore, and we sent one of our number to warn Cortes. While this was happening many more canoes loaded with warriors came up and assailed us with darts, arrows, and stones. We repelled them also, and two of our number were wounded in the head. Then, as it was night and very dark, these canoes went off to join the captains of the whole fleet, and they all made for another landing-place where the canals were deeper. As they were not used to fighting at night, they then united with the squadrons Guatemoc had sent overland, which already numbered more than fifteen thousand.

As soon as daylight came, we saw all the Mexican bands closing in on the court where we were encamped. But they did not catch us napping. We charged through them, the horsemen from one direction where the ground was dry, and we and the Tlascalan allies from another. We wounded three of their captains, who died next day, and our allies made a good capture, taking those five chieftains from whom we learnt about Guatemoc's orders.

Many of our soldiers were wounded in the battle, but this engagement was not the end of the fighting. Following on the heels of the enemy, our horsemen met the ten thousand warriors whom Guatemoc had sent as a reinforcement to help those he had sent in advance. The Mexican captains who came with this force carried swords they had captured from us, and made great demonstrations of the valour with which they would use them, crying out that they would kill us with our own arms. The horsemen were afraid when they came up with them, for the Mexican bands were numerous and they were few. So they turned aside in order not to encounter them until Cortes and the rest of us could help them. When we heard this, every horseman who was left in the camp instantly leapt into the saddle, even though both mount and rider were wounded, and we all marched out behind them. Soldiers, bowmen, and Tlascalan allies, we charged them all together, and so impetuously that we broke their ranks and were able to fight them hand to hand. Our good sword-play then made them give up their unlucky enterprise and leave the field to us.

We captured some other chiefs there, and learnt from them that Guatemoc had ordered the dispatch of another great fleet of canoes, and another army of warriors overland. He had told his men that, being weary from our recent engagements and having many dead and wounded, we would now suppose that no more bands would be sent against us and become less vigilant. Then, with the large force he was sending, he would be able to defeat us. When we heard this we became even more watchful than before; and it was agreed that we should wait for no more attacks but leave the town next morning. We spent the rest of the day attending to the wounded, cleaning our weapons, and making arrows.

It seems that there were many rich men in this city who had very large houses full of cloaks and cloth and Indian shirts, all of cotton and gold feather-work and many other things. While we were busy, the Tlascalans and certain soldiers found out where these houses were, for some of the Xochimilcan prisoners went with them to show them. The houses stood in the lake, and were approached by a causeway, on which were two or three small bridges which spanned deep channels; and when they reached them our soldiers found them unguarded and full of cloth. So they loaded themselves and the many Tlascalans with this cloth and with some gold ornaments, and brought their booty to the camp. On seeing this, some other soldiers also set out for the houses, but while they were taking the cloth out of the large wooden boxes in which it was stored, a great fleet of Mexican warriors arrived and fell on them, wounding many of them and carrying off four of them alive, whom they took to Mexico. The rest, however, escaped.

When these four prisoners were brought before Guatemoc, he learnt how few we were that followed Cortes, and how many of us were wounded, and everything he wanted to know about our expedition. After getting this information, he had the arms, feet, and heads of our unfortunate companions cut off, and sent them round to various towns of our allies and those who had made peace with us, with the message that he did not think one of us would be left alive to return to Texcoco. Then he offered their hearts and blood to his idols.

Guatemoc promptly sent many more flotillas of warriors over the lake, and other companies by land, with orders that we must not be allowed to leave Xochimilco alive. Though I am tired of narrating our many battles and skirmishes with the Mexicans in these few days, yet I cannot omit any of them. As soon as dawn broke there came such a host of Mexicans by the inlets and along the causeways and overland, that we could hardly break through them. We left the town, however, for a great square near by in which they used to hold their markets, and halted there with all our baggage, ready for the march. Cortes then began to speak to us of our dangerous situation, for we knew very well that the whole power of Mexico and its allies would be lying in wait for us at the difficult places on the roads, at the creeks, and on the canals. He said that it would be a good thing, therefore, and it was his command, that we should march unencumbered, and leave our baggage and booty, which would impede us when it came to fighting. On hearing this we cried out with one voice that, with God's blessing, we were men enough to defend our property and persons, and his also, and that it would be great cowardice to do such a thing. When Cortes heard our wishes, he said he prayed God to help us. Knowing the strength and power of the enemy, we then arranged the order of march, putting the wounded and the baggage in the middle, sending one half of the horsemen ahead, posting the other in the rear, and keeping our crossbowmen and also our allies in the middle as a security, since it was the Mexicans' habit to attack the baggage. We could make no use of our musketeers, however, for they had run out of powder. In this order we set out.

When Guatemoc's army saw that we were retiring from Xochimilco, they thought that we were frightened and did not dare to meet them, which was true. A great host of them started off at once and came straight at us, wounding eight soldiers, two of whom died a week later. Their intention was to break our ranks and overrun the baggage. But as we marched in the order I have described, they were unable to do so. However, all along the road, until we reached a large town called Coyoacan, which is about six miles from Xochimilco, sudden attacks were continually made on us from positions we could not approach. For the Mexicans were able to assail us with darts and stones and arrows, and then take refuge in the neighbouring creeks and ditches. We arrived at Coyoacan, which stands on level ground, at about ten o'clock in the morning, and found the place deserted. We decided to spend the rest of the day there and the next also, so that we could attend to the wounded and make arrows, for we knew that we should have to fight many more battles before returning to our camp at Texcoco.

Then, early on the second morning, we resumed our march in our accustomed formation, following the road to Tacuba, a distance of about six miles from our starting-point. At one place on the road we were attacked by three parties of warriors, and repelled all three attacks, our horsemen pursuing them over the level ground until they took refuge in the creeks and canals.

As we went on our way, Cortes rode aside with ten horsemen and four young pages to prepare an ambush for the Mexicans who were attacking us from the creeks. Now the Mexicans made a show of retreating, and Cortes with his horsemen and servants followed them. But when he looked round he saw, lying in wait, a great company of the enemy, who attacked him and his horsemen, wounding the horses. Indeed, if they had not retired at once they would all have been killed or taken prisoner. As it was, the Mexicans seized two of Cortés' young pages and carried them alive to Guatemoc, who had them sacrificed.

We arrived at Tacuba with our banners flying, and with all our army and baggage. The rest of the horsemen had already come in with Pedro de Alvarado and Cristóbal de Olid. But Cortés and the ten horsemen with him did not appear, and we suspected that some disaster must have overtaken them. So Pedro de Alvarado, Cristóbal de Olid, and some other horsemen went in search of them, in the direction of the creeks where we had seen them turn off. At that moment the two pages who had escaped came in, and after telling their story, they said that Cortés and the others were following slowly because their horses were wounded. While they were still talking, Cortés himself arrived, at which we all rejoiced, though he himself was so sad that he was almost in tears.

By the time he arrived in Tacuba it was raining heavily, and we sheltered for nearly two hours in the great courts. Cortés, with some of his captains and the treasurer Alderete, who was sick, and Friar Melgarejo, and many of us soldiers, ascended the lofty *cue* of that town, which commanded a fine view of the city of Mexico near by and of the whole lake and most of the towns I have mentioned, which are built on it. When the friar and the treasurer saw all these great cities standing in the water, they were astonished. And when they gazed on the great city of Mexico, and the lake crowded with canoes, some loaded with provisions, others going to fish, and others empty, they were even more amazed, and said that our coming to New Spain was the act not of human beings but of the great Mercy of God, who had decreed that we should hold it and protect it. They said also, as they had said before, that they never remembered to have read in any history of vassals who had done such great services to their king as we had. But now they said it with greater assurance, and promised to report our story to His Majesty.

A consultation was now held among our captains on whether we should inspect the causeway, for it was very close to Tacuba, where we were. As we had no powder and very few arrows, and most of the soldiers in our army were wounded, and as we remembered that it was little more than a month since Cortes had attempted to forced his way along this causeway with a great number of soldiers and had run into such danger that he had been afraid of defeat, it was agreed that we should march on, for fear we might have to fight another battle with the Mexicans at some time in the day or night. For Tacuba is very close to their great city, and Guatemoc might send his great army to capture some of our men alive.

So we began our march, and passed through Atzcapotzalco, which we found deserted. Then we went on to Tenayuca, a large town, which was also deserted and which we called the city of snakes, on account of the three serpents they kept in their temple and worshipped as gods. From there we went on to Cuauhtitlan, and all that day the rain did not stop beating down. We marched along with our arms in our hands, for we were never parted from them by night or day, and we were almost collapsing under the weight of our armour and the drenching rain. When we arrived at this last town, we found it empty too. It did not stop raining all night long and the mud was very deep, and all night the inhabitants of the place and some Mexicans yelled at us from the canals and from other positions where we could do them no harm. It was too dark and wet for us to organize our system of sentinels and patrols. No order was kept, and we could not find the men who were put on guard. I say this because I was given the first watch, and neither officer nor patrol visited me, and it was the same throughout the camp.

Next day we continued our march to another large place, where there was also a great deal of mud, and we found it deserted. On the second day we passed through other deserted towns, and on the third we reached a place called Acolman, which was a dependency of Texcoco. When they heard in Texcoco that we were coming they came out to receive Cortes, and we met many Spaniards who had just come from Castile. Captain Gonzalo de Sandoval also welcomed us with many soldiers and with him came the lord of Texcoco, who, as I have already said, was called Don Fernando. Indeed, Cortes was very well received both by our men and by the newcomers from Spain, but he was even more cordially welcomed by the inhabitants of the neighbouring towns, who brought him food.

That night Sandoval returned to Texcoco with all his soldiers to protect his camp, and the next morning Cortes and the rest of us continued our march to Texcoco. We pressed on, weary and wounded, leaving many of our comrades behind us dead or in the hands of the Mexicans and about to be sacrificed. But instead of resting and healing our wounds, we had to meet a conspiracy organized by certain persons of quality, who were partisans of Narvaez.

Now it appears that a close friend of the Governor of Cuba, Antonio de Villafana by name, a native of Zamora or Toro, with other soldiers of Narvaez' party – I will not mention their names for honour's sake – had planned to stab Cortes to death on his return. This was to be the manner of it. A ship having just arrived from Spain, one of the plotters was to bring to Cortes when he was dining with his captains at table a heavily sealed letter purporting to come from Castile, and to say that it was from his father, Martin Cortes; and when he was reading it they were to stab him with daggers, together with any of us captains or soldiers who might try to protect him.

However, when all this had been discussed and prepared, it pleased Heaven that the conspirators should reveal their plan to two important persons who had taken part in our expedition. They had chosen one of them to be captain-general after the murder of Cortes; and they had elected various soldiers of Narvaez' party to fill the posts of chief constable, lieutenant, paymaster, treasurer, and steward. Judgeships, governorships, and other offices had also been filled in anticipation; and they had even divided our goods and horses among their own following. This plot was not discovered until two days after our return to Texcoco. And, God be praised, it was not carried out, or New Spain would have been destroyed and all of us with it. For factions would immediately have arisen, and all sorts of follies would have been committed.

It appears that a soldier revealed the affair to Cortes, who immediately extinguished the fire before it could spread further, for the soldier swore that many men of rank were involved.

As soon as he was informed, Cortes gave the informer large presents, and promised him more. He then quickly and secretly conveyed the news to all our captains, Pedro de Alvarado, Francisco de Lugo, Cristobal de Olid, Andres de Tapia, Gonzalo de Sandoval, and myself; also to the two magistrates officiating that year, Luis Marin and Pedro de Ircio, and to the rest of his adherents.

Once informed, we made ready, and went without delay to Antonio de Villafana's quarters, where we found him and many of his fellow plotters. With the aid of four constables, whom Cortes had brought with him, we seized Villafana; whereupon the captains and soldiers with him attempted to run away. But Cortes ordered them to be stopped and detained. At the moment of Villafana's arrest, our Captain snatched from his breast a document bearing the signatures of all the participants in the conspiracy. On it he read the names of many important persons. But being unwilling to disgrace them, he spread the report that Villafana had swallowed the memorandum before he could see it or read it.

In his statement Villafana admitted the whole truth. But the regular magistrates sitting with Cortes, and the camp commander, Cristobal de Olid, examined many good and trustworthy witnesses before passing the death sentence. Villafana was hanged from the window of his own quarters, after making his confession to Father Juan Diaz.

Although many were arrested at the time in order to frighten them and to suggest that further punishments were intended, Cortes did not wish anyone else to be disgraced. Unpleasant though the affair was, the moment was inopportune. He therefore concealed his feelings.

Cortes at once agreed to have a personal guard, under the command of Antonio de Quiñones, a gentleman from Zamora, who with six soldiers, good courageous men, watched over him day and night. And he requested us whom he knew to be his friends to take good care of him henceforth. As for those who had taken part in the conspiracy, though he often conferred great favours on them, he distrusted them always.

Let us leave this matter, and speak of Cortes' proclamation

that all the Indian men and women whom he had captured in our expeditions must within two days be brought for branding to a place specified for the purpose. I will say no more about the conduct of the auctions than I have already said in describing the two previous brandings. But bad though it was before, this time it was even worse. After subtracting the royal fifth, Cortes took his own fifth, and pickings for about thirty captains. And if any sound and handsome Indian women were sent to the branding, they were stolen away by night from among the others, and did not appear again. Thus many of the captured women were not sold, but later were hired by us as free servants.

The Siege and Capture of Mexico

WHEN justice had been done on Antonio de Villafana and his fellow conspirators had quieted down, Cortes was informed that the launches were ready and their rigging and sails in place, that their oars were well made, and there were spare oars for each launch, and that the channels through which they were to pass had been deepened and broadened. He then sent a request to all friendly towns in the region of Texcoco to make eight thousand copper arrowheads each, to the standard of some patterns from Spain that had been sent round, and to make and trim for him eight thousand arrows of a good kind of wood, patterns of which had also been circulated; and he gave them a period of eight days in which to deliver the arrows and arrowheads to our camp. They brought them in the specified time, more than fifty thousand arrowheads and as many thousand arrows, the former better than their Spanish models, and these were divided among all the crossbowmen, who were told to polish, oil, and feather them. He also ordered the horsemen to have their horses shod and to get their lances ready, and to parade each day on horseback and gallop, and train their horses to turn quickly and to skirmish.

Then Cortes sent messengers with letters for our friend Xicotenga the Elder, and his son Xicotenga the Younger, and to his brothers, and to Chichimecatecle, informing them that after Corpus Christi we were going to set out against Mexico and blockade it. He told them to send twenty thousand warriors from Tlascala, Huexotzinco, and Cholula. For they were now all friends and comrades, and they all knew the time of meeting and the plan, he having sent them information by their own men, who were continually leaving our camp, laden with the spoils of our expeditions. Cortes also warned the people of Chalco and Tlamanalco and their vassals to be ready when he sent to summon them, and told them that we were going to invest Mexico, and when we should set out. He sent the same information to Don Fernando, the lord of Texcoco, and to his chieftains and vassals and to all the other towns friendly to us. All replied that they would obey his orders.

Then Cortes decided that on the second day of the Feast of the Holy Spirit a review should be held in the great courts of Texcoco. Eighty-four horsemen were present, and six hundred and fifty soldiers with sword and shield and many with lances, and a hundred and ninety-four crossbowmen and musketeers, and from these were chosen crews to man the thirteen launches. Twelve crossbowmen and musketeers were to go on each; but they were not to row, for twelve additional men were picked to man the oars, six on each side. Besides these there was a captain for every launch, so that each carried twenty-five men, which amounts to upwards of three hundred in all. Cortes also distributed among them all the boat-guns and falconets we possessed and the powder he thought they would need. Having done this, he proclaimed the rules which we must observe:

First, no man should dare to blaspheme Our Lord nor his Blessed Mother, nor the apostles, nor any of the saints, under heavy penalties.

Second, that no soldier should ill-treat our allies, who had come to help us, or take anything from them even if it was captured booty; neither men nor women prisoners, gold, silver, nor *chalchihuites*.

Third, that no soldier should dare to leave the camp by day or night to go to any allied town, either to fetch food or for any other reason, under heavy penalties.

Fourth, that all soldiers should wear very good armour, well quilted, and a gorget, headpiece, leggings, and shield.

Fifth, that no one should on any account gamble for a horse or arms, under heavy penalties.

Sixth, that no soldier, horseman, crossbowman, or musketeer should sleep except in complete armour and with his sandals on his feet, except in case of severe wounds or sickness.

Further rules were proclaimed to be observed on campaign: that anyone sleeping on guard or quitting his post should be punished with death, and that no soldier should go from one camp to another without his captain's permission, under the same penalty.

After the review Cortes discovered that there were not enough seamen to row the launches. The crews of the ships which we had destroyed and the sailors from Narvaez' ships and those from Jamaica had been put on a list and warned that they would have to row. But including them all, there were still not sufficient men, and some of them refused the task. Cortes then made an inquiry to discover who were sailors or who had been seen to go out fishing, and any men who came from Palos or Moguer or any other port were ordered to man the launches, under severe penalties for refusal. Even if they claimed high birth, he still made them row. Thus he got together a hundred and fifty oarsmen; and they suffered far less hardship than we who fought on the causeways, and got rich plunder into the bargain. Cortes then chose his captains and gave them his orders, telling each what to do, to what part of the causeway he was to go, and with which of our captains there he was to cooperate.

As soon as these orders had been given, a message was brought to Cortes that the Tlascalan captains were approaching under the supreme command of Xicotenga the Younger, who had two of his brothers with him and was accompanied by another great force under the command of Chichimecatecle, also a company from Huexotzinco and another from Cholula. The Cholulans, however, were few in numbers, because, from what I observed, although they never again sided with the Mexicans after we punished them, they did not side with us either, but watched events.

When Cortes heard that Xicotenga and his brothers and captains were approaching a day before their time, accompanied by Pedro de Alvarado and others, he went out a mile to receive them, and greeted and embraced them all. They marched in fine order, all very brilliant, beneath their great devices, each company separately with its banners streaming, and the white bird, like an eagle with wings outstretched, that is their badge. The ensigns waved their banners and standards, and all carried bows and arrows, two-handed swords, javelins, and spear-throwers. Some also had double-edged swords and long or short lances. Marching in good order, in their feathered head-dresses, they whistled, shouted, and cried: 'Long live our lord the Emperor!' and 'Castile! Castile!' and 'Tlascala! Tlascala!' They took more than three hours entering Texcoco.

Cortes ordered that our allies should be given good quarters and provided with everything we had in our camp. Then, after many embraces and promises to make them rich, he took his leave, telling them that he would send his orders next day, but that they should rest now, for they were tired.

Cortes appointed Pedro de Alvarado captain of a hundred and fifty soldiers, thirty horsemen, and eighteen musketeers and crossbowmen. With him he sent his brother, Jorge de Alvarado, Gutierrez de Badajoz, and Andres de Monjaraz, with fifty soldiers each and exactly a third of the musketeers and crossbowmen. Pedro commanded the horsemen himself, and was commander of all three companies, and he was given eight thousand Tlascalans as well. I too was sent with him, and we were told to take up our position in the city of Tacuba.

Cortes then gave Cristobal de Olid, who was quartermaster, thirty horsemen, a hundred and seventy-five soldiers, and twenty crossbowmen and musketeers, and put three captains under him: Andres de Tapia, Francisco Verdugo, and Francisco de Lugo, among whom he divided this force exactly, leaving Cristobal de Olid the horsemen and the supreme command over the three companies. He too was given eight thousand Tlascalans, and he was told to go and establish his camp in the city of Coyoacan, six miles from Tacuba.

Gonzalo de Sandoval, the chief constable, was given another division of twenty-four horsemen, fourteen musketeers and crossbowmen, and a hundred and fifty soldiers, also more than eight thousand Indian warriors from Chalco and Huexotzinco and other friendly places through which he had to pass. As captains he was given his friends Luis Marin and Pedro de Ircio, among whom his force was divided, while he retained command of the horsemen and was set over his two comrades. His orders were to establish his camp near Iztapalapa and attack it, doing all the damage he could until he should receive other instructions. He did not leave Texcoco until Cortes, who himself commanded the launches, was ready to put them on the lake.

As we were to set out next morning, the companies of Tlascalans were now sent ahead as far as the Mexican border, in order to avoid congestion on the road. But they were careless in their order of march, and neither Chichimecatecle nor any of the other captains noticed that Xicotenga, their supreme commander, was not with them. When Chichimecatecle finally inquired what had become of him, it was discovered that he had secretly returned to Tlascala during the night, and was planning to seize the Caciqueship, vassals, and lands of Chichimecatecle for himself. The reasons which the Tlascalans gave for his action were that once the Tlascalans, and especially Chichimecatecle, had gone to the war, he knew there would be no one to oppose him. Xicotenga the Elder, being his father, would help him, Mase Escasi was dead, and the only man he feared was Chichimecatecle. They said they had always known that Xicotenga had no wish to take part in the war against Mexico, for they had heard him say many times that all of us and of them would be killed.

On receiving this news Chichimecatecle, whose lands and vassals were in danger, turned very swiftly back from the march, and returned to Texcoco to inform Cortes, who immediately dispatched five Texcocan chiefs and two from Tlascala, all friends of Xicotenga's, to force him to come back. They were to tell him that Cortes begged him to return and fight his enemies the Mexicans, and to remind him that if his father Don Lorenzo de Vargas were not old and blind he would certainly do so, and that as all the Tlascalans were loyal servants of His Majesty, it was not right that he should dishonour them as he was now doing.

To this Xicotenga answered that if his father and Mase Escasi had taken his advice, Cortes would not have obtained such complete authority over the Tlascalans, and that, to waste no more words, he did not intend to return.

On receiving this answer, Cortes at once ordered a constable, four horsemen, and five chiefs from Texcoco to go with all speed and hang him wherever they caught him. 'There is no reforming this *Cacique*,' he said. 'He will always be a traitor and a villain and a plotter of evil,' and he added that this was no time to bear with him or to forgive the past. On hearing this Pedro de Alvarado put in a strong plea for Xicotenga; and Cortes answered him favourably, but secretly he ordered the constable and the horsemen to kill him, which they did. They hanged him in a town which was subject to Texcoco, and thus put an end to his treacheries. Some Tlascalans said that Xicotenga's father Don Lorenzo de Vargas had sent a message to Cortes, saying that his son was wicked and he would not vouch for him, and begging Cortes to kill him.

Because of Xicotenga's treachery, we stayed at Texcoco for another day, and departed on the next, which was 13 May, both divisions together, for both had to take the same road and to spend the night at Acolman. So Christobal de Olid sent men ahead to that town to secure quarters, and green branches were hung above the roof of each house to show that it was his. Consequently, when we arrived under Pedro de Alvarado there was nowhere for us to lodge. The men of our company had already half drawn their swords against Cristobal de Olid's men, and even the captains had defied one another. Fortunately there was no lack of gentlemen on both sides to intervene and somewhat appease the clamour, though all of us were still disgruntled. A message was sent to Cortes, and he dispatched Friar Pedro Melgarejo and captain Luis Marin in all haste. He also wrote to the captains and the rest of us, scolding us for our conduct. When the two emissaries arrived we made friends; but from that time onwards the two captains Pedro de Alvarado and Cristobal de Olid remained on bad terms.

Next day the two divisions continued their march, and we spent the night in a large town which we found deserted, for we were now in Mexican territory. We passed the following night in another large town named Cuauhtitlan, and on the day after moved through Tenayuca and Atzcapotzalco, all three of which were also deserted. On the evening of the last day we came to Tacuba and at once took up our quarters in some large houses and halls, for this place too was deserted. Our Tlascalan allies also found quarters there, and on that evening they visited the farms belonging to these towns, and brought in food to eat. We set a good watch and posted our sentinels carefully for, as I have said, Tacuba is close to Mexico.

When night fell we heard loud shouting from the lake. The Mexicans were abusing us with the taunt that we were not men enough to come out and fight them. They had many canoes full of warriors, and the causeways were crowded with fighting men, and the purpose of their mockery was to provoke us into fighting them that night. But we had gained experience from our battle on the causeways and the bridges, and refused to come out till next day, which was Sunday. Then when Father Juan Diaz had said mass and we had commended ourselves to God, we decided that both divisions should go together to cut off the city's water supply at Chapultepec, which was about a mile and a half from Tacuba.

As we went to break the pipes we found many warriors waiting for us on the road, for they were well aware that this would be the first damage we could inflict on them. When they met us, near some difficult ground, they began to shoot arrows and darts and to hurl stones, so that three of our men were wounded. But we quickly put them to flight, and our Tlascalan allies pursued them so successfully that they killed twenty and took six or eight prisoners. Once these bands were dispersed we broke the pipes which supplied the city, and the water did not flow into Mexico again so long as the war lasted. When we had accomplished this, our captains agreed that we should now reconnoitre, advance along the causeway from Tacuba, and endeavour to seize a bridge. But when we reached the causeway, armed canoes were so thick on the lake and there were so many warriors on the causeway itself, that we were filled with astonishment; and they fired so many darts, arrows, and stones at us that more than thirty of us were wounded at the first encounter. Nevertheless we advanced along the causeway towards the bridge, and they retreated before us in order, as I understand, to trap us on the other side. For once we had crossed, such a host of warriors descended on us that we could not repel them. The causeway was only eight yards wide. So what could we do, against a force that assailed us from both sides and shot at us as a sitting target? Our crossbowmen and musketeers fired continuously at their canoes, but hardly did them any damage, for they were very well protected by wooden bulwarks. Then, when we attacked the bands that were fighting on the causeway itself, they immediately jumped into the water; and there were so many of them that we could do nothing against them. Our horsemen were useless, for the Indians wounded their horses from one side or the other, hurling darts from the water, into which, as I have said, they leapt when pursued.

We fought them on the causeway for about an hour, and they pressed us so hard that we could resist no longer. Finally we saw a great fleet of canoes approaching from another direction to cut off our lines of retreat. Seeing this, and realizing that our Tlascalan allies were greatly obstructing the causeway and that if they jumped off they could not fight in the water, we decided, captains and soldiers alike, to attempt no further advance and to retire in good order.

When we reached dry land, hard pressed by the Mexicans and pursued by their howls, shouts, and whistles, we thanked God for our escape from the fight. For eight of our soldiers had been killed and more than a hundred wounded. Yet, even so, they howled insults at us from the canoes. But our friends the Tlascalans challenged them to come ashore, saying that they would fight them even if they were double their numbers. These were our first moves, to cut off their water supply and reconnoitre the lake, but we did not gain much honour by them.

Next morning Cristobal de Olid said he wished to go to his station at Coyoacan, nearly five miles away, and although Pedro de Alvarado and other gentlemen begged him to keep the two forces together, he insisted on departing. For he was a very brave man, and he said that it had been Pedro de Alvarado's fault that we had done badly on the previous day. So he went to the post that Cortes had assigned to him, and we stayed in camp. But it was wrong to separate the two divisions. If the Mexicans had known how small our numbers were, they would have attacked both companies separately in the four or five days that we were apart, before the arrival of the launches, and we should have been hard pressed and have suffered great losses.

As it was, we remained in Tacuba and Cristobal de Olid in his camp, and neither party dared to reconnoitre any further or to advance along the causeways. Every day we had skirmishes, with large bands of Mexicans, who came on land to fight us.

Meanwhile Gonzalo de Sandoval set out from Texcoco four days after the feast of Corpus Christi, and came to Iztapalapa. Almost all his route was through friendly territory which was subject to Texcoco. But when he reached Iztapalapa, he began to fight and to burn many of the houses that stood on dry land. But before many hours had passed great bands of Mexicans came to the aid of that city, and Sandoval had a stiff battle with them. During the fighting they saw great smoke-signals going up from a hill on the lakeside, and answering signals from other towns on the lake. They were summoning all the canoes from Mexico and the towns around the lake, for they saw that Cortes had now set out from Texcoco with the thirteen launches. Once Sandoval had left, Cortes delayed no longer; and the first thing he did on entering the lake was to attack a rocky island near Mexico on which many Mexicans had collected. Every canoe in the whole of the city, and in every town on or near the lake, had come out against him. For this reason the attack on Sandoval somewhat slackened, but as at that time most of the houses stood on the water, Cortes could not do them much harm. At the beginning, however, he killed many of the enemy, and with the help of his large force of allies captured and made prisoner many of the people of these towns.

When Cortes saw so many fleets of canoes converging on his thirteen launches, he was very frightened, and this was not un-reasonable, since there were more than a thousand canoes. So he abandoned the fight at the island and stationed himself out in the lake, so that if he found his men hard pressed he could sail out freely and hurry to any place he chose. He ordered the launch captains not to attack or bear down on the canoes until the land-breeze freshened, for it was just beginning to blow. When the canoes saw the launches halting, they thought that it was for fear of them, and the Mexican captains spurred them on, telling all their people to go in at once to attack them. At that moment a very strong, favourable breeze sprang up. The time was now suitable, and our oarsmen put on a great spurt, and Cortes ordered them to attack. Many of the canoes were overturned and many Indians were killed and captured, and the remaining craft made off to take refuge among the houses on the lake and in other places where our launches could not reach them. This was the first battle on the lake, and Cortes won the victory. Praise be to God for it all! Amen.

After this Cortes brought his launches towards Coyoacan, where Cristobal de Olid had his camp,[1] and fought many bands of Mexicans who were lying in wait for him in difficult places, hoping to capture the launches. As he was fiercely attacked from the canoes on the lake and from some *cues* on the causeway, he ordered four cannon to be taken out of the launches, with which he killed and wounded many Indians. But the gunners were in such a hurry that they carelessly set fire to their powder, and some of them even had their hands and faces scorched. Then Cortes promptly dispatched a very fast launch to Sandoval's camp in Iztapalapa to bring all the powder that was there, and he wrote to Sandoval that he must not move from his position.

All this time I was at Tacuba with Pedro de Alvarado, and I will relate what we did in our camp. Knowing that Cortes was going about the lake, we pushed forward along our causeway, and with greater caution than before pushed ahead as far as the first bridge, the crossbowmen and musketeers working together, some loading while the others fired. Pedro de Alvarado ordered the horsemen not to advance with us, but to stay on dry land and protect our rear, for he feared that the towns through which we had passed might attack us on the causeway. So, sometimes attacking and sometimes on the defensive, we fought every day, losing three soldiers in these engagements, and at the same time we filled in the awkward places on the causeway.

1. Actually, according to his own third letter, Cortes first captured the rocky island, chasing the enemy's canoes back towards Mexico, and then landed on the Iztapalapa causeway, where it was joined by another causeway which came from the direction of Coyoacan. Here he established a camp.

Seeing that he could do no harm to the people of Iztapalapa – for they were in the water – though they could wound his soldiers, Sandoval decided to attack a small town and group of houses that stood in the lake. Having succeeded in effecting an entry, he was able to begin the attack. But while the fighting was going on, Guatemoc sent many warriors to the help of the inhabitants, to destroy and break open the causeway by which Sandoval had advanced; and to surround his troops and leave them no way of escape he sent many warriors to the other side also.

While standing with Cristobal de Olid, Cortes saw the great fleet of canoes making towards Iztapalapa, and decided to go in that direction with his launches and the whole of Olid's company, to look for Sandoval, he on the lake with the launches and Olid with his men along the causeway. As they went forward, they saw a swarm of Mexicans breaking up this causeway, from which they concluded that Sandoval was in a certain group of houses, towards which they rowed the launches. They found him there fighting Guatemoc's warriors; and when the combat slackened a little, Cortes ordered him to abandon his camp at Iztapalapa and go by land to blockade the other causeway, which runs from Mexico to a town once called Tepeaquilla, but now Our Lady of Guadalupe, the place of many miracles.

As Cortes and all our captains and soldiers realized that without the launches we could not advance along the causeways to attack Mexico, he sent four of them to Pedro de Alvarado, and kept six in his own camp, which he now shared with Cristobal de Olid. He sent two more to Gonzalo de Sandoval on the Tepeaquilla causeway, and ordered that the smallest should not be sent on the lake again, since it was now light and the canoes might overturn it. He had the soldiers and oarsmen of its crew distributed among the other twelve launches, for twenty of their complement had already received very severe wounds.

When this reinforcement reached our camp at Tacuba, Pedro de Alvarado ordered two of the launches to move to one side of the causeway and two to the other, and the fighting went very much in our favour. For the launches routed the canoes which had been attacking us from the water, and so we were able to capture several bridges and barricades. During this fight, however, the enemy discharged upon us so many stones from their slings, so many darts, and so many arrows that although all our soldiers wore armour they were wounded on the head and body, and a bitter battle went on until night parted us. I must explain that from time to time the Mexicans relieved one band by another, a change which we observed by the marks and distinguishing signs on their armour. As for the launches, they were checked by the darts, arrows, and stones that fell on them, thicker than hail, from the high rooftops. I do not know how else to describe it, and no one would understand me who was not there. But they really were more numerous than hailstones, and quickly covered the causeway. Whenever we left some bridge or barricade unguarded, after having captured it with great efforts, they would retake it that night, deepen the channel, strengthen the defences, and even dig holes under the water into which we should stumble and fall when the moment came to retire after the next day's fighting. Then they would be able to overwhelm us from their canoes. For they had posted many of them for this purpose in places where our launches could not find them, so that when we were trapped in the pits they could attack us both by land and water; and to prevent our launches from coming to our aid they had fixed many concealed stakes in the water on which they would get impaled.

We fought in this way every day, and, as I have already said, our horsemen were of little use on the causeways. For if they charged or pursued the enemy's bands, the Mexicans immediately jumped into the water. Other bands too were posted behind breastworks which the enemy raised on the causeways; and these were armed with long lances and even longer scythes, made from the arms they had captured when they defeated us so severely in Mexico. With these lances, and great showers of darts and arrows shot from the lake, they wounded and killed the horses before the riders could do the opposing squadrons any harm. Moreover, those horsemen who owned their mounts were unwilling to risk them, for at that time horses cost eight hundred or even a thousand and more pesos, and more were not to be had. But in any case they could have caught very few of the enemy on the causeway.

Now when we fell back at nightfall, we cauterized our wounds with burning oil, and a soldier called Juan Catalan made a cross and said a prayer over them. We certainly found that our Lord Jesus Christ gave us strength, as well as showing us mercies every day, for they healed very quickly.

Wounded and bandaged with rags, we had to fight from morning till night, for if the wounded had not fought but stayed behind in camp, there would not have been twenty sound men in each company to go out.

When our Tlascalan allies saw the soldier Catalan curing us by making the sign of the cross over our wounds and broken heads, they went to him too; and there were so many of them that he could hardly attend to them in a day.

As for our captains and our standard-bearer and his guard, they were covered with wounds and their standards were ragged. Indeed I should say that we needed a new standard-bearer every day, for we were so badly battered that no one could carry the standards into battle a second time.

What is more, we had hardly enough to eat. I do not speak of maize-cakes, for we had plenty of them, but of nourishing food for the wounded. The wretched stuff on which we existed was a vegetable that the Indians eat called *quelites*, supplemented by the local cherries, while they lasted, and afterwards by prickly pears, which then came into season.

Events in Cortes' camp and in Sandoval's were much the same as in ours. Not a day passed without great companies of Mexicans coming to attack them and, as I have said, their attacks lasted from dawn till nightfall. For this purpose Guatemoc had chosen captains and squadrons to reinforce each causeway, and he warned Tlatelolco and all the lakeside towns which I have so often mentioned that when a signal was raised on the great *cue* of Tlatelolco, their men must come up, some in canoes and some by land. The Mexican captains had received well concerted orders, too, on how and when and to what points they must bring assistance.

Now I will explain the way in which we changed our order

and method of fighting. It was like this. When we saw that however many water obstacles we captured each day, the Mexicans returned and opened them again, and that in our assault a few were killed and most of us wounded, we decided to take up our station on the causeway, in a small square where there were some temple towers which we had already captured. Here there was room for us to set up our shelters, which were so poor that when it rained we all got wet. Indeed they were fit for nothing but to protect us from the dew. The Indian women who made our bread we left in Tacuba, with all the horsemen and our Tlascalan allies to guard them, and also to watch the passes, in case the enemy should come down from the near-by towns and attack our rearguard while we were fighting on the causeway.

Once we had set up our shelters in this square, we endeavoured to destroy any houses or groups of buildings we captured and to fill up any water obstacles. We pulled the houses down to the ground, for if we set fire to them they took too long to burn, and one did not catch alight from another, because, as I have several times said, they all stood in the water, and the only way of passing from one to another was over bridges or by canoe; and if we tried to swim across, the enemy did great execution on us from the flat roofs. We were safer, therefore, when the houses were demolished.

Once we had captured a barrier or bridge or strong-point at which they had put up great resistance, we tried to guard it by day and night. Our watches were organized in this way : All our companies were on guard together. The first, of just over forty soldiers, was on duty from sunset until midnight, and another company of forty men took over from midnight until two hours before dawn. However, the first company did not leave their post, but slept there on the ground. This second period is called the 'sleeping-watch'; and when it was over another company came to the dawn-watch, which lasted for the two hours until day. But those who had done the 'sleeping-watch' did not leave the spot either. When morning came, therefore, there were a hundred and twenty soldiers all on guard together. On some nights, even, when we thought there was great danger, we all watched from dawn till daybreak, for fear that a heavy attack by the enemy might break our defences. For we had been warned by some Mexican captains whom we had taken in battle that Guatemoc had made a plan, which he had discussed with his officers, for breaking through our line on the causeway, either by day or night. Then when he had overwhelmed us in our sector, he would quickly defeat and rout Cortes and Sandoval on the other two causeways. He had also arranged that the nine lakeside towns, Tacuba itself, Atzapotzalco, and Tenayuca, should unite and, on a chosen day, attack us from the rear, breaking our position on the causeway. Also, one night, they were to seize the Indian women who made our bread in Tacuba, and capture our baggage. On learning this, we warned our horsemen in Tacuba and our Tlascalan allies to keep watch all night and remain on the alert.

Guatemoc carried out this plan as he had made it. On several occasions great bands came at midnight to attack us and break through, and were followed by others in the 'sleeping-watch' and the dawn-watch. Sometimes they came noiselessly and sometimes with loud yells and whistles, and when they reached the place where we were keeping watch some let fly darts and stones and arrows, while others came on with lances. But although we sustained some wounds, we held our position and sent many of them back wounded. The large bands of warriors who came to seize our baggage were defeated by our horsemen and the Tlascalans; and as it was night they did not make much of a stand.

Despite rain, wind, and cold, we kept watch in the way I have described; and although wounded we were forced to stay there in the midst of the quagmires. We had only a miserable supply of maize-cakes, vegetables, and prickly pears to eat, and in addition there were the hardships of the fighting, which the officers said were unavoidable.

Then, in spite of all our precautions, the enemy would break some bridge or causeway that we had captured but could not defend in the night. Next day, however, we would recapture it and build it up again. Then the Mexicans would return, break it once more, and strengthen their position with barricades. This went on until the enemy changed their method of fighting, as I will tell in due course.

Let us leave these daily battles, and those others fought by Cortes and Sandoval, and say what an advantage we had gained by preventing food and water getting to the enemy along the three causeways. But since our launches were stationed at our camps, they were only useful to protect our rear from warriors in canoes and others who attacked from the roof-tops during the fighting. The Mexicans, however, were able to bring in much food and water from the nine towns around the lake, which sent them supplies in canoes by night; and from other friendly villages they received maize, poultry, and all they required. To interrupt these supplies, it was agreed between our three camps that two launches should patrol the lake by night and destroy all the canoes they could or, if they could capture any, should bring them to the camps. Although we missed these two launches as a guard and reinforcement during the night fighting, the plan was a good one. For even if many loaded canoes managed to get through, our launches served a useful purpose in interrupting the Mexicans' supplies of food and water. Moreover the enemy took no precautions when bringing supplies in their canoes, and so no day passed in which the patrolling launches did not bring in some prizes, with many Indians hanging from their yards.

Let us leave this and tell of the strategem which the Mexicans employed to capture our launches and kill their crews. It was like this. As I have said, every night and in the early mornings, our men went out on the lake searching for canoes, and overturned them from their launches, capturing many of them. The Mexicans decided to arm thirty pirogues, and at night they posted all thirty, covered over with branches, among some reed-beds, in a place where the launches could not see them. Then before nightfall they sent out two or three canoes with strong oarsmen, which appeared to be carrying provisions or water. On the course that the Mexicans thought the launches would follow in attacking these canoes, they had driven a number of stout timbers pointed like stakes, on which they would get impaled. So, as the canoes crossed the lake and approached the reed-beds, showing every sign of fear, two of our launches set out in pursuit. The two canoes made a show of retiring to the land at the place where the thirty pirogues were lying in wait; and the launches followed them. But when they reached the ambush all the pirogues came out together and attacked them, quickly wounding all the soldiers, oarsmen, and officers; and the launches could not escape in either direction on account of the stakes that had been planted. Thus they killed a certain Captain de Portilla, an excellent soldier who had fought in Italy, and wounded Pedro Barba, another very good officer, whose launch they captured and who died of his wounds three days later. These two launches belonged to Cortes' camp, and their loss distressed him greatly. But within a few days the enemy planted other very successful ambushes, which I will describe in due course.

I will now go on to speak of the severe fighting that was all the time going on in Cortes' camp and in Gonzalo de Sandoval's. But by far the heavier engagements were fought by Cortes. For he had ordered that all houses should be pulled down and burnt and the bridged channels filled up; and what he gained each day was thus consolidated. He sent an order to Pedro de Alvarado to be sure that we never crossed a bridge or gap in the causeway without first blocking it up, and to pull down and burn every house. Then we had to fill up the gaps and bridges with the mud-bricks and timber of the demolished houses; and our Tlascalan allies helped us manfully in all this warfare.

Now when the Mexicans saw us levelling the houses and filling up the bridges and gaps, they decided on another way of fighting. They would lift a bridge, leaving a very deep and wide channel for us to wade across, which in places was out of our depth. For under the water they dug many pits, which we could not see, and they erected walls and barricades on both sides of the gap. They also drove in many stakes or heavy pointed timber in places where our launches would run on them, if they came to our assistance while we were fighting to capture this fortification. For they well understood that we must first destroy the barricade, and then cross that channel of water, before we could approach the city. At the same time they kept ready in hidden places many canoes, fully manned with warriors and strong oarsmen. Indeed, one Sunday morning squadrons of warriors fell on us from three directions, attacking us so hard that it was all we could do to prevent them from overwhelming us.

At this time Pedro de Alvarado gave orders that half the horsemen who had remained in Tacuba should sleep on the causeway, where they would be in less danger than before, since no roofs were standing, nearly all the houses having been demolished. In fact, they could now ride down some parts of the causeway without their horses being wounded from the roofs or the canoes.

To continue my story, these three bands came on very boldly, one from the direction of the broad open channel, another from some houses that we had demolished, and the third to attack us in the rear from the direction of Tacuba. Thus we were more or less surrounded. The horsemen with our Tlascalan allies, however, broke through the band that had taken us from the rear and we resisted the other two so valiantly that we drove them to retreat. But their retreat proved to be a feint. We thought we had captured the first of their barricades, while in fact they had abandoned it. Imagining we had gained a victory, we leapt through the water, and where we crossed there were no pits. We pressed on with our advance among some large houses and temple towers, and the enemy still made a show of retreating. But they went on shooting darts, and stones from their slings, and plenty of arrows; and when we least expected it, a host of warriors sprang on us from a place we could not see, many more joined in from the roofs and houses, and those who had appeared to be retreating suddenly turned round to attack us so hard that we could not hold our ground. We then decided to retire very cautiously. But in the channel we had captured at our first crossing, which had been free from pits, the enemy had stationed such a fleet of canoes that we could not cross at this place. They forced us to cross at another where, as I have said, the water was very deep and they had dug many pits. Being pursued in our retreat by such a host of warriors, we swam or leapt through the water, and nearly all our men fell into these pits. Then the canoes attacked us, and the Mexicans seized five of our comrades, whom they took to Guatemoc alive. Nearly all of us were wounded. For the launches we were expecting could not come to our aid, being impaled on the stakes that the enemy had fixed there. At the same time they too were overwhelmed by such a rain of darts and arrows that two soldiers were killed at the oars, and many others wounded. To return to the pits in the channel, I think it was a wonder we were not all killed there. For myself, I was seized by a great number of Indians, but I managed to free my sword-arm and the Lord Jesus Christ gave me strength to deal them a few good thrusts, with which I saved myself, though I had a severe wound in the other arm. Once safely out of the water, I lost all sensation and could not stand on my feet or take breath, so exhausted was I by my efforts to free myself from that rabble, and by copious loss of blood. I declare that when they had me in their claws I was mentally commending myself to our Lord God and Our Lady, His blessed Mother; and He it was that gave me strength to save myself. Thanks be to God for the mercy He granted me.

There is another thing I wish to mention. When Pedro de Alvarado and his horsemen had thoroughly routed the bands that had attacked us in the rear from the direction of Tacuba, only a single horseman passed the water and the barricades, a man who had recently come from Spain; and both he and his horse were killed. The cavalry were already advancing to our assistance when they saw us retiring. If they had crossed we should have been compelled to turn back against the Indians, and if they had then been forced to retreat, none of them or their horses or any of us would have survived. For the enemy's dispositions were so cunning that they would have fallen in the pits, and there were a great number of warriors who would have killed their horses with lances, which they had brought for the purpose, and by attacking from the many flat roofs all around, for this was in the heart of the city.

Flushed with their victory, the Mexicans continued through-out that day, which, as I have said, was a Sunday, to send such vast hoards of warriors against our camp that we could not drive them off. They certainly expected to rout us. But with the aid of some bronze cannon and by dint of hard fighting and by all the companies keeping guard every night, we managed to hold our own.

When Cortes received news of this state of affairs he was very much annoyed. He immediately sent a launch to Pedro de Alvarado with written orders that he was never on any account to leave a gap unblocked, and that all the horsemen were to sleep on the causeway with their horses saddled and bridled all night long. He insisted that we should not attempt to advance a single step until we had filled up that great opening with bricks and timber, and that every precaution should be taken in the camp.[1] When we saw that the great disaster we had suffered was our own fault we then and there began to fill in the opening. Though it cost us great labour and many wounds which the enemy inflicted on us while we were at work, and although six of our soldiers were killed, we had it blocked in four days.

Each night we kept watch on the place itself, all three companies together in accordance with Cortes' orders; and the Mexicans were very close to us as we watched. For they too had their sentinels, and changed them by watches just as we did. They lighted great fires that burnt all night, but their sentinels stood away from them so that we could not distinguish them from a distance. Although we could not see the Indians who were watching, because of the brightness of their fires, yet we always knew when they changed guard, for then they came to feed the fire. As this was a season of heavy rains, on many nights their fire was put out. But they always lit it again, noiselessly and without exchanging a word, for they communicated by whistling.

Very often when we knew they were about to change their guard our musketeers and crossbowmen fired random shots at them. But they did them no harm, for the Mexicans were in a

1. Cortes himself says in his third letter that he visited Pedro de Alvarado's camp and was astonished to find how much he had done, and how far he had penetrated into the city.

position where we should not have been able to attack them at night even if we had wished to do so, on account of another wide and deep channel which they had excavated, and of the barricades and ramparts they had raised. But they shot plenty of missiles at us.

Let us turn from the subject of these sentinels to that of our daily battle on the causeway. Fighting in regular order, we captured the opening I have mentioned where the enemy kept guard. But so many warriors attacked us every day, and so many missiles fell on us, that even though we exercised great caution and wore good armour we were all wounded. Then when we had fought all day and it was growing late, and there was no possibility of a further advance, but only of retreat, the enemy would throw in many companies that they had been keeping for this moment. For they believed that if they attacked very vigorously as we retired, they would be able to rout us. So they came on as bravely as tigers and fought us hand to hand. When we got to know this plan of theirs we made the following dispositions for our retreat. The first thing we did was to get our Tlascalan allies off the causeway. They were very numerous, and the Mexicans, being cunning, would have liked nothing better than to see us obstructed by our friends. Thus they made fierce attacks on us from two or three directions, hoping to catch us between them and cut some of us off. So if we had been impeded by the Tlascalans we should not have been able to fight them everywhere. Once our allies were no longer hampering us, we retired to our camp without ever turning our backs but always facing the enemy. Some of the crossbowmen and musketeers shot while others loaded, and our four launches in the lake, two on either side of the causeway, protected us from the great fleets of canoes and the many stones which were piled on the rooftops and in the houses ready to be hurled down. Yet despite all our caution every one of us was in great hazard of his life until we got back to our shelters. There we cauterized our wounds with oil and bandaged them with native cloth. We dined off maize-cakes brought to us from Tacuba, and such of us as had them ate vegetables and prickly pears. After this we at once mounted guard at the water-channel I have mentioned, and returned to the fight next day. We had no alternative, for the enemy battalions began to attack us early in the morning, shouting their abuse, and even got as far as our camp. Such was the nature of our ordeal.

But let us leave our camp, which was Pedro de Alvarado's, and return to Cortes. The enemy attacked his quarters too, by night and day, killing and wounding many soldiers. He kept two launches employed all night chasing the canoes that brought food and water into Mexico, and one of them captured two chieftains from one of these provisioning canoes, from whom Cortes learnt that forty pirogues and other canoes were once again lying in ambush to capture one of our launches. Cortes flattered these two prisoners, presenting them with cloaks and promising that he would give them land after we had captured Mexico. Then he asked them through our interpreters where the pirogues were, for they would not be in the same place as before. They pointed out the place where they were stationed, and also warned us that many heavy timber stakes had been driven in at certain points, to impale our launches should they turn in flight from their pirogues, so that they could seize and kill the crews.

On receiving this warning, Cortes got six launches ready to go that night, covered with plenty of foliage, to take up their position in some reed-beds about three-quarters of a mile from where the pirogues were hidden. They were rowed with muffled oars, and their crew kept watch all night. Then, early next morning, Cortes ordered a launch to be sent out as if in pursuit of provisioning canoes, with the two Indian chiefs on board to point out the exact position of the pirogues. At the same time the Mexicans sent out their two decoy canoes, which purported to carry supplies, and they went in the direction of the ambush in the hope that our launch would pursue them. Each party had its own idea, and the ideas were in fact the same. When the launch sent out by the cunning Cortes saw the canoes which the Indians used as bait, it began to pursue them, and the two canoes pretended to run for the land, where their pirogues were lying in ambush. Our launch then put up a show of not daring to approach the shore and being about to retire.

When the pirogues and the other canoes saw it turning away, they all came out after it most furiously, rowing as hard as they could in pursuit. The launch then made off, as if in flight, towards the place where the other six launches were concealed, and the pirogues continued to follow. At that moment a gun was fired as a signal for our launches to emerge. They came out with a great rush, and attacked the enemy craft, which they overturned, killing many warriors and taking many prisoners. The launch which we had sent out as a decoy was now some way off, but it returned to assist the others. A good capture of prisoners and canoes was made, and after that the Mexicans did not dare to lay any more ambuscades, or to bring in food and water as openly as before.

Now when the lakeside towns saw that we were victorious every day both land and water, and that, while the people of other towns had made friends with us, we continued to make war on them, doing them great harm and making many prisoners, they came together, as it seems, and decided to ask Cortes for peace. With great humility they asked for pardon if they had in any way offended us, and pleaded that they had been acting under orders and could not have done otherwise. Cortes was delighted by these overtures, and when the news spread to Pedro de Alvarado's and Sandoval's camp, we soldiers were equally pleased. With a smile on his face, and comforting words, Cortes granted them pardon, but said that they deserved severe punishment for helping the Mexicans. The towns that made peace were Iztapalapa, Churubusco, Culuacan, Mixquic, and all those on the fresh-water lake. Cortes told them that we should not shift our camp till the Mexicans either sued for peace or were destroyed in the fighting, and ordered them to aid us in our war with all the canoes they possessed, to come to build shelters for him, and to bring him food. They promised to obey and built him some shelters, but brought no food or very little, and that grudgingly. Our shelters were never built, so we of Pedro de Alvarado's company continued to get wet. For, as everyone who has been in this country knows, in June, July, and August it rains every day here.

But to return to the causeway and our daily battles with the

Mexicans, we succeeded in capturing many temple-towers and houses, and in mastering more openings and channels and bridges between houses, all of which we blocked with the bricks and timbers of the houses that had been pulled down. We kept guard on these channels, but despite all our precautions the enemy came back and deepened and widened them, and erected more barricades. Our three companies considered it disgraceful that some of us should be filling up crossings and gaps and bridges while others were meeting the Mexicans face to face. So, to avoid quarrels over who should be fighting and who should be filling in channels, Pedro de Alvarado ordered us to take turns, one company labouring and guarding the work one day and another the next, until all three companies had had their turn. By this arrangement every building we captured was razed to the ground, and our Tlascalan allies helped us. So we went on penetrating into the city. But when the time came for retreat, all three companies had to fight together, because that was when we were in the greatest danger.

But let us leave our camp for those of Cortes and Sandoval, which were continuously attacked by day and night, both overland and by fleets of canoes on the lake. They could never shake the enemy off. Cortes' men endeavoured to capture a bridge over a deep opening, which was very difficult to take. The Mexicans had erected many barricades and ramparts, so that it was impossible to cross except by swimming. Whenever an attempt was made hosts of warriors were waiting for our men with arrows and slings and their various kinds of swords and lances, and the lake was full of war-canoes. Near the barricades were many flat roofs from which volleys of stones descended, and here again the launches could be of no assistance because of the stakes they had placed there. In capturing this fortress, bridge, and opening, Cortes' troops suffered great losses. Four of his soldiers were killed in the fighting and more than thirty were wounded; and as it was already late when they effected the capture, they had no time to block the channel. They made their retreat with much difficulty and in great danger, carrying their own wounded and many more Tlascalans who had been hurt.

Let us now speak of another way in which Guatemoc ordered his companies to fight, and for which he had his whole force prepared. It was on the following day, the feast of Saint John, and exactly one year since we had first entered Mexico to relieve Pedro de Alvarado and had been so severely defeated. It appears that the Mexicans had kept count of this, for Guatemoc ordered that we should be attacked at all three camps by his whole army and with the greatest possible vigour, both on land and by water. The attack was timed for the 'sleeping-watch', and in order that the launches should not be able to help us, stakes had been placed in most parts of the lake to impale them. The enemy came along at such a furious pace that had it not been for those who were on watch – more than a hundred and twenty very experienced soldiers – they would have broken into our camp. As it was we were in very great danger. However, by fighting in good order we withstood them. But fifteen of our men were wounded, two of whom died of their wounds within a week.

In Cortes' camp the situation was very difficult also. Our troops were reduced to the greatest straits, and many were killed and wounded; and the same thing happened in Sandoval's camp. They attacked us like this on two successive nights, and many Mexicans were killed and very many wounded in these encounters. Realizing, however, that these two nights of fighting had gained them nothing, Guatemoc, his captains, and *papas* decided to come with all their combined forces at the down-watch and attack our camp in Tacuba. Advancing fearlessly, they invested us on two sides, and had almost defeated and cut us off when, thanks be to Jesus Christ, we mustered the strength to turn and close our ranks. Under the partial protection of the launches we advanced shoulder to shoulder, cutting and thrusting as we went, and drove them back a little. Our horsemen were not idle, and our crossbowmen and musketeers did what they could, but they had enough work in breaking up yet other forces which attacked us from the rear. In that battle eight of our men were killed and many more wounded, including Pedro de Alvarado, who was hit on the head. If our Tlascalan allies had slept on the causeway that

night, we should have been seriously hampered by their numbers and in great danger; but thanks to our past experience we
had no concern on that score, since we had got them away
quickly and they were back in Tacuba.

Seeing that it was impossible to fill in every channel and gap
that we captured in the daytime and that the Mexicans reopened and refortified each night, and that all of us together
fighting, filling in, and keeping watch was very hard labour,
Cortes decided to hold consultations with the captains and
soldiers in his camp, and wrote to us in Alvarado's camp, and
to those in Sandoval's, to learn the opinion of us all. What he
asked us was whether we approved of a rapid advance into the
city as far as Tlatelolco, which is the great market of Mexico
and much larger and broader than that at Salamanca. If we
could capture it, he thought it would be good to pitch all three
camps there, since from that base we should be able to fight in
the streets of Mexico without all the labour of our nightly
retreats and of filling in and guarding the bridges.

As is usual in such discussions, there were many different
opinions. Some of us said that it was not a good idea to take up
our position so far inside the city, but that we should go on as
we were, fighting and pulling down and burning the houses.
The strongest argument put forward by those of us who held
this opinion was that if we took up our position in Tlatelolco
and left the causeways and bridges unfortified and unguarded,
the Mexicans, being so strong in warriors and canoes, would
break them down again and we should lose our mastery of
them. They would then attack us with their powerful forces by
night and day, and as they always had plenty of stakes in position, our launches would not be able to help us. By the plan
Cortes was proposing, it would thus be we who were besieged,
and the enemy would be left in possession of the shore, the
countryside, and the lake. We wrote him our opinion of his
plan so that we should not fall into the same devilish trouble
as when we were escaping from Mexico.

Cortes listened to our opinions and the reasons with which
we supported them. But the sole outcome of all this discussion
was that next day we were to advance with all possible strength

from all three camps, horsemen, crossbowmen, musketeers, and soldiers, and push forward into the great market square of Tlatelolco. When all was ready in the three camps, and warnings had been sent to our Tlascalan allies, the men of Texcoco, and those of the other towns who had recently sworn obedience to His Majesty and were to bring their canoes to help our launches, we started from our camp on Sunday morning, after mass. Cortes too set out from his camp, and Sandoval led his men forward; and each company advanced in full force, capturing barricades and bridges. The Mexicans fought like brave men, but Cortes made great gains, and so did Gonzalo de Sandoval. As for us, we had already captured another barricade and bridge, which was very difficult because Guatemoc had great forces guarding them. Many of our men were wounded, one so severely that he died a little later, and more than a thousand of our Tlascalan allies were injured. Still, we followed up our victory in high spirits.

To return to Cortes and his men, they captured a deepish water-opening with a very narrow causeway across it, which the Mexicans had constructed most cunningly. For they had cleverly foreseen just what would happen; which was that after his victory Cortes and his men would press along the causeway, which would be crowded with our allies. They decided therefore that at this point they must pretend to be in flight, but continue to hurl javelins, arrows, and stones and to make little stands as though trying to put up some resistance, until they lured Cortes on to follow them.

When the Mexicans saw that Cortes was indeed following up his victory in this way, they simulated flight, as they had planned. Then, as bad fortune follows on good and great disasters succeed great prosperity, so in his headlong pursuit of the enemy, either out of carelessness or because Our Lord permitted it, Cortes and his men omitted to fill in the channel they had captured. The causeway had been deliberately built very narrow, and it was interrupted by water in some places, and full of mud and mire. When the Mexicans saw him cross that channel without filling it in they were highly delighted. They had assembled great bands of warriors under very valiant captains and posted many canoes on the lake in places where our launches could not reach them on account of great stakes. All was prepared for the moment when such a furious army of shrieking, shouting, and whistling Mexicans fell on Cortes and his men that they could not stand up to the shock of their charge. Our soldiers, captains, and standard-bearers then decided to retreat in good order. But the enemy continued to charge them furiously, and drove them back to that difficult crossing. Meanwhile our allies, of whom Cortes had brought great numbers, were so confused that they turned and fled, offering no resistance. On seeing them run away in disorder Cortes tried to hearten them with cries of: 'Stop, stop, gentlemen! Stand firm! What do you mean by turning your backs?' But he could not halt them.

Then, at that gap in the causeway which they had neglected to fill, on that little, narrow, broken causeway, the Mexicans, aided by their canoes, defeated Cortes, wounding him in the leg, taking sixty-six of his soldiers alive, and killing eight horses. Six or seven Mexican captains had already seized our Captain, but the Lord was pleased to help him and give him strength to defend himself, although wounded. Then, in the nick of time, that very valiant soldier Cristobal de Olea came up to him and, seeing Cortes held by so many Indians, promptly killed four of them with mighty thrusts of his sword; and another brave soldier called Lerma helped him. Such was the personal bravery of these two men that the Indian captains let Cortes go. But in defending him for the second time Olea lost his life and Lerma was almost killed. Then many other soldiers rushed up and, although badly wounded, grasped Cortes and pulled him out of his dangerous position in the mud. The quartermaster Cristobal de Olid also ran forward, and they seized Cortes by the arms to drag him out of the mud and water, and brought him a horse, on which he escaped from death. At that same moment his steward Cristobal de Guzman arrived with another horse. Meanwhile the Mexican warriors went on fighting very bravely and successfully from the rooftops, inflicting great damage on us and capturing Cristobal de Guzman, whom they carried alive to Guatemoc; and they continued to pursue Cortes and his men until they had driven them back to camp. Even after that disaster, when they reached their quarters the Mexicans continued to harry them, shouting and yelling abuse and calling them cowards.

But to turn from Cortes and his defeat to our army under Pedro de Alvarado, on the causeway from Tacuba. We were advancing most victoriously when suddenly and unexpectedly we saw a great number of Mexican bands advancing against us, with handsome standards and plumes. Uttering loud yells, they threw in front of us five heads, streaming with blood, which they had just cut off the men of Cortes' company whom they had captured.

'We will kill you too,' they cried, 'as we have killed Malinche and Sandoval, and all the men they brought with them.' With these words they closed in on us, and neither cut nor thrust, nor crossbow nor musket could keep them off. They rushed at us as if we were a target. Even so, we did not break our ranks at all as we retired. We at once commanded our Tlascalan allies to get quickly out of our way in the streets and on the causeways and at the difficult places, and this time they did so with a will. When they saw those five bloodstained heads, they said that Malinche and Sandoval and all the *Teules* with them had been killed, and that the same would happen to us, and to them, the Tlascalans. They were very much frightened, for they believed what they said.

As we were retreating, we heard the sound of trumpets from the great *cue* of Huichilobos and Tezcatlipoca, which dominates the whole city, and the beating of a drum, a very sad sound as of some devilish instrument, which could be heard six miles away; and with it came the noise of many kettle-drums, conches, horns, and whistles. At that moment, as we afterwards learnt, they were offering the hearts and blood of ten of our comrades to these two idols.

But let us return to our retreat and the great attack they made on us from the causeway, the rooftops, and the canoes on the lake. At that moment we were attacked once more by fresh bands whom Guatemoc had just sent, and he had ordered his horn to be sounded. The blowing of this horn was a signal that his captains and warriors must now fight to capture their enemies or die in the attempt, and as soon as this sound struck their ears, his bands and companies, hurling themselves on us with a terrifying and indescribable fury, endeavoured to drag us away. Even now, when I stop to think, I seem to see it all and to be present at that battle once more. It was our Lord Jesus Christ, let me repeat, who gave us strength, for we were all wounded. It was He who saved us, for otherwise we should never have reached our huts, and I praise and thank Him for it, that I escaped that time, as on other occasions, from the power of the Mexicans.

The horsemen charged repeatedly, and with two cannon which we placed near our huts, and which were loaded and fired by turns, we managed to hold our own. The causeway was choked with Mexicans, who pursued us as far as the houses, as if we were already conquered, and hurled javelins and stones at us. But, as I have said, we killed many of them with these cannon. The most useful man that day was a gentleman called Pedro Moreno Medrano, who now lives at Puebla. He acted as gunner, because our proper artillerymen had been either killed or wounded. He was a good soldier, and gave us great assistance. While we were defending ourselves like this, hard pressed and wounded, we did not know whether Cortes and Sandoval and their armies had been killed or routed, as the Mexicans had told us when they threw down those heads, which they had brought tied together by the hair and beards. We could get no news of them, for they were fighting about a mile and a half away, and the place where the Mexicans had defeated Cortes was even further off. We were very distressed, therefore, but by keeping together in one body, both wounded and sound, we withstood the fury of the attack, which the Mexicans believed would annihilate us. For they had already captured one of our launches, killing three soldiers and wounding the captain and the rest of the crew, though it had afterwards been rescued by another launch whose captain was Juan Jaramillo; and yet another was impaled in a place from which it could not move. Its captain was Juan de Limpias, who lost his hearing at that time, and now lives at Puebla. He himself fought so valiantly, and so encouraged the soldiers who were rowing the launch, that they broke the stakes and got away, all badly wounded, thus saving the craft, which was the first to break the stakes, a great thing for us all.

To return to Cortes, when he and nearly all his men were either killed or wounded, the Mexican bands made an attack on his camp, and cast in front of the soldiers who were defending it another four heads, dripping with blood, which were those of four men captured from Cortes' own army. But they said they were the heads of Tonatio – that is of Pedro de Alvarado – and of Sandoval, Bernal Díaz, and another *Teule*, and that they had already killed us all at Tacuba. It is said that Cortes was even more distressed than before, and that tears sprang to his eyes and the eyes of all those who were with him. Nevertheless he did not seem to weaken. He at once ordered Cristobal de Olid, the quartermaster, and his captains to be sure that the many Mexicans who were pressing in on them did not break into the camp, and to see that his men held together, the sound and the wounded alike. He then sent Andres de Tapia with three horsemen post-haste overland to Tacuba, to see if we were alive, and to tell us, if we had not been defeated, to keep watch by day and night, also in a single body. But we had already been doing this for some time. Tapia and his three horsemen came as hard as they could, though he and two of them were wounded, and when they reached our camp and found us fighting the Mexicans who were gathered against us, they rejoiced in their hearts. They told us how Cortes had been defeated and conveyed his message to us, but they did not care to tell us how many had been killed. They gave the number as about twenty-five, and said that the rest were well.

Sandoval and his men had advanced victoriously along the streets in the quarter they were invading. But after the defeat of Cortes, the Mexicans turned on them in such force that they could make no headway. Six soldiers were killed and all the rest injured, including Sandoval himself, who received three wounds, in the thigh, the head, and the left arm; and when the struggle was at its height, the enemy displayed six heads of Cortes' men whom they had killed, saying that these were the heads of

Malinche, Tonatio, and other captains, and that Sandoval and his companions would meet with the same fate. They then made a fierce attack. When he saw the heads Sandoval told his men to show a bold spirit and not be dismayed. He warned them too that there must be no confusion on the narrow causeway as they retreated, and ordered his allies, who were numerous, to leave it immediately, since they would hamper him. Then, with the help of his two launches and his musketeers and cross-bowmen, he very laboriously retired to his quarters, with all his men badly wounded and discouraged, and six of them dead. Once he was clear of the causeway, although still surrounded by Mexicans, he encouraged his people and their captains, charging them to be sure to keep together by day and night and thus prevent the camp from being overwhelmed.

On receiving captain Luis Marin's assurance that this would be done, wounded and bandaged with rags though he was, Sandoval took two horsemen and rode post-haste to Cortes' camp; and when he saw Cortes, he exclaimed : 'Oh, my lord Captain, what is this? Are these the counsels and strategems of war that you have always impressed on us? How did this disaster happen?' And Cortes answered him, with the tears starting to his eyes : 'Sandoval, my son, my sins are the cause of this. But I do not deserve as much blame as my captains and soldiers say. It is Julian de Alderete, the treasurer, who was at fault. I told him to fill in that opening where they defeated us. But because he has no experience of war, and is not used to receiving orders from captains, he did not do so.' Then the treasurer himself answered – for he was standing beside Cortes, having come to see Sandoval and find out if his army was dead or defeated – that Cortes was to blame and not he, since during his victorious advance Cortes had been so eager to follow up his advantage that he had cried : 'Forward, gentlemen !' and had never ordered them to fill in the dangerous gap at the bridge. If Cortes had given him that order, said the treasurer, he and his company and the allies would have carried it out. Alderete also blamed our Captain for not ordering the hosts of allies to clear off the causeway in good time, and there was some further angry argument between the two which I will not record. Just at that moment the two launches which Cortes kept under his command beside the causeway came in. There had been no news of them since the defeat. It appears that they had been caught on some stakes and, according to their captains' reports, surrounded by canoes which had attacked them. They all came in wounded, and said that in the first place God had aided them with a wind, and then by making every effort with their oars they had broken the stakes and escaped. Cortes was very pleased, for up to that time (although he had not said so in order not to dishearten the soldiers) he had given these launches up for lost, having heard nothing of them.

After this, Cortes strongly urged Sandoval to ride post-haste to our camp at Tacuba and see whether we were defeated, or how we stood; and if he found us alive, he was to help us to defend our camp from their assaults, and he instructed Francisco de Lugo to accompany him, for he knew very well that there were Mexican companies on the road. Indeed he told Lugo that he had already sent Andres de Tapia with three horsemen to get news of us, and feared they might have been killed on the way. Then, after taking his leave of him, he turned to embrace Sandoval, to whom he said: 'See, my son, I cannot go everywhere, because I am wounded. So I entrust you with the task of ensuring the safety of all three camps. I know that Pedro de Alvarado and all his comrades have fought valiantly, like true gentlemen. But I fear the great forces of these dogs may have overwhelmed them. As for me and my army, you can see our condition.'

Sandoval and Francisco de Lugo rode post-haste to our position, arriving a little after dusk, and found us fighting with the Mexicans who were trying to get into our camp by way of some houses we had pulled down. Others were attacking along the causeway, and many canoes were assaulting us from the lake. They had already driven one launch aground, killing two of its crew and wounding all the rest; and Sandoval saw me with six other soldiers above our waists in the lake, helping to push it off into deep water. Many Indians were attacking us, with swords captured when Cortes was defeated or with flint-edged broadswords, trying to prevent us from rescuing the launch, which, to judge by their efforts, they intended to drag off with their canoes. Indeed, they had already attached several ropes to it in order to tow it into the city. When Sandoval saw us in this condition, he cried: 'Brothers, put your backs into it and see that they do not get the launch!' And we made such an effort that we dragged it to safety, even though, as I have said, two of its crew were killed and all the rest wounded.

Just then many companies of Mexicans came down the causeway, wounding us all, including the horsemen. Sandoval too received a stone full in the face. But Pedro de Alvarado and some other horsemen went to his assistance. As so many bands were coming on, and only I and twenty soldiers were opposing them, Sandoval ordered us to retire gradually in order to save the horses; and because we did not retire as quickly as he wished he turned on us furiously and said: 'Do you want me and all my horsemen to be killed because of you? For my sake, Bernal Díaz, my friend, please fall back!' Then Sandoval received another wound, and so did his horse. By this time we had got our allies off the causeway; and facing the enemy and never turning our backs, we gradually retired, forming a kind of dam to hold up their advance. Some of our crossbowmen and musketeers shot while others were loading, the horsemen made charges, and Pedro Moreno loaded and fired his cannon. Yet despite the number of Mexicans that were swept away by his shot we could not keep them at bay. On the contrary, they continued to pursue us, in the belief that they would carry us off that night to be sacrificed.

When we had retired almost to our quarters, across a great opening full of water, their arrows, darts, and stones could no longer reach us. Sandoval, Francisco de Lugo, and Andres de Tapia were standing with Pedro de Alvarado, each one telling his story and discussing Cortes' orders, when the dismal drum of Huichilobos sounded again, accompanied by conches, horns, and trumpet-like instruments. It was a terrifying sound, and when we looked at the tall *cue* from which it came we saw our comrades who had been captured in Cortes' defeat being dragged up the steps to be sacrificed. When they had hauled them up to a small platform in front of the shrine where they kept their accursed idols we saw them put plumes on the heads of many of them; and then they made them dance with a sort of fan in front of Huichilobos. Then after they had danced the *papas* laid them down on their backs on some narrow stones of sacrifice and, cutting open their chests, drew out their palpitating hearts which they offered to the idols before them. Then they kicked the bodies down the steps, and the Indian butchers who were waiting below cut off their arms and legs and flayed their faces, which they afterwards prepared like glove leather, with their beards on, and kept for their drunken festivals. Then they ate their flesh with a sauce of peppers and tomatoes. They sacrificed all our men in this way, eating their legs and arms, offering their hearts and blood to their idols as I have said, and throwing their trunks and entrails to the lions and tigers and serpents and snakes that they kept in the wild-beast houses I have described in an earlier chapter.

On seeing these atrocities, all of us in our camp said to one another: 'Thank God they did not carry me off to be sacrificed!' My readers must remember that though we were not far off we could do nothing to help, and could only pray God to guard us from such a death. Then at the very moment of the sacrifice, great bands of Mexicans suddenly fell upon us and kept us busy on all sides. We could find no way of holding them. 'Look!' they shouted, 'that is the way you will all die, as our gods have many times promised us,' and the threats they shouted at our Tlascalan allies were so cruel and so frightening that they lost their spirit. The Mexicans threw them roasted legs of Indians and the arms of our soldiers with cries of: 'Eat the flesh of these *Teules* and of your brothers, for we are glutted with it. You can stuff yourselves on our leavings. Now see these houses you have pulled down. We shall make you build them again, much finer, with white stone and fine masonry. So go on helping the *Teules*. You will see them all sacrificed.'

Guatemoc did something more after his victory. He sent the hands and feet of our soldiers, and the skin of their faces, and the heads of the horses that had been killed, to all the towns of our allies and friends and their relations, with the message that as more than half of us were dead and he would soon finish off the rest, they had better break their alliance with us and come to Mexico, because if they did not desert us quickly he would come and destroy them.

The Mexicans went on attacking us by day and night; and we all kept guard together, Gonzalo de Sandoval, Pedro de Alvarado, and all the other captains included. So although great bands of warriors came by night, we were able to repel them. Both by day and night half the horsemen remained in Tacuba and the other half on the causeway. But this was not all the harm we suffered. The enemy returned and reopened all the channels that we had blocked since we had first advanced along the causeway, and built even stronger barricades than before. Then our friends from the cities on the lake who had recently allied themselves to us and were coming to help us with their canoes decided that they had 'come for wool but gone away shorn'. For many of them lost their lives and many went home wounded, and more than half their canoes were destroyed. But even so they did not help the Mexicans any more, for they loathed them. They stood aside, however, and watched events.

Then Gonzalo de Sandoval and his fellow captains and soldiers who had come to our camp thought they had better return to their posts and report the state in which they had found us. They told Cortes that Pedro de Alvarado was exercising great caution; and Sandoval, who felt friendly towards me, told him how he had found me and other soldiers fighting up to our waists in the water. He said that but for us the crew of the stranded launch would all have been killed, and said many things in my praise which became known throughout the camp but which I will not repeat here. When Cortes realized that we were exercising great caution, he was much relieved, and from that time onwards he ordered the men of all three camps to fight the Mexicans neither too much nor too little. By this he meant that we were not to worry about capturing any bridge or barricade, and only to go out to fight in defence of our camp. Day had hardly dawned, however, when they attacked it again, hurling all their missiles and shouting hideous abuse. But as we were protected by a very deep channel we remained for four days without crossing it.

[For five days the three forces of Spaniards stayed in their respective camps, sustaining and repelling repeated attacks.]

Let us cease talking of the great attacks they made on us, and tell how our allies the Tlascalans and the people of Cholula and Huexotzinco, and even those of Texcoco, Chalco, and Tlamanalco, decided to return home and went off without the knowledge of Cortes, Pedro de Alvarado, or Sandoval. The only chiefs who remained in Cortes' camp were Ahuaxpitzactzin, the brave man who was afterwards baptized Don Carlos and was the brother of Don Fernando, the lord of Texcoco, and some forty of his relatives and friends; and in Sandoval's camp another *Cacique* from Huexotzinco with about fifty men; and in our camp two sons of Lorenzo de Vargas, and Chichimecatecle the brave, with about eighty Tlascalans, his relations and vassals. Of the twenty-four thousand allies we had brought with us, only about two hundred remained in our three camps; all the rest had gone home.

When we found ourselves abandoned by our allies, Cortes and Sandoval asked those who remained in their respective camps why the rest had gone. They replied that they had observed the Mexicans consulting their idols during the night, and the idols had promised that we and they would all be killed. Our allies had believed this to be true and had departed in fear. What made this prophecy seem more credible to them was that many of us had indeed been killed and all the rest wounded, and they themselves had lost more than twelve hundred men. They feared, therefore, that the rest of us would be killed too. Moreover, Xicotenga the Younger, whom Cortes had hanged, had always told them that he knew by his magic we should all be killed and not a Tlascalan would remain alive. These were the reasons for their desertion.

Although Cortes showed his distress in private he told them with a cheerful smile that they need not be afraid, for what the Mexicans said was a lie intended to discourage them. He made them such promises and spoke to them so affectionately that he gave them the courage to stay, and we did the same to Chichimecatecle and the two young Xicotengas. In his conversation with Cortes, Don Carlos, who was a brave man, answered: 'Lord

Malinche, do not be distressed that you cannot fight the Mexicans every day. Get your leg well, and follow my advice, which is to stay in camp for some days and tell Tonatio and Sandoval to do the same. But keep the launches busy by day and night, to prevent their bringing in food or water. There are so many thousand bands of warriors in the city that they are bound to eat up all the provisions they have, and the water they are now drinking is brackish, for it comes from pools they themselves have dug. They are catching the rainwater and making do with that. But if you stop their food and water, how can they go on? They will suffer worse from hunger than from war.'

When this was translated for him, Cortes threw his arms round Don Carlos's neck and thanked him, and promised that he would give him towns. Many of us soldiers had already discussed the idea, but we were so impatient that we did not want to wait so long before advancing into the city. When Cortes had thoroughly considered the *Cacique*'s advice (although we had already sent a proposal to the same effect, and his own captains and soldiers had made the same suggestion) he sent two launches to Sandoval's camp and two to ours, with orders that we should wait another three days before entering the city. As the Mexicans were then victorious he did not dare to send one launch alone, and therefore sent them in pairs.

One thing was of great help to us, that our launches now had the courage to break the stakes placed in the lake to impale them. They did it by rowing with all their strength, and to give their spurt greater impetus they started it some distance back, and got the wind into their sails as well. So they became masters of the lake, and of a good many isolated groups of houses; and when the Mexicans saw this they lost some of their spirit.

But to return to our battle. Having now no allies, we ourselves began to fill in the great channel, which, as I have said before, was close to our camp. The first company on the rota worked hard at carrying bricks and timber, while the other two companies did the fighting. (I have explained our system of rotation before.) And in the four days that we all worked together we had it completely blocked and levelled off. Cortes did the same in his camp, where they followed the same plan, and he worked himself, carrying bricks and timber, until the bridges and gaps were filled and the causeway secure enough to allow of a safe retreat. Sandoval too followed the same course. With our launches close by and no longer afraid of their stakes, we then began to advance little by little.

[The fighting continued in the same way as before, the Spaniards advancing each day along the causeways, though this time without allies, and retiring each night. The Mexican attacks were persistent, but thanks to the relative freedom of the launches and the effectiveness of Pedro Moreno's cannon, the danger diminished. Each night, however, the Mexicans sacrificed a further batch of the prisoners taken from Cortes, and this continued for ten successive nights.]

Each day we had very hard battles, but we continued to capture bridges and barricades and to master the channels; and our launches were of great assistance, since they could go wherever they wished on the lake and were not afraid of the stakes. Twelve or thirteen days had now passed since Cortes' defeat, and Don Carlos saw that we were recovering strength. Realizing that the Mexicans had been wrong when they said they would kill us all within ten days, which was what their idols had promised them, he sent to advise his brother Don Fernando to send Cortes all the warriors he could get from Texcoco, and within two days of his sending this message more than two thousand warriors arrived.

When Cortes saw this fine reinforcement he was highly delighted and spoke most flatteringly to them. At the same time many Tlascalans returned with their captains, and a *Cacique* named Tepaneca from Topeyanco was their commander. Many Indians also came from Huexotzingo and a very few from Cholula. When Cortes heard the news, he ordered that all our allies should come to his camp when they arrived, so that he could speak to them. But before they came he ordered guards of our soldiers to be placed on the roads, to protect them in case the Mexicans attacked, and when they stood before him, he made them a speech through Doña Marina and Jeronimo de Aguilar, saying that they well understood the good will he had felt and still felt towards them, both for the obedience they had given to His Majesty and for the good work they had done for us. If, when we reached the city, he had ordered them to join us in destroying the Mexicans, it had been his intention, he said, to benefit them and send them home rich, and give them vengeance on their enemies. Our purpose in capturing that great city would not be merely to benefit him. Although he had always found them willing and they had helped him in every way, he continued, we had sent them off the causeways each day because we were less hampered when we fought without them, since, as he had told them before, He who gave us victory and aid in everything was our Lord Jesus Christ in whom we believed. Because they had deserted at the most critical moment of the war, and left their captains in the lurch when the fighting was hardest, they deserved execution. But since they did not understand our laws and ordinances he pardoned them. However, so that they should understand the situation better, he pointed out that we were still pulling down houses and taking barricades without them; and he ordered them to kill no Mexicans in future, for he wished to win them by kindness. After making this speech, he embraced Chichimecatecle and the two young Xicotengas and Don Carlos, and promised that he would add to the territory and vassals they then held. He then sent them away, each one to his own camp.

I am tired of writing about battles, and was even more tired when I had to take part in them, and my readers may well be just as tired of my prolixity. For ninety-three days [1] we were fighting continuously, but I must now be excused if I call no more battles to mind.

To return to our story, as we advanced from all three camps into the city, we came to the pool from which they drew the brackish water I have spoken of, and destroyed it so that they should make no more use of it. It was guarded by some Mexicans with whom we had a brush. But we could now move freely along all the streets we had captured, for they had been levelled and were no longer broken up by channels. Consequently our horsemen had freedom of manoeuvre.

As soon as Cortes saw that we were capturing bridges, cause-

1. This figure is probably incorrect.

ways, and barricades in the city and destroying the houses, he ordered three Mexican captains, men of importance whom we had captured, to go to Guatemoc and induce him to make peace. The chieftains replied that they dared not carry such a message, for their lord Guatemoc would certainly have them killed. Nevertheless, after further conversations in which Cortes made them promises and gave them some cloth, they set out. The message they carried to Guatemoc was that Cortes had a great regard for him as a close relative and son-in-law of his friend the great Montezuma, and that he would be sorry if that great city were totally destroyed. To avoid the daily slaughter of its inhabitants and their neighbours, therefore, he begged Guatemoc to make peace, and promised not only to pardon in His Majesty's name all the deaths and damage they had inflicted on us, but to do him some favours also. He reminded the prince that he had already sent this message four times, but owing to his youth and bad advisers, and principally because of the evil counsel offered him by his idols and their *papas*, Guatemoc had refused to make peace and had preferred war. But already he had seen what slaughter these battles cost him, how all the cities and towns in the neighbourhood were now on our side, and that every day more were rising against him. While condoling with him on such a loss of vassals and cities, Cortes said that we knew they had exhausted their provisions and run out of water; and he said other things that were much to the point. Although this message was thoroughly explained to them by our interpreters, the three chieftains asked Cortes for a letter, not because it would be understood but because they knew that when we sent a message or command it was always on paper – which they call *amales* in their language – as a sign that it was an order.

When the three messengers appeared before Guatemoc with tears in their eyes, they conveyed to him the burden of Cortes' message; and when Guatemoc heard it, as we afterwards learnt, he burst into a rage with them, in the presence of his captains, for daring to bring such a proposal. He was, however, as we afterwards learnt, inclined to make peace, and he called together his chieftains and captains and the *papas* of his idols to discuss the matter, telling them that he had no wish to fight against Malinche and the rest of us. He said in his address that he had done all he could to beat us in war and had changed his method of fighting many times, but that we were men of such a kind that whenever they thought they had conquered us we turned on them more vigorously than before. Moreover, he knew that we had recently been joined by great hosts of allies and that all the cities were against him, and that our launches had now broken through their lines of stakes, and our horsemen were galloping through all the streets of the city. Guatemoc put before them their many other difficulties with food and water, and begged or commanded each one of them to give his opinion and not be fearful of speaking the truth. The reply of Guatemoc's counsellors seems to have been : 'Great lord, you are our king and you exercise your office nobly. You have shown your courage in all things, and the kingdom is yours by right. The peace you speak of as good is illusory. Consider how, ever since the *Teules* entered this land and this city, things have gone from bad to worse with us. Think of the benefits and presents that your uncle the great Montezuma bestowed on them and of his death. Think of the fate of his successor, your cousin Cacamatzin, and of what befell your relations, the lords or Iztapalapa, Coyoacan, Tacuba, and Talatzingo, and the sons of our great Montezuma. All are dead. All the gold and riches of this city have been destroyed, and they have enslaved and branded the faces of all your subjects and vassals at Chalco and Tepeaca and at Texcoco, and in all your cities and towns. But before this, consider what your gods have promised you and reflect well upon it. Do not trust Malinche and his flattering words. It is better that we should all die fighting in this city than see ourselves in the power of those who would enslave us and torture us for gold.'

At the same time the *papas* also announced that for the past three nights, at the time when they offered the sacrifice, their idols had promised them victory. Then Guatemoc replied somewhat angrily : 'If that is what you want, take good care of the maize and provisions we possess, and let us all die fighting. From now on, let no one dare ask me to make peace or I will have him killed.' Then they all promised to fight night and day in defence of the city. When this was settled they arranged with the people of Xochimilco and other towns to bring water in canoes by night, and dug pools in other places where some existed, although it was rather brackish.

Cortes and the army waited two days for their reply without advancing any further into the city. Then to our surprise great bands of Indian warriors came against all three camps and attacked us fiercely, like brave lions who hoped to carry us off. This is what happened at Pedro de Alvarado's camp, but they say that the attacks on Cortes and Sandoval were just as fierce, and that despite the number of Indians they killed and wounded they could scarcely hold their own. In the course of battle, Guatemoc's horn would be sounded, and then we had to close our ranks to avoid being overwhelmed. For, as I have said before, in their endeavours to lay hands on us they impaled themselves on our swords and lances. Being already used to these attacks, however, for some of us were killed and wounded every day, we fought them off hand to hand for six or seven days in succession, inflicting great casualties on them. They were not discouraged by this, however, for they cared nothing for death in battle. They said, as I remember : 'Why does Malinche ask us every day to make peace with you? Our idols have promised us victory, we have plenty of food and water, and we shall not let one of you survive. So do not talk to us any more about peace: words are for women, arms for men.' With these words they came on us like mad dogs, without a thought for their lives, and the fighting lasted till nightfall, when we cautiously retired to our huts.

We held out like this for many days, during which time things changed for the worse once more, and the Mexicans collected an army from the three provinces of Matlazingo, Malinalco, and another whose name I forget (it was twenty-five or thirty miles from Mexico) to fall on us from the rear and attack our camps. At the same time the Mexicans themselves planned to come out from the city, and thus we should be caught between two forces and, as they expected, routed.

Matlazingo and Malinalco and Tulapa were among the places

to which Guatemoc had sent the heads of the horses and the flayed faces and hands and feet of the soldiers they had sacrificed; and when they received his message the prince's relations in these towns had promptly assembled all the forces they could raise to come to the assistance of Mexico and their kinsman Guatemoc. They were already on their way against us when they passed three towns of our allies, which they began to attack, robbing their farms and maize-fields, and killing their children for sacrifice. These towns sent post-haste to Cortes for help and assistance, and he at once dispatched Andres de Tapia with twenty horsemen, a hundred soldiers, and many of our Tlascalan allies to help them; which they did so effectively that they drove the enemy back to their towns and then returned to camp.

Cortes was delighted by the news of their defeat, but almost immediately other messages came from the town of Cuernavaca to claim assistance against the people of these same three provinces, who were descending upon them. This time he sent Gonzalo de Sandoval with twenty horsemen and eighty soldiers, the soundest in all three camps – myself and some of my friends among them – and many of our allies. God knows that those who remained behind were in danger of their lives, for they were all wounded and had no restoratives. A great deal might be told about what we did under Sandoval's command, and how he defeated the enemy. But I will confine myself to saying that we quickly returned to relieve our own camp, bringing with us two chieftains of Matlazingo, and leaving the towns at peace again.

[Cortes once more requested Guatemoc to sue for peace, but was refused. The enemy's attacks were intensified, but then began to flag. The Spaniards' powder ran out in all three camps, but a new ship arrived, and supplies were sent up from Vera Cruz.]

To return to our conquest of the city. To be brief, Cortes settled with his captains and soldiers that we should push forward until we reached Tlatelolco, the great market-place where there were seven lofty *cues* and shrines, and our three companies advanced each from its own side, capturing bridges and barricades. Cortes got as far as a small square in which there were some other shrines and small towers, and in one of the houses there were some upright posts on which they had put the heads of many of our Spaniards whom they had killed and sacrificed during the recent battles. Their hair and beards had grown much longer than they were in life; which I would never have believed if I had not seen it. I recognized three of my fellow soldiers, and to see them in this condition saddened our hearts. We left them where they were for the time being, but they were taken down twelve days later, when we took away those and other heads that had been offered to the idols and buried them in a church that we built, which is called the Martyrs, near the bridge named Alvarado's Leap.

Enough of this. Let me say that Pedro de Alvarado's men advanced fighting till they reached Tlatelolco. There were so many Mexicans guarding their idols and tall shrines and they had raised so many barricades that it took us quite two hours before we could capture them or get inside. Now that the horses had room to gallop, they were of great assistance even though most of them were wounded, for the horsemen speared many Mexicans. As the enemy were so numerous, our ten companies were divided into three parts to fight against them; and Pedro de Alvarado ordered one, under the command of Gutierrez de Badajoz, to ascend the hundred and fourteen steps of the *cue* of Huichilcbos. He fought very well against the enemy warriors and against the many *papas* in the shrines. But the Mexicans attacked him so hard that they sent him rolling down ten or twelve steps, and we had to go promptly to his rescue. As we advanced the enemy bands kept close to us, and we were in great peril of our lives. Nevertheless we climbed to the top, set the shrines on fire, burnt the idols, and planted our banners there; and after we had fired the shrines we fought on the ground until nightfall, but we could do nothing against so many warriors.

Next day, when Cortes and his captains saw from where they were fighting in a distant quarter of the city the great blaze of the tall *cue* burning (for the Mexicans had not put the fire out) and our banners planted at the top, he was greatly delighted and wished that he were there himself. They even say he was envious, but he could not have got there, for he was nearly a mile away and there were still many bridges and channels to be captured. Wherever he turned he was fiercely attacked; and he could not penetrate as fast as he wished into the heart of the city, as we of Alvarado's company had done. However, within four days both Cortes and Sandoval joined us, and we could pass along the streets from one camp to another over demolished houses and over bridges, barricades, and channels, every one of which had been levelled.

Guatemoc and all his warriors were now retreating to a part of the city that stood in the lake, for the houses and palaces in which he had lived were razed to the ground. Yet every day they came out to attack us, and pursued us as hotly as ever as soon as the time came for us to retreat. When some days had passed and Cortes saw that they were not coming to sue for peace and had no thought of doing so, he consulted all our captains and decided that we must lay some ambuscades. This is how we did it. From all three camps we collected about thirty horsemen and a hundred soldiers, the most active and pugnacious that Cortes could find, and he sent to summon a thousand Tlascalans from all three camps. Then we took up our position in some large houses that had belonged to a Mexican lord. This we did early in the morning, and Cortes then advanced along the streets and causeways with the rest of his horsemen, and his soldiers, crossbowmen, and musketeers, fighting in the usual way and pretending to be filling in the bridge over a certain channel. The Mexican bands detailed for the task were already fighting him, also many others whom Guatemoc had sent to guard the bridge. On seeing the enemy's great numbers, Cortes pretended to retreat, and ordered that the allies should be got off the causeway, so that the Mexicans should believe he was retiring. They came and followed him, at first slowly, but when they saw him act as if he were really in flight, all the troops on the causeway came after him and attacked him. As soon as he knew that they had advanced just beyond the houses in which the ambush was placed, he ordered two shots to be fired close together, as a signal for us to emerge from our hiding place. The horsemen came out first, followed by all of us soldiers, and we fell on the enemy unopposed. Cortes then quickly faced his men about, and our friends the Tlascalans did great damage to the enemy. Thus many of them were killed and wounded, and thereafter they did not follow us when we retired. Another ambush was laid for them in Alvarado's camp, but it came to nothing.

When we were all in Tlatelolco, Cortes ordered all the companies to take up their quarters and keep watch there, because we had almost two miles to come from our camp to the place where we were then fighting. We spent three days there without doing anything of importance. For Cortes ordered us not to advance any further into the city or demolish any more houses since he intended to summon the enemy once more to make peace. So while we were in Tlatelolco, Cortes sent to Guatemoc begging him to surrender and not to be afraid. He undertook with solemn promises that the prince's person should be scrupulously respected and honoured, and that he should continue to rule Mexico and all his territory and cities just as before; and Cortes sent him a gift of provisions – maize-cakes, poultry, prickly pears, and chocolate – for he had nothing else to send. Guatemoc consulted his captains, and the advice they gave him was to say that he desired peace but would wait three days before giving an answer. Then, when this time had elapsed, Guatemoc and Cortes would meet to discuss terms, but in the interval he would have the opportunity to learn more fully the wishes of his god Huichilobos in this matter, also to mend bridges, make openings in the causeway, prepare arrows, javelins, and stones, and build barricades.

Guatemoc sent four Mexican chieftains with his reply, and we believed that his desire for peace was genuine. Cortes ordered that these messengers should be given plenty to eat and drink, and then sent them back to Guatemoc with more food of the same kind as before. Then Guatemoc sent other messengers with a gift of two fine cloaks, and they said the prince would come as soon as everything was ready. To waste no more words on this matter, Guatemoc never intended to come, for his counsellors had advised him not to trust Cortes, and had reminded him of the fate of his uncle the great Montezuma and his relations, and of the destruction of all the Mexican nobility. They advised him to plead illness, and then to send out all his warriors in the hope that his gods would be pleased to grant them the victory they had so often promised.

We waited for Guatemoc in vain. But no sooner did we understand his deceit than many battalions of Mexicans came out under their distinguishing signs in the direction of our camp and Sandoval's. They seemed to have started the battle all over again. As we were somewhat off our guard, believing that they had already settled for peace, many of our men were wounded, three of them mortally. They also wounded two horses, but they did not get away with much advantage, for we paid them out well. After this onslaught Cortes ordered us to attack them again and advance into those parts of the city where they had taken refuge. When they saw us capturing the whole city, Guatemoc sent two chieftains to tell Cortes he wished to speak to him across a channel. Cortes was to stand on one bank and he on another, and they fixed the time for the morning of the next day. Cortes kept the appointment, but Guatemoc refused to come. He sent some chieftains instead, to explain that their master dared not appear for fear we would shoot at him with our guns and crossbows during the conversations and he would be killed. Cortes then swore to him that he would not be harmed in any way, but to no purpose. They would not believe him, and said they knew the value of his word. Just then two of the chieftains who were speaking to Cortes took some maize-cakes, the leg of a fowl, and some cherries out of a bag that they were carrying, and sat down to a leisurely meal, so that we should suppose that they were not hungry; and on seeing this, Cortes sent them word that since they did not want to make peace, he would soon enter all their houses to see if they had any maize or any more poultry. We went on in this way for another four or five days without attacking them, and during this time many poor Indians who had nothing to eat came to our camp exhausted with hunger. In view of this, Cortes ordered that we should not attack, for perhaps they would change their minds about ending the war. But even though we sent to entreat them, they would not make peace.

There was a soldier in Cortes' camp who said that he had been in Italy, in the Great Captain's company, and was in the affair at Garellano and other great battles. He talked a good deal about war-engines, and said he could make a catapult in Tlatelolco which, if they were to bombard the quarter of the city into which Guatemoc retreated, would make them sue for peace in two days. He talked so much about it, for this man was a great talker, that Cortes promptly set to work on the catapult. They brought lime and stone and wood, as the soldier requested, and carpenters and nails and all that was needed for its construction. They made two slings of strong rope and cords, and brought up great stones bigger than demijohn jars, and when the catapult was made and rigged as he desired, the soldier said that it was ready to be discharged. So they placed a suitable stone in the sling, but all it did was to rise to the height of the catapult and fall back to its original place. Cortes was very annoyed with the deviser of the catapult and with himself for having believed him. He said the man had proved that nothing was more prejudicial to war than talk, and that the whole matter had been one of talk for talking's sake; and he at once ordered the catapult to be taken to pieces. Cortes now knew that the Mexicans did not wish for any sort of peace, so when he saw that the catapult was quite useless, he ordered Gonzalo de Sandoval to invade that part of the city in which Guatemoc had taken refuge with all the flower of his captains and of the Mexican nobility, but not to kill or wound any Indians unless they should attack him, and if they did so, only to defend himself and do them no harm. He was, however, to destroy their houses and the many defences they had erected in the lake. Cortes himself ascended the great *cue* of Tlatelolco to watch Sandoval's advance.

Sandoval went forward vigorously with his launches towards the place where Guatemoc's houses stood, and when Guatemoc found himself surrounded he was afraid he would be taken or killed. He had prepared fifty large pirogues with good oarsmen, so that when he saw himself hard pressed he could escape and hide in some reed-beds, from which he would be able to reach land and conceal himself again in another town, and had given instructions to his captains, and the principal persons whom he had with him in that part of the city, that they should do the same.

When they saw the launches getting in among the houses, these people embarked in their fifty canoes, in which they had already placed Guatemoc's property, gold, and jewels, and all his family and women. Then he himself embarked and shot out into the lake, accompanied by many captains. At the same moment many more canoes set out, and soon the lake was full of them. Immediately on receiving news that Guatemoc was escaping, Sandoval ordered all his launches to stop destroying the houses and defences and follow the flight of the canoes. He told them to keep track of where Guatemoc was going, and not to molest him or do him any harm, but simply to try to capture him.

Sandoval instructed a certain Garcia Holguin, a friend of Sandoval's who was captain of a very fast launch with good sails and good sailors, to follow him in the direction in which they said Guatemoc and his pirogues were going, and capture him if he could overtake him. Sandoval himself went in another direction with a number of other launches. It pleased our Lord God that Garcia Holguin should overtake Guatemoc's fleet, which by its rich decorations, its awnings, and royal seat he recognized as the craft in which the Lord of Mexico was travelling. Holguin signed to them to stop, but they refused, so he made as if to shoot at them with muskets and crossbows. This alarmed Guatemoc, who cried out: 'Do not shoot. I am the king of this city. Guatemoc is my name. Please do not interfere with the things I am taking with me, or disturb my wife or relatives, but take me at once to Malinche.' Holguin was delighted to hear these words, and embraced Guatemoc very respectfully. He placed him in the launch with his wife and about thirty chieftains, seating him in the poop on some cloths and mats, and gave them some of his own food to eat, and he touched nothing in the canoes that carried Guatemoc's property, but brought them along with the launch.

By this time Gonzalo de Sandoval had ordered all the launches to come back, for he knew that Holguin had captured Guatemoc and was taking him to Cortes. On receiving the news he told the oarsmen in his own launch to make all possible speed and, overtaking Holguin, claimed the prisoner. Holguin refused his demand, saying that he and not Sandoval had made the capture. Sandoval replied that this was so, but that he was commander of the launches and Garcia Holguin sailed under his command and banner, and that it was for reasons of friendship and because Holguin's launch was the fastest that he had ordered him to follow and take Guatemoc, who must now be surrendered to him as commander. Holguin, however, persisted in his refusal; and at that moment another launch went at high speed to Cortes to ask for a reward for the good news. Cortes was still at Tlatelolco, not far away, watching Sandoval's advance from the top of the *cue*, and when he was informed of the dispute between Sandoval and Holguin he at once dispatched Captain Luis Marin and Francisco de Verdugo to summon them both to come immediately in their launches, and to bring Guatemoc and his wife and family with every mark of respect. He said he would himself settle whose prisoner Guatemoc was and to whom the honour of his capture was due. While they were bringing him in, Cortes ordered as good a guest-chamber to be prepared as was possible at that time, with mats and cloths and seats, and plenty of Cortes' own food. Sandoval and Holguin soon arrived with Guatemoc, and both together led him up to Cortes. On appearing before him Guatemoc treated our Captain with great respect, and Cortes, embracing him joyfully, treated him and his captains with a great show of affection. 'Lord Malinche,' said Guatemoc, 'I have assuredly done my duty in defence of my city and my vassals, and I can do no more. I am brought by force as a prisoner into your presence and beneath your power. Take the dagger that you have in your belt, and strike me dead immediately.' He sobbed as he spoke and the tears fell from his eyes, and the other great lords whom he brought with him wept also. Cortes answered him very kindly through our interpreters that he admired him greatly for having had the bravery to defend his city, and did not blame him at all. On the contrary, he thought rather well than ill of him for having done so. What he wished, however, was that he had sued for peace of his own accord when his defeat was certain, and had thus prevented so much of his city from being destroyed, and so many of his Mexicans from losing their lives. But now all this had happened, there was no help for it. Nothing could be mended. Let his spirit and the spirit of his captains be at rest. For he should rule over Mexico and his provinces as before.

Guatemoc and his captains thanked Cortes for this assurance. Then Cortes asked after his wife and the other great ladies, wives of other captains, whom he knew to have come with the prince; and Guatemoc himself answered that he had begged Gonzalo de Sandoval and Garcia Holguin to leave them in their canoes while he came to learn Malinche's orders. Cortes at once sent for them, and ordered that they should be given of the best we had in the camp to eat. Then, as it was late and it was beginning to rain, he arranged for them to be sent to Coyoacan and, taking Guatemoc, his family, and household, and many other chieftains with him, he ordered Pedro de Alvarado, Gonzalo de Sandoval, and the other captains each to go to his own camp and quarters. We went to Tacuba, Sandoval to Tepeaquilla, and Cortes himself to Coyoacan. Guatemoc and his captains were captured on the evening of 13 August 1521. Thanks be to our Lord Jesus Christ and Our Lady the Virgin Mary, His Blessed Mother.

It rained and thundered that evening, and the lightning flashed, and up to midnight heavier rain fell than usual. After Guatemoc's capture all we soldiers became as deaf as if all the bells in a belfry had been ringing and had then suddenly stopped. I say this because during the whole ninety-three days of our siege of the capital, Mexican captains were yelling and shouting night and day, mustering the bands of warriors who were to fight on the causeway, and calling to the men in the canoes who were to attack the launches and struggle with us on the bridges and build barricades, or to those who were driving in piles, and deepening and widening the channels and bridges, and building breastworks, or to those who were making javelins and arrows, or to the women shaping rounded stones for their slings. Then there was the unceasing sound of their accursed drums and trumpets, and their melancholy kettle-drums in the shrines and on their temple towers. Both day and night the din was so great that we could hardly hear one another speak. But after Guatemoc's capture, all the shouting and the other noises ceased, which is why I have made the comparison with a belfry.

Guatemoc was very delicate, both in body and features. His face was long but cheerful, and when his eyes dwelt on you they seemed more grave than gentle, and did not waver. He was twenty-six, and his complexion was rather lighter than the brown of most Indians. They said he was a nephew of Montezuma, the son of one of his sisters; and he was married to one of Montezuma's daughters, a young and beautiful woman.

Before we go any further, let me relate how the dispute between Sandoval and Garcia Holguin ended. After telling them a story about a similar quarrel in Roman times between Marius and Cornelius Sulla, Cortes said he would refer the question to His Majesty, as to which of the two he would permit to incorporate the capture in his coat-of-arms, since the decision must come from Spain; and two years later an order came from His Majesty that in the ornaments of his coat-of-arms Cortes should have seven kings: Montezuma, the great lord of Mexico; Cacamatzin, the lord of Texcoco, and the lords of Iztapalapa, Coyoacan, Tacuba, and another, a nephew of Montezuma, to whom they said the Caciqueship of Mexico would fall – he was lord of Matlazingo and other provinces – and lastly this Guatemoc about whom the dispute arose.

Now to speak of the dead bodies and heads that were in the houses where Guatemoc had taken refuge. I solemnly swear that all the houses and stockades in the lake were full of heads and corpses. I do not know how to describe it but it was the same in the streets and courts of Tlatelolco. We could not walk without treading on the bodies and heads of dead Indians. I have read about the destruction of Jerusalem, but I do not think the mortality was greater there than here in Mexico, where most of the warriors who had crowded in from all the provinces and subject towns had died. As I have said, the dry land and the stockades were piled with corpses. Indeed, the stench was so bad that no one could endure it, and for that reason each of us captains returned to his camp after Guatemoc's capture; even Cortes was ill from the odours which assailed his nostrils and from headache during those days in Tlatelolco.

The soldiers in the launches came off best and gained most spoil, because they were able to go to the houses in certain quarters of the lake where they knew there was cloth, gold, and treasure. They also searched the reed-beds in which the Mexicans had hidden their property when we were assaulting some quarter or group of houses. Under cover of chasing the canoes that were bringing in food and water, they would sometimes capture some chieftains fleeing to the mainland to take refuge in the towns of their neighbours the Otomis, and would rob them of everything they had. We soldiers, on the other hand, who were fighting on the causeways and on land, gained no profit, but plenty of arrows and lance-thrusts and wounds from darts and stones. For when we captured houses, the inhabitants had already carried off any property they possessed, since we could not go through the water without first blocking the gaps and bridges. Therefore, as I said when speaking of Cortes' search for sailors to go in the launches, they were better off than we who fought on land. This was clearly proved when Cortes demanded Montezuma's treasure from Guatemoc and his captains. They told him that the men in the launches had stolen most of it.

As there was such a stench in the city, Guatemoc asked Cortes' permission for all the Mexican forces who remained there to go out to the neighbouring towns, and they were promptly told to do so. For three whole days and nights they never ceased streaming out, and all three causeways were crowded with men, women, and children so thin, sallow, dirty, and stinking that it was pitiful to see them. Once the city was free from them Cortes went out to inspect it. We found the houses full of corpses, and some poor Mexicans still in them who could not move away. Their excretions were the sort of filth that thin swine pass which have been fed on nothing but grass. The city looked as if it had been ploughed up. The roots of any edible greenery had been dug out, boiled, and eaten, and they had even cooked the bark of some of the trees. There was no fresh water to be found; all of it was brackish. I must also remark that the Mexicans did not eat the flesh of their own people, only that of our men and our Tlascalan allies whom they had captured. There had been no live births for a long time, because they had suffered so much from hunger and thirst and continual fighting.

Cortes ordered a banquet to be held in Coyoacan to celebrate the capture of the city, and got plenty of wine for the purpose from a ship that had just come from Spain to Villa Rica, also some pigs that had been brought to him from Cuba. He invited all of us captains and soldiers whom he thought worthy of consideration, from all three camps. But when we came to the banquet there were not enough seats or tables for even a third of the invited guests. Consequently there was much disorder. So many discreditable things occurred, indeed, that it would have been better if the banquet had never been held.[1]

Now that our daily and nightly battles with the Mexicans are far away in the past, for which I give great thanks to God who delivered me from them, there is one thing that I wish to relate, which happened to me after seeing the death by sacrifice of the sixty-two soldiers who were carried off alive. What I am going to say may seem to some to arise from my lack of any great inclination for battle. But, on the contrary, anyone will see on reflection that it was due rather to the excessive daring with which I had to risk my life in the thickest of the fighting. For great courage was at that time required of a soldier. I must say that when I saw my comrades dragged up each day to the altar, and their chests struck open and their palpitating hearts drawn out, and when I saw the arms and legs of these sixty-two men cut off and eaten, I feared that one day or another they would do the same to me. Twice already they had laid hands on me to drag me off, but it pleased God that I should escape from their clutches. When I remembered their hideous deaths, and the proverb that the little pitcher goes many times to the

---

1. Bernal Díaz describes a general scene of drunkenness, ending in a dance in which the soldiers, still wearing their cotton armour, led out such Spanish ladies as were there. He scratched this paragraph out in his manuscript, however.

fountain, and so on, I came to fear death more than ever in the past. Before I went into battle, a sort of horror and gloom would seize my heart, and I would make water once or twice and commend myself to God and His blessed Mother. It was always like this before battle, but my fear quickly left me.

It must seem very strange to my readers that I should have suffered from this unaccustomed terror. For I had taken part in many battles, from the time when I made the voyage of discovery with Francisco Hernandez de Cordoba till the defeat of our army on the causeway under Alvarado. But up to that time when I saw the cruel deaths inflicted on our comrades before our very eyes, I had never felt such fear as I did in these last battles. Let those experienced in soldiering, who have been at times in great peril of death, say whether my fear is to be attributed to faint-heartedness or to excessive valour. For, as I have said, my own opinion is that having to thrust myself when fighting into such dangerous positions, I was bound to fear death more at that time than at others. Besides, I was not always in good health. I was many times severely wounded, and for this reason was not able to go on all the expeditions. Still, the hardships and risks of death to which I was personally exposed were not insignificant, either before the capture of Mexico or afterwards.

The first orders Cortes gave to Guatemoc were that the conduits from Chapultepec should be repaired and restored to their former condition, so that the water could flow again into the city; that the streets should be cleared of the bodies and heads of the dead, which should be buried, so that the city should be left clean and free from any stench; that all bridges and causeways should be thoroughly restored to their former condition, and the palaces and houses rebuilt so as to be fit for habitation within two months. He marked out the parts in which the Indians were to settle, and those which were to be left clear for us.

Guatemoc and his captains complained to Cortes that many of our men had carried off the daughters and wives of chieftains, and begged him as a favour that they should be sent back. Cortes answered that it would be difficult to take them from their present masters, but they might seek them out and bring them before him, and he would see whether they had become

Christians or preferred to go home with their fathers and husbands, in which case he would order them to be given up. So he gave the Mexicans permission to search in all three camps, and issued an order that any soldier who had an Indian woman should surrender her at once if she of her own free will wished to return home. Many chieftains searched from house to house and persevered until they found them. But there were many women who did not wish to go with their fathers or mothers or husbands, but preferred to remain with the soldiers with whom they were living. Some hid themselves, others said they did not wish to return to idolatry, and yet others were already pregnant. So they did not bring back more than three, who by Cortes' express command were handed over to them.

Everyone was agreed that all the gold and silver and jewels in Mexico should be collected together. But this seems to have amounted to very little. For there was a report that Guatemoc had thrown all the rest into the lake four days before we captured him, and that the Tlascalans and the people of Huexotzingo and Cholula and all the rest of our allies who had taken part in the war, also the *Teules* themselves who went about in the launches, had stolen their share. The officers of the Royal Treasury publicly proclaimed therefore that Guatemoc had hidden the treasure, and that Cortes was delighted since he would not have to give it up but could keep it all for himself. For this reason these officers decided to torture Guatemoc and his cousin the lord of Tacuba, who was his great favourite. Cortes and some of the rest of us were very much distressed that they should torture a prince like Guatemoc for greed of gold. Thorough inquiries about the treasure had been made, and all Guatemoc's stewards had said that there was no more than the king's officials already had, which amounted to three hundred and eighty thousand gold pesos, and had been melted and cast into bars, and mulcted of the royal fifth and another fifth for Cortes. On finding that the sum was so little, Cortes' enemies among the Conquistadors, and Narvaez' men who distrusted him, told the treasurer Julian de Alderete that they suspected him of opposing the arrest and torture of Guatemoc and his captains only because he wanted to keep the gold for himself. So, to avoid making any accusations against Cortes, who could not prevent their action, they tortured Guatemoc and the lord of Tacuba by burning their feet with oil, and extorted the confession that four days before they had thrown the gold into the lake, together with the cannon and muskets they had captured from us when they drove us out of Mexico. The place Guatemoc indicated was the palace in which he had lived, where there was a large pond, from which we fished up a great golden sun like the one that Montezuma had given us, and many jewels and articles of small value which belonged to Guatemoc himself. The lord of Tacuba said that in his house at Tacuba, about twelve miles away, he had some gold objects, and that if we would take him there he would tell us where they were buried and give them to us. Pedro de Alvarado and six soldiers, myself among them, took him there. But when we arrived he said he had only told us this story in the hopes of dying on the road, and invited us to kill him, for he possessed neither gold nor jewels. So we returned empty-handed. The truth is that Montezuma's treasure-chamber, of which Guatemoc took possession at his death, did not contain many jewels or golden ornaments, because all the best had been extracted to form the magnificent offering that we had sent to His Majesty, which was worth twice as much as the fifth deducted for him and Cortes' own fifth as well. This we sent to the Emperor by Alonso de Avila, who had just returned from the island of Santo Domingo.

We captains and soldiers were all somewhat sad when we saw how little gold there was and how poor and mean our shares would be. The Mercedarian friar, Pedro de Alvarado, Cristobal de Olid, and other captains told Cortes that since there was so little gold, the entire share that would fall to us ought to be divided among those who were maimed and lame and blind, or had lost an eye or their hearing, and others who were crippled or had pains in their stomachs, or had been burnt by the powder, or were suffering from pains in their sides. They said that it was only right that it should all be given to them, and that the rest of us who were more or less sound ought to approve. After due consideration they repeated this to Cortes, believing that he would increase our shares, for there was a strong suspicion that he had hidden all the gold away and ordered Guatemoc to say he had none.

Cortes replied that he would see we came out all right, and would take measures to that effect. As we were all anxious to see what our share would be, we were in a hurry for the accounts to be issued. After making the calculation, they told us a horseman would receive eighty pesos, and a crossbowman, musketeer, or shield-bearer fifty or sixty – I do not remember which – and when we heard this figure not a single soldier was willing to accept his share.

While Cortes was at Coyoacan, he lodged in a palace with whitewashed walls on which it was easy to write with charcoal and ink; and every morning malicious remarks appeared, some in verse and some in prose, in the manner of lampoons. One said the sun, moon, and stars, and earth and sea followed their courses, and if they ever deviated from the plane for which they were created, soon reverted to their original place. So it would be with Cortes' ambition for command. He would soon return to his original condition. Another said that he had dealt us a worse defeat than he had given to Mexico, and that we ought to call ourselves not the victors of New Spain but the victims of Hernando Cortes. Another said he had not been content with a general's share but had taken a king's, not counting other profits; and yet another: 'My soul is very sad and will be till that day when Cortes gives us back the gold he's hidden away.' It was also remarked that Diego Velazquez had spent his whole fortune and discovered all the northern coast as far as Panuco, and then Cortes had come to enjoy the benefit and rebelliously taken both the land and the treasure. And other words were written up too, unfit to record in this story.

When Cortes came out of his quarters of a morning he would read these lampoons. Their style was elegant, the verses well rhymed, and each couplet not only had point but ended with a sharp reproof that was not so naïve as I may have suggested. As Cortes himself was something of a poet, he prided himself on composing answers, which tended to praise his own

great deeds and belittle those of Diego Velazquez, Grijalva, and
Francisco Hernandez de Cordoba. In fact, he too wrote some
good verses which were much to the point. But the couplets
and sentences they scrawled up became every day more scurrilous, until in the end Cortes wrote: 'A blank wall is a fool's
writing paper.' And next morning someone added: 'A wise
man's too, who knows the truth, as His Majesty will do very
soon!' Knowing who was responsible for this (a certain Tirado,
a friend of Diego Velazquez and some others who wished to
make their defiance clear) Cortes flew into a rage and publicly
proclaimed that they must write up no more libels or he would
punish the shameless villains.

Many of us were in debt to one another. Some owed fifty or
sixty pesos for crossbows, and others fifty for a sword. Everything we had bought was equally dear. A certain surgeon
called Maestre Juan, who tended some bad wounds, charged
excessive prices for his cures, and so did a sort of quack by the
name of Murcia, who was an apothecary and barber and also
treated wounds, and there were thirty other tricks and swindles
for which payment was demanded out of our shares. The
remedy that Cortes provided was to appoint two trustworthy
persons who knew the prices of goods and could value anything
that we had bought on credit. An order went out that whatever
price was placed on our purchases or the surgeons' cures must
be accepted, and that if we had no money, our creditors must
wait two years for payment. And I must say that in the end,
in compensation for slaves sold by auction, the remaining gold
all fell to the King's officials.

When Cortes found that many of the soldiers were still in-
solently demanding larger shares, and saying that he had stolen
everything for himself, and begging him to lend them money,
he decided to free himself from their clutches and send them
to settle in any province that seemed to him suitable. He ordered
Gonzalo de Sandoval to go to settle at Tuxtepec and punish
the Mexican garrisons that had killed seventy-eight persons and
six Spanish ladies of Narvaez' party who had stayed there. He
was to found a town there to be called Medellin, and then to go
on to Coatzacoalcos and form a settlement at that port. He

also ordered one Castaneda and Vicente Lopez to go to con-
quer the province of Panuco, and Rodrigo Rangel to stay at
Villa Rica as before, and Pedro de Ircio with him. He sent Juan
Alvarez the younger to Colima, and a certain Villafuerte to
Zacatula, and Cristobal de Olid, who had recently married a
Portuguese lady, to Michoacan, and he sent Francisco de Orozco
to settle in Oaxaca.

When the news spread through all these distant provinces
that Mexico was destroyed their *Caciques* and lords could not
believe it. However, they sent chieftains to congratulate Cortes
on his victories and yield themselves as vassals to His Majesty,
and to see if the city of Mexico, which they had so dreaded, was
really razed to the ground. They all carried great presents of
gold to Cortes, and even brought their small children to show
them Mexico, pointing it out to them in much the same way
that we would say : 'Here stood Troy.'

But let us leave this topic for another that richly deserves
explanation. Many interested readers have asked me why the
true Conquistadors who won New Spain and the great and
strong city of Mexico did not stay to settle, but went on to
other provinces. I think this question is justified, and I will give
them an answer. Learning from Montezuma's account-books the
names of the places which sent him tributes of gold, and where
the mines and chocolate and cotton-cloths were to be found,
we decided to go to these places; and our resolve was strengthened when we saw so eminent a captain and so close a friend
of Cortes as Gonzalo de Sandoval leaving Mexico, and when we
realized that there were no gold or mines or cotton in the
towns around Mexico, only a lot of maize and the *maguey*
plantations from which they obtained their wine. For this
reason we thought of it as a poor land, and went off to colonize
other provinces. But we were thoroughly deceived.

I remember that when I went to ask Cortes for leave to go
with Sandoval he said to me : 'On my conscience, Señor Bernal
Díaz del Castillo, you are making a mistake. I wish you would
stay here with me. But as you want to go with your friend Sandoval, go and good luck to you. I shall always consider your
wishes, but I know very well that you will be sorry you left.'

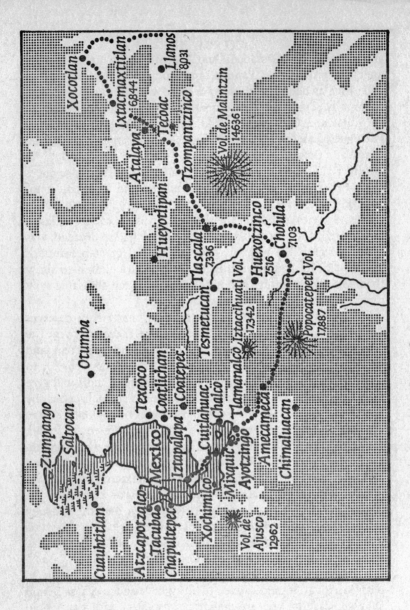

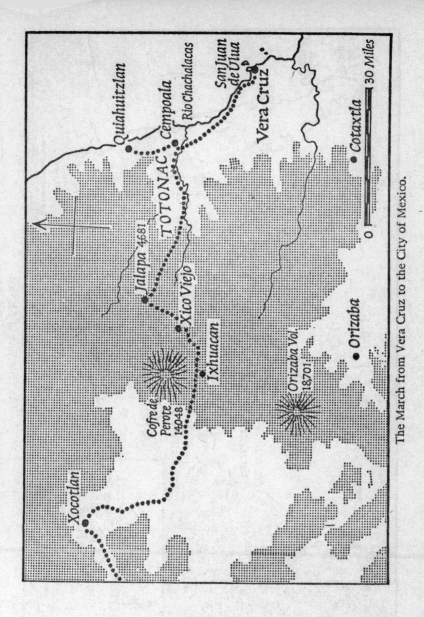

The March from Vera Cruz to the City of Mexico.

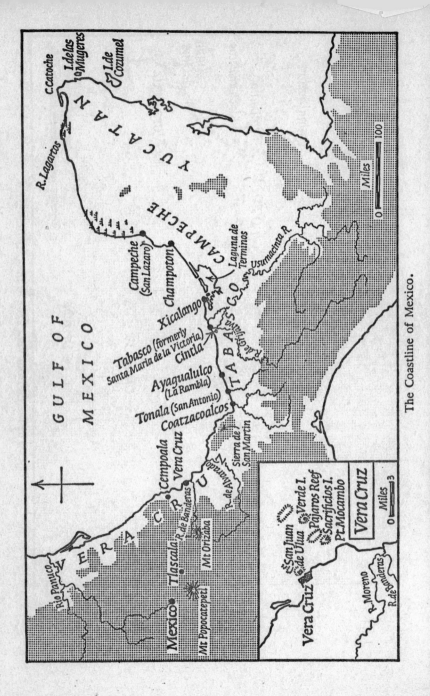

The Coastline of Mexico.

C. Catoche
I. de las Mugeres
I. de Cozumel

YUCATAN

R. Lagartos

CAMPECHE

Laguna de Terminos

Usumacinta R.

Campeche (San Lazaro)
Champoton

GULF OF MEXICO

Xicalango

TABASCO

R. de Grijalva

Tabasco (formerly Santa Maria de la Victoria) Cintla

Ayagualulco (La Rambla)

Tonala (San Antonio)
Coatzacoalcos

sierra de San Martin

Cempoala
Vera Cruz

VERACRUZ

R. de Banderas

R. de Alvarado

Tlascala
Mt Orizaba

Río Panuco

Mexico
Mt Popocatepetl

Miles
0   100

Vera Cruz

San Juan de Ulua
Verde I.
Pajaros Reef
Sacrificios I.
Pt. Mocambo

Vera Cruz

R. Moreno

R. de Banderas

Miles
0   3